Public Service Delivery in India

Public Service Delivery in India

Understanding the Reform Process

Edited by

VIKRAM K. CHAND

UNIVERSITY PRESS

OXFORD
UNIVERSITY PRESS

YMCA Library Building, Jai Singh Road, New Delhi 110 001

Oxford University Press is a department of the University of Oxford. It furthers the University's objective of excellence in research, scholarship, and education by publishing worldwide in

Oxford New York
Auckland Cape Town Dar es Salaam Hong Kong Karachi Kuala Lumpur
Madrid Melbourne Mexico City Nairobi New Delhi Shanghai Taipei Toronto

With offices in
Argentina Austria Brazil Chile Czech Republic France Greece Guatemala
Hungary Italy Japan Poland Portugal Singapore South Korea Switzerland
Thailand Turkey Ukraine Vietnam

Oxford is a registered trademark of Oxford University Press
in the UK and in certain other countries

Published in India
by Oxford University Press, New Delhi

First published 2010

ISBN-13: 978-019-806845-7
ISBN-10: 019-806845-X

Typeset in 10/12 Minion Pro
by Excellent Laser Typesetters, Pitampura, Delhi 110 034
Printed at Artxel, New Delhi 110 020
Published by Oxford University Press
YMCA Library Building, Jai Singh Road, New Delhi 110 001

Contents

Tables and Figures

TABLES

FIGURES

Abbreviations

ABIDE	Agenda for Bengaluru Infrastructure Development
ACA	Additional Central Assistance
ADB	Asian Development Bank
AMC	Ahmedabad Municipal Corporation
APERC	Andhra Pradesh Electricity Regulatory Commission
APGENCO	Andhra Pradesh Power Generation Corporation Limited
APIO	Assistant Public Information Officer
APTRANSCO	Transmission Corporation of Andhra Pradesh Limited
BARC	Bihar Administrative Reforms Commission
BATF	Bangalore Agenda Task Force
BBMP	Bruhat Bengaluru Mahanagar Palike
BDA	Bangalore Development Authority
BESCOM	Bangalore Electricity Supply Company
BMP	Bangalore Mahanagar Palike
BMTC	Bangalore Metropolitan Transport Corporation
BOOT	Build, Own, Operate and Transfer
BPSM	Bihar Prashasnik Sudhar Mission
BSUP	Basic Services for Urban Poor
BWSSB	Bangalore Water Supply and Sewerage Board
CAA	Constitutional Amendment Act
CDMA	Code Division Multiple Access
CDP	City Development plan
CEO	Chief Executive Officer
CESC	Calcutta Electric Supply Corporation
CPI (M)	Communist Party of India (Marxist)
CRC	Citizens Report Cards
CSO	Civil Society Organization

DMRC	Delhi Metro Rail Corporation
DPEP	District Primary Education Programme
DPR	Detailed Project Report
DPC	District Planning Committee
DPSC	District Primary School Council
DoS	Department of Shipping
DoT	Department of Telecom
GoAP	Government of Andhra Pradesh
GoB	Government of Bihar
GEB	Gujarat Electricity Board
GERC	Gujarat Electricity Regulatory Commission
GoG	Government of Gujarat
GoI	Government of India
GIDB	Gujarat Infrastructure Development Board
GIIC	Gujarat Industrial Investment Corporation
GoK	Government of Karnataka
GMB	Gujarat Maritime Board
GSM	Global System for Mobile Comminication
GoWB	Government of West Bengal
IAS	Indian Administrative Service
IFAI	Federal Institute for Access to Public Information
JNPT	Jawaharlal Nehru Port Trust
JNNURM	Jawaharlal Nehru National Urban Renewal Mission
KSCB	Karnataka Slum Clearance Board
MPC	Metropolitan Planning Council
MTNL	Mahanagar Telephone Nigam Limited
MoU	Memorandum of Understanding
NCTD	National Capital Territory of Delhi
NGO	Non-governmental Organization
NSICT	Nava Sheva International Container Terminal
NTP	National Telecom Policy
O&M	operations and maintenance
PAC	Public Affairs Centre
PIO	Public Information Officer
PMC	Patna Municipal Corporation
PPP	public–private partnership
PSE	Public Sector Enterprise
PUA	Patna Urban Agglomeration
RTI	Right to Information
RWD	Rural Works Department

SEB	State Electricity Board
SES	Senior Executive Service
SFC	State Finance Commission
SISI	Sistema de Solicitudes de Información
SIC	State Information Commissioner
SOE	State-owned Enterprise
SP	Superintendent of Police
SSA	Sarva Shiksha Abhiyan
SWM	Solid Waste Management
TAMP	Tariff Authority for Major Ports
TDSAT	Telecom Dispute Settlement Appellate Tribunal
TRAI	Telecom Regulatory Authority of India
ULB	Urban Local Body
ULCRA	Urban Land Ceiling and Regulation Act
VRS	Voluntary Retirement Scheme
WBPDCL	West Bengal Power Development Corporation Limited
WBSEB	West Bengal State Electricity Board
WBERC	West Bengal Electricity Regulatory Commission

Acknowledgements

Improving the quality of public service delivery is a crucial step towards achieving the overarching objective of inclusive growth in India. I am indebted to a long list of individuals who commented extensively on chapters of the book including: Anupama Dokeniya, Stephen Howes, and Sanjay Pradhan (Chapter 2); Dwaipan Bhattacharyya and Verena Fritz (Chapter 3); Vinaya Bhargava, and James Manor (Chapter 4); Amit Kapur and Ashish Khanna (Chapter 5); Om Prakash Mathur and Chetan Vaidya (Chapter 6); Ranjana Mukherjee, Naresh C. Saxena, and Chunlin Zhang (Chapter 7); and Marcos Mendiburu, Richard Messick, and Naseer Ahmad Rana (Chapter 8). Others who provided comments on different sections of the manuscript included Ahmad Ahsan, Arnab Bandyopadhyay, Bhavna Bhatia, Richard Clifford, Dipak Dasgupta, Kwawu Mensan Gaba, William Kingdom, Mohan Nagarajan, John Speakman, and Sri Kumar Tadimalla. I am grateful to Joel Hellman, James Manor, Samuel Paul and Naresh C. Saxena, for comments on the volume. I would like to thank Dipak Dasgupta, Shantayanan Davarajan, and Joel Hellman for stimulating discussions on the themes of this work. A word of thanks is due to Pinaki Joddar, Kaushik Sarkar, and Monika Sharma, all of whom provided research assistance as well as to Vidya Kamath for administrative support. I would like to thank the Department of Administrative Reforms and Public Grievances, Ministry of Personnel, Public Grievances and Pensions, Government of India for their comments. Finally, I would like to thank Oxford University Press and Adil Tyabji for doing an excellent job in readying the manuscript for publication.

Vikram K. Chand

Acknowledgements

[illegible]

1

Context, Complexity, and Contingency

Understanding the Process of Reforming Public Service Delivery in India

VIKRAM K. CHAND

This book examines processes of change and reform in public service delivery in a range of states, sectors, and time periods. Understanding exactly how change takes place is a key objective of this work. What emerges from the seven studies of reform processes included in this volume is a picture of considerable complexity, the importance of context, the role of leadership in fashioning a strategy that seizes opportunities for change, and the presence of unpredictability, uncertainty, and contingency. Reformers often groped their way step by step towards reform, not knowing at the outset how the enterprise would turn out. Experimentation, trial-and-error, and learning from past experience played a crucial role in the process of effecting change. Reform in this sense was anything but the execution of a blue-print designed in advance and seamlessly implemented. Instead, the process of reform involved mastering 'the science of muddling through' or 'bricolage'—putting together different pieces of the puzzle in ways that advanced reform in a mostly incremental fashion.[1] Serendipity, including the presence of key civil servants at a particular juncture in key departments along with an authorizing environment at the top, also played a key role.

Tinkering or small changes on the margin emerged as the most powerful form of effecting reform; constant tinkering on the margin could eventually add up to major shifts over time, but in a way that did not trigger counter-reform pressures that might derail the process entirely.[2] Couching reform strategies in the metaphors and language understood by elites and masses alike often helped push the process along in our studies.[3] The reforms studied here reveal an extraordinary creativity with which reformers juggled different factors often in an unstable environment, experimenting with different institutional forms as they searched for solutions that might work. What emerged was a quilt of changes uniquely stitched together rather than the mechanical application of 'best practices', a half-hearted attempt to straightjacket (or wish away) an inevitably unruly reform process.

Goals also shifted over time: as one challenge was overcome, the calculus of opportunities and constraints facing reformers changed, leading to a refashioning of goals. Successful reforms emerged primarily out of a dynamic home-grown process rather than a strategy designed ex ante revolving around international models of change.[4] Identifying the incentives reinforcing (or limiting) change was crucial for understanding reform processes as a whole.[5] Many solutions to problems (some even regarded as 'best practices') have failed for want of a proper understanding of the incentives facing local actors in particular settings.[6] Intentions could thus diverge from outcomes. Reform solutions displayed considerable variety, which is another way to say that functions did not map into particular forms clearly or consistently.[7] Although reform was mostly a messy process involving considerable uncertainly and luck, the results did approximate standard reform goals in terms of better public service delivery and faster growth. There was agreement on what the results of reform should be but no standard path to get there.[8] In the cases studied here, elements of complexity also included Centre–state dynamics, the nuances of particular states and sectors, and variations in state capacity.[9]

A key finding emerging from these case studies is the role of ideas in the reform process: ideas of change could bubble to the surface from below; they could find their way into reform strategies through engagements with external actors, such as the Central government; and international ideas could work their way into the fabric of domestic reform debates through a process of transmutation involving the interaction of local reform movements and global networks over time.[10]

EXPLAINING CASE SELECTION

This volume examines change in several states, sectors, and issue areas; the choice of case studies was eclectic but all were major cases sharing the fact of change. We chose three states for special study: Bihar, West

Bengal, and Gujarat. The three states varied significantly in their growth trajectories.[11] Gujarat was among the fastest growing states with a buoyant industrial sector: The state grew at an annual average of 8 per cent between 1994–5 and 1999–2000 and 8.8 per cent between 2000–1 and 2007–8. West Bengal, a state long in industrial decline, but with a growing agricultural economy, performed reasonably well in the 1990s growing at an annual average of approximately 7.1 per cent between 1994–5 and 1999–2000. A significant deceleration of growth, however, occurred between 2000–1 and 2003–4 when the average annual rate of growth slowed down to 5.3 per cent, thus heightening pressures to boost employment through greater private investment, for example. West Bengal did better in the latter half of the decade with the annual average growth rate picking up to 7.6 per cent between 2004–5 and 2007–8. Overall, the state grew at an annual average of 6.4 per cent between 2000–1 and 2007–8. On the other hand, a combination of poor governance and low public investment severely limited annual average gross state domestic product (GSDP) growth in Bihar to only 4.7 per cent between 1994–5 and 1999–2000. This pattern of low growth persisted in the early 2000s with Bihar growing at only 4.5 per cent between 2000–1 and 2003–4. However, a dramatic change occurred between 2004–5 and 2007–8 when the annual average growth of GSDP increased to 11.3 per cent compared to 11.1 per cent for Gujarat and far ahead of West Bengal's 7.6 per cent for the same period.

Bihar offers a model of a very poor state in eastern India that has successfully pursued a range of reforms that have considerably improved the prospects for economic growth and poverty alleviation. West Bengal is an example of the use of incremental strategies to improve the functioning of public sector enterprises and the power sector to promote economic growth in a state long dominated by the left.[12] Gujarat is an altogether different model relying on the efficient delivery of economic services to attract investment by a bureaucracy intent on pursuing consistently high growth in a state known historically for its industrial base and commercial acumen. The shift in Bihar towards a new emphasis on delivering public services and fostering growth; the incrementalism of West Bengal; and the long-term developmentalist focus of Gujarat are all examples from which one can absorb lessons about how change happens on the ground.

In terms of sectors, we focus on regulation in infrastructure as well as the delivery of urban services. Effective regulation is crucial to break investment barriers in sectors, such as telecommunications, ports, and power, to ensure a level playing field between incumbents and private investors, set objective rules of the game, separate policymakers from providers, and protect consumers from predatory behaviour. Reforming regulation in infrastructure is thus likely to have a major effect on India's overall development prospects. The reason for focusing on the urban sector is that it represents a laboratory of change. Transforming India's cities will make a crucial difference to the quality of life of many Indians who are likely to migrate to urban centres in the future and foster an environment conducive to technological change, investment, and innovation in India's fast growing cities.

In terms of issue areas, this volume focuses first on the question of how to balance greater autonomy with accountability to improve the delivery of public services through the use of executive agencies on the lines of New Zealand, the UK, Australia, and Japan. Second, it focuses on how India might absorb lessons for the effective implementation of the Right to Information (RTI) Act, 2005, from countries such as Mexico, South Africa, and Canada. India has a long home-grown movement that succeeded in propelling the enactment of a pioneering right to information law that itself constitutes best practice; the chances, therefore, of adapting and extending from elsewhere successful practices relating to implementation are thus good. On the other hand, there are few local precedents of the executive agency model being successfully applied in India for a variety of reasons; attempts to restructure the delivery of public services along these lines are thus likely to be more difficult.

HOW DID CHANGE HAPPEN?

Understanding Processes of Changes at the State Level

The Importance of Leadership

The emergence of a leadership oriented towards development in Bihar resulted in a multi-pronged approach to reforming public services and faster economic growth.

A major shift took place in Bihar in 2005 with the rise of a reform coalition.[13] This shift was the product of long administrative neglect and social polarization that resulted in a virtual breakdown of the delivery of public services. Law and order collapsed while public spending ground to a halt. The breakdown of the state translated into almost non-existent public services, especially outside Patna, including non-functional schools and primary health clinics and dilapidated roads. In effect, reform ideas had become sufficiently popular with citizens that they chose to support a new alternative to resolving the state's problems. Bihar is clearly a case of change driven by ideas from below and executed by a reform-oriented leadership.[14]

Public expectations drove the new focus on development as the main goal of state policy. In a sense, voters, and political actors, learnt from the past, resulting in a major reshaping of the policy framework. The key focus of the new government was to restore public confidence by reasserting the rule of law. This involved a series of changes ranging from reorienting the police from merely filing a charge-sheet to focusing more on successful prosecution to improved coordination between the judiciary, the state government, and local police to better investigative techniques. It also involved structural changes, such as the adoption of a Police Act designed to reduce interference in the working of the police force as well as the hiring of some 70,000 ex-servicemen on a contractual basis to enforce law and order in particularly difficult areas. These changes resulted in the virtual disappearance of the kidnapping-for-ransom industry in Bihar, along with a steep fall in road hold-ups and bank robberies, and murders more generally.

Meanwhile, public spending on social and economic services jumped dramatically, aided by a decision to activate spending by significantly decentralizing financial powers at all levels of the administrative hierarchy. In health, education, and roads, the government was woefully understaffed: staffing concerns were alleviated by hiring new doctors in the health department and engineers on contract for road construction, as well as some 170,000 teachers controlled directly by local Panchayati Raj Institutions (PRIs). For road construction, simple changes like hiring an outside company to assist the Rural Works Department with the preparation of detailed project reports allowed the government to access precious funds from the Central government's Pradhan Mantri Gram Sadak Yojna (PMGSY) to improve rural road connectivity across the state.

Some real innovations occurred as well. In order to improve the quality of health services, the government chose to outsource monitoring to a private company. This company was made responsible for collecting data on the performance of health facilities in the state's blocks and for uploading it onto the department's website, thus allowing the secretary (Health) to track performance on a daily basis. In order to make it easier for citizens to file requests under the RTI, the government set up a call centre to process such requests efficiently. This initiative, Jaankari, has been nationally hailed as a best practice, making access to information relatively easy in a context marked by high illiteracy and disempowerment. Another significant achievement was the passage of the landmark Panchayati Raj Act in 2006 that earmarked 50 per cent of all elected positions in rural local government for women within the reserved and unreserved categories. It also granted village assemblies (Gram Sabhas) the power to select beneficiaries for government programmes and monitor implementation through social audits, for example. The Act also provided for the creation of a parallel structure of Gram Kutcheris (village courts) designed to resolve minor disputes and help decongest the court system.

The government appointed experienced civil servants to key departments important for the reform process and gave them the necessary autonomy and stability of tenure to achieve results in the context of a favourable authorizing environment. The results have indeed been positive, although challenges remain, stemming from weak capacity (especially at the lower levels of the civil service), the need to beef up monitoring further, and the problem of case backlogs in the judicial system. In the roads sector, a big effort has been made to upgrade major district roads: some 3,432 km have been refurbished between 2006–7 and 2008–9. In health, the number of out-patients visiting a government hospital rose, on average, from 39 per month in January 2006 to 4,380 in October 2008.[15] In education, enrolment at the primary and upper primary levels rose by 8 per cent between 2006–7 and 2007–8, while the number of out-of-school children fell steeply by 77 per cent between 2006–7 and 2008–9 (World Bank 2010: 10). The pupil–teacher ratio improved from 63:1 to 53:1 as a result of hiring the first round of 100,000 teachers, and may fall further to the national norm of 40:1 when teachers hired in the second round are actually placed in schools.

The persistence of reform over a period of almost five years appears to have improved economic outcomes as well. Bihar thus presents a fascinating case study of how changes in institutions, including better law and order, roads, and administration, fuelled economic growth in an unprecedented manner.[16] The multi-pronged approach of the government towards reform revealed a certain agnosticism about what might constitute the 'binding constraint' to Bihar's economic growth. It simply used common sense to attack the most visible problems ranging from law and order to low public spending to focusing on roads, health, and education all at once.[17] The willingness of the government to engage with a variety of actors, including think-tanks, foreign and Indian universities, the Planning Commission, and other agencies indicated a new openness to ideas that flowed from the change in the policy framework sparked by voter fatigue with the old way of doing business. Although several important reforms occurred in many areas, Bihar is still a case of incremental, albeit rapid, reform: most changes involved getting the existing machinery of administration to work better through changes in rules, better enforcement, and improved monitoring, along with efforts to address capacity problems by allowing much new recruitment, private contracting, and outsourcing. Partly because of the low base that Bihar started with on most parameters, these changes on the margin had a pronounced effect: in aggregate terms, GSDP grew significantly from an annual average of 4.5 per cent between 1999–2000 and 2003–4 (the pre-reform period) to 10.7 per cent between 2004–5 and 2008–9 (the reform period) (Central Statistical Organization various years).

Seizing Opportunities for Change

Changing incentives produced uneven reform in West Bengal; the reform process was aided by incremental tactics and strategies. Reformers seized the opportunities for change, especially in the area of the power sector. Effective communication was a critical part of the reform process, as was support furnished by external actors.

If Bihar is a case of incremental reform telescoped into a compressed time frame, West Bengal represents an incremental approach to adjusting policy in response to altered incentives, but over a longer time period. Sumir Lal addresses the core question of what drives the reform of public services, in the context of a puzzle in the Indian state of West Bengal—its push to improve industrial investment services while focusing less on human development. Through comparative case studies of the state's public enterprise and power sectors on the one hand, and its elementary education sector on the other, he finds a successful reform programme with important theoretical lessons, in the first case, while in the second a host of perverse incentives and tangled accountability relationships continue to prevail.

A combination of fiscal distress combined with a change in the overall framework of economic policy at the Central government level after 1991, and the growing need to boost employment rates in the state led to a shift in West Bengal towards a renewed emphasis on industrialization fuelled by private capital. The government announced a new industrial policy to welcome foreign and domestic investors. It also began the process of reforming its public sector enterprises in the late 1990s. The strategy for reforming public enterprises involved building ownership by helping employees own the problem; including all those who could influence the outcome of change in the discussions about restructuring; concentrating first on those directly affected by change, especially employees; and proceeding in small, realistic, and sequential steps. Ownership and inclusion complemented an incremental strategy towards reforming public sector enterprises (PSEs) beginning from the inside-out, that is with employees first.

Reform was couched in terms of improving the business performance of PSEs rather than privatization, reform, or restructuring. The emphasis was on communicating the dire financial position of PSEs in regular meetings between senior management, supervisors, and workers' unions: as a result, the unions themselves internalized the need for structural change. Only after three years of such mostly private discussions was the process of actual restructuring begun. At this stage, the government approached a bilateral agency for support to finance a voluntary restructuring programme; unions were involved in the selection of the consultants who would oversee the administration of the voluntary retirement scheme (VRS); comparisons with other similar schemes in other countries were deliberately downplayed; and the consulting team was composed entirely of Indians, mostly Bengalis, for cultural sensitivity. The government then engaged in another round of face-to-face meetings with employees and party forums to communicate the fact that PSEs were overstaffed and lacked capital; that change was inevitable because the government lacked the funds to keep these PSEs afloat and inaction would simply result in closure; and that inefficient PSEs absorbed funds badly needed to spur growth and reduce poverty. The first phase of the PSE restructuring programme was almost completed by 2006–7 with over 6,000 employees taking advantage of the VRS and 21 PSEs being closed down entirely.

A similarly measured strategy was put in place to rescue the power sector. The West Bengal State Electricity Board (WSEB) in the late 1990s was running up losses of around Rs 12 billion a year, which the financially strapped state government could simply not cover. Again the government did not rush headlong into restructuring, but preferred to focus first on financial improvements and better management. The reform process was carefully sequenced to ensure the cooperation of employees without alienating powerful middle class consumers with tariff hikes in the absence of improvements in service quality. The old Board of WSEB was asked to quit and reconstituted with a trusted Indian Administrative Service (IAS) officer at its helm to spearhead the reform process. A joint management council consisting of unions, management, and associations was established to create and monitor new performance targets and develop accountability measures. Talk of restructuring was muted but the implication was that it would occur if the unions failed to take remedial actions immediately. The chairman also suspended several corrupt WSEB officials with the backing of political leadership; this was followed by the passage of anti-theft law in December 2001 and stringent actions against government departments that had not paid their dues to WSEB. As a result of these measures, employee productivity rose significantly between 2004–5 and 2007–8 and WSEB's commercial performance also improved considerably.

At this stage the government decided to proceed with the unbundling of WSEB into separate generation, transmission, and distribution companies. Clearly, enough preparatory reform had occurred to begin the process of unbundling. Also, the government wanted to take advantage of the Centre's Accelerated Power Development and Reforms Programme (APDRP) which involved the exchange of soft loans for the fulfilment of reform targets. The passage of the Central Electricity Act in 2003 provided an additional spur for unbundling. Initially, the unions objected to unbundling as a form of privatization, but the government was able to take them along during the three-year period set aside to achieve this goal.

What explains the relative success of the transformation of West Bengal's power sector? Taking the reform process forward incrementally gave employees time to adjust to its inevitability. Involving the unions up-front before any reforms were implemented greatly helped reassure employees. West Bengal was also fortunate that it did not have to contend with a powerful farmer lobby intent on obtaining free power for electric pumps sets (most agriculture in West Bengal is rain fed). On the other hand, the government had a major incentive to reform the power sector which was pivotal for its plan to industrialize the state, attract investment, and win over the growing urban middle class. Incentives furnished by the Central government also helped nudge the West Bengal government to cross the Rubicon of unbundling. The appointment of empowered technocrats with the full support of the state government in both the PSE and power sector cases was a key factor in the execution of reforms. The need for the Communist Party of India (Marxist), CPI(M), to take along unions and employees thus led to a series of tactical innovations based on consultation, careful sequencing, and incremental steps towards reform that ultimately worked. In short, the reform process was highly opportunistic depending on contextual factors specific to West Bengal (for example, the strength of unions, the absence of a farmer lobby, and the fiscal crisis) to shape its course.

On the other hand, the government was distinctly less successful in improving human development outcomes, especially in education. No political party in West Bengal has historically made education a priority with public spending on education remaining relatively low throughout. The CPI(M)'s striking achievements in redistributing land and reactivating PRIs in the state were not matched by a similar breakthrough in education. Indeed, the attention of the state (the policymaker) has clearly been focused on these other areas of reform. High rates of absenteeism and poor learning outcomes clearly indicate low levels of teacher commitment. The inspection system that must undergird an effective school system has also largely atrophied. Lal argues that this reflects the strength that teachers have acquired as an organized interest group within the system. Because teachers play a crucial role in garnering support for the existing order (not just in West Bengal but in several other states as well), they have had a critical advantage in dealing with the state. As a consequence, teachers in West Bengal have become relatively wealthy as a result of higher salaries (compared to market rates) and additional income in the form of fees received for private tutoring. At the same time, parents, especially from marginal communities, while wanting quality education, have been unable to press for it effectively.

Lal concludes his essay by comparing the incentives facing reformers in the power/PSE sector on the one hand, and education on the other. In the first case, incentives clearly favoured reform, but significantly less so in the second case. If the state's fiscal crisis compelled the government to restructure the power sector, the availability of large Central funds for education may have bailed out the state government, diluting the incentives for reforms. If the reform of the power sector was fuelled by the politically influential urban middle classes and industry, the 'clients' in the education sector were dispersed, marginal, and powerless. If the media in big cities was gripped by the story of PSE and power sector reforms, little attention was paid to the need to improve education in rural areas. Finally, the process of restructuring the PSE/power sectors was more manageable than in the education sector, which involved much larger numbers, dispersed over a large geographical area, and multiple institutional actors. In the end, Lal does not see a contradiction between a renewed focus on education and the state's industrialization policy, arguing that a well-educated labour force is a prerequisite for inclusive growth. In fact, he argues that the key to reforming the education sector in West Bengal lies in applying the lessons learnt in reforming the PSE and power sectors, such as painstaking consultation with unions/ employees, an incremental and well-sequenced approach to change, and creating institutional focal points to drive the reform process with full ownership by the leadership. At key points, external actors played a positive role with a bilateral donor agency stepping in to fund a VRS and the Central Electricity Act offering a new framework for thinking about how to reform the sector. Couching reform in terms most likely to appeal to employees and other groups initially set against change pointed to the importance of effective communication strategies.

Reform in a High Growth State

A high growth state reforms economic and other services to stay ahead of other states. The successful pursuit of reforms in Gujarat reflected several factors: a positive historical legacy; strong state capacity; support from the private sector; a willingness to allow reformers to experiment and develop new reform designs through a process of learning and trial and error; and a measure of luck. External actors reinforced an essentially home-grown reform process at critical junctures.

Gujarat's gross domestic product (GDP) grew at 10.2 per cent per annum during 2002–7 (Government of Gujarat, 2008). Initial conditions favoured its development: the state has a strong industrial base, a large private sector, and a high degree of state capacity, that is, a system able to translate policy changes into concrete results on the ground. This historical legacy clearly made reforms easier to pursue and shaped the nature and course of the process.

It is also worth noting the close relationship between the private sector and the state in Gujarat, translating into a high degree of policy convergence. The Gujarati state is highly entrepreneurial, always looking for opportunities to foster economic growth. Even during the restrictive licence raj, Gujarat's government made strenuous efforts to divert licences to the state and then promptly involved the private sector in manufacturing through the concept of 'joint sector' companies.

Gujarat is also well known for its high level of state capacity. State capacity is a complex concept but in the end it implies the ability to implement policy decisions effectively. Because of this ability to translate policy into action, Gujarat does have a reputation of being able to extend credible commitments to investors interested in working in the state, explaining the state's popularity with large Indian business firms as a destination for investment in a range of activities. The state also possesses strong mobilization abilities, as evidenced by the campaign to boost the enrolment of girls in schools in Gujarat. Effective top-down monitoring is also a feature of governance in the state through the use of overlapping committees, working groups, and institutions, as well as regular interaction between the political leadership and senior civil servants to resolve problems.[18] As Aseema Sinha notes, even in the early 1990s Gujarat benchmarked itself not with the rest of India but with the Asian tigers in South-East and East Asia.

The change in the national model after 1991 compelled Gujarat to alter its approach to economic growth in the state. Institutions were no longer needed to funnel Central production quotas to Gujarat, but to spur private investment by improving infrastructure. Fiscal constraints also played a role in pushing the state towards reform in the mid-1990s. While a large loan from a multilateral lending institution in 1996–7 helped catalyse some of these reform ideas and provided cover for civil servants who believed in them, the loan itself came because of Gujarat's prior commitment to core reform ideas expressed in the State Finance Commission of 1994. In this sense, reform was clearly home-grown and not the result of external involvement. The proceeds from this loan were used to finance the state government's privatization programme by offering a voluntary retirement scheme to some 14,000 employees, especially from the decaying Gujarat State Textile Corporation. High levels of political commitment, tight monitoring by senior civil servants, and the availability of funds for the VRS were all critical factors in the success of Gujarat's privatization programme from the mid- to late-1990s.

The government quickly realized that infrastructure development was the key to the state's prospects in the post-1991 liberalization era. In 1995, it adopted a new industrial policy, a new energy policy, and a new IT policy. It also created the Gujarat Infrastructure Development Board (GIDB) to act as a nodal agency for infrastructure development by catalysing private sector investment. The Gujarat Maritime Board Act was amended in 1995 to allow two IAS officers to head it instead of the engineers who ran it in the past. A new ports policy was announced in 1995, designed explicitly to develop Gujarat as a major source of cargo traffic as an alternative to Bombay (now Mumbai). The private sector was viewed a key factor in port development, albeit in collaboration with the government, an extension of the old joint stock concept. As ports developed, so did industry around ports and employment. Politicians quickly realized the potential of port development for Gujarat as a whole, including the power sector which relied heavily on imported coal for the operation of thermal generating plants. New rules were adopted to explicitly promote public–private partnerships (PPPs) in ports based on competitive bidding and, in 2007, viability gap funding. Today, the state has India's only chemical-handling port, one of three liquefied natural gas (LNG) terminals, and India's largest private port. Gujarat currently handles approximately one-third of India's total cargo traffic and two-thirds of non-major port traffic, a stunning achievement.

Major changes occurred in the power sector in Gujarat between 2003 and 2009. The Gujarat Electricity Board (GEB) was divided into six corporate entities without privatization or removing any employees. From a utility that lost Rs 1,932 crore in the early 2000s, the GEB registered a modest profit of Rs 200 crore in 2006–7 along with a significant reduction of losses on account of transmission and distribution. Sinha argues that this process was one that took place in fits-and-starts during which decision makers learnt from the past. That the authorizing environment facilitated this transition is not in doubt but the process of reform itself involved a good deal of what Sinha calls 'non-linearity' and pure luck.

Gujarat had tried to reform its power sector in the mid-1990s but the sequencing was not quite right. The government negotiated power purchase agreements with private sector producers at adverse rates instead of tackling the issue of improving the working of GEB head-on. Adverse power purchase agreements worsened the financial straits of the GEB, which, in the absence of tariff hikes, had to bear the costs of this. As GEB approached financial bankruptcy in 2002, a series of reforms focusing on GEB itself followed. Procurement procedures were tightened to reduce costs; defaulters, especially industries, were compelled to pay their dues; and high-interest loans taken by GEB were refinanced. The political leadership took a strong stand on power theft, giving GEB the space to crack down on transmission and distribution losses. Finally, power purchase agreements were renegotiated over a period of one year, greatly improving the financial position of the GEB. That this was done voluntarily through negotiation minimized any damage to the credibility of the government in the eyes of investors. A key serendipitous factor in the success of the reforms in power lay in the fact that the chairperson of GEB (a highly regarded civil servant) was at the same time secretary of the state's energy department as well as the chairperson of its energy-related public sector enterprises. This was truly a fortuitous circumstance, a case of the right person in the right positions at the right time to push the reform process forward. Learning from the past; designing an incremental programme focusing first on the GEB itself, then the renegotiation of PPPs, and later unbundling; and contingent factors thus all came together to create a successful reform experience.

Finally, Gujarat has in recent years done much to improve the enrolment of girls in primary schools around the state. The groundwork for boosting the enrolment of girls in primary schools was laid by District Primary Education Programme (DPEP), a Central government programme that focused on backward districts in states, such as Gujarat, in its second phase. As a result of the boost in enrolment, the demand for better infrastructure in schools (for example, functioning toilets, more classrooms, drinking water facilities) multiplied in the state.

The success of DPEP was quickly absorbed by the political leadership in Gujarat. The leadership launched a massive campaign across the state to promote the enrolment of children in school, involving senior civil servants, local district officials, and ministers. The campaign was also closely synchronized with aggressive monitoring of the targets and objectives set by the Central government programme of Sarva Shiksha Abhiyan (SSA), which also sought to boost enrolment, particularly of girls, and improve quality of education. In this sense, a Central government programme fully owned by the state government resulted in what Sinha calls a 'convergent framework' that helped raise school enrolments across the state, along with a highly visible campaign to achieve this objective.

Given Gujarat's special characteristics, one could ask whether other states could learn from its experience. Clearly, there is much to learn from Gujarat despite its somewhat unique experience. One common lesson emerging from the Gujarat experience is the importance of building state capacity to achieve development goals through better programme monitoring, closer coordination with the private sector to fashion a strategy for growth, and the use of the state apparatus to campaign for development objectives.

Putting in place competent civil servants to implement a politically supported reform programme (along with stability of tenure for them) is certainly another lesson that Gujarat offers to other states, but this is only part of the story. It is precisely the autonomy to experiment with the development of a reform strategy within a supportive authorizing environment that affords the civil servant the room to search for solutions to complicated problems, eliminating some possibilities and pursuing others. The search for a solution is inevitably laden with uncertainty, risks, and choices through which the reform process unfolds: it involves much more than simply asking a civil servant to carry out a pre-determined set of plans. Autonomy is thus a prerequisite for unleashing the creativity and experimentation needed to find solutions to the pressing dilemmas faced by the state.

Again, as in West Bengal, external actors helped nudge the reform process further along. A loan from a multilateral development agency made it easier for reformers to argue the case for the reform ideas that they supported anyway with sceptics; the loan also helped finance a VRS programme that facilitated the process of privatization. These reform ideas were shaped primarily by Gujarat's internal deliberations primarily at the level of senior civil servants and politicians in response to locally perceived challenges with strong input from the private sector. Central programmes also helped shape the process of educational reforms: DPEP first focused the state government on the issue of the enrolment of girls, while SSA provided a further incentive to continue doing so.

Gujarat also offers a range of models through which public service delivery reform can occur, starting from concepts such as the joint sector company to a variety of PPPs to outright control by the private sector (in case of some ports in Gujarat) that could be emulated by other states, recognizing that these concepts were common in Gujarat long before they became popular in India as a whole. Gujarat also shows what can happen when the state government supports the effective implementation of a Centrally sponsored scheme, such as the SSA. Such schemes are far more likely to succeed when state governments own their objectives than when they do not. Gujarat illustrates the importance of credibility for development: the ability of the state to provide a credible framework of rules for infrastructure development and investment and also to revise those rules periodically to reflect changes on the ground points to the importance of getting rules right and taking feedback from key stakeholders seriously in formulating them.[19]

Understanding Processes of Change in Sectors

The Challenge of Regulation in Infrastructure

Home-grown ideas helped the reform process in telecommunications and the power sector, particularly in Andhra Pradesh. On the other hand, weak incentives limited the development of ports. High-level support was necessary to overcome vested interests opposed to the reform process. Political economy factors played an important role in the differential levels of success of the reform process in all three sectors.

Effective regulation in infrastructure is crucial to promote accountability by separating policymakers from providers; to foster private sector participation by ensuring a level playing field between incumbents and new investors; and to protect consumers from predatory behaviour. The growth of effective regulation in the telecommunications sector has opened the door to a flood of private investment with growth exceeding all expectations. In January 2010, India crossed the 580 million telephone mark and its tele-density per hundred people was 49.5 (data available with Telecom Regulatory Authority of India [TRAI] on http://www.trai.gov.in/Default.asp).

What explains the remarkable growth of the telecommunications sector in India? Telecommunications reform has a long history in India, going back to the 1980s when the Department of Telecommunications (DoT) was separated from the Department of Posts in 1981, which helped the government to focus more closely on reforming the sector. The Prime Minister's Office (PMO) also took the lead throughout the process of reform, beginning with the decision to corporatize DoT by creating the Mahanagar Telephone Nigam Limited Company (MTNL) to serve Delhi and Mumbai. At the insistence of Prime Minister Rajiv Gandhi in the late 1980s, the Centre for the Development of Telematics (CDoT) was created to develop telecom switches, resulting in the creation and proliferation of the Rural Automatic Exchange (RAX) switch. Most rural networks in India today are served by RAX switches. Telecom reform—and the direct involvement of the PMO in promoting it—was thus already an established fact by the end of the 1980s.

The National Telecom Policy (NTP) of 1994 allowed private sector entry in basic fixed telephony but did not set up a regulatory mechanism to ensure fair treatment of new players. Complaints about the fairness of the bidding process that ensued led to the creation of a relatively weak regulator, the TRAI, in 1997. At the time, the incumbent—the DoT-supported MTNL—sought to obtain licence-free entry into the Global System for Mobile Communications (GSM) cellular telephony business, resulting in a crisis of private investment in the sector. The intervention of the PMO—driven by pressure from India's emerging software industry and the recognition that India's economic power globally depended on the success of its IT and telecom sectors—led to a decision to reinforce the regulator and thereby create a clear level playing field between state-owned incumbents and private players. In 2000, TRAI was given additional authority in the area of licensing and a Telecom Dispute Settlement Appellate Tribunal (TDSAT) was established. TDSAT had the sole authority to mediate disputes between the DoT and service providers, barring an appeal to the Supreme Court. As a result, private sector investment in the GSM cellular business boomed, aided by the fact that the provision of mobile telephony services was intrinsically a less capital-intensive business than fixed line services. Meanwhile, the foreign equity limit in the sector was raised from 49 per cent to 74 per cent between 2004 and 2006, adding to the rate of fast growth in the sector.

The long history of home-grown reform efforts in the sector, the involvement of the PMO in pushing along the process of reform, and the resultant creation of an independent regulator were critical factors in the success of telecom reform in India. It is worth noting that telecom reform was a subject entirely in the hands of the Central government with consumers who were willing and able to pay higher tariffs early on, especially in urban areas. In the end, however, tariffs fell steadily as volumes expanded, while quality improved at the same time.

Reform has been slower in the ports sector for several reasons. Although India depends heavily on ports to fuel trade (Indian ports carry 70 per cent of all trade in terms of value and 95 per cent in terms of volume), unlike telecom, there has been less focus at the highest levels of government on this crucial issue. The PMO, for example, has not been directly engaged with the issue in the way it was in the case of telecom. The reasons for this are unclear, but one could surmise that vested interests opposed to reform were stronger in ports than in the telecom sector. The Department of Shipping (DoS) remains the most powerful decision-maker in the area of major ports; the Tariff Authority for Major Ports (TAMP) has no licensing authority, only tariff-setting authority. It depends heavily on the DoS for appointments and financial resources. The ports sector, in comparison to telecom, thus lacks a clear separation between the policymaker and the provider; in the absence of a powerful regulator, private investment in ports has been limited and modernization has not taken off in the way that one would hope given the centrality of the sector for India's overall growth prospects.

There is little history of home-grown efforts to reform the major ports sector, though, as we saw earlier, a handful of states have taken the lead in this area, particularly Gujarat, largely on their own initiative. The rules governing the functioning of major ports have also discouraged their competitiveness in relation to other ports, such as Dubai, Singapore, and Colombo. Port trusts responsible for governing landlord ports have been dominated by representatives of the government and trade unions. Port trusts have often had a vested interest in prolonging cargo storage to earn higher demurrage charges, as Rahul Mukherji points out. Rules governing bidding in ports favoured higher bids because they yielded higher royalties to the port trusts, thus discouraging participation by the private sector. Nor does TAMP take royalty payments into account when determining costs as a basis for tariff setting. Treating royalty as an ingredient of cost would yield more realistic tariff rates for private operators. Also, while India has one of the lowest cargo charges in the world, vessel-related charges levied by port trusts are far above international benchmarks. This is not to say that there have been no successful examples of reforms in the major ports sector—the creation of a privately operated container terminal in the Jawaharlal Nehru Port Trust in Mumbai has certainly improved the quality of port services there. Yet, the absence of a strong regulator, along with rules that act as a disincentive for investment, has limited the growth of the sector to a level that is clearly far below its real potential.[20]

On the other hand, Andhra Pradesh has done well in the area of power sector reform, despite the fact that it has a large farmer community dependent on the use of electric pump-sets for irrigation. Mukherji attributes the relatively good performance of the power sector in Andhra Pradesh to the fact that the state had by the mid-1990s already developed a powerful home-grown set of ideas to grapple with the problem. A 1995 report by a committee constituted by the state government underscored the need to expand generation capacity by involving the private sector in light of the state's fiscal crunch, highlighted the problem of agricultural tariffs, supported the unbundling of the state electricity utility, pointed to the need to reduce power theft and adopt new technology, and endorsed the creation of an independent regulatory authority to rationalize the tariff-setting process (Bhaya 1995).

The political leadership strongly supported the reform of the state's power sector. The availability of a large pool of technocratic talent in the civil service helped steer the reform process in a skilful manner. Andhra Pradesh passed an Electricity Reform Act in 1998, unbundled the state electricity utility into two separate generating (APGENCO) and transmission companies (APTRANSCO). In 2000, APTRANSCO was further unbundled into four distribution companies. In a way, the state benefited from the fact that APGENCO was relatively efficient with a plant-load factor of 84 per cent (April 2007—January 2008); the rise of less efficient independent power producers with a guaranteed rate of return underlined the need to assure a level playing field, this time in favour of the state incumbent vis-à-vis private players. The Andhra Pradesh Electricity Regulatory Commission (APERC) was established in 1999. APERC's first tariff order was issued in 2000 after a series of public hearings, which increased the legitimacy of the new regulator. The political leadership gave the regulator considerable space to perform autonomously in its early years, setting its course for the future. The government also got tough on power theft, as in West Bengal and Gujarat, but it was difficult to measure accurately the decline in the level of theft because it was easy to post losses due to theft to unmetered agricultural consumption.[21] Because of the relatively high quality of generation and a fall in industrial power tariffs, the number of industrial users grew, allowing the state to cross-subsidize agricultural consumption in the process and offset to some extent the losses entailed by the decision to provide free power to farmers.

Mukherji argues that the decision to provide such free power is a regressive one, more likely to favour large and middle-sized farmers over small and marginal ones who rely more on rain-fed agriculture and ponds for water. He also notes a significant decline in the quality of free power, resulting in frequent motor burn-outs and higher maintenance charges (more costly for small farmers than large ones), power wastage, and the risk of electrocution. The paradox is that the majority of farmers, especially poorer ones, would have preferred to pay for better quality power than get low quality, free power. In this area, however, the regulator was unable to intervene to check the influence of richer farmers in shaping agricultural power tariffs. This was in sharp contrast to West Bengal where all rural consumption was metered and farmers benefiting from rain-fed agriculture and abundant groundwater did not need to use electric pumps on the same scale as in Andhra Pradesh. The relative absence of a sizeable farmer lobby dependent on irrigation pump-sets made it easier to reform the power sector in West Bengal. In Andhra Pradesh, on the other hand, the presence of a strong farmer lobby heavily dependent on irrigation pump-sets made it more difficult to reform the sector in the absence of a countervailing movement against the costs of free power by marginal and small farmers who gained little from such subsidies compared to large farmers.

Urban Reforms in Three Cities

The ability (and need) of cities to respond to Central incentives for urban reform furnished by the Jawaharlal Nehru National Urban Renewal Mission (JNNURM) depended on contextual factors, such as the commitment of the state government to reform; the capacity of urban local bodies to absorb Central funds; and the prior trajectory and history of reforms. JNNURM provided a central reference point for establishing common standards and ideas of good governance in urban areas.

The institution of a comprehensive Central programme—the JNNURM in 2005—has provided a vital impetus for urban reform. Darshini Mahadevia does not seek to assess the impact of JNNURM itself; rather, her main goal is to contextualize the intersection of this programme with the urban reform process in three cities/states: Ahmedabad in Gujarat, Bangalore in Karnataka, and Patna in Bihar.[22] These cities were chosen for three main reasons: they are all corporation cities; they have different institutional models for delivering services (for example, direct provision in the case of the Ahmedabad Municipal Corporation, provision mostly by parastatals in Bangalore, and provision mostly by government departments in Patna); and they vary in rank in terms of the release of Additional Central Assistance (ACA) funds from JNNURM and the enactment of reforms needed to access such funds. Ahmedabad ranks 12th out of 62 JNNURM cities based on a combination of these criteria; Bangalore 23rd, and Patna 44th. These rankings are clearly not objective: some cities with a strong resource base may have less need to access funds available under the programme, while others may have already enacted some of the reforms required under JNNURM.

JNNURM had a major effect on Bihar, where the urban policy framework has been significantly reformed. On the other hand, many of the reforms that now constitute part of JNNURM were already in place in Bangalore before the programme and many of the reforms that took place later might have happened anyway. The same could be said of Ahmedabad, though JNNURM clearly offered an incentive to raise participation in city governance. Both Bangalore and Ahmedabad had the necessary capacity to absorb JNNURM funds, which may explain their greater use of funds under the programme compared to Patna. Where state governments did not wish to cooperate (for example, by strengthening the local funding base of cities or decentralizing public service delivery to urban local bodies [ULBs]), these reforms were not carried out, at least not in the three cities under study.

The state government in Bihar has responded to the incentives offered by JNNURM for urban policy reform. It repealed the Urban Land Ceiling and Regulation Act (ULCRA) in August 2006; stamp duty has been cut steeply from 18 per cent to 5 per cent; bye-laws have been amended to improve the process of approvals for building construction, while provisions have been made for rainwater harvesting and structural safety; and the process of property registration has been simplified through computerization. The task of planning has been transferred from the Patna Regional Development Authority to the Patna Municipal Corporation (PMC) and District Planning Committes (DPCs).

On the other hand, capacity remains low in the Patna Urban Agglomeration (PUA) area consisting of the PMC and adjoining municipalities. The shift to double-entry municipal accounting has been difficult given the lack of trained accountants. The frequent transfer of urban functionaries, especially chief executive officers, has disrupted the thread of continuity needed to implement reforms effectively. The lack of technical capacity to prepare detailed project reports (DPRs) necessary to access JNNURM funds under the programme has limited usage. Because PUA municipalities lack capacity to deliver services, the state government has been compelled to create an Urban Infrastructure Development Corporation to help implement projects supported by the Urban Infrastructure and Governance (UIG) component of JNNURM. Low capacity has limited the ability of PUA municipalities to absorb JNNURM funds and achieve some reform milestones, despite the positive changes in the urban policy framework in Bihar.

Neither Ahmedabad nor Bangalore face a lack of capacity to deliver municipal services. In fact, both cities have been leaders in urban reform. Ahmedabad distinguished itself by being the first city to raise funds by issuing municipal bonds worth Rs 100 crore in 1998 without any state guarantee. The repeal of ULCRA, a key JNNURM milestone, took place as early as 1999 in Karnataka. In 2000, the introduction of a more transparent self-assessment scheme for property taxes led to a large revenue increase for the Bangalore city corporation. Bangalore was the first municipal corporation to adopt the double-entry accounting system. In 2002, the city moved to a sophisticated fund-based accounting system that allowed for better tracking of funds. Both cities have done well on e-governance, including providing records (such as birth and death certificates) online, delivering several services electronically, including property tax payments, and e-procurement (in the case of Bangalore).

Given their prior trajectory of urban reforms (stemming in part from their larger resource base and capacity relative to many other cities), the impact of JNNURM in Bangalore and Ahmedabad has been less extensive. In both cases, JNNURM has solidified the development of new participatory structures. Bangalore now has 33 functioning ward committees. In Ahmedabad, the state government enacted a community participation law in 2007 and proceeded with the creation of ward committees. The 2007–8 Ahmedabad city budget was prepared on the basis of submissions by these ward committees. The construction of new housing units for slum dwellers has been facilitated by JNNURM's Basic Services for the Urban Poor (BSUP) component in both cities, although Ahmedabad went further by allotting land to construct new dwelling units for the poor rather than only upgrading existing ones in situ. E-Governance continued to make rapid progress in the two cities, but this may well have happened without JNNURM.

On the other hand, where the respective state governments were reluctant, reforms were more difficult to accomplish in those areas, despite incentives offered by JNNURM. In Bangalore, for example, no serious attempt was made to move away from the parastatal route for delivering services to direct provision by ULBs, although parastatals were asked to enter into contractual agreements with city governments. These contracts were intended to give ULBs greater control, for example, by spelling out in legal terms what was expected from parastatals. Parastatals performed quite well in Bangalore, as evidenced by report cards of the Public Affairs Centre (PAC), which noted high levels of satisfaction with city services.[23] The public at large was thus not necessarily in favour of restructuring the parastatal model, underlining the larger point that the institutional form of delivering public services may not matter all that much as long as it works. In both city corporations, the state governments enlarged the boundaries of the two cities without adequate consultation, leading to a fall in property tax coverage and collection (new areas incorporated had not been adequately assessed beforehand). Neither state has shown much interest in financial devolution to city governments, with the Gujarat government abolishing octroi, a major source of ULB revenue and a 'bad' tax by any account, but without compensation for the loss of revenue.

Cities have responded in their own particular ways to this important initiative depending on their past experiences with urban reform, the priorities of state governments, and the capacity to carry out reforms on the ground. Clearly, these contextual factors had a significant effect on how JNNURM played out locally. It is also important to note that JNNURM has established for the first time a clear understanding of common ideas about what constitutes urban reform in the Indian city of today.

Understanding Processes of Change in Issue Areas

International experience indicated that the use of executive agencies could improve the delivery of some public services, but these ideas did not find much resonance in India. On the other hand, global experience relating to the right to information was seamlessly adapted to the Indian setting. The presence of an organic movement for RTI shaped largely by home-grown processes explains its superior ability to successfully integrate global practices. On the other hand, there was less receptivity to the executive agency model among policymakers and fewer precedents to support its application on the lines of the UK or New Zealand.[24] *Autonomy in the Indian setting was more the result of serendipity than design on the whole.*

The Executive Agency Model and Civil Service Reform in India

Several countries—particularly the UK, New Zealand, Sweden, Japan, and Australia—have adopted the executive agency model to deliver public services more effectively. Executive agencies have the following common characteristics across countries: they are concerned exclusively with service provision, not policymaking, which remains with the parent ministry. They are commonly headed by a chief executive officer (CEO) who is recruited from the open market or the regular civil service; CEOs are given autonomy over staffing and financial decisions, including the freedom to recruit staff from the private sector at market rates. In exchange for autonomy, CEOs enter into a performance agreement with the minister of the department, specifying clearly the outputs expected of the agency within a hard budget envelope set by the minister concerned. The agency delivers an annual performance report that is tabled in the legislature, thereby retaining the principle of legislative oversight. Several countries have created a Senior Executive Service (SES) to staff higher posts in the civil service and CEO positions in executive agencies. Typically, SES positions are filled on the basis of competitive recruitment from both the regular civil service and the private sector; appointees are given fixed-term assignments on a contractual basis with compensation packages that mirror market salaries so as to draw the best talent into government.

As S.K. Das notes, the executive agency model has proven to be successful in many countries. In the UK, for example, there are some 140 executive agencies in existence, covering a range of services such as the issuance of passports and drivers' licences; the collection of income taxes, customs duties, and excise levies; prison management; child support; and even weather forecasting. An independent review commissioned by the UK government in 2002 concluded that the executive agency model has brought about 'revolutionary changes' and created a more 'responsive and accountable framework' for delivering services. Similar reforms in New Zealand during the 1980s also helped improve the country's fiscal position by substantially cutting unit costs across agencies. Sweden has had a version of the executive agency model in place for a very long time.

Annual public surveys reveal high levels of satisfaction among Swedish users of such services. Japan has also recently begun a transition to the executive agency model, despite some opposition from the traditional civil service. By 2004, the country had 105 Independent Administrative Institutes and 224,000 civil servants attached to them.

One cost of the executive agency model noted in the literature (see Nunberg, 1994: 29) is the problem of 'enclaving'—the risk that individuals recruited to a particular agency will suffer from tunnel vision and loyalty to that agency alone rather than the civil service as a whole. Others have pointed out that the executive agency model can upset the balance of pay and seniority grades in the civil service. In Sweden, for example, the CEOs of executive agencies are often paid more than high-level civil servants working in policymaking ministries. One way around the problem of 'enclaving' is to create an SES that would involve choosing senior policymakers and CEOs on a competitive basis, knitting them in a common institutional framework.

While Indian policymakers have recognized the importance of both autonomy and accountability as important factors in service provision and created a host of boards, companies, and societies to deliver services, these have not always performed in the way that they were intended. Das notes that for the most part half-hearted autonomy has been combined with weak accountability, resulting in a situation sometimes even worse than direct ministerial control. More often than not such bodies have worked in the Indian setting mainly for serendipitous factors. The example of the Delhi Metro Rail Corporation (DMRC) is a case in point. Because the DMRC is a joint venture between the Government of India and the Government of the National Capital Territory of Delhi (NCTD), it does not need to report to a particular Central or state ministry. Its chairman is so well regarded by virtue of his long-standing reputation as an outstanding innovator and administrator of complex projects that he has been given space to run DMRC in an autonomous fashion. The authorizing environment for the DMRC is also much stronger than in the case of other bodies; DMRC projects are approved by a Group of Ministers (GoM) committee specially created for this purpose. Generally though, most societies, boards, or companies created in India to deliver public services do not enjoy the same level of autonomy or the tight accountability arrangements that go along with the executive agency model in other countries. Boards are not always chaired by professionals, CEOs have limited scope for managing staff or varying salary scales, and CEOs themselves often enjoy only an uncertain tenure.

The Second Administrative Reforms Committee has openly endorsed the idea of adopting the executive agency model on a wide scale in India (Second Administrative Reforms Commission, 2008: 303). Yet, there appears to be little broader support for its adoption. The Draft Civil Services Reform Bill (2009) does not, for example, contain a provision for creating executive agencies on the lines of other countries or the establishment of an SES. In short, a good idea that has worked well globally lacks resonance within policymaking circles in India. Politicians may worry that creating an executive agency might undermine their control over the functioning of such an agency, while civil servants may be concerned about the erosion of the core values of a unified civil service. These are legitimate concerns and much more will need to happen before policy elites turn wholeheartedly to the executive agency model. The decision of the government to turn over the issuance of passports to a private company is a positive step in this direction.[25]

If politicians can see that they will be able to claim credit for the resulting improvements in public service delivery and if senior civil servants come to realize that they will be able to clinch most of the positions in a future SES, as in Australia, then opposition to the executive agency model may dissipate. Some conditions needed to implant the executive agency model already exist, such as the prior existence of a rules-based civil service from which it is possible to carve out executive agencies in the first place, and the large availability of talent from inside and outside government to manage and staff them effectively. But for this model to be widely implemented will require high-level ownership; a communication strategy that convinces those opposed to the model that they could gain from it in the end; and more public pressure to improve public service delivery systems generally.

Implementing the Right to Information in India

Fostering greater access to information about government programmes and schemes is an important tool to empower citizens to access public services more effectively by making them more aware of their rights, allowing them to cross-check official claims with the actual state of affairs, and pushing officials to be more transparent in their dealings with the public. Ensuring access to information can also have significant multiplier effects by aiding the delivery of other public services as well.[26]

The adoption of a revised Indian RTI law in 2005 marked a watershed in the history of governance reform in India. The RTI Act (2005) applies to both Central and state governments. It provides for an independent channel of appeals in the form of the Central and State Information Commissions, permits the imposition of penalties on public information officers (PIOs), places a host of implementation obligations on the executive, and has wide provisions for proactive or suo motu disclosure. These are all regarded as 'best practices' in freedom of information laws around the world over. In fact, the Indian Act contained a number of innovations that themselves could be considered valuable additions to the stock of 'best practices'. The Act, for example, defines 'information' in broad terms including any material recorded in any form, a standard global best practice, but adds a fascinating twist: it includes 'samples' as a form of recorded information. This mirrors the uniquely Indian experience of taking samples from construction projects, including roads or buildings, to verify if they meet the standards set out in written agreements with contractors in public hearings, for example. Another example is the provision that information be released within 48 hours when it concerns the life and liberty of a person rather than the standard period of 30 days. This provision, as Toby Mendel argues, reflects the Indian experience of linking the use of RTI to the supply of human entitlements necessary for the right to life, such as minimum wages, access to food, and shelter.

The Indian Act provides for unusually strong proactive disclosure requirements that surpass many other Acts around the world. It provides, for example, for the suo motu release of information relating to 'the manner of execution of subsidy programmes, including the amounts allocated as well as the details of beneficiaries of such programmes' (Section 4, 1b, XII) as well as the 'particulars of recipients granted concessions, permits, or authorizations' (Section 4, 1b, XIII). Government authorities are also asked to 'publish all relevant facts while formulating important policies' or announcing decisions that affect the public (Section 4, 1c). The proactive disclosure provisions also cover (as do several others Acts) budgetary transparency questions, including information on budget allocations, plans, expenditures, and disbursements (Section 4, 1b, XI).

The Indian RTI Act not only successfully integrate global best practices, but produced several innovations as well. This outcome reflects the development of a large home-grown movement around RTI in India that was able to employ what was useful in the global toolkit relating to RTI through its international networks, while at the same time developing new tools to address distinctly Indian challenges.

The history of the RTI movement in India is long and complex.[27] In 1975, for example, the Supreme Court in a landmark case ruled that the public had a 'right to know'. In 1982, the Court again ruled that right to information was a fundamental right under the Indian Constitution. The Bhopal gas tragedy in 1984 also led to demands by civil society, particularly environmentalists, for greater transparency. The 1990s were marked by a new development: the proliferation of grassroots organizations seeking to use access to information to secure basic entitlements for the poor. In Rajasthan, for example, the Mazdoor Kisan Shakti Sangathan (MKSS) found that securing access to documents to prove that workers had worked at all was necessary to ensure the payment of minimum wages, including muster rolls as well as details of public works sanctioned by the government. In 1994, the MKSS held public hearings (*jansunwai*s) to audit government works in front of the local community, a process that uncovered ghost works and ghost workers.[28] Under considerable pressure, the Government of Rajasthan proceeded to enact its own RTI law in 2000. Meanwhile, RTI was also used effectively to enforce entitlements for poorer urban residents in Delhi where a local non-governmental organization (NGO), Parivartan, successfully used the Delhi Right to Information Act to expose the diversion of subsidized food to the open market by fair price shop dealers in collusion with government food inspectors as well as ghost workers.

The widespread use of RTI as an instrument to reduce corruption in development programmes was thus the hallmark of the Indian RTI movement and its singular contribution as well. Finally, various states, such as Maharashtra, Karnataka, Tamil Nadu, Rajasthan, Madhya Pradesh, and Goa, had already adopted their own RTI Acts long before a national law was in place. These states' experiences provided an important laboratory for experimenting with RTI across the country and developing a broad consensus in favour of a national RTI law. The first national law was adopted in 2002 but it lacked an independent appeals process, failed to provide for the imposition of penalties, and applied only to the Central government. With the strong support of the National Advisory Council, a revised law was adopted in 2005 that remedied these weaknesses and set a new standard for RTI around the world. The concept of RTI thus resonated in India because of the RTI movement's ability to give it a thrust that was deeply relevant to ordinary citizens in both rural and urban areas.

The challenge is to effectively implement the law across a vast and complex country. Mendel examines some of these challenges ranging from overcoming an entrenched tradition of secrecy, making access to records easier, to engaging the public in support of RTI. Based on an analysis of how other countries, such as Mexico, Canada, and South Africa, have approached such challenges, he suggests ways in which the Indian RTI movement and policymakers might address them as well. Given the ferment surrounding RTI in India, it is likely that many of these ideas ranging from the greater use of information technology to manage records to fostering incentives for PIOs to comply with the provisions of the Act to involving civil society actors and the media will find resonance and eventually be implemented in the Indian setting. In fact, three evaluations have already been conducted by Indian actors to benchmark the implementation of RTI in the country.[29]

Civil society, information commissions, and Central and state governments are thus clearly wrestling with how to take the process forward in a creative and organic fashion. Some best practices in implementation have already begun to emerge from this process, including Jaankari in Bihar; the development of comprehensive request tracking system in Orissa; the practice of sending an SMS to brief an appellant on the status of his/her appeal in the case of the Andhra Pradesh Information Commission, along with an electronic case-tracking system; the use of videoconferencing to facilitate hearings by the Central Information Commission; and a system to rank compliance with the RTI law by public authorities in Uttarakhand developed by the state Information Commission.[30] India may thus turn out to be as adept at integrating and innovating new best practices in RTI implementation as it was in designing the law itself, once again drawing on its home-grown RTI movement. Indeed, RTI has now emerged as a key part of India's democratic culture and folklore.[31]

IN CONCLUSION

This volume demonstrates the complexity of reform processes. It shows how reforms depend critically on contextual factors, such as the history of reform ideas, the capacity of the state to execute reform, and the nature of the state itself including its relationships with key actors, such as the private sector and unions. Context is important in a broader sense as well: It defines the issues that need to be addressed and offers a set of opportunities and constraints that policymakers cannot ignore in formulating policy options. A key part of the reform process involves shifting the context by rearranging relationships among key actors and adjusting mutual expectations and perceptions.

Two elements linked to the context of reform merit special mention here: the role of ideas and state capacity in the reform process. Ideas could take the form of a desire for change among the public at large (as in

Bihar); they could emerge from internal discussions among policy elites and related players, such as the private sector (as in Gujarat); they could be shaped by the policy framework provided by external actors, such as the Central government in the case of urban reforms; finally, ideas derived from global experience were more likely to be integrated and accepted when a home-grown movement already existed that could absorb (and modify) them, as was the case of India's RTI movement.

Capacity also played a key role in the process of implementing reform in the cases studied. Capacity involves several dimensions, such as the ability to monitor the progress of reform, coordinate the actions of different players, and mobilize administration for the achievement of goals. Gujarat clearly scored high on state capacity, unlike Bihar which continues to wrestle with the problem of weak capacity especially at lower levels of administration. Bihar, however, offers telling examples of how to overcome such constraints through large-scale hiring on contract, outsourcing, and the use of information technology to monitor important programmes.

Contingency is a critical factor in an unfolding reform process. While the authorizing environment may be positive and the capacity of the civil service high, individual reformers often have to deal with the unpredictable as they develop reform strategies. Their ability to seize opportunities when they arise, fend off threats when they appear, and take calculated risks to promote reform cannot be underestimated. Balancing several factors at once in a shifting and uncertain environment requires strategies to makes sense of complexity. Reformers do this in a variety of ways: they choose a particular sequence or path of change which automatically rules out the pursuit of other possible paths, they listen to signals from some quarters, but not others, and they view context through the filters of their own worldviews. Complexity thus comes into focus, allowing for the emergence of a more concrete reform path. This reform path is mostly non-linear in character, marked by trial and error, experimentation, and gradual learning as some options are discarded in favour of others, some strategies pursued and others left by the wayside. A prerequisite for the creative learning necessary to produce genuine reform is a measure of autonomy that allows for the space needed to make mistakes, learn from them, and then go back to the drawing board to do better the next time around.

Tactics are a crucial part of the reformers' repertoire ranging from preparing the ground for change well beforehand through extensive consultation, sequencing reform in a way that minimizes disruption from groups which could derail the process altogether, to even the framing of terms and symbols associated with the process of change. All of the reforms examined occurred more or less incrementally. Yet, incremental reforms can over time themselves generate a major change but without the pain associated with more abrupt shifts. Incremental reforms are reassuring in the sense that each step can be viewed as potentially reversible, thus defusing opposition and allowing government to move forward. Yet, as such incremental steps build rapidly on each other, the direction of change as a whole will become irreversible (or reversible at an ever increasing cost). Incremental reforms also allow reformers to assess how they are doing and adjust course if necessary. Shifting goalposts are thus an inevitable part of any reform process. Reformers must face the right incentives to implement change; otherwise even the most desirable of changes have no chance of succeeding. Understanding and correctly identifying those incentives in a particular historical, economic, and social setting over time is a critical part of the process of successful reform.

All this suggests that there is no single magic bullet to achieve reform, no blueprint that can simply be applied to a situation to 'fix' it, no best practice that is a best practice everywhere at any time. Reform is an art that cannot be reduced to a set of formulas learnt and applied like a diligent student. It has a life of its own involving a complex process of learning by doing, making decisions without complete information and with only a partial knowledge of consequences, and contending with pulls and counter-pulls. This is not to say that reformers cannot benefit (sometimes greatly) from experiences elsewhere but to make the point that learning is likely to occur best when integrated with an organically shaped strategy and movement for change.

NOTES

1. See the classic article by Lindblom (1959); see also Lindblom (1979). For a good discussion of the concept of 'bricolage' in development, see Scott (1998: 324); see also, Claude Levi-Strauss (1966), and Hirschman (1965b).
2. On the logic of incrementalism, see North (1990: Chapter 11, 92–104).
3. On the importance of 'framing' reform ideas, see Campbell (1998).
4. On the difficulties of applying international models in the field of legal reform, for example, see Pistor (2002). On the problem of 'dirigisme' in development thinking, see Sabel and Reddy (2007).
5. For an excellent discussion of incentives, perverse and positive, as they face particular decision-makers in particular contexts, see Easterly (2002: especially Part III).

6. This is pointed out in embarrassing detail (for the development community) by Easterly (2002: Part II).

7. On the heterogeneity of institutional forms for delivering public services, all of which could equally serve similar purposes, see Woolcock and Pritchett (2002).

8. On the many paths to change, see Rodrik (2007). This point is reiterated in The World Bank (2008).

9. For a discussion of the dimensions of state capacity, see Fukuyama (2004).

10. The literature on ideas and policymaking is voluminous. A few examples of this rich literature include Sikkink (1991); Pierson (1993); Campbell (1998); and Blyth (2002).

11. Central Statistical Organization, Ministry of Statistics and Programme Implementation, Government of India at http://mospi.nic.in/rept%20_%20pubn/ftest.asp?rept_id=nad03_1993_1994&type=NSSO, accessed on 10 May 2010 for 1993–94 to 1999–2000; See also, http://mospi.nic.in/rept%20_%20pubn/ftest.asp?rept_id=nad03_1999_2000&type=NSSO for subsequent years (2001–2 to 2007–8) accessed on 10 May 2010.

12. The reformist orientation of the Communist Party of India (Marxist) in West Bengal provided an interesting example of change at the state level sometimes at variance with the positions of the national party politburo.

13. For an insightful analysis of shifts in policy, see Hall (1993).

14. When this threshold was crossed, as opposed to being manifested in an election, is difficult to say. The notion of 'thresholds' is inevitably subjective in nature. For a summary of the literature on 'thresholds' of change, see Collier and Norden (1992).

15. Government of Bihar, Finance Department (2009: 164).

16. Bihar thus vindicates the proposition of institutional economists that institutions (rules and norms) are crucial for economic growth. Clearly, improvements in law and order translated into a more favourable environment for economic activity, contract enforcement, and the security of property rights. More efficient administration and investments in key sectors, particularly roads, obviously played a part in this as well. For works in this tradition, see North (1990). See also North (1981); World Bank (1998); and Williamson (2005).

17. Rodrik (2007) urges readers to identify binding constraints to growth. While in principle identifying a binding constraint to growth might seem a sensible approach, in practice binding constraints are hard to identify. This does not mean that Bihar's reformers did not have some idea of prioritization—clearly, law and order, roads, and the social sectors were at the top of their initial agenda; power sector reform, on the other hand, was given less priority. The idea that one can identify a binding obstacle and then attack it to achieve change has been questioned by Albert O. Hirschman. See his brilliant article, 'Obstacles to Development: A Classification and Quasi-Vanishing Act' (Hirschman 1965a).

18. On the importance of top-down monitoring in another context, see Olken (2007).

19. On the importance of credible commitments for development, see the classic piece by North and Weingast (1989).

20. North notes that the wrong rules can foster a low productivity trap. If these rules persist over time, the costs of overturning them are inevitably high as actors benefiting from such rules become entrenched. See North (1990).

21. Power theft in Andhra Pradesh is believed to have fallen from 37.9 per cent in 2000/1 to 19.06 per cent in December 2007.

22. See the chapter by Mahadevia in this volume for an explanation of why these cities were chosen for examination.

23. For a detailed study of report cards, see Balakrishnan (2006).

24. On the role of resonance in translating policy ideas from one setting to another, and the factors that shape such resonance see, in the Latin American context, Sikkink (1991).

25. The appointment of a former CEO of Infosys to manage India's highly complex, unique ID number project appears to be another step in the direction of moving towards an 'executive agency' model.

26. On this issue see, in the Indian context, Pandey et al. (2008). Based on a cluster randomized control trial, the authors show how a systematic information campaign improved learning outcomes, teacher effort, as well as the delivery of benefits, such as stipends, uniforms, and the midday meal.

27. The story of India's RTI movement is eloquently told by Singh (2007).

28. Singh (2007: 6). See version provided to this author by Shekhar Singh; for published version of the same article see Singh (2007).

29. See Department of Personnel and Training (DoPT) (2009). The DoPT study was prepared by PricewaterhouseCoopers and converged with the findings of another major study by the RTI Assessment and Analysis Group (RaaG) and the National Campaign for the People's Right to Information (NCPRI) (2009). The DoPT/PWC study can be accessed at http://rti.gov.in/rticorner/studybypwc/index-study.htm, accessed on 15 January 2010. The RaaG/NCPRI executive summary is available at http://rti-assessment.org/exe_summ_report.pdf, accessed on 15 January 2010. The third study is that prepared by a sub-committee constituted by the Central Information Commission to explore ways of strengthening RTI. See Annual Convention of Information Commissioners (2009).

30. Centre for Good Governance (2009).

31. In the first 30 months of the operation of India's RTI Act, some 2 million requests for information were filed (1.6 million from urban areas and 400,000 from rural areas). Over 30 per cent of all rural applicants were drawn from people who were below the poverty line, compared to 15 per cent of all urban applicants. See RaaG/NCPRI (2009).

BIBLIOGRAPHY

Acemoglu, Daron and James Robinson (2006), 'Economic Backwardness in Political Perspective', *American Political Science Review*, 100(1): 115–31.

Annual Convention of Information Commissioners (2009), (Briefing Book) *Report of the Sub-Committee of the Chief Information Commissioner, Central Information Commission*. New Delhi: Central Information Commission.

Balakrishnan, Suresh (2006), 'Making Service Delivery Reforms Work: The Bangalore Experience', in Vikram K. Chand (ed.), *Reinventing Public Service Delivery in India*, pp. 157–85. Delhi: Sage Publications.

Bhaya, Hiten (chair) (1995), *The Report of the High Level Committee: Guidelines on Restructuring and Privatisation of Power Sector and Power Tariff*. Hyderabad: Government of Andhra Pradesh.

Blyth, Mark (2002), *Great Transformations: Economic Ideas and Institutional Change in the Twentieth Century*. New York: Cambridge University Press.

Campbell, John L. (1998), 'Institutional Analysis and the Role of Ideas in Political Economy', *Theory and Society*, 27(3): 377–409.

Central Statistical Organization (various years) at http://mospi.nic.in/rept%20%20pubn/ftest.asp?rept id=nad03 1993 1994&type=NSSO, data for 1993–4, to 1999–2000, Ministry of Statistics and Programme Implementation, Government of India, accessed on 10 May 2010.

Central Statistical Organization (various years) at http://mospi.nic.in/rept%20%20pubn/ftest.asp?rept id=nad03 1999 2000&type=NSSO, data for 2001–2, to 2007–8, Ministry of Statistics and Programme Implementation, Government of India, accessed on 10 May 2010.

Central Statistical Organization (various years), 'Gross State Domestic Product at Factor Cost by Industry of Origin at 1999–2000 Prices as on 29-01-2010' for Bihar, available at www.mospi.nic.in, accessed on 8 February 2010.

Centre for Good Governance (2009), *Innovations/Good Practices (National and International) in Implementation of the Right to Information Act, 2005*. Hyderabad: Centre for Good Governance.

Collier, David and Deborah Norden (1992), 'Strategic Models of Political Change in Latin America', *Comparative Politics*, 25(2): 229–43.

Department of Personnel and Training (2009), *Final Report: Understanding the Key Issues and Constraints in Implementing the RTI Act*. New Delhi: DoPT, Government of India, June, available at http://rti.gov.in/rticorner/studybypwc/index-study.htm, accessed on 15 January 2010

Easterly, William (2002), *The Elusive Quest for Growth: Economists' Adventures and Misadventures in the Tropics*. Cambridge, MA: The MIT Press.

Fukuyama, Francis (2004), *State Building: Governance and World Order in the Twenty-First Century*. Ithaca, NY: Cornell University Press.

Government of Bihar, Finance Department (2008), *Economic Survey, 2007–2008*. Patna: Government of Bihar.

_________ (2009), *Economic Survey, 2008–2009*. Patna: Government of Bihar.

Government of Gujarat (2008), *Socio-Economic Review: Gujarat State, 2007–2008*. Gandhinagar: Government of Gujarat Press.

Hall, Peter A. (1993), 'Policy Paradigms, Social Learning, and the State: The Case of Economic Policymaking in Britain', *Comparative Politics*, 2(3): 275–96.

Hall, Peter A. and Rosemary Taylor (1996), 'Political Science and the Three New Institutionalisms', *Political Studies*, XLIV: 936–7.

Hirschman, Albert O. (1965a), 'Obstacles to Development: A Classification and Quasi-Vanishing Act', *Economic Development and Cultural Change*, 13(4): 385–93.

_________ (1965b), 'Models of Reform-Mongering', in Albert O. Hirschman, *Journey of Progress: Studies of Economic Policymaking in Latin America*. Garden City: Doubleday.

Levi-Strauss, Claude (1966), *The Savage Mind*. Chicago: The University of Chicago Press.

Lindblom, Charles E. (1959), 'The Science of Muddling Through', *Public Administration Review*, 19(2): 79–88.

_________ (1979), 'Still Muddling, Not Yet Through', *Public Administration Review*, November–December, 39(6): 517–26.

North, Douglass C. (1981), *Structure and Change in Economic History*. New York: W.W. Norton and Co.

_________ (1989), 'Institutions and Economic Growth: An Historical Introduction', *World Development*, 17(9): 1319–32.

_________ (1990), *Institutions, Institutional Change, and Economic Performance*. New York NY: Cambridge University Press.

North, Douglass C. and Barry Weingast (1989), 'Constitutions and Commitments: The Evolution of Institutions Governing Public Choice in Seventeenth-Century England', *The Journal of Economic History*, 49(4): 803–32.

Nunberg, Barbara (1994), *Managing the Civil Service: Reform Lessons from Advanced Industrialized Countries*, World Bank Discussion Paper 204. Washington D.C.: World Bank.

Olken, Benjamin A. (2007), 'Monitoring Corruption: Evidence from a Field Experiment in Indonesia', *Journal of Political Economy*, 115(21): 200–48.

Pandey, Priyanka, Sangeeta Goyal, and Venkatesh Sundararaman (2008), 'Community Participation in Schools: The Impact of Information Campaigns in Three Indian States', Policy Research Working Paper No. 4776, Impact Evaluation Series, No. 26. Washington D.C.: World Bank, South Asia Region.

Pierson, Paul (1993), 'When Effect Becomes Cause: Policy Feedback and Political Change', *World Politics*, 45(4): 595–628.

Pistor, Katharina (2002), 'The Standardization of Law and Its Effect on Developing Economies', *American Journal of Comparative Law*, 50(97): 97–130.

Roberts, Alasdair S. (forthcoming 2010), 'A Great and Revolutionary Law? The First Four Years of India's Right to Information Act', *Public Administration Review*, 70(6), November–December.

Rodrik, Dani (2007), *One Economics, Many Recipes: Organizations, Institutions, and Economic Growth*. Princeton, NJ: Princeton University Press.

RTI Assessment and Analysis Group (RaaG) and the National Campaign for the People's Right to Information (NCPRI) (2009), *Safeguarding the Right to Information: Report of the People's RTI Assessment, 2008—Revised Executive Summary and Draft Agenda for Action*. New Delhi: RaaG/NCPRI, October, available at http://rti-assessment.org/exe_summ_report.pdf, accessed on 15 January 2010.

Sabel, Charles and Sanjay Reddy (2007), 'Shaking up International Development: Learning to Learn: Undoing the Gordion Knot of Development Today', *Challenge*, 50(5): 73–92.

Scott, James (1998), *Seeing Like the State*. New Haven, CT: Yale University Press.

Second Administrative Reforms Commission (2008), *Tenth Report: Refurbishing of Public Administration*. New Delhi: Government of India.

Sikkink, Kathryn (1991), *Ideas and Institutions: Developmentalism in Brazil and Argentina*. Ithaca, NY: Cornell University Press.

Singh, Shekhar (2007), 'Social Mobilization and Transparency: The Indian Experience', in Ann Florini (ed.), *The Right to Know: Transparency in an Open World*, pp. 19-53. New York: Columbia University Press.

Telecom Regulatory Authority of India, http://www.trai.gov.in/Default.asp

Williamson, Oliver (2005), 'The Economics of Governance', *American Economic Review*, 95(2): 1–18.

Woolcock, Michael and Lant Pritchett (2002), 'Solutions when the Solution is the Problem: Arraying the Disarray in Development', Working Paper No. 10, September. Washington D.C.: Center for Global Development.

World Bank (1998), *Beyond the Washington Consensus: Institutions Matter*. Washington D.C.: World Bank.

_________ (2008), *The Growth Report: Strategies for Sustained Growth and Inclusive Development*. Washington D.C.: World Bank.

_________ (2010), 'Sarva Shiksha Abhiyan: Eleventh Joint Review Mission', 15–29 January (Aide Memoire). Washington D.C.: World Bank, South Asia Region.

2

Transforming Governance in a Lagging State

The Case of Bihar

VIKRAM K. CHAND

Bihar, traditionally regarded as the country's worst governed state, has experienced a sea change since November 2005 when a new coalition government was elected to power and then embarked on a wide-ranging set of reforms. The key common thread underlying all the reform initiatives of the government has been the construction of a functioning state capable of delivering public goods such as security, health, and education more effectively and with less corruption. It is worth noting that in several areas of governance reform, Bihar has sought to actively learn from other states, taking advantage of other reform experiences and adapting them to suit itself rather than attempting to reinvent the wheel. Best practices abound in areas relating to implementation of the Right to Information (RTI) law in Bihar; public–private partnerships (PPPs), outsourcing, and hiring new technical staff on contract have been the norms in key sectors, such as roads, health, and education; and a pioneering decentralization law has opened the door to a potentially powerful third tier of government. The turnaround has of course not been without its challenges: capacity, especially at lower levels of administration, remains weak but the prospects of overcoming these continuing challenges have considerably improved.

KEY DRIVERS OF CHANGE IN BIHAR: FROM IDENTITY POLITICS TO DEVELOPMENT

Jeffrey Witsoe refers to the rise of the backward castes in Bihar between 1990 and 2005 as an 'incomplete revolution'.[1] The government's principal objective at the time was to promote the caste empowerment of the other backward classes (OBCs) in a bid to loosen the control of the forward castes which ruled the roost in Bihar's feudal–agrarian society. The government succeeded in empowering the OBCs politically. However, economic divisions persisted between the 'upper' backward castes—which had gained access to land at the expense of the zamindars during the post-independence period and adopted an increasingly commercial approach to agriculture—and the 'lower' backward castes who were left behind, along with the Scheduled Castes, Dalits, and other such groups. In the process of empowering the OBCs and lower castes, the state de-institutionalized the power of the elite civil service; the judiciary, as an independent organ of government, fared better and served as a check on the populist tendencies of Bihar's politics during the period.

In the end, the legitimacy of forward caste rule in Bihar was shattered by the state's initiatives to empower the lower castes as well as the burgeoning Naxal movement in the countryside, and development, measured in terms of the effective delivery of public services, suffered with the whittling away of the bureaucracy's ability to function. Law and order collapsed, with Bihar becoming notorious for its flourishing kidnapping industry; teachers and doctors failed to perform their duties citing insecurity in the state's far-flung blocks as a reason; private industry fled the state; and the civil service, mirroring the lack of development focus at the top and fearful of becoming embroiled in anti-corruption investigations, put the brakes on capital investment and spending. In consequence, Bihar in 2005 had some of the country's worst roads, and the lack of road connectivity between villages and larger cities constituted a major bottleneck for the development of rural prosperity and a return to normalcy in the countryside.

On the other hand, there is no question that lower caste empowerment has occurred through their incorporation into the political process. However, economic empowerment resting on an effective model of development was neglected. This in turn created a unique opportunity for the new approach adopted by the combine that won power in November 2005. The fact that conditions in the state had deteriorated to such a degree and for so long effectively meant that the only legitimate alternative that the government could offer was a focus on development. The tenor of public opinion in 2005 in Bihar pointed virtually unidirectionally towards a focus on development. Support from the Central government, Bihar's many academic and non-governmental institutions, the Bihari diaspora in India and abroad, and a private sector more interested in investing in the state has clearly helped the new government to move ahead as it pursues wide-ranging reforms.

Public expectations and support clearly drive this transformation. An obvious risk is that the government will not be able to satisfy public demand for change, resulting in a return to apathy. However, so far this has not occurred: polls showed that well into its third year in office, the political leadership in Bihar remained popular with voters.[2] The incumbent coalition government, with its claims to have improved public services, performed well in the 2009 elections to the Lok Sabha, winning 32 out of 40 parliamentary seats in the state. Candidates linked to criminal factions lost in the elections, signalling a major change in the tolerance of the electorate for such candidates.

This chapter examines the reforms implemented in Bihar over the last five years to improve governance and public service delivery, as well as the reasons underlying the success documented here and the prospects for the sustainability of the reform process over time.

REASSERTING THE RULE OF LAW

Perhaps the most significant sign of decay of the state in Bihar was the near complete breakdown of the rule of law. This is where the most dramatic turnaround occurred in the performance of the state during the first 30 months of the government.

Eliminating Interference

The principal objective of the government was to eliminate political interference in the prosecution of criminals. The government has succeeded in punishing notorious criminals linked not only to opposition parties but also its own party. The message that the government will not protect the powerful has gone out loudly and clearly, reversing the impunity that criminals in politics enjoyed in the past. In order to shield the police more effectively from interference, Bihar became one of the first states to adopt a model police act to govern the state police.

The Police Act 2007 provides for a tenure of minimum two years for senior police officers, including the director-general of police (DGP), additional director generals (ADGs), inspector-generals (IGs), deputy inspector generals (DIGs), and district superintendents of police (SP), as well as more junior officers, such as station house officers (SHOs). The adoption of minimum tenures for police officers has made it more difficult to use the threat of transfers to affect the outcome of a police inquiry. The Police Act also creates a State Police Board, consisting of the chief secretary, the home secretary, and the DGP to review the performance of the police and implement changes designed to improve its functioning. It also establishes District Accountability Authorities consisting of the district magistrate (DM), additional DM, and the district SP to monitor the progress of complaints filed against police officers with the department.[3] The Act also mandates the separation of the investigation and law and order wings, thus shielding officers working on investigations from being re-deployed to tasks that might distract them from their core function. It is worth noting that not all states have adopted a police act, notwithstanding a Supreme Court directive to do so: Uttar Pradesh, for example, has refused to adopt such an act, fearing that the control of the police would slip out of the hands of the executive. Bihar, therefore, should be commended for taking such bold measures to depoliticize and professionalize the working of its police force.

Raising Conviction Rates

The government has sought to boost the conviction rate for criminals prosecuted under both the Arms Act and the Indian Penal Code (IPC). Rather than take any single big measure to achieve this objective, the government took numerous smaller ones in relation to the police, the judiciary, and the local administration. First, the government sought to reorient the police away from the old practice of filing charges against an offender, but then doing very little to mount an effective prosecution. SPs were told in no uncertain terms that they should focus on getting a conviction, not just filing a charge-sheet with a court. This, in turn, compelled the police to prioritize cases, focusing on those affording the highest prospect of obtaining a conviction, and also on improvement of investigative techniques and the handling of expert witnesses.

Minor changes added up to a great deal: for example, a small change in police procedure allowing the storage of exhibits used in cases in police district headquarters, rather than where the crime occurred, made it easier to produce such evidence in district courts and prevent tampering by local elements seeking to derail proceedings. A special court set up to try a dreaded criminal-cum-politician meted out a conviction (in 2008) that boosted the credibility of the Bihar government. SPs were told that their own performance would be evaluated in terms of the number of convictions they secured, not just on the basis of the charge-sheets filed.

Second, the government actively sought to bolster the capacity of the judiciary. The new government quickly approved a significant pay rise for judges, provided a generous sum of money for computerization, and sanctioned the hiring of over 300 new civil judges. The state government, the police, and the high court conferred together for the first time in decades to frame a strategy to achieve higher convictions in the bid to tackle lawlessness. The high court in turn began actively monitoring pendency rates in criminal proceedings, exerting pressure on judges to try cases faster. It created a mobile court that could move from district to district dispensing justice: the mobile court was a symbol of the high court's desire to address the problem of slow justice in Bihar. Third, the government responded to the poor training and shortage of police officers on the ground by hiring on contract some 7,000 ex-servicemen from the army to help maintain order. This is a novel approach to policing in India.

The first year of the new government was marked by a rapid increase in conviction rates. In 2006, 6,839 criminals were brought to justice compared to 9,853 in 2007, 12,007 in 2008, and 13,146 in 2009, as shown in Figure 2.2 (Data provided to author by the Police Department, Government of Bihar). Overall, 41,845 criminals have been convicted since January 2006 in trial courts across the state. Convictions over four years clearly show a rising trend based on a three-month moving average, notwithstanding a temporary dip between February and October 2007 after which convictions once more gathered pace (Figure 2.1).

One explanation for the dip was simply that the easiest cases had been tackled first, while the more complex ones requiring greater investigation were taken up subsequently. Convictions, however, resumed their upward path through 2008 and 2009, as the leadership stayed the course and the system adjusted to the pursuit of the more complex cases. A comparison of conviction data across four years shows a clearly rising trend by year (Figure 2.2).

Crime Trends in Bihar

Prior to 2005, neither crime nor conviction figures were reliable; the government simply did not focus on the collection of these numbers as an input into policy formulation. Given the law and order situation in Bihar prior to the declaration of President's Rule in February 2005, and

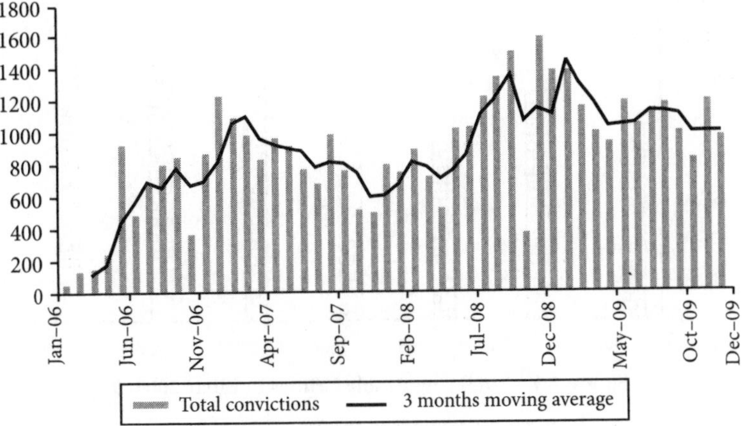

Figure 2.1 Monthly Conviction Rates in Bihar: January 2007 to December 2009[4]

Source: Data provided by the Police Department, Government of Bihar.

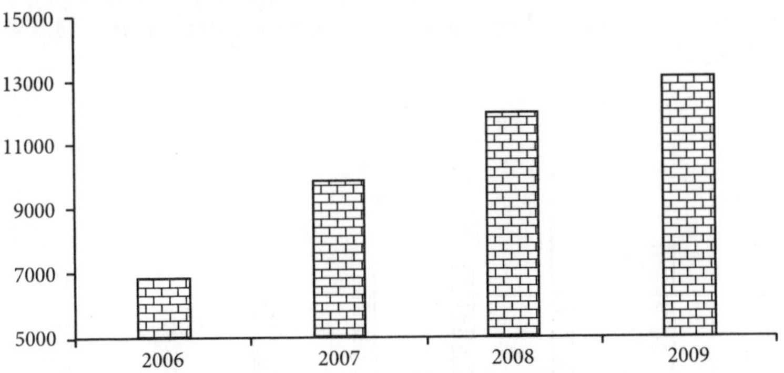

Figure 2.2 Annual Convictions in Bihar: 2006–9

Source: Data provided by the Police Department, Government of Bihar.

the political dimensions of the problem, the government understandably had less interest in such numbers. Since 2005, the total number of cognizable crimes committed has shown a small, but steady, upward trend from 104,778 in 2005 to 130,693 in 2008 and 133,525 in 2009 (Figure 2.3). This largely reflects a greater willingness on the part of the Bihar police to register crimes in the first place, along with more accurate data collection relating to crime in all its forms rather than an increase in crime rates per se.

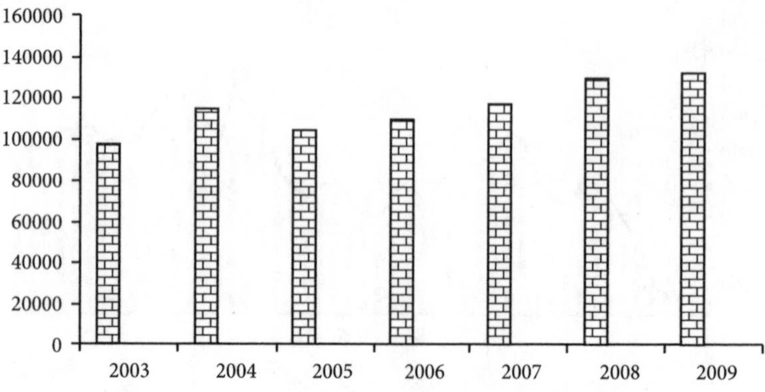

Figure 2.3 Total Cognizable Crimes in Bihar 2003–9

Source: Data provided by the Police Department, Government of Bihar.

On the other hand, there was a significant decline in some categories of major crime that could scare off investment, particularly kidnappings-for-ransom, road hold-ups, and bank robberies (see Figure 2.4 and Table 2.1).

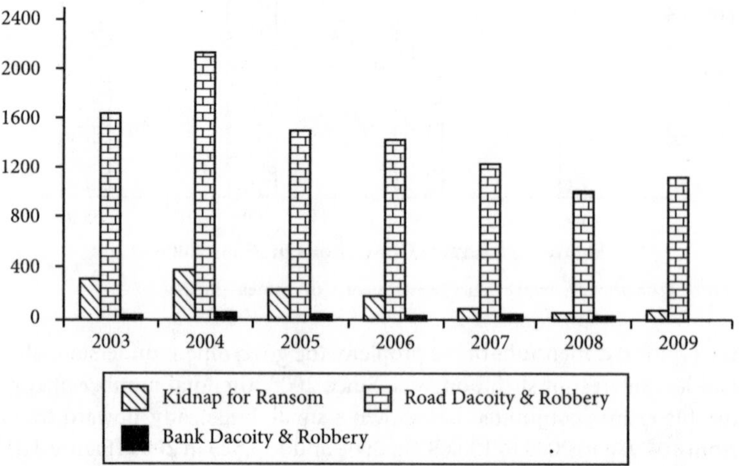

Figure 2.4 Kidnappings for Ransom, All Road Attacks (Dacoities and Robberies), All Bank Assaults (Dacoities and Robberies), 2003–9

Source: Data provided by the Police Department, Government of Bihar.

Kidnappings for other reasons (for example, murder, elopements treated as kidnappings) fell between 2004 and 2007, but not as sharply as kidnappings for ransom (Table 2.1). The number of murders fell by 18 per cent between 2004 and 2008. Bank robberies and dacoities were virtually eliminated between 2004 and 2009, falling by 86 per cent, while road hold-ups were halved in the same period.

Table 2.1 Bihar: Crimes by Category/Total Crime, 2004–9[5]

Year	Kidnappings (Excluding for Ransom)	Kidnapping for Ransom	Road Dacoities/ Robberies	Bank Dacoities/ Robberies	Murder	Total Cognizable Crimes
2004	2,566	411	2,162	57	3,861	115,216
2005	2,226	251	1,534	34	3,423	104,778
2006	2,301	194	1,462	20	3,225	110,716
2007	2,092	89	1,260	28	2,963	118,176
2008	2,735	66	1,043	23	3,029	130,693
2009	3,142	80	1,163	9	3,152	133,525

Source: Data provided by the Police Department, Government of Bihar.

The Problem of Social Conflict in Rural Areas

Another dimension to the law and order problem in Bihar is the issue of Naxal violence, feeding on deep injustices in the state's agrarian social structure. Curiously, the turnout in Naxal-affected districts of Bihar in the 2005 assembly elections was about the same as in non-Naxal districts, indicating that the population in Naxal areas was just as interested in participation in the political system as others. The Naxal movement in Bihar has gone through several stages, beginning first as a social movement seeking the redress of grievances of scheduled and lower caste marginal labourers or sharecroppers, then evolving into attacks on landlords and conflict with upper caste gangs, such as the Ranvir Sena, and finally becoming a movement engaged in violent conflict with the symbols of the state, particularly the police.[6]

The state's approach to the Naxal movement has become more sophisticated with time: the holding of local panchayat elections has opened up political space for marginal rural population to make their demands known to the state; the electoral process was also not interrupted by the Naxals. The government for its part has not vilified the Naxals, preferring instead to adopt a low-key approach to tackling the problem. It has tried hard to improve the provision of public services at the local level by introducing the 'Apki Sarkar, Apke Dwar' (ASAD) programme designed to provide essential services at a single place in selected gram panchayats.[7] The phrase 'apki sarkar, apke dwar' translates literally as 'your government at your doorstep'. The programme is significant because it marks a first step in the process of reclaiming an administrative presence in villages that have been marked by a history of social conflict. The Naxal problem has deep social roots in Bihar, but the current regime has clearly crafted a political and administrative strategy to address the problem in a way that stands a good chance of working over time. Indeed, the number of violent attacks in Bihar stemming from this problem has declined from 382 in 2004 to 79 in 2008; the number of civilian deaths has also fallen sharply during the same period from 199 to 43; and the number of attacks specifically on police targets has fallen from 19 to five.[8]

COMBATING CORRUPTION IN GOVERNMENT

The 2005 Centre for Media Studies (CMS)/Transparency International (TI) survey ranked Bihar as the most corrupt state in India (Figure 2.5). Historically, corruption in Bihar appears to be endemic but petty in nature, focusing on rent-seeking in procurement, transfers of civil servants, and public service delivery. The problem with this form of petty corruption is that it is largely at the expense of the poor. The school teacher who

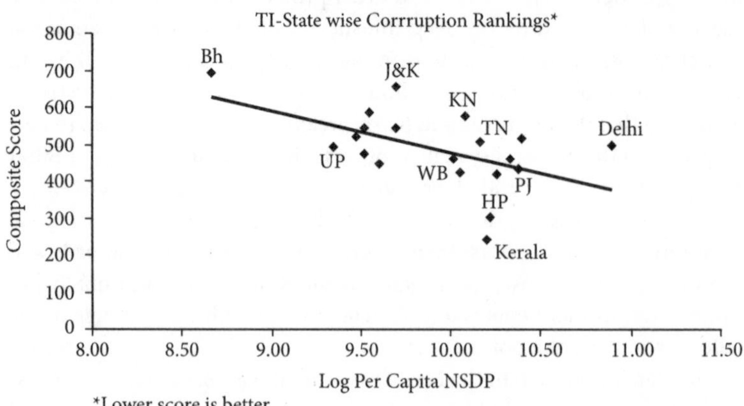

Figure 2.5 Corruption Rankings by State, 2005

Source: Ranking derived from Centre for Media Studies/Transparency International, 2005. Rankings matched against per capita net state domestic product (NSDP) figures.

Note: Although suggestive in some ways, this scatter plot does not necessarily point to a consistent relationship between higher corruption and lower per capita income in Indian states.

bribes an education officer to wink at her absence from the classroom ultimately interferes with the goal of raising literacy; the doctor who neglects his duties at the local primary health centre (PHC) in favour of private practice ends up depriving the poor of access to health care; the wholesale diversion of food from the public distribution system affects the nutritional status of vulnerable groups. Reducing corruption in delivering services and making progress in achieving the Millennium Development Goals (MDGs) are thus intimately related objectives.

The CMS/TI survey covered 20 major states. The least corrupt ones were Kerala at the top (lowest corruption ranking), followed by Himachal Pradesh, and Gujarat. The most corrupt states included Bihar at the bottom (highest corruption ranking) (see Center for Media Studies/ Transparency International 2005). The study ranked Uttar Pradesh as 10th, significantly better than Bihar.

Strengthening Anti-Corruption Enforcement in Bihar

A key objective of the new government was to strengthen anti-corruption enforcement. A perennial problem of anti-corruption enforcement across many Indian states has been lack of institutional autonomy. Vigilance investigations have been used by members of one political party to harass their opponents in the opposition, especially in states where the political culture is more polarized. In Bihar, misdirected vigilance efforts designed more to harass individuals than curb corruption actually discouraged civil servants from taking decisions or embarking on major spending projects. Therefore, a key priority of the new government was to step up targeted vigilance activities against corrupt officers without reinforcing risk-averse behaviour. Quite the contrary, targeted vigilance activity was crucial to restraining corruption in a context in which public expenditure was exploding in Bihar for the first time in decades.

Improving the Performance of Anti-Corruption Institutions

There is no doubt that the government has stepped up vigilance activity in the state. A Special Vigilance Unit (SVU) has been created to pursue cases against high-level civil servants. So far five cases have been filed and are currently being investigated against senior officials. The SVU is led by an IG of police and staffed by five retired officers from the Central Bureau of Investigation (CBI) of the rank of SP and eight inspectors/ sub-inspectors. The SVU's budget in financial year 2006–7 was in the region of Rs 2.87 crore (Data provided to author by State Vigilance Unit, Government of Bihar).

If the SVU was designed to tackle high-level cases, the Vigilance Bureau was intended to address corruption across the civil service. The activity of the Vigilance Bureau has burgeoned across all types of cases (Figure 2.6). Disproportionate asset cases registered, for example, rose from only one in 2005 to 10 each in 2006 and 2007.[9] The number of simple trap cases registered (where an individual is caught red-handed taking a bribe) has surged from seven in 2005 to 60 in 2006, 108 in 2007, and 78 in 2008 (Data provided to author by the Vigilance Bureau, Government of Bihar). Expressed differently, the annual average of trap cases filed between 1996 and 2005 was 4.5 compared to 82 between 2006 and 2008. The total number of cases registered shot up from 21 in 2005 to 104 in 2006, 133 in 2007, and then fell slightly to 110 in 2008. Again it is worth noting that the annual average of total cases filed between 1996 and 2005 was 28.5 compared to 116 between 2006 and 2008. Most cases focused on corruption in public services involving block education extension officers (BEEOs), supply inspectors in the public distribution system (PDS), jail superintendents, district forest officers, assistant engineers, clerks, civil surgeons, and block development officers, among others. Of the 246 trap cases filed in 2006, 2007, and 2008, the highest number was in the education department followed by home, revenue, personnel, and health.

The Vigilance Department is, therefore, doing two things right. It has become much more active than in the past, as the surging case load numbers indicate. This activity is likely to send a clear signal that corruption

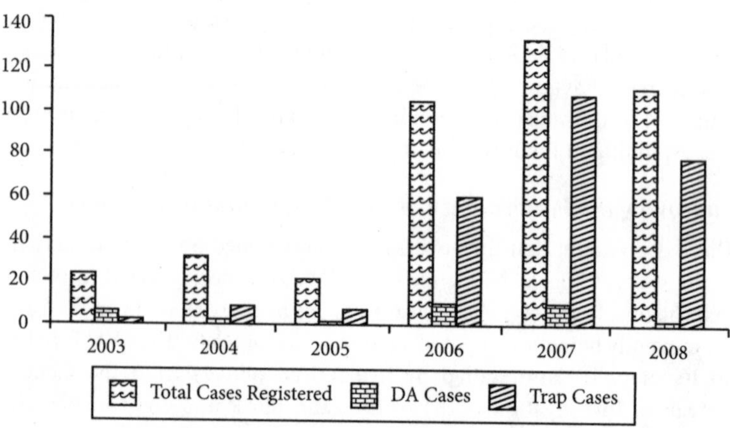

Figure 2.6 Cases filed by the Vigilance Bureau: Total, DA, and Trap Cases

Source: Data provided by the Vigilance Bureau, Government of Bihar.

will be dealt with firmly by the government. In addition, it has focused on corruption that affects ordinary citizens the most, particularly in the public delivery system. It has proposed a pay hike of 15 per cent for police officers deputed to the Vigilance Bureau and an accelerated promotion scheme to motivate such officers to perform better and also to attract staff. The Vigilance Bureau has succeeded in drastically shortening the time that it takes to bring a suspect to book to less than 90 days between filing a first information report (FIR) and deciding whether to file formal charges, drop the case, or refer it back to the originating department for a disciplinary inquiry. Most important of all, the government is no longer dragging its feet on granting permission to prosecute corrupt officers.[10] If such permission often took years to obtain in the past, in most cases it now takes no more than 30 days. Old cases filed between 1985 and 2002 that were pending investigation have been closed or prosecuted. Currently, 52 cases filed between 2003 and 2006 are still under investigation (Data provided to author by the Vigilance Bureau, Government of Bihar).

Senior vigilance officers from the corruption control squad have publicized their mobile telephone numbers, thus allowing members of the public to report corruption more easily and without having to visit the Bureau. The vigilance department has even conducted a survey involving services such as hospitals, registration, integrated child development services, and land mutation to assess public satisfaction and identify processes vulnerable to corruption.

Disappointingly, however, for all this effort, verdicts have been issued in only 11 cases filed since 2005 (eight of which resulted in convictions).[11] Even if verdicts were painfully slow in coming, the fact that eight out of 11 cases went in favour of the government indicates much improved case preparation. The Bureau has sought to improve its conviction record in anti-corruption cases by commissioning a special court, in addition to the three other special vigilance courts currently functioning in Bihar, earmarked only for trap cases in order to boost the conviction rate. The government has sought to strengthen its hand in dealing with the problem of corruption by passing The Bihar Special Courts Act 2009, which authorizes the state government to create new special courts to try cases under the Prevention of Corruption Act, 1988. The Bihar Special Courts Act also allows the government to confiscate ill-gotten assets from public servants found by a trial court to have engaged in corruption (with provisions for restitution of such property with interest if the accused wins the case on appeal).[12] This bill has now received presidential assent and is the first of its kind in any Indian state. Its passage sends a powerful signal that corruption will not be tolerated by the government and that consequences will follow if a public servant engages in corrupt behaviour.

Anti-Corruption Institutions: How Autonomous?

If interference by the leadership in vigilance matters has ceased in Bihar, the government has still not been able to come to a consensus about creating an institutional mechanism to protect the autonomy of the Vigilance Bureau. The case for an autonomous vigilance function rests on preventing interference from politicians generally, not necessarily the leadership. The government has drafted a bill establishing an autonomous State Vigilance Commission on the lines of the Central Vigilance Commission (CVC), but has yet to decide whether to go forward with its adoption (Government of Bihar 2007d). The government could also consider departing from the CVC model by appointing members of civil society to the State Vigilance Commission, if established.

Another way of bolstering the autonomy of the Vigilance Bureau would be to place it under the state's Lok Ayukta or ombudsman. The Lok Ayukta in Bihar has the power to investigate and recommend action in cases involving grievances relating to maladministration as well as allegations of corruption involving ministers (except the chief minister) and other appointed public servants (Government of Bihar 2001: 1). The Lok Ayukta in Bihar, however, lacks its own investigative staff and has to rely on the Vigilance Bureau for this. The Lok Ayukta also has no suo motu powers, allowing him to take cognizance, for example, of an offence on the basis of media reports rather than a formal complaint. Nor can he hold government officials in contempt for failing to cooperate with an investigation. Bihar could consider adopting the Karnataka model where the Vigilance Bureau has effectively been placed under the superintendence of the Lok Ayukta, thereby bringing a measure of autonomy to anti-corruption investigations. So far, however, there is no support in Bihar for either placing the Vigilance Bureau under the Lok Ayukta or strengthening the office of the latter, for example, by granting him suo motu powers.[13]

Promoting Transparency through the Right to Information

The government has also sought to discourage corruption by aggressively implementing the RTI law in Bihar. The State Information Commission (SIC), which began its work in August 2006, has significant achievements to its credit. Given Bihar's high level of illiteracy, some citizens might have been expected to have difficulty framing a formal request for information under the new law. In order to surmount this obstacle, the Bihar government has launched a call centre to assist callers with processing requests for information, popularly called 'Jaankari' (information).[14] Callers can simply make their requests orally over the telephone to call centre operators, outsourced to Bharat Sanchar Nigam Limited (BSNL), who then transform the oral request into a written one, identify and relay the request to the correct department, and then check back with the requester to see if the information has actually been received. If there is no response, Jaankari staff then file a first appeal with the secretary of the department, and, if necessary, file a second appeal with the SIC.

No other state has created such a call centre to process requests for information on behalf of citizens. Jaankari has 10 employees trained to deal with requests for information over the telephone, and the telephone numbers of the call centre have been widely publicized. The number of calls received every month by Jaankari operators has risen dramatically from 123 in January 2007 to 2,452 in March 2009, while the numbers of applications resulting from such calls shot up from 24 in January 2007 to 600 in March 2009 (Figure 2.7). In January 2007, none of the 24 applications filed resulted in either a first or second appeal, but by March 2009, the appeal rate had grown considerably: of 600 applications filed

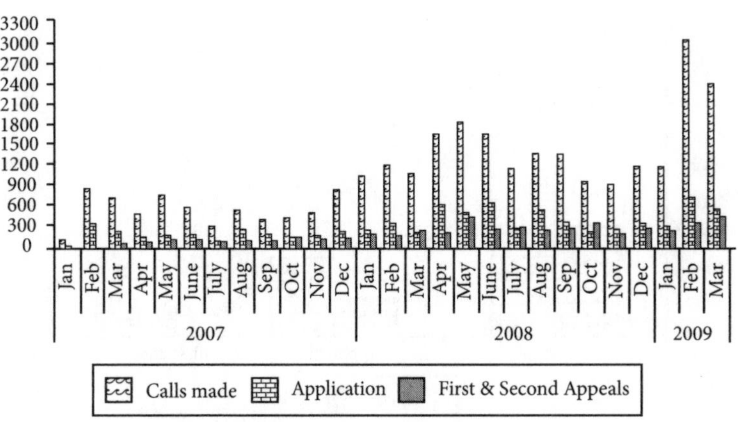

Figure 2.7 Calls, Applications, and Appeals in *Jaankari*, January 2007 to March 2009

Source: Data provided by the State Information Commission, Bihar.

that month, 343 resulted in a first appeal, and of these, 137 ended up in a second appeal with the SIC.

Overall, the number of calls received at the Jaankari centre between January 2007 and December 2008 totalled 22,504, while the number of applications filed during the same period stood at 7,070 (Figure 2.8). Of these requests for information, over 60 per cent ended up in a first or second appeal. Jaankari is clearly a best practice in implementing access to information laws around the world, especially in poorer settings marked by high levels of illiteracy.

In addition, the number of appeals/complaints from all sources (not just Jaankari) filed with the SIC has exploded, rising from 155 in April 2007 to 1,032 in March 2009 (Figure 2.9).

The ability of the SIC to dispose of cases has, however, suffered with the increase in appeals. According to data provided by the Commission, while 112 of the 155 appeals/complaints filed with it in April 2007 were resolved during that month itself (a disposal rate of 72 per cent), the situation was quite different two years later when only 472 cases were resolved in March 2009 out of the 1,032 new cases filed that month (45 per cent). In 2008, the Commission received 9,871 cases (including a carryover from previous year), but resolved only 4,987 (a disposal rate of less than 51 per cent). The number of pending cases at the end of December 2008 was thus 4,884 (Figure 2.10). In order to deal with the situation, the Commission recently decided not to hear cases in the

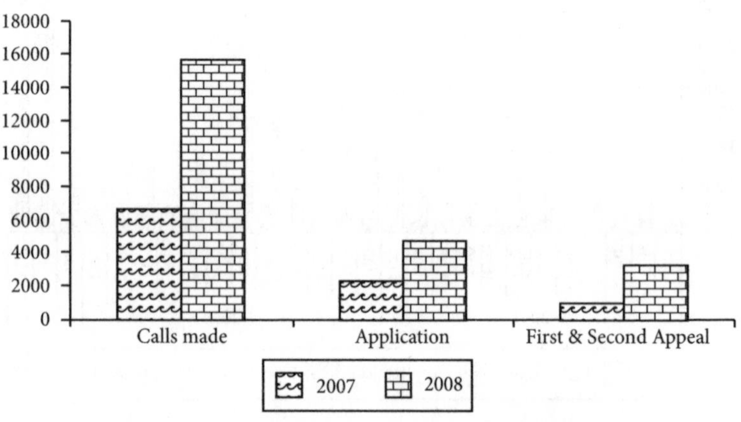

Figure 2.8 Annual Calls, Applications, and Appeals: Jaankari, 2007 and 2008

Source: Data provided by the State Information Commission, Bihar.

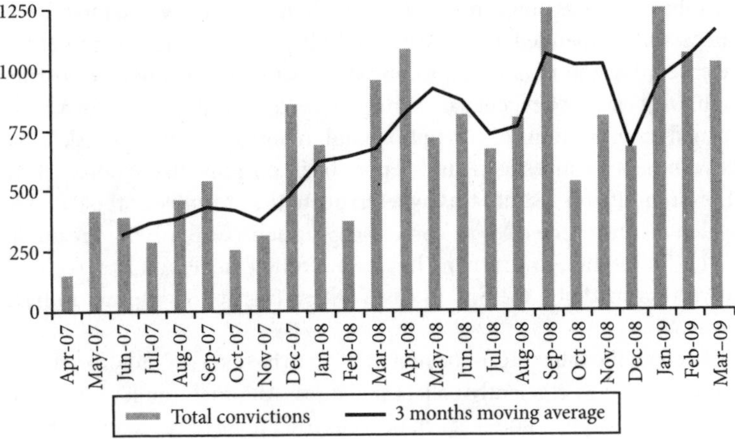

Figure 2.9 Appeals/Complaints, State Information Commission: April 2007 to March 2009

Source: Data provided by the State Information Commission, Bihar.

absence of a first unsuccessful appeal at the departmental level. Earlier the Commission had been less fastidious, admitting cases directly, and thereby allowing requesters to bypass the first layer of internal appeal. The government could consider appointing additional information commissioners to tackle the burgeoning case load.

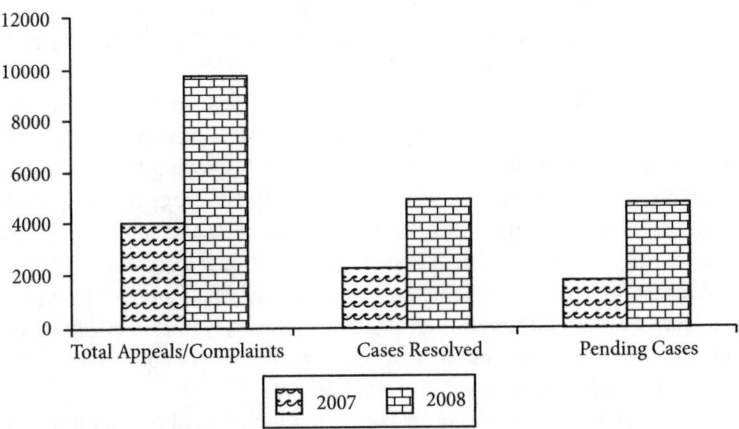

Figure 2.10 Pending Cases, State Information Commission: 2007 and 2008

Source: Data provided by the State Information Commission, Bihar.

Bihar's SIC has pioneered best practices in two other ways. First, it has successfully expanded its mandate not only to compel the government to release information, but also to probe cases that reveal possible corruption. In at least two recent cases, the process of appealing for information turned up indications of corruption, and in both cases, the SIC asked the government to investigate and report back on remedial actions taken. The Commission justifies this by referring to the preamble of the RTI Act, which mentions the need to 'contain corruption' (Gupta 2006: Preamble, p. 1). So far the government has been willing to respond to requests for action made by the SIC in cases where corruption appears to have occurred.

Second, the Bihar SIC is the first in India to have successfully developed a mechanism to efficiently collect penalties. Although the RTI Act contains a penalty provision that can be levied on Public Information Officers (PIOs) for failing to release information covered by the Act, it does not specify how this penalty can be collected other than by enforcing payment through a civil proceeding. In Bihar, penalties are deducted directly from the pay cheque of the PIO concerned in the form of an order issued to the Treasury. The proceeds of penalty deductions are then credited to the government's receipt account for fees paid for filing applications under the RTI Act. The SIC has levied penalties in 140 cases since its inception in August 2006 and penalties have been paid in all cases except where the Commission has chosen to rescind them. The Bihar government has been scrupulous in following SIC orders. In no case has an order by the Commission to release information not been carried out in Bihar.

The political will to push implementation of the RTI Act clearly exists in Bihar. The government, at the request of the SIC, has taken steps to release the beneficiary lists of major government schemes, such as the Indira Awas Yojna (IAY) housing programme. Most primary health centres in the state now have a large notice board displaying the medicines available free of cost as well as the prices of those drugs that require a payment, along with the stock position and doctors and nurses on duty. Muster rolls and measurement books for the National Rural Employment Guarantee Scheme are available for inspection in blocks and even in some panchayat offices, although such availability is surely uneven, despite the push by the state government and the Commission to comply with the suo motu disclosure provisions of the RTI Act.

Given the political support for the implementation of the Act in Bihar (viewed by state officials as an essential prong of their strategy to improve programme delivery), PIOs have on the whole been supportive. The

Commission has relied heavily on the Bihar Public Administration and Rural Development Organization (BIPARD) to train PIOs and widely publicize the Act. BIPARD has overseen the distribution of training manuals prepared by non-governmental organizations (NGOs) for implementing the RTI Act to PIOs and state officials. Publicity and training are likely to receive an additional fillip in the wake of the creation of a new Government of India programme to provide funds to state governments for such activities, free from a matching grant requirement.[15]

RESTRUCTURING GOVERNMENT TO PROVIDE PUBLIC SERVICES

A perception survey conducted in 2004 by the Public Affairs Centre, Bangalore (now Bengaluru), ranking public services across states placed Bihar at the bottom of 16 major states in the overall provision of services (Figure 2.11). By contrast, Uttar Pradesh ranked ninth in the survey. Bihar did slightly better in education and PDS where it ranked twelfth in the quality of service provision; in health it ranked 14th, close to the bottom; and 16th in the provision of drinking water and transport services.

Clearly, Bihar residents were among the most dissatisfied in India with the state of their public services. The new government thus had its work cut out for it when it assumed office in late 2005. In order to shift the focus of the government decisively towards providing better services to

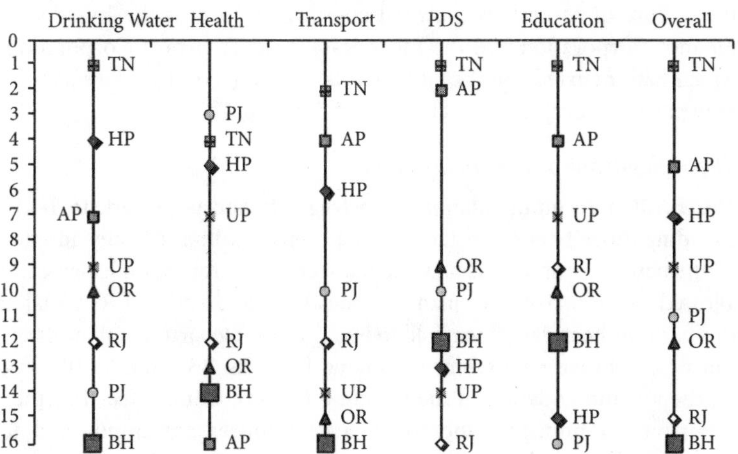

Figure 2.11 Public Perceptions of the Quality of Services (16 Major States)

Source: Samuel Paul et al. (2005: 930).

the population, the new leadership created an Administrative Reforms Commission to recommend ways in which the government could be reformed to function better. This was the first time any government in Bihar since the 1950s had paid attention to administrative reform issues. The new government also sought to boost public spending by decentralizing financial powers to the degree possible without inviting trouble. In roads, health, and education, the government sought to fill vacant technical positions on contract and outsource key tasks to the private sector in order to overcome capacity constraints within the bureaucracy. Finally, it enacted a new Panchayati Raj Act that sought to devolve power to local government in a way never seen before in Bihar.

Administrative Reform

The Bihar Administrative Reforms Commission (BARC) recommended significant changes in the functioning of the bureaucracy, not all of which were accepted by the government. It asked the government to consider reducing the number of departments from 47 to 36, in line with the constitutional provision that the size of the cabinet in any state should not exceed 15 per cent of the strength of the legislative assembly, which in Bihar translated into 36 ministers only.[16] While the size of the cabinet was actually lower than 36 at least for the first year of the government, there was no support for drastically pruning the number of departments beyond a modest reduction from 47 to 44. The BARC also proposed the closure of several state-owned enterprises, such as the Bihar State Finance Corporation and the Bihar State Road Transport Corporation, which had incurred significant losses, but these recommendations were only partially accepted (Government of Bihar 2007b).

The Delegation of Financial Powers

The BARC's recommendation to delegate financial powers to boost spending capacity at lower levels was, however, enthusiastically adopted by the new government. Departmental secretaries, for example, were not allowed to authorize new 'plan' schemes beyond a value of Rs 25 lakh; this has now been raised ten-fold to Rs 2.5 crore. Departmental ministers can now approve new schemes ranging from Rs 2.5 crore to 10 crore on the recommendation of the Standing Finance Committee. Together, departmental ministers and the finance minister are empowered to approve new spending ranging from Rs 10 crore to 20 crore, while expenditure exceeding Rs 20 crore has to be authorized by the cabinet. For new schemes under the 'non-plan' head, secretaries can authorize expenditure of up to Rs 1 crore, ministers from Rs 1–5 crore, and the cabinet above Rs 5 crore. The reforms have empowered government to spend money on public services in a way that was inconceivable in the past, thereby correcting in some measure the systematic under-funding of public services, particularly health, education, and roads in Bihar.

The Problem of Civil Service Transfers

On the other hand, the BARC's recommendation that transfers of state civil servants (excluding the Indian Administrative Service [IAS]) be decided by an establishment committee at different levels has been ignored. Indeed, the government has chosen instead to do away with establishment committees (with the exception of the police governed by the new Police Act), allowing ministers to issue orders directly to transfer gazetted officers, while heads of department have been given the authority to transfer non-gazetted officers directly. The result is that ministers can exercise a disproportionate influence in deciding the transfer of officers.

Historically, civil service transfers have been a difficult matter in many states: in 'wet' departments, where opportunities for rent-seeking abound, posts can be bought and sold;[17] the post of the block development officer (BDO) is often subject to such pressures because of its importance in the implementation of development programmes. Patronage has also been rife: an officer's personal loyalty to a minister based on caste or other factors might carry the day in selecting him/her for a coveted post, resulting in the politicization of the civil service.[18] This is not to say that the government is not aware of the problem: it has limited the transfer season to only once a year, rather than twice, banned the use of influence to obtain transfers, and put in place an automatic review by the next higher authority for any transfer occurring outside the season. In addition, the government has created a high-level committee chaired by the chief secretary to monitor compliance with the norm of spending at least three years in post stipulated by the state's transfer policy, especially for classes I and II supervisory posts in departmental cadres. This is an important step that will, if effectively implemented, help inject some stability and accountability in the functioning of the civil service in Bihar.

Transfers of senior IAS officers entail even more complex issues. Frequent transfers have left the senior civil service in disarray in several states and undermined its independence, with negative effects on performance. The new government was clearly committed to stable tenures for IAS officers. It sought to place the right person in the right position to spearhead the government's reform programme in key sectors, such as roads, health, education, finance, and other areas. Top civil servants in the secretariat thus enjoyed a measure of autonomy not seen in Bihar in decades, raising morale and performance. On the other hand, the government was reluctant to provide formal protection to civil servants by adopting the new IAS cadre rules issued by the Ministry of Personnel in Delhi, which provide for an average minimum tenure of two years for IAS posts, such as principal secretary, secretary, and district magistrate, with exceptions for deputation, retirement, promotion, or long leave.[19]

The autonomy, and stable tenures, granted to key players in the reform programme does not, however, appear to have more broadly translated into longer tenures. As of 1 June 2008, the average tenure for principal secretaries was one year, secretaries a little over a year, and DMs around eight months (Table 2.2). The tenures of DMs may have been higher a few months earlier because the government transferred many DMs as recently as March 2008, thus lowering the average tenure significantly; most of the DMs transferred had served for a reasonable period in their previous posts.

Table 2.2 Average Tenures in Bihar in the IAS, 1 June 2008

Category	Average Tenure (in years)
Principal secretaries	1.01
Secretaries/additional secretaries	1.28
District magistrates[20]	0.64
Other IAS officers	1.02
All IAS officers	0.98

Source: Data calculated from Government of Bihar, Personnel and Administrative Reforms Department, *Gradation List of IAS* (as on 1 June 2008).

Reinvigorating Public Service Delivery in Three Sectors

The government has focused on three crucial sectors for development at the outset: roads, health, and education. At the time it assumed office, Bihar's road network was in deplorable condition, reflecting poor maintenance, the effects of periodic flooding, and under-investment. In education, Bihar suffered from the worst indicators of any state with 2 million out-of-school children in the 6–13 year age bracket, high levels of teacher absenteeism, and a literacy rate of 48 per cent (see Government of Bihar 2007a: 104–14; see also Government of Bihar 2008: vii). The health sector was plagued by lack of infrastructure, absenteeism, and shortages of qualified personnel; only 5 per cent of the rural population actually used the public health system, the rest paying from their personal resources for care from the private sector.[21] The common challenges faced by all the three sectors included: (1) low levels of capacity to deliver services, (2) poor monitoring of performance, (3) lack of robust accountability arrangements, and (4) the need to strengthen decentralization.

Addressing the Problem of Capacity

Hiring New Staff on Contract According to the BARC, serious staff shortages existed in the Road Engineering Organization (REO) and the road construction departments. REO, for example, in 2006 had a sanctioned strength of some 1,816 engineers at all levels of which 272 positions were vacant (Government of Bihar 2007b: 45). The situation was more serious in the road construction department, which had 4,617 sanctioned posts of which some 1,133 were vacant, though not all these positions were of a technical nature (Ibid.). In order to address staff shortages, all three departments moved to hire technical personnel on contract, rather than on a permanent basis. The roads department, for example, hired some 450 junior engineers on one year, renewable contracts in fiscal year 2006–7. The rural works department (RWD), which focuses on rural roads, has also sought to improve its working by raising the number of divisions from 45 to 80, while maintaining equivalent staffing norms for all of them. The demand for additional staff in the newly created divisions dedicated to project management, quality control, and procurement has been met largely through the redeployment of surplus engineers from the irrigation department. This has entailed no additional expenditure, yet capacity has been consequently enhanced.

In health, the state embarked on an ambitious plan to get its district hospitals, sub-divisional hospitals, and primary healthcare centres functional after a long period of neglect. The state was desperately short of medical officers, auxiliary nurse midwives (ANMs), and other skilled staff. In order to address these shortages, the health department has hired on contract some 400 specialists and 1,200 medical officers, and 1,122 ANMs. In addition, the state has sought to lure private practitioners to treat patients in PHCs by paying them monthly honoraria. By early 2009, the health department had filled up some 58 per cent of its regular and contractual posts, totalling 4,105 new doctors (2,712 regular and 1,393 on contract) (Government of Bihar 2009: 163). In primary education, the government has allowed the newly elected panchayats to recruit some 100,000 schoolteachers. While there have been complaints of irregularities in the hiring of these teachers, there is very little dispute about the need to recruit them in the first place. This has been followed by a second round of recruitment of another 70,000 teachers with improved safeguards, including the development of standardized recruiting criteria. An audit of the process by a reputable third-party agency concluded that the exercise was, by and large, free of problems.

Outsourcing to the Private Sector It is also necessary to note that existing technical staff often lack the capacity to deliver services effectively. Recruited long ago, largely isolated from developments in their field, and overburdened with administrative tasks, such officers sometimes lack both the motivation and the ability to perform. The government has recognized the problem by resorting to outsourcing very substantially, especially in roads and health. The road construction department and the RWD have, for example, outsourced project preparation to outside consultants from the private sector. Both departments have together outsourced the preparation of engineering designs for some 18,000 km of new roads; designs have been completed for 13,000 km. The timely completion of designs has in turn allowed the government of Bihar to access some Rs 32 billion in funding for new roads from the Central government's Pradhan Mantri Gram Sadak Yojna (World Bank, 2009: 10). In health, pathology, and radiology services have been outsourced to private companies on contract, as have hospital maintenance and ambulance services.

Freeing up Time to Focus on the Essential A key problem in large departments is that top managerial time is consumed with non-essential matters, such as transfers and postings, answering court summons, and responding to legislative questions. In a small way, the education department in Bihar has begun reversing this process by reducing the department's involvement in legal cases. In a large department like education, disputes over promotions, transfers, and annual confidential reports can often spill over into the filing of legal cases, which then consume a considerable amount of managerial time. The department has sought to obviate the need for legal action by resolving staff grievances as quickly as possible. It has also chosen to comply with court orders right away rather than file an automatic appeal unless there is a strong prospect of winning the case. The effort by the education department paralleled a wider move across the Bihar government to reduce litigation by the government, a major cause of court congestion. The office of the advocate-general is being much stricter in allowing appeals to go forward, and departments are being encouraged to comply routinely with court orders rather than rushing to file an appeal. The education department is a leader here in one other respect: it has issued strict orders prohibiting other agencies from using teachers for non-teaching purposes, barring oversight of the mid-day meal programme, an action which will surely have a positive effect on teacher attendance in Bihar.

Even so, notwithstanding all this, the government's efforts to better manage its case load have had only limited results. In fact, the total number of contempt cases pending against the government has risen steadily from 1,895 in 2005 to 4,760 in May 2009 (see Figure 2.12). In higher education alone, contempt cases rose from 58 in 2006 to 518 in 2009, reflecting in part disputes over delayed payments of salary arrears (Data provided to author by Law Department, Government of Bihar). It is safe to say that the number of contempt cases would have been still higher but for the measures taken by the government to stem them.

Better Performance Monitoring

All three departments are dealing with the problem of performance management in creative ways. New contract teachers are subject to the supervision of the panchayats that hired them. Panchayats may stop paying teacher salaries in the event of non-attendance. Regular teachers can only be removed by the education department on the

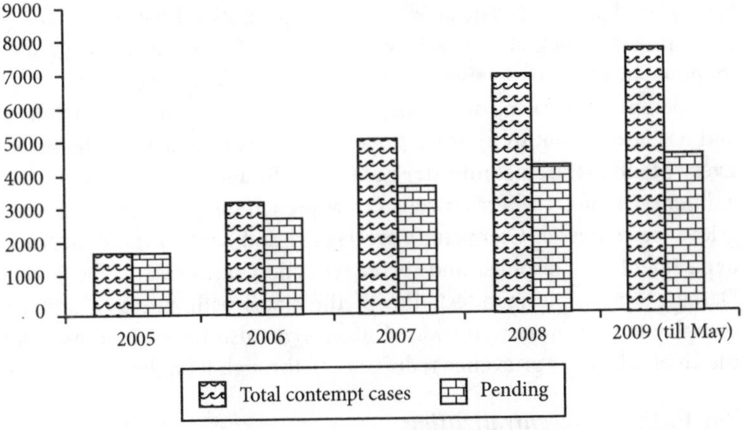

Figure 2.12 Contempt Cases against the Government of Bihar

Source: Data provided by the Law Department, Government of Bihar.

recommendation of the school management committee. In health, data centres managed by a private company have been established at the block level to collect information on the number of patients visiting a health facility, each doctor's patient list, and the drugs prescribed by her/him. This makes it possible to track the number of patients seen by a doctor on a daily, monthly, or yearly basis, and compare the performance of doctors and facilities. This information is collected on a central server, accessible to top health officials in Patna, and will also be placed on a public website. In roads, third-party monitoring of the quality of new road construction has become routine in Bihar, while the commissioning of a Geographic Information System (GIS) based Road Information System (RIS) should enhance the department's ability to monitor its operations and projects more closely.

Strengthening Accountability Arrangements

In health, the state has introduced the Rogi Kalyan Samiti (RKS) model that allows district and sub-divisional hospitals to create autonomous societies that can monitor the quality of services and raise funds through modest user fees earmarked for maintenance and the purchase of necessary equipment or supplies.[22] In education, the decision to allow Panchayati Raj institutions (PRIs) to hire contract teachers will over time make for closer accountability of teaching staff to the local community. In all three departments, the provision of information has become an important tool for accountability. In health, as noted earlier, all PHCs have placed a list of crucial information on notice boards, including free drugs in stock at the facility, the prices of other drugs, and staff in attendance. In roads, the government has made a major effort to be transparent in releasing information relating to contracts and tenders, and has also sought to improve the quality of its feedback mechanisms. Every Monday the chief minister holds a public audience (each week has a different subject) where citizens can approach him and his officers for grievance redressal. Complaints are tagged and sent to the concerned department for a response and corrective action, if necessary. The 'Janata Darbar' is a visible manifestation of the state's willingness to address complaints in a meaningful way. Citizens can also file complaints with the chief minister's grievance redressal cell through its website.

The Push for Decentralization

One of the most significant achievements in governance reform in Bihar has been the passage of a landmark new Panchayati Raj Act in

2006, replacing an earlier law passed in 1993 (Government of Bihar 2006). The new Act empowers women by earmarking 50 per cent of all elected positions for them (this also covers the chairpersons of the gram panchayat and panchayat samiti at the block level, and the zilla parishad at the district level) within the reserved and unreserved categories. The Act also clearly establishes that the village assembly, gram sabha, has the right to select beneficiaries for government programmes and monitor their implementation through social audits, for example, and vote on the budget. The Act also allows the gram panchayat to remove its elected head, the *mukhiya*, by passing a vote of no-confidence. In order to limit irresponsible use of this provision, the Act stipulates that (a) a vote of no-confidence cannot be passed in the first two years of the term of the mukhiya, and (b) at least a year has to elapse between one vote of no-confidence and another. In order to strengthen the foundations of local justice, the Act provides for the creation of a parallel structure of gram kutcheris or village courts, designed to resolve minor cases involving members of the panchayat, each gram kutcheri being assisted by a *nyaymitra* or friend of the court and a trained lawyer. The Act also contains stiff penalties for interfering with the conduct of local elections through voter intimidation, booth capturing, and tampering with ballots or the count, common in Bihar in the past.

Clearly, the Bihar Panchayati Raj Act 2006 provides sufficient legal authority to the PRI system to function effectively. The panchayat elections held in 2006 opened up political space at the local level (Table 2.3). In Naxal-infested areas, this may have afforded an opportunity for some of their sympathizers or even members to participate in the political process for the first time, although the elections were, at least officially, held without regard to party labels. That is, the candidates did not formally contest along party lines, but as individuals.

Table 2.3 Distribution of Panchayat Members/Chairpersons in Bihar, 2006

Gram panchayat members	115,876
Gram kutcheri members	115,876
Panchayat samiti members	11,566
Zilla parishad members	8,463
Gram panchayat mukhiyas	8,463
Gram kutcheri sarpanches	8,463

Source: Data provided by the Panchayati Raj Department, Government of Bihar.

THE IMPACT OF REFORM: SOME EVIDENCE

Public Spending Patterns

The impact of these changes is becoming apparent. Public spending on roads, health, and education has increased significantly. Total expenditure increased from Rs 215 billion in 2005–6 to Rs 350 billion in 2008–9. The share of non-wage expenditure (for example, capital outlays, operation and maintenance [O&M]) in total expenditure increased from 50 per cent in 2006–7 to 57 per cent in 2008–9 (preliminary estimates). New development expenditure almost trebled from Rs 49 billion in 2005–6 to Rs 141 billion in 2008–9. Expenditure on the social sectors, that is education, health, water supply, and sanitation, increased by nearly 40 per cent in 2007–8 and 60 per cent in 2008–9 (preliminary estimates). Agriculture, irrigation and flood control, energy and road sectors currently account for over 60 per cent of expenditure on economic services. The increase in public expenditure has thus been complemented by a necessary focus on development priorities.[23]

Roads

The consequences of this are clear. In the roads sector, a total of 773 km of the national highway network was renovated in fiscal year 2006–7 and another 552 km in the first nine months of 2007–8 (Government of Bihar 2008: 128). A big effort has been made to upgrade major district roads: some 3,432 km have been refurbished between 2006–7 and 2008–9. As noted earlier, the outsourcing of the preparation of designs for rural roads has greatly increased the ability of the RWD to tap funds under PMGSY.

The Social Sectors: Health and Education

In health, the number of outpatients visiting a government hospital rose, on average, from 39 per month in January 2006 to 4,380 in October 2008 (Government of Bihar 2009: 164). There has been a striking improvement in the percentage of the population now fully immunized, from approximately 18.6 per cent in 2005 to 53 per cent in 2008 (Data provided by Health Department, Government of Bihar). The number of institutional deliveries has also shot up from 112,371 for fiscal year 2006–7 to 838,481 in 2007–8, and 780,000 in 2008–9 (through December 2008). Medicines are also being provided free to patients.

In education, enrolment at the primary and upper primary levels rose by 8 per cent between 2006–7 and 2007–8, while the number of out-of-school children fell steeply by 77 per cent between 2006–7 and 2008–9.

The pupil–teacher ratio improved from 63:1 to 53:1, as a result of hiring the first round of 100,000 teachers, and will fall further to the national norm of 40:1 when teachers hired in the second round are actually placed in schools. The government in 2008 extended its mid-day meal scheme to cover children in Classes VI to VIII, thereby increasing its reach to nearly 11 million children. The mid-day meal scheme introduced in Bihar in 2005 covered 75.7 per cent of all children enrolled in primary school in 2009–10 compared to 60 per cent in 2006–7 (Government of Bihar, 2010: 166). Of course, learning outcomes will be the real test of improvements, but a good start has been made in the education sector in Bihar.[24]

Survey Data

The ADRI Survey

A user survey in November 2006 by the Asian Development Research Institute (ADRI) captured early uneven improvements in public services across five representative districts: Patna and Bhojpur located in the south-west quadrant of Bihar, both relatively well off; Saran in the lower half of northern Bihar with good irrigation systems and moderate income levels; Lakhisarai, less well off than Saran, with hilly terrain and low population density; and Araria in the north-east, the poorest of the five districts in the sample.

Some limited progress is apparent from the survey in infrastructure (Table 2.4). All five districts experienced a significant increase in road works. Village drainage improved far more in Patna and Saran than in the other districts, such as Araria where no improvements were apparent. The picture on the availability of electricity was highly uneven: 72 per cent of the respondents in Patna noted having electricity; while 48.3 per cent in Saran and 46.7 per cent in Bhojpur mentioned an improvement in the availability of electricity, unlike Lakhisarai and Araria, where only 17.7 and 25 per cent, respectively, did so.

Table 2.4 Improvements in Infrastructure in Five Districts in Bihar

Percentage of Respondents Reporting Improvements	Araria	Bhojpur	Saran	Patna	Lakhisarai
Roads	50	45.8	60	58.3	37.7
Village Drainage	0	16.7	37.5	55.1	28.8
Electricity	25	46.7	48.3	72.5	17.7

Source: Asian Development Research Institute (2007: 61).

Users were relatively satisfied with the quality of service received at district hospitals, ranging from 75 per cent in Bhojpur to 47.5 per cent in Patna (Asian Development Research Institute 2007: 63). However, satisfaction with the performance of PHCs was significantly lower across the five districts studied, ranging from 45.8 per cent in Saran to 16.7 per cent in Araria. Regularity of attendance by doctors was reported by 54.1 per cent of all respondents in Saran, 45.8 per cent in Bhojpur, 43.3 per cent in Patna, 42.2 per cent in Lakhisarai, and only 16.7 per cent in Araria, a remote region prone to severe flooding during the monsoons. Fewer respondents agreed that free medicines were regularly available: while 58.3 per cent in Bhojpur acknowledged the regular availability of free medicines, the percentages were only 37.5 in Saran, 36.6 in Patna, 33.3 in Araria, and 26.6 in Lakhisarai. With the exception of Araria, respondents agreed that an improvement had taken place over the preceding year in health delivery, ranging from 64.1 per cent in Saran to 46.6 in Patna.

Between 14.1 and 7.5 per cent of the respondents across the sampled districts reported having a member of the family being recruited as a teacher over the past year; only 3–5 per cent of these families mentioned paying a bribe to get a teacher appointment (Ibid.: 66), belying the widespread impression that such recruitment was tainted by corruption in several places.[25] The survey revealed that only a small percentage of the respondents had received job cards under the National Rural Employment Guarantee Programme (NREGP), ranging from a high of 25 per cent in Saran to a low of 17.7 per cent in Lakhisarai.[26] Knowledge of the programme itself was, however, substantially higher, ranging from 50 per cent in Saran to 33.3 per cent in Bhojpur (Ibid.: 67).

There was considerable variation across the five districts in views of the police: 55.8 per cent in Patna felt that the police were active in maintaining law and order in comparison to 45.5 per cent in Lakhisarai, 40 per cent in Saran, 39.2 per cent in Araria, and 18.3 per cent in Bhojpur (Ibid.: 69). The higher figure for Patna may indicate that the government has succeeded most impressively in bringing law and order under control in the capital of the state, although the rule of law appears to be improving in other districts too. The need to use a 'connection', such as a Member of Legislative Assembly (MLA) or a mukhiya, to contact the police was relatively infrequent, ranging from 26.6 per cent in Lakhisarai to 10 per cent in Patna (Ibid.: 69).

The Hindustan Times/C Fore Survey

In early 2008, an opinion survey by the *Hindustan Times* in collaboration with a research organization showed major improvements in perceptions of governance in Bihar (*Hindustan Times* 2008). Over 38 per cent of respondents stated that they felt 'far safer' and 31 per cent a 'lot safer' in Bihar. Sixty-one per cent of those surveyed felt that hospitals were being run better, 65 per cent thought that the education system had 'improved a lot', and 49 per cent stated that the bureaucracy was more responsive. Forty-one per cent felt that roads were much better compared to 14 per cent who stated that they were 'just the same' and 6 per cent who felt they were 'worse'. Respondents were divided over the question of corruption: 38 per cent felt corruption had 'gone down' while 31 per cent felt it was 'still rampant' and 19 per cent felt that corruption levels were the same as before. Finally, 73 per cent felt that governance was more efficient that in the past, while 68 per cent felt that Bihar had 'turned the corner', indicating a high level of optimism about the future.

Economic Outcomes

The persistence of reform over almost five years is yielding results in terms of aggregate and sectoral economic outcomes. In aggregate terms, gross state domestic product (GSDP) grew significantly from an annual average rate of 4.5 per cent between 1999–2000 and 2003–4 (the pre-reform period) to 10.7 per cent between 2004–5 and 2008–9 (the reform period), although with fluctuations in individual years primarily stemming from the volatility of agricultural production (data provided by Central Statistical Organization, 2010). Even if one takes population growth into account, the annual average growth rate of per capita income at constant prices rose from 2.2 per cent between 1999–2000 and 2003–4 to 9 per cent between 2004–5 and 2008–9.

The annual average growth rate for construction rose from 7.2 per cent between 1999–2000 and 2003–4 to 37.1 per cent between 2004–5 to 2008–9. This massive increase in construction activity indicates a greater willingness to invest in property correlated with an improved law and order situation as well as feeding into a general economic upturn. The same story is indicated by the growth of 'trade, hotels, and restaurants' from an annual average of 11.2 per cent between 1999–2000 and 2003–4 to 16.3 per cent between 2004–5 and 2008–9. Indeed, taking the number of tourist arrivals as an indication of improved conditions in Bihar, these increased dramatically from 6.9 million in 2005 to 10.5 million in

2009. The number of motor vehicles in Bihar also rose by 239 per cent in 2007 alone, reflecting greater consumer spending, better infrastructure, and heightened economic activity, while the number of mobile phones rocketed to 12 million from only 1 million in 2004. Communications as whole grew from an annual average of 10.2 per cent between 1999–2000 and 2003–4 to 18.4 per cent between 2004–5 and 2008–9.

Manufacturing recovered from a negative average annual growth rate (–2.2 per cent between 1999–2000 and 2003–4) to a much better 7.1 per cent between 2004–5 and 2008–9. Services registered an increase in the average annual growth rate from 5.4 per cent between 1999–2000 and 2003–4 to 10.9 per cent between 2004–5 and 2008–9 (Figure 2.13). While the roots of economic growth are complex, it is not unreasonable to suppose that the faster growth experienced by Bihar after 2004 is linked to improvements in the rule of law, more efficient and larger public expenditures, and better infrastructure.

THE ROAD AHEAD: SUSTAINABILITY AND CHALLENGES

Much has been accomplished in Bihar over the past five years. A basic shift has occurred towards a focus on improved governance and public

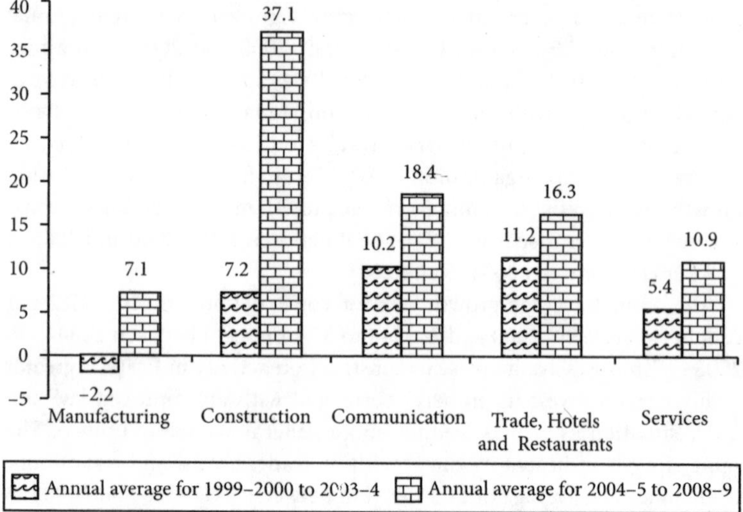

Figure 2.13 Annual Average Growth Rates by Sector: Comparing Time Periods

Source: Central Statistical Organization, 2010.

service delivery. Significant progress has been made on the ground in several critical areas, ranging from the restoration of law and order to much improved health and educational services, and progress on infrastructure starting with the pivotal roads sector. These changes in Bihar have in turn triggered much faster growth by sector and also in aggregate terms. One can therefore establish a clear connection between improvements in institutional quality (for example, the rules and framework governing economic activity) and economic activity itself. These changes are likely to be sustainable regardless of which party is in power.

Reforms have continued apace for the last five years, triggering a major change in expectations. Citizens in Bihar have now become accustomed to expecting improvements in the performance of the state and are not likely to vote in a party that fails to deliver on this. The basic discourse in Bihar has shifted towards providing good governance. All political parties in Bihar, for the most part, favour change. It is remarkable that the current changes in governance have occurred in a coalition setting, putting to rest concerns that such an arrangement implies a drag on reform. The fact that governance has been at the forefront of politics in Bihar for almost five years implies that turning back will be no easy proposition: the people have tasted the fruits of a functioning state and going back will be difficult for any government, irrespective of its composition.

The reasons for the success of the reforms discussed in this chapter are clearly the following: (a) the willingness of voters to extend a clear political mandate for change entailing major reforms in governance and public service delivery, along with their basic desire for change in the framework of politics in Bihar; (b) the ability of the government to appoint seasoned civil servants to key reform posts and give them relative autonomy and stability of tenure to execute reforms in their respective domains; and (c) the willingness of the Bihar government to engage with key outside players to reinforce its reform programme, including universities, the Government of India, and the private sector, thereby signalling an openness to new ideas and thinking, as well as adopting blueprints from other states to improve the working of public services (for example, e-governance).

Even so, the road ahead is littered with challenges that have not been fully addressed. Governmental capacity remains the principal constraint to development. It is worth noting that Bihar has one of the lowest tax–GDP ratios in India, conventionally an indicator not just of fiscal health but also of administrative capacity. In 2007–8, Bihar's tax–GDP ratio stood at only 2.39 per cent compared to 6.86 per cent in Tamil Nadu, 6.13 per cent in Andhra Pradesh, and 5.87 per cent in Karnataka (Majumdar, n.d.: slide 13). The very low tax–GDP ratio implies not only less revenue for developmental expenditure but also a more fundamental lack of capacity across the board.

That is not to say that the state has not sought to improve its capacity over the past five years. Clearly, the state, which had almost ceased to exist in Bihar, has now re-emerged as a functioning entity devoted to wealth creation. The most visible result of a functioning state is the improved law and order situation, as well as the rapid increase in public expenditure on roads, schools, and health clinics. The government has established a special entity, the Bihar Prashasnik Sudhar Mission (BPSM), to drive administrative reforms in selected departments and district collectorates.

Nonetheless, more inevitably needs to be done. Staffing gaps remain a serious problem, especially in health, roads, and police (the state still has a very low ratio of police officers to population), while the judiciary remains understaffed in relation to its case load. Much has happened to revitalize PRI institutions in Bihar; yet, it is not clear that the thousands of people elected as local government officials have the capacity or resources to administer public services effectively or whether departments have engaged in the mapping of activities necessary to concretely devolve functions to the third tier of governance.

Individual departments too continue to labour under capacity constraints. The RWD still lacks the ability to meet one of its basic functions: the routine maintenance of rural roads under its care; nor does it have the technical skills to effectively manage contracts. It should be noted that procurement remains a problem in infrastructure: national contractors have not shown great interest in participating in the growth of the roads sector in Bihar, particularly because of the availability of more profitable projects elsewhere in India. Therefore, the road construction department and the RWD have been obliged to rely more on local contractors, who often lack the necessary equipment, financial base, and skilled labour to efficiently execute a programme. It should be noted that the problem does not lie with the procurement process itself, but more with the weak capacity of contractors within Bihar and the reluctance of national contractors to bid for projects given the availability of greener pastures elsewhere. Because execution of projects was so slow in the past, existing staff is often ill-equipped to deal with the challenges of higher spending levels. Engineers lack the ability to execute, manage, or supervise projects; accountants are poorly trained, especially in Bihar's districts and blocks;

and a large number of doctors and teachers still possess only basic skills. Training and exposing the state's professional cadres more fully to the latest techniques in their field is thus a priority going forward.

Cadres critical for local development, particularly BDOs, are overburdened. In Gaya, for example, a field trip revealed that the BDO was tasked with supervising some 33 schemes and serving as the block electoral officer, the circle officer, and PIO all at once. Streamlining the work of BDOs is thus an important step towards improving the effectiveness of local administration.

Another major challenge ahead will be the task of monitoring delivery of programmes and schemes to ensure quality. There is no doubt that considerable progress has been made in key sectors, such as health and education, but quality will be an important issue in the future. The Government of Bihar has created a central monitoring and evaluation cell, which has in turn reached out to senior state cadre officials across departments to serve as focal points for monitoring in their respective domains. The health department's successful initiative to monitor the working of the health system in the state's districts and blocks by outsourcing this activity has already been noted. The government's Janata Darbar has furnished an excellent mechanism to relay citizen feedback directly to the chief minister for corrective action. Both the education and roads department have used third parties to monitor the quality of their initiatives, the hiring of teachers in the case of education and the quality of execution of construction in the case of rural roads.

The payoffs to good monitoring can be very high indeed, as demonstrated by the example of Tamil Nadu where social programmes are known to function well partly for this reason. Yet, information widely known at the local level often fails to reach the ears of decision-makers in Patna. In order to further improve monitoring, the government could take several possible steps. It could revitalize the traditional inspection system, requiring government officials to travel regularly to the field to personally inspect the performance of programmes and schemes at the cutting-edge level. It could continue to outsource monitoring to private players, who do not have an interest in misrepresenting data, to get feedback on a real time, continuing basis, as has happened in health, for example. It could also develop parsimonious, but relevant, performance indicators to track progress in outputs and outcomes on the ground. It could also turn to PRIs and NGOs to play an active role in monitoring rural programmes, where information is likely to be relatively scarce, using techniques such as social audits. Finally, for monitoring to be effective, senior policymakers need to take feedback seriously and adjust course accordingly.

Finally, the achievements in reasserting the rule of law in Bihar are certainly impressive. On the other hand, it will become necessary over time to build the capacity of the judiciary to process cases faster. Bihar still suffers from a large backlog of cases: the hiring of new judges, the creation of additional mobile courts, the development of alternative dispute-resolution mechanisms, the creation of new courts, and the application of information technology for case-load management, along with a substantial increase in funding for the reform of the state's judicial system, will be necessary to fully capitalize the gains already made in improving public order. Alongside this, the government will, and already does, face the risk of decentralized corruption by lower-level officials who deliver services at the cutting-edge level, especially as public expenditure rises dramatically. The creation of an independent State Vigilance Commission to coordinate the fight against corruption, and better monitoring using information technology and other means, can help address the problem over time, along with more effective implementation of the state's RTI Act, for example, through the appointment of additional commissioners to tackle case pendency. While high-level corruption in Bihar has declined considerably and the vigilance bureau has become more active, those who deliver services at the cutting edge should get the message that corruption will be swiftly detected and punished in one way or another.

There is much to celebrate in Bihar's success in recent years and the turnaround is undoubtedly real and here to stay. Many of the changes that have occurred look so stunning because they start from a low base. That is no reason for discouragement, only a measure of realism in understanding the task ahead. Even so, challenges exist to be overcome and there is much in Bihar's recent history to be optimistic about the ability of the government and citizenry to address them successfully with persistence and patience.

NOTES

1. See Witsoe's (2006) article on the politics of caste empowerment in Bihar between 1995 and 2005.

2. The chief executives of Bihar and Gujarat were rated as the most popular in India by the news-magazine *India Today* in February 2007. See *India Today* (2007). In February 2008, however, the chief executive of Bihar was still ranked among the country's five best, but at the fourth position. See Damodaran (2008).

3. See Bihar Police Act 2007 published in Government of Bihar (2007c).

4. Note that all data relating to crime in Bihar, including convictions, has been put on the web at http://biharpolice.bih.nic.in. This itself is a significant advance in transparency.

5. Bank dacoities are different from bank robberies in that they involve more people in the commissioning of the crime (five at a minimum) and are thus viewed as being more serious; the same goes for road hold-ups. I have collapsed dacoities and robberies into a single category in Table 2.1, as the psychological impact of a single incident is often the same regardless of how many people were involved in the crime.

6. For more on the evolution of the Naxalite movement, see Mehta (2008), especially pp. 10–12. Mehta argues that the shift in tactics of the Naxal movement towards targeting symbols of the state reflects its desire to set the terms of eventual incorporation in the political process on terms more favourable than could be accomplished without violence.

7. See notes from field trip to Sikaria Village, Jehanabad District, where a pilot of the ASAD programme has been put in place, 23 May 2008 (with Ahmad Ahsan). The World Bank mission notes are available with the author. See also Singh (n.d.).

8. This is according to the government's own statistics. See Government of Bihar (2009).

9. Note that the number of DA cases filed in 2008 fell to just two but then rose again to eight in the first five months of 2009.

10. Permission is required from the appointing authority to prosecute a public servant for corruption.

11. This low conviction rate in vigilance cases does not mean that the accused will not spend any time in jail. Once charge-sheeted, an accused is usually arrested pending bail. If the high court denies bail, then it can take up to one year for the Supreme Court to intervene and grant bail.

12. See a draft of The Bihar Specials Courts Bill 2009, as passed by the state assembly (Government of Bihar 2009b).

13. Most states, barring noteworthy exceptions such as Karnataka and Madhya Pradesh, have been reluctant to empower their Lok Ayuktas in this fashion.

14. For more on the initial conceptualization of Jaankari, see Kumar (n.d.).

15. A matching contribution from the state government is required in the case of land and buildings for state information commissions but not for the purposes of training and publicity.

16. Bihar's legislative assembly consists of 243 members, of which only 15 per cent can be members of the cabinet, resulting in a maximum cabinet size of 36.

17. See the classic article by Wade (1985). See also Wade (1982).

18. For an excellent overview of the problem of transfers, see also Bagchi (2007), especially chapters 7, 8, and 9.

19. Government of India (2006). The Ministry of Personnel is the cadre controlling authority for the IAS as a whole, a Union service, whether in the Government of India or the states.

20. Includes collectors-cum-district magistrates, DMs, and assistant collectors.

21. Including an indeterminate number of quacks.

22. For more on the RKS model as it originally evolved in Madhya Pradesh, see Sadanandan and Kumar (2006).

23. World Bank fiscal data on Bihar. See The World Bank, INDIA First Bihar Development Policy Loan/CREDIT (Loan Number 4879-IN and Credit Number 4380-IN) Second Tranche Release Document, p. 7.

24. World Bank data on education in Bihar. See The World Bank, INDIA First Bihar Development Policy Loan/CREDIT (Loan Number 4879-IN and Credit Number 4380-IN) Second Tranche Release Document, p. 10.

25. On the other hand, one would not expect a respondent to admit to paying a bribe in a survey of this kind. So the numbers may understate the payment of bribes to secure teacher appointments.

26. The distribution of job cards has since gathered momentum across Bihar. Data for 2007–8 indicates that job cards had been issued to 8.1 million households (Government of Bihar, 2009a: 174).

BIBLIOGRAPHY

Asian Development Research Institute (ADRI) (2007), *Ideas Behind Recent Economic Reforms in Bihar and their Impact*. Patna: ADRI.

Bagchi, Sanjoy (2007), *The Changing Face of Bureaucracy*. New Delhi: Rupa.

Centre for Media Studies/Transparency International (2005), *India Corruption Study*, vol. I. New Delhi: CMS/TI.

Central Statistical Organization (2010), 'Gross State Domestic Product at Factor Cost by Industry of Origin at 1999–2000 Prices as on 29-01-2010' for Bihar. Delhi: CSO, Ministry of Statistics and Programme Implementation, available at www.mospi.nic.in, accessed 8 February 2010.

Damodaran, Ashok (2008), 'Winners and Losers', *India Today*, 8 February.

Das, Arvind N. (1992), *The State of Bihar: An Economic History without Footnotes*. Amsterdam: VU University Press.

Government of Bihar (GoB) (2001), *The Bihar Lok Ayukta Act, 1973, The Bihar Lok Ayukta (Condition of Service) Rules, 1974, and the Bihar Lok Ayukta (Investigation) Rules, 1980* (Compendium). Patna: Superintendent Secretariat Press.

_________ (2006), 'The Bihar Panchayat Raj Act', *Bihar Gazette*. Patna: Finance Department, Government of Bihar, April.

Government of Bihar (GoB) (2007a), *Economic Survey, 2006–2007*. Patna: Finance Department, GoB.

_________ (2007b), *Report of the Bihar State Administrative Reforms Commission (Part 1)*. Patna: GoB.

_________ (2007c), *Bihar Gazette: Extraordinary Issue*, Bihar Police Act, 2007. Patna: GoB, 30 March.

_________ (2007d), The Bihar State Vigilance Commission Bill, 2007 (unpublished). Patna: GoB.

_________ (2008), *Economic Survey 2007–2008*. Patna: Finance Department, GoB.

_________ (2009a), *Economic Survey, 2008–2009*. Patna: Finance Department, GoB.

_________ (2009b), *Draft Bihar Special Courts Bill*. Patna: GoB.

_________ (2010), *Economic Survey, 2009–2010*. Patna: Finance Department, GoB.

Government of India (2006), *The Gazette of India: Extraordinary Issue*, Notification dated 24 August 2006. New Delhi: Ministry of Personnel, Public Grievances, and Pensions.

Gupta, Om Prakash (2006), *The Right to Information Act, 2005 & The Right to Information Rules, 2005 with the Official Secrets Act, 1923*. Allahabad: Sagar Law House.

Hindustan Times (2008), 'The Bihar Turnaround', 22 January, pp. 1 and 18, Delhi edition.

India Today (2007), 'Mood of the Nation Poll', 12 February.

Kumar, Chanchal (n.d.), *Project Report on Jaankaari: ICT-Based Facilitation Center under the RTI Act*. Patna: Chief Minister's Secretariat.

Majumdar, Subhakriti (n.d.), 'Challenges of Tax Administration in Bihar', powerpoint presentation slide 13. Patna: GoB.

Mehta, Pratap Bhanu (2008), 'The Political Economy of Development in Bihar: An Agenda for Public Investment', paper produced for the World Bank, New Delhi, April.

Mooij, Jos (2001), 'Food and Power in Bihar and Jharkhand: PDS and Its Functioning', *Economic and Political Weekly*, 36(4): 3289–95, 3297–9.

Paul, Samuel, Suresh Balakrishnan, K. Gopakumar, Sita Shekhar, and M. Vivekananda (2005), 'State of India's Public Services: Benchmarks for the States', *Economic and Political Weekly*, 39(9): 920–33.

Sadanandan, Rajeev and N. Shiv Kumar (2006), 'Rogi Kalyan Samitis: A Case Study of Hospital Reforms in Madhya Pradesh', in Vikram K. Chand (ed.), *Reinventing Public Service Delivery in India: Selected Case Studies*, pp. 186–224. New Delhi: Sage Publications.

Sharma, Alakh N. (2005), 'Agrarian Relations and Socio-Economic Change in Bihar', *Economic and Political Weekly*, 40(10): 960–72.

Singh, Sanjay Kumar (n.d.), 'Aap Ki Sarkar, Aap Ke Dwar (District Gaya)', unpublished document.

Subramanian, T.S.R. (2004), *Journeys Through Babudom and Netaland: Governance in India*. New Delhi: Rupa.

Wade, Robert (1982), 'The System of Administrative and Political Corruption: Canal Irrigation in South India', *Journal of Development Studies*, 18(3): 287–328.

———— (1985), 'The Market for Public Office: Why the Indian State is Not Better at Development', *World Development*, 13(4): 467–97.

Witsoe, Jeffrey (2006), 'Social Justice and Stalled Development: Caste Empowerment and the Breakdown of Governance in Bihar', in *India in Transition: Economics and Politics of Change*, pp. 1–42. Philadelphia: University of Pennsylvania, Center for the Advanced Study of India.

World Bank (2004), *Bihar: Toward a Development Strategy. A World Bank Report*. Washington D.C. and New Delhi: World Bank.

———— (2009), INDIA First Bihar Development Policy Loan/CREDIT (Loan Number 4879-IN and Credit Number 4380-IN), Second Tranche Release Document, p. 10 (unpublished document). Washington D.C.: World Bank.

3

Drivers of Reform

Examining a Puzzle in West Bengal

SUMIR LAL

In its search for solutions, the development discourse has moved from the purely economic, and from an alternating faith in the state and the market, to recognition of the role of institutions[1] in the success or failure of public policy, development effort, and public service provision. However, institutions are not static or monolithic, and in order to be activated, amended, or sustained, they rely on drivers emanating from underlying power structures and individual or collective agency. Thus, to examine institutions purposefully you need to examine relationships, behaviours, incentives, and interests, and the interplay among them, of the individuals, groups, and organizations of which they are constituted, and with which they interact. A growing body of literature acknowledges this prior and very real political dimension of development, and in particular addresses the political economy of reform.

Building on this line of inquiry, this chapter examines the question: when and how does reform of a public service occur? That is, when do long-term perverse or low performance incentives change in the direction of providing better services, or greater accountability, especially to poor clients? Here I do so by examining an example of (so far) successful reform and another of inadequate reform within the same political and institutional sphere, namely, the regional state[2] of West Bengal in eastern India. By comparing the two cases after controlling for external political, social, historical, and fiscal variables, we are able to discern the conditions that make the same set of individuals in broadly the same circumstances actively, and skilfully, it might be said, pursue reform in one case while passively avoiding it in the other.

These two case studies are: first, West Bengal's (as yet insufficiently studied) innovative and theoretically significant approach to restructuring its public sector enterprises and, in a related parallel effort, its power sector; second, its disappointing performance in the field of elementary education. The two cases epitomize a contradiction in contemporary West Bengal: much government energy directed to improving investor services and industrial and urban infrastructure, while remaining indifferent to human development outcomes. Politically, this is a puzzle. At the time of independence in 1947, West Bengal was India's leading industrial state. However, by the 1970s it had slipped steeply from this position, in some part due to the militant trade-unionism espoused by the Communist Party of India (Marxist), CPI (M), during the 1960s and early 1970s.

The CPI (M), in coalition with a group of fellow left-wing parties, collectively called the Left Front, has ruled the state continually since 1977, winning impressive majorities in every state election since then.[3] The Left Front government has been responsible for what is widely acclaimed to be one of the most successful land reform and decentralization operations in India, benefiting millions of poor farmers. Even so, today, a government of such political orientation has attempted to reform its industrial sector and make it productive, while failing to adequately provide an essential service such as elementary education to its apparently natural constituency of poor citizens. Therefore, to improve our general understanding of the intersection of politics with development, it is pertinent to ask what drove reform in one area but not the other.

It can be argued that comparing a commercial sector comprising manufacturing companies and power utilities with a sprawling social service like elementary education is akin to comparing apples with oranges. Governing policies, scales of operation, nature of clients, measurability of outcomes, role and interest (or lack of them) of private capital, market orientation (or its absence), and structure of the sectors are vastly different. True, but some critical issues that bedevil education—the state government's fiscal limitations, politically powerful unions on which the ruling party is dependent, poor governance and work culture, unclear lines of accountability—are exactly those that characterized the power sector 10 years ago and seemed just as immutable. If anything, the variation in the outcomes of the two sectors begs a comparison. This is not just to satisfy academic curiosity, but also to identify practical lessons from the successful case that may be replicable in the second precisely because they emerge from the same governance context.[4]

There is another significant commonality to the two otherwise dissimilar sectors: both grossly ill-serve the poor, especially the bottom quintile which has little or no access to the services of either. However, the power sector retains an elite clientele while the elite has, for the most part, altogether exited the public education system. In this lies the nub. This chapter will contend that a strong client for a particular service, in combination with external stimuli such as incentives offered by the federal government, or the regional state's own fiscal distress, will drive reform in that sector. Where such stimuli are wanting and the client is weak, it is not politically rational for the government to pursue a goal of universal public service provision.[5] This is an important understanding for the development community, even if not a remarkably fresh insight for close observers of developing-country politics. As development academics and practitioners have progressed from recognizing the role of institutions to acknowledging that understanding their political economy is critical, to their latest notions, such as demand-driven governance, they have agonized much over the question of political accountability. Why do poor people, even in democratic societies (such as India), apparently not hold their leaders to account for poor services? I conclude simply that this is the wrong question to ask, because in these societies poor people do hold their leaders accountable, but for other things (such as physical and economic security), not public services. Winning political strategies are forged accordingly. However, I will also show that such strategies cannot pay off in perpetuity.

This argument is not a hypothesis that I set out to test. I begin with the simple question articulated earlier and proceed towards a causally-reached answer.[6] The conclusion, when it comes, is not definitive, but the best possible and open to revision. Generic inferences are drawn, but this is not an attempt to verify a general theory: the focus is endogenous. The material I work with comes from first-hand accounts from key participants in the processes described, garnered through free-wheeling interviews with politicians, bureaucrats, businessmen, and trade union leaders, and close observers of them such as academics and journalists. This is supplemented by references to the most recent scholarship on West Bengal. Given the choice of its subject, the question it seeks to answer, and its empirical source, this chapter is of necessity overt in its identification of participants and motives. Without such frankness, its argument would lack clarity, but its standpoint is that of a disinterested, academic, and, to the extent that is consciously possible, non-partisan observer.

THE FRAMEWORK

In examining the two disparate sectors, I apply the service delivery framework developed in the World Bank's *World Development Report (WDR) 2004*. Premising that 'successful services for poor people emerge from institutional relationships in which the actors are accountable to each other' (World Bank 2004: 46), the *WDR* identifies four service-related actors—citizens/clients, politicians/policymakers, organizational providers, and frontline professionals—and the following relationships of accountability that connect them: voice and politics connecting citizens and politicians; compacts connecting politicians/policymakers and providers; management connecting provider organizations with frontline professionals; and client power connecting clients with providers (Figure 3.1).

The *WDR* also develops concepts of 'long' and 'short' routes of accountability.[7] Client power connecting clients and providers is the direct, 'short route' of accountability. When such client power is weak or not possible to use, clients must use voice and politics in their role as

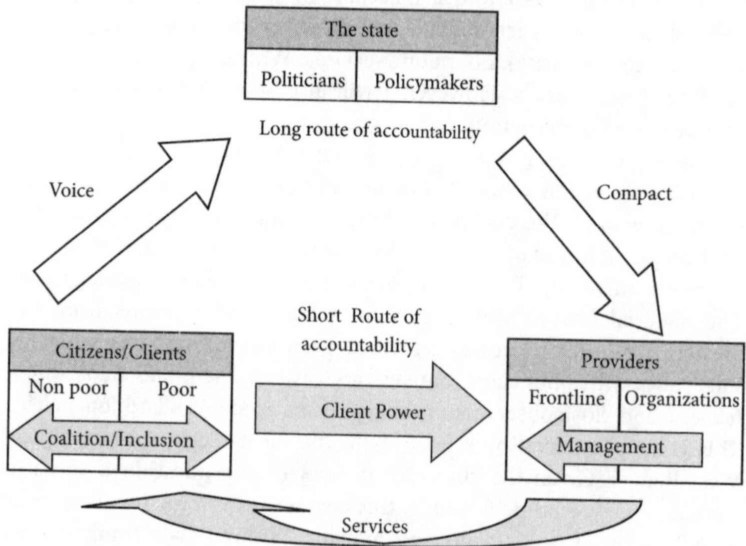

Figure 3.1 The Service Delivery Framework

Source: World Bank (2004).

citizens to hold politicians accountable, and politicians/policymakers must in turn use the compact to do the same with providers. The combination of the two is the roundabout, 'long route' of accountability.

This framework and its accompanying concepts prove useful in identifying West Bengal's strategies in its successful public sector and power reform, as well as to examine the weaknesses in its elementary education delivery system. This is, however, an idealized framework: the real world is far more complex. Another World Bank study (World Bank 2008: 15–16) points out in the context of rural India: there are five levels of democratically elected representatives; there are levels of civil servants operating at the same level as these elected representatives, but without direct responsibility to them; all these levels of civil servants have powers to delegate to providers the delivery of services; and there are competing relationships of accountability altogether outside this framework, such as those between politicians and their parties. The power of citizens/clients is greatest over local politicians, but the accountability of service-providers is usually to state civil servants. The chain of accountability thus breaks down (Figure 3.2). The education case study, in particular, will reflect this reality.

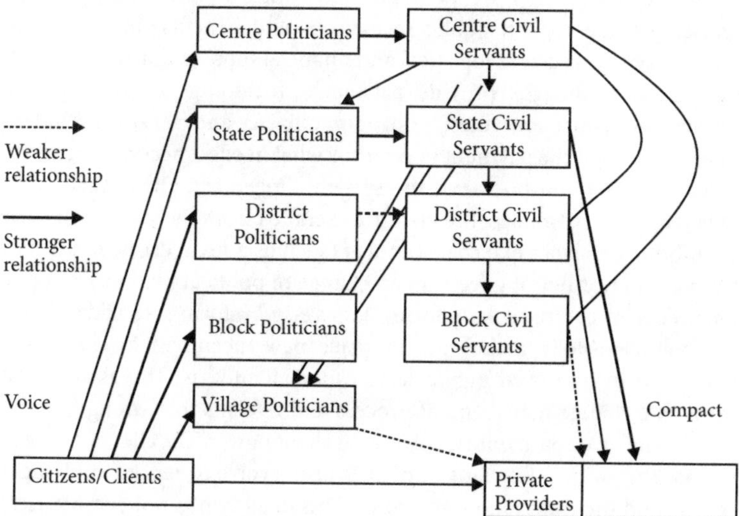

Figure 3.2 Reality Check: The Accountability Tangle in Rural India

Source: World Bank (2008).

Figure 3.2 also graphically depicts the true nature of the 'state' (in its broader, conceptual sense). Usually conceived of as a single, powerful entity—Hobbes's Leviathan—the state is actually a 'divided leviathan' (Sinha 2005: 4–5). Arguing in the context of industrial policy in India, Sinha contends that 'the national framework that governs industrial change in India was, and continues to be, a combined product of central rules of the game, sub-national strategic choices, and regional institutional variation. Regional politics, a product of sub-nationalist movements and electoral compulsions, emerges as a salient factor' (Ibid.). In other words, the regional states are powerful components of the 'ensemble of institutions' that comprise the Indian state, with autonomy to respond with politically determined strategies to 'rules of the game' emerging from the Centre,[8] and to the proclivities of their own constituents. That slices of the national state possess this autonomy of political choice and action is important to our understanding of West Bengal's approaches in both our cases and enhances the validity of the generic inferences we draw.

With these factors in mind, we can modify the *WDR*'s theoretical framework to conceptualize a model that reflects the actual politics of service delivery in a typical developing country (Figure 3.3). In a business-as-usual scenario, the relationships between politicians, service-providers, and clients are perverse but symbiotic: politicians protect service-providers (with public sector jobs and benefits) in return for political services such as logistical and financial support during elections; to citizens, politicians provide patronage, including access to public service, in return for votes; non-poor citizens and service-providers interact through the payment of rents for what in effect becomes a private service (or the non-poor exit the system altogether). Other than what they receive as patronage, the poor are excluded from the service. In such equilibrium, only an external stimulus (such as a fiscal crisis, incentives from a superior tier of government, change of political regime, or donor intervention) can provoke reform. A *successful* reform scenario will see the politician/policymaker put in place new incentives for providers that result in improved public services for all citizens. This is achieved through a change management process and reforms that strengthen the short route of accountability, enhancing client power. The clients' broader relationship with politicians *may* over time evolve to voice (implying a say beyond the transaction of a vote). This depiction is not symmetrical as in the *WDR*, but is busier at the provider apex, because that indeed is where most tangles, and solutions, lie. This model can apply equally to a wide-scale electric supply system as to a microcosmic village community

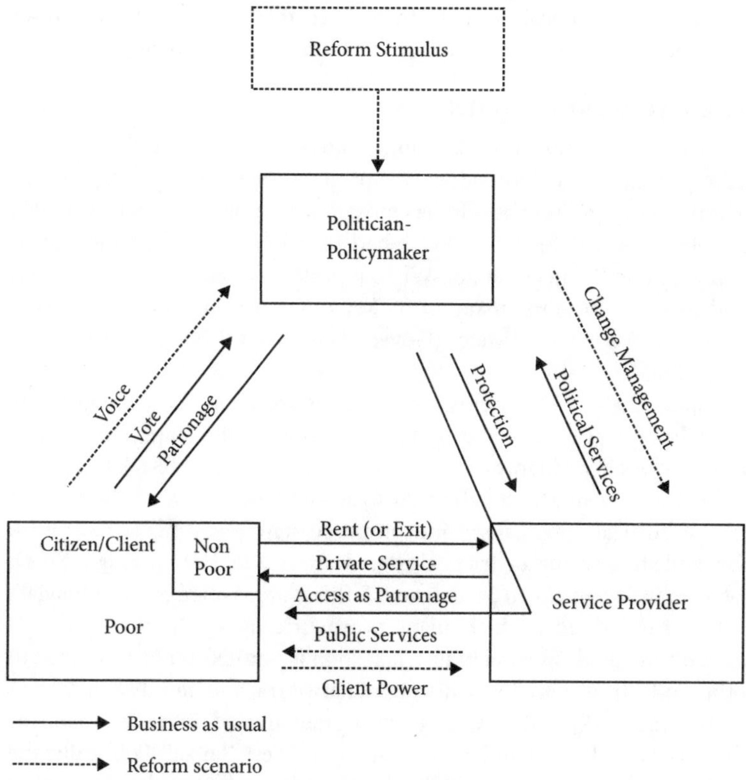

Figure 3.3 The Politics of Service Delivery

Source: Author.

managing a school. It best encapsulates the West Bengal story described here, and captures both our cases, disparate as they may be.

We now move to our study proper. In the section entitled 'The Two West Bengals', I describe the structural political economy of West Bengal. The sections on 'Power and Public Sector Reform' and 'Elementary Education' are the two case studies. In 'Addressing the Puzzle', I compare the two to isolate the drivers of action in one and inaction in the other, and examine what political accountability and rationality mean in the context of West Bengal. This leads to discussion of a current dilemma in West Bengal: tension over land allotments to industrial investors; and thence to the conclusion that there is a limitation to what might so far have been a politically rational strategy in the matter of public services, and that West Bengal needs to turn no further than to its own power sector to understand how to reform its human development sectors.

THE TWO WEST BENGALS

West Bengal is ranked ninth among India's 15 major states in terms of both per capita state gross domestic product (GDP) and per capita consumption expenditure. It is India's most densely populated state, with 904 people per sq km. In 1999–2000, it had 18 million rural poor, the fourth-worst among the major states. While it performs well in some education and health indicators, many of its key outcomes in these sectors trail the other major Indian states (Government of West Bengal 2004; World Bank 2005).

Sinha (2004, 2005) yields a specific insight about West Bengal: 'the spatial political economy of industrialization in the state'. Historically, industry has been highly concentrated around the city of Kolkata (earlier named as Calcutta), and through to contemporary times, the bulk of new industrial applications and proposed new investments have been for Kolkata and the districts clustered around it: Haora, Hugli, South 24-Parganas, and North 24-Parganas.[9] This is aggravated by West Bengal's urban–rural divide, which maps symmetrically on to the industry–agriculture divide as rural industrialization is non-existent (in contrast to other industrial states like Gujarat, Maharashtra, and Tamil Nadu).

In other words, the state is starkly demarcated into an urban, industrial West Bengal and a rural, agrarian West Bengal. Politically, the former comprises a vast middle-class of government and public sector employees and private sector professionals, industrial workers, a (largely non-indigenous) business and entrepreneurial class, and the urban poor. The latter comprises agricultural labourers, marginal farmers, and (in the absence of a large landlord class) a dominant middle peasantry, besides rural-based government employees, and the self-employed.

An important dimension of the political economy of West Bengal is that, unlike most Indian states, its dominant political class is urban-based. This is the Bengali Hindu, upper-caste dominated middle class. Its peculiarities are its lack of ties either to the land or to capitalist enterprise, and its ethic of educational and cultural achievement. By the weight of its demography, West Bengal is a rural, agricultural state, and about three-quarters of its legislative districts are rural. This notwithstanding, it is this urbanized middle class that dominates every sphere of public life, including the ideological and organizational leadership of all political parties. This dominance emerges from its early exposure to Western ideas, monopolization of education, openness to radical political thought (possibly because of its disconnect from both agrarian and industrial productive activity), the absence of competing capitalist or landed classes, and its being accepted as an 'objective' arbiter in the countryside because of its lack of vested interest in land.[10]

A word about West Bengal's much-acclaimed land reform and decentralization. Under the land reform programme, the rights of 1.68 million sharecroppers (or *bargadars*) were recorded in a process known as Operation Barga, introduced by the Left Front shortly after it came to power. This gave sharecroppers security of tenure, hereditary rights of cultivation, a three-fourth share of the crop, and a certificate that worked as a form of identity to secure loans. Further, about a million acres of vested land were distributed among 2.5 million beneficiaries (roughly half an acre each), and half a million households were given title to homestead plots. The bulk of the land reform programme occurred during the Left Front's first term (1977–82), and the programme wound down by about 1985, though some land redistribution continued into the 1990s. In 2000, the number of recorded bargadars accounted for 20.2 per cent of agricultural households. The land covered amounted to 1.1 million acres or 8.2 per cent of arable land in the state (Government of West Bengal 2004: 29–30). As about 18–22 per cent of arable land is believed to be under sharecropping, it is clear that the Left Front both achieved a lot[11] and left a significant portion undone. The Left Front distributed land that had already been vested by earlier governments and took no radical measures to collect more land to redistribute. Also, while it recorded sharecropper rights, it did not go to the next step and give them title. In this way, it maintained the balance between its constituencies of dominant middle farmers and the rural poor.

In implementing the land reform, a 'mechanism of vigilance and public pressure' was required at the local level to counter resistance from the lower rungs of the bureaucracy and dominant rural classes (Bhattacharyya 1994: 75; 2006: 103). The Left Front thus revived the moribund panchayats,[12] with elections in 1978 to become the channels that would identify beneficiaries and settle disputes. This process of decentralization has an important bearing on our education story, as we shall see later.

On the urban–industrial side, West Bengal under the Left Front had, prior to the Centre's liberalization reform (initiated in 1991), followed 'a self-defeating economic strategy [that] was politically rational' (Sinha 2004). This consisted of ideological opposition to private industry, alongside a policy of confrontation with the Centre over public investment. This played to the proclivities of the dominant class in the state and helped the Left Front mobilize electoral support. Then, however, the impact of China's reforms, the Soviet collapse, and the reduced federal role in resource allocations after 1991 led to much debate within the party. By 1994, it 'realized it had to swim with the tide',[13] and that year West Bengal announced a new industrial policy that sought to welcome private and foreign investors.

The 1994 policy did not result in immediate gains for the state, largely due to systemic and institutional weaknesses in the field of investor services.[14] A fresh impetus was provided after a generational change in leadership in 2000, which was followed by the Left Front's sixth and seventh consecutive state election victories in 2001 and 2006. During this period the state has pushed aggressively to invite investors, propelled by its fiscal situation (a huge debt burden that crowds out development expenditure), and lately, the visible aspirations of a new twenty-first century urban generation seeking opportunities in the modern economy. Playing catch-up with the information technology (IT) boom that was driving growth in other states, West Bengal launched an IT policy in 2000 to promote Kolkata as a destination, which has met with some success. This process has resulted in a departure from the earlier anti-industry, anti-Centre postures.[15] 'The shift is from "capital is bad", to "capital is bad but we won't say it is", to "capital is good and welcome",' a leading Kolkata industrialist said.[16] The change is visible in the city with private sector entry in housing, hotels, healthcare, English-medium schools, and engineering colleges.

While these benefit the urban middle class, a major challenge for West Bengal is the extent of poverty and unemployment. Poverty has declined significantly in the state since the 1980s, but in recent years it has done so at a rate that is less than that of India as a whole. The slowdown has been especially marked in rural areas: real agricultural wages grew by 4.2 per cent during 1987–93, but by only 1.8 per cent in 1993–9 (World Bank 2005). One result is a growing disparity in urban and rural incomes. In 2000–1, the per capita income of Darjeeling, the second-ranked district after Kolkata, was only 55.6 per cent of Kolkata's. In 1980–1, it had been 70.8 per cent (Government of West Bengal 2004). The incidence of poverty follows the same pattern. In 1999–2000, some 84 per cent of the poor in West Bengal lived in rural areas, where the poverty head count ratio was 31.7 per cent, more than double the urban ratio of 14.7 per cent (World Bank 2005). In both urban and rural areas, the number of marginal workers has increased more rapidly than main workers.[17] The major decline in urban areas has been in organized sector employment: the ratio of organized sector workers to total workers decreased from 12 per cent in 1990 to 8.7 per cent in 2000 (Government of West Bengal 2004).

POWER AND PUBLIC SECTOR REFORM: THE EXEMPLAR

Theoretical Significance

In this section, we will examine how West Bengal, very quietly and with great political skill, has gone about reforming its public sector enterprises (PSEs) and, in particular, its power sector. In describing the process, we uncover the political drivers. The process is in itself important as well, because West Bengal's approach to this very sensitive task provides an object lesson on how reformers can address apparently insurmountable challenges of political economy.

The formal literature on the political economy of reform is rife with game theory analyses of winners versus losers, of the presumed immutability of interest groups, and of the importance of aligning incentives. While these provide us with an understanding of the conditions under which reform can succeed, there is little guidance in the literature on how a political practitioner, juggling simultaneous and opposing demands from multiple constituencies, might actually go about achieving those conditions in real life. West Bengal's success with PSE and power sector reform helps address this theoretical gap by providing empirical evidence for one potential strategy, which works as follows:

1. *Ownership*: convert assumed losers (and therefore opponents) of reform into allies by making them own the problem and so develop incentives to resolve it.[18]
2. *Inclusion*: ensure that all those who wield actual political power in the situation, whether formal or informal, are included in the process of evolving a solution to the problem that has been collectively recognized.[19]
3. *Inside-out*: in the first instance, focus on the internal stakeholders (in this case, public sector employees).[20]
4. *Incrementalism*: proceed in realistic, sequential, and measured steps.

In short, first align the incentives of the immediate ring of stakeholders to the reform through a process of change management, and thus reinforced, move outwards to other stakeholders rather than, as the literature generally suggests, divide stakeholders from the very outset into a zero-sum game between presumed winners and losers. In the context of our theoretical model, what West Bengal did was to focus, first and foremost, on the vexed policymaker–service provider axis of the accountability triangle.

Restructuring Public Sector Enterprises

The story[21] begins in the late 1990s when West Bengal's fiscal deficit had risen to unmanageable levels: according to some estimates, up to nearly 10 per cent of the state's GDP. By 1998, the state's department of public enterprises—created to oversee 23 sick companies that had been nationalized over the years largely to prevent worker layoffs—was doing nothing more than doling out huge sums to subsidize the salaries of over 8,500 unproductive employees (on the combined payroll).

The situation was dire. The state government was reaching its fiscal limits, and such largesse was unsustainable.[22] It was, however, a political non-starter to speak of reform with its connotations (in the 1990s) of privatization and retrenchments. Public sector employees on the factory floor as well as in supervisory and managerial cadres were, after all, unionized, and the majority belonged to the CPI (M)-affiliated Centre of Indian Trade Unions (CITU). They were a critical, organized electoral base for the state's ruling party.[23]

There was only one way forward: improve the business performance of the PSEs *without terming the process privatization or even reform or restructuring*. In 1998–9, the new senior bureaucrat in the Department of Public Enterprises, Sunil Mitra, began holding quarterly meetings with a panel from each enterprise, representing senior management, supervisory levels, and worker unions. At these meetings, the government bluntly laid bare the financial situation and called for improvements that would not require fresh investments. The meetings began jointly to set quarterly targets and assess quarterly performance.

The approach in these meetings was non-ideological and apolitical, with no blame-shifting about the past, and a restricted focus on improving the present. Masty (2008: 364) observes: 'This did give labour leadership an essential sense of shared ownership of the problems together with management and government.' This series of meetings had twin benefits: personnel across the 23 units discovered common issues and problems; and, most importantly, through the shared, discursive process, *the need for structural change became self-evident* to all the participants. The process led to incremental improvements in PSE productivity and financial performance, breeding political support as the state's top leadership, reformers in the party, and the departmental minister began to see political gain in the exercise.

The decision to involve the unions in these business planning meetings was inspired, but it was no more than a clear-eyed recognition of political reality. The fact that in any event employees dictated terms to PSE managements, and the sheer formal power of CITU within the CPI (M) and Left Front would have rendered 'dead on arrival' any move not involving the unions.[24] In this connection, reformers in the political leadership were playing a simultaneous troubleshooting role, talking with state-level CITU leaders in party forums, and with the individual leaders of the unions of the 23 PSEs.[25] The political tactic at play here was the recognition that first-order stakeholders such as union leaders had their own stakeholders, and it was necessary to work both through and around those relationships. Within the party, a two-way consultative process ensued. The reformist leadership, led by the chief minister[26] and the politically weighty state industries minister, made presentations, drafted articles and resolutions, and issued diktats; and, party members, many of them resistant, responded with discussion and debate.

The result was the creation of an incipient coalition for reform, comprising senior bureaucrats, public sector managers, union leaders, and reformists within the political layers. Thus empowered and confident, the department leadership was able to convince the state cabinet in early 2001 about the urgent need for PSE restructuring: by then, the government was subsidizing 69 companies[27] to the extent of Rs 50 billion a year, which was roughly equivalent to the state's budgetary deficit. The party was sufficiently convinced to place public enterprise reform in its manifesto for the state election that year, and after a convincing victory, the chief minister called for strong action in that area.

It was therefore only after three years of under-the-radar preparatory work, and after seeing through an election, that the government attempted actual restructuring of the state public sector. It is pertinent to note that the CPI (M) at the national level has consistently opposed the federal government's public sector disinvestment programme, a position backed by many of its cadres and affiliated unionized workers in West Bengal. The party's critique is based on its ideological commitment to the principle of state ownership and objections to the federal government's attempts to sell off profitable companies. The Left Front government in West Bengal had to ensure that its reform policy did not contradict the CPI (M)'s central party line. Its reform coalition therefore emerged with a three-pronged approach: the government would shut down the completely unviable companies, partially privatize (up to 74 per cent) those needing fresh capital and technology, and retain and restructure the potentially viable. The PSE department's 23 companies would form the pilot to test this framework. Later, more companies from other departments were included, taking the total during this phase to 34.

The important political factor to note is that resistance to reform was internal to the Left Front: the differing views, incentives, and interests of its state and national leaderships, its party cadres, and its public sector worker-supporters. During this period, the principal opposition party, Congress, was not only complicit in the reform (it was a Congress government that had initiated liberalization reform at the Centre), but was also in disarray in the state.[28]

With displacement of workers now explicitly on the agenda, the state government approached the UK Department for International Development (DFID) for a grant to finance a redundancy fund. Even at this stage, it required an intense two-day debate in the party office for the sceptics to give the go-ahead. DFID provided Rs 20.87 billion, and the project consultants PricewaterhouseCoopers (PwC) entered the process in 2002. Labour suspicions were addressed by involving unions in the assessment of the consultants, downplaying global comparisons and received wisdom about privatization programmes ('international best practice' was not a welcome phrase), and ensuring that the PwC team comprised almost wholly of Indians, predominantly Bengalis. (Another act of cultural sensitivity was retaining the respected social and spiritual organization, Ramakrishna Mission, for counselling and retraining activities.)

Continuing to innovate its tactics as it proceeded, the department now embarked on an intensive phase of face-to-face meetings with PSE managers, union leaders, relevant bureaucrats, and workers. Mitra wrote detailed letters to these stakeholders, describing the issues and the agreements reached at each meeting. Transparency was a key principle: letters and minutes of meetings were made accessible to every worker. While building trust and credibility, this also served to ensure that union leaders stayed honest to the process. Objections and concerns were answered and widely distributed.

The critical ingredient of the process was the consistency of the reform coalition's messages, whether in party forums or with employees. First, the undeniable fact that most PSEs suffered from overstaffing and insufficient capital; second, the inevitability of change as the government had no more capital to invest, and inaction could only result in closure and job losses; third, the moral high ground: public enterprises absorbed funds needed for the state's economic growth and poverty alleviation (this argument was particularly effective in discouraging pleading for special consideration by any one group); and finally, the government's commitment to respect stakeholder concerns, particularly those of workers.

It is worth pausing to examine why these messages were *credible*. One, stakeholders had been allowed to recognize and 'own' the problem, and therefore did not suspect the government's motives. Two, the CPI (M)'s intimate relationship with the key stakeholder (employees) helped engender trust. Three, the stakeholders had been involved in the evolution of the solution. Four, the department *behaved* credibly through its transparent and consultative approach. Thus, much of the success was based on what the literature calls the 'institutional design' of the reform programme.

A pivotal aspect of the approach was its eschewing publicity, even though there was a general excitement in the local media about the state's new, investor-friendly industrial and IT policies.[29] The managers of the reform programme were very clear that their focus had first to be internal. Only after the primary stakeholders had been directly convinced and brought on board, were secondary stakeholders reached through the media, whose support reinforced the government's confidence that the powerful middle class was behind it.

Over the period 2003–5, carefully customized redundancy packages were evolved for the different companies in consultation with the employees. These had significant safety net provisions to protect the many redundant workers who were likely to be too old and under-qualified to find other jobs.[30] Other policy measures that evolved as a result of this consultative process included contractual restrictions on successful private bidders to prevent asset-stripping, and committing them to strict timelines for implementing business plans. These ensured that the reform was seen as an attempt to revitalize the units and generate jobs, and not merely as a bankruptcy bailout for the government. This is another important theoretical point: the positive way in which the programme was framed was itself a result (and proof of the virtue) of consultation.

The programme's first success was the partial privatization of Kolkata's historic Great Eastern Hotel. (Two attempts to privatize it in previous years had failed in the face of political and worker resistance.) The first phase of the PSE restructuring programme was largely completed by 2006–7, by when over 6,000 employees had availed of the redundancy payouts; 21 companies had been shut down; four were converted into joint ventures; and four had been retained by the state government after restructuring. Interestingly, these latter eight companies are all back in the black.

A second phase is now underway involving 28 PSEs[31] and the state power sector. DFID has granted Rs 18.40 billion for this phase, which follows the pattern of Phase 1, but with greater emphasis on capacity building and skill development in areas like human resource management, financial management, information solutions and management, project management, procurement, inventory management, regulatory matters, and customer services.

Reforming the Power Sector

Most companies in the first phase of PSE restructuring were from the manufacturing sector. With the inclusion of the power sector in the second phase, action moved to the somewhat more complex arena of public utilities. (Power companies, as one of my interviewees put it, interface with the public every second.) Attempts to reform the power sector in India's states began in the 1990s, driven by three principal considerations: increase generation, rescue state governments from the financial haemorrhaging of the public sector state electricity boards (SEBs),[32] and improve the delivery of this essential public service to consumers. Various reform models with different emphases have been tried during this period. By the late 1990s, most attention had shifted to governance issues within the sector with a focus on improving the distribution end.[33] These efforts culminated in the federal Electricity Act of 2003.[34]

In April 2007, West Bengal became the fourth state after Maharashtra, Assam, and Gujarat to restructure and corporatize its SEB under the 2003 Act. (Some other states had undergone the process using their own legislations.) West Bengal's relatively smooth ride in achieving this major reform is a story worth telling because of the very thoughtful process it followed. As a late starter down the path of power reform, the West Bengal government learnt from the experience of other states, several of which had faced intense political resistance from both employees and consumers, particularly on the issues of tariffs and subsidies, and SEB restructuring. It did not rush into restructuring and focused first on financial improvement: a strategy that subsequently helped to relieve the pressure for short-term revenue-generation measures like tariff hikes ahead of quality improvements, which had alienated consumers in several other states. Second, it focused on improving the utility's corporate governance and managerial capacity, believing that this, as in the PSE case, would create and sustain internal drivers for reform. Third, it kept business plans realistic, feasible, and achievable. The reform was carefully phased, the measured approach being essential to its strategy of gaining employee support at each step along the way, while not alienating middle-class consumers through tariff measures or service deterioration.

Electricity in West Bengal is generated, transmitted, and distributed through a mix of federally owned, state government-owned, and private entities. The state government's entities handle 54 per cent of generation capacity and 62 per cent of distribution capacity. The focus of this account is primarily on the West Bengal State Electricity Board (WBSEB), the most important of these organizations and the central subject of the reform. Back in the 1970s and 1980s, West Bengal and Kolkata were synonymous with power blackouts, and WBSEB was known as an inefficient organization with an overstaffed, indisciplined, and highly politicized and unionized workforce. Augmentation of generation capacity had improved the state's power supply situation during the 1990s, but WBSEB remained a loss-making and inefficient organization.

The power reform timeline runs parallel to that of the PSE restructuring. By the end of the 1990s, WBSEB was running up annual losses of over Rs 12 billion, owed the federal power suppliers over Rs 26 billion, and was itself owed Rs 12 billion by CESC, the private sector supplier to Kolkata.[35] The state's fiscal crisis made this situation untenable. At the same time, the Left Front had begun wooing industrial investors, for whom an effective power sector was a prerequisite. One competitive edge that West Bengal had over other states was its relatively comfortable power supply situation; what it needed to do to impress investors was efficient delivery.

In January 2000, the government got the entire WBSEB management board to quit, and reconstituted it with a bureaucrat, Gyan Dutt Gautama, as chairman, the first IAS[36] officer in the post after decades of engineers in charge. Similar to what was happening on the PSE side, Gautama formed a joint management council of unions, associations,[37] and management that together began to set and monitor performance targets, and introduce accountability measures with the aim of achieving financial and technical efficiencies. The new chairman repeatedly toured the districts, speaking to SEB workers, engineers, and union representatives with the blunt message that the government could no longer protect the organization or workers. Dialogue with union leaders continued at the political level. At this stage, there was no overt 'reform' programme being pushed. Rather, the leadership deliberately used that idea as a threat: if you do not improve your performance, then we will have no option but to reform (that is, privatize) because the government cannot help you any longer. The political leadership backed Gautama when he matched this blunt message with strong action. He was permitted to take exemplary disciplinary steps, instituting over 600 proceedings, including some arrests and dismissals, during his three-year stint. On one particular day, he suspended as many as 28 people. The unions were initially agitated, but soon got the message and resistance began ebbing.[38] These measures were accompanied by softer ploys, such as appeals to the engineers' professional self-respect and social conscience.[39]

West Bengal passed an anti-power-theft law in December 2001, which was implemented with much fervour. Another dramatic step was to send notices to other government departments that had not paid their electricity dues. The Asansol Waterworks, Salt Lake Municipality, and Kalyani general hospital were among those that briefly had their connections cut. These were promptly restored when their bosses and consumers protested, but the message was clear, most importantly to WBSEB staff, that their management was serious. The board began collecting its dues, including the money owed by CESC. (Some astute denial of power to Kolkata and the resultant media and public pressure helped push this along.) WBSEB's own debt of Rs 26 billion was securitized by the government. Its operating losses saw dramatic declines and it turned in profits from 2005 (Figure 3.4).

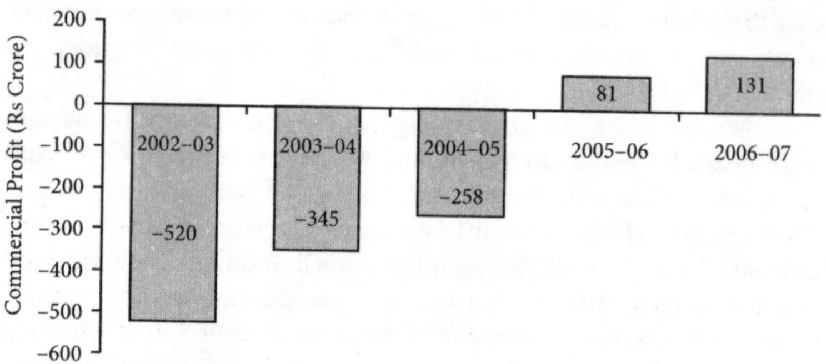

Figure 3.4 WBSEB Commercial Performance

Source: Government of West Bengal (2008).

A brief pause here to examine the political process at work. Clearly, the new WBSEB management enjoyed complete political backing,[40] and it is easy to see why. The government's fiscal desperation was, of course, the immediate factor. More importantly, however, the political leadership and, after a point, the unions could see that only winners would emerge from improved WBSEB performance: the industrial and urban middle classes were clear beneficiaries and, in contrast to many other states, there were no large, politically influential farmers using electric pumps and resisting measures such as anti-theft (and later, metering).[41] Conversely, the powerful urban middle class (whose political importance I described in the section 'The Two West Bengals') could turn against the government and potential investors would lose interest in the state if service did not improve. The political opposition parties had remained viable in urban West Bengal despite their overall weakness in the state during this period, so this was an important consideration. This political incentive, coupled with the deliberate fear-mongering about possible privatization, forced the employees to fall in line.

The important nuance, however, is that though the positive political fallout and its reinforcing effects were external to WBSEB (among consumers), the focus of the reform managers remained narrowly internal on ensuring the alignment of employees and their political mentors with the reform. The combination of joint business planning, carrot and stick measures,[42] political pressure, confidence induced by improved productivity, and trust in government (because of the way it was conducting the simultaneous PSE restructuring), led, by 2003, to employee buy-in to the idea of actual restructuring.

Notwithstanding its financial turnaround, it was clear that WBSEB could not continue running in its present form. At its core, it remained an outmoded and inefficient organization. The state government felt pressure, among other things, to augment generation, further improve efficiencies and performance, avail of new financing options, improve trading of surpluses, avoid losing high-paying industrial consumers to competitors, expand rural electrification (only 20 per cent of rural households in West Bengal are electrified), modernize technology, management, and business practices, and improve the organization's credit rating and debt-worthiness.[43] The West Bengal government was keen to avail of the Centre's Accelerated Power Development and Reform Programme (APDRP),[44] and then came the Electricity Act, which set in place a competitive power market and provided it with the alibi to proceed with unbundling WBSEB into separate generation, transmission, and distribution companies.[45] The state initiated this formal process of reforming its power sector in October 2005, full five years after first unleashing Gautama on WBSEB. By this time, Sunil Mitra had moved from the PSE department to the power department.[46]

The process of restructuring WBSEB into two successor entities, the West Bengal State Electricity Transmission Co. Ltd (WBSETCL) and the West Bengal State Electricity Distribution Co. Ltd (WBSEDCL), comprised a diagnostic review from November 2005 to December 2006, structural change during March–May 2006, and implementation of action plans from May 2006 to January 2007. A transition period of three years was envisaged, after which decisions on further restructuring would be taken.[47] Throughout, the strategy adhered to its non-negotiable principles: gain internal ownership each painstaking step of the way, avoid tariff shocks to consumers, and keep business plans and targets modest and realistic.[48]

The unions initially strongly opposed the idea of restructuring WBSEB, seeing it as a prelude to privatization. However, as in the PSE case, the government was able to gain their trust and eventually acquiescence. West Bengal was primarily aided by the fact that recruitment freezes in earlier decades had resulted in a high age profile of WBSEB employees: an average of 51 in 2005. Moreover, most managers would retire by 2010, so the issue was not retrenchment, but the criteria for transferring personnel to the successor companies, issues relating to seniority, promotions, and career development, capacity-building and skills development, security of pensions and post-retirement benefits, and the contours of an early retirement scheme. In a process mirroring that of the ongoing PSE exercise, packages and policies were evolved in consultation with the employees. The consultation process focused largely on compensation, transfer, and retirement issues, but also included such steps as sharing and obtaining feedback on the terms of reference for the project consultants, conducting consumer surveys and sharing the findings, holding workshops and discussions on each phase, meeting employee representatives to address doubts, and inviting written comments from the unions when finalizing the reports for each phase. The timeline for the project was undoubtedly slower, but that much sure.

Today, the two new companies have been constituted without past liabilities. The process of transferring WBSEB employees to them was possibly the smoothest of all such efforts in India, with most issues resolved to the mutual satisfaction of employees and government. Where, in 1985, WBSEB had 45,000 employees for 1.7 million consumers, its two successors today have less than 22,000 employees for nearly 7 million consumers (Table 3.1). The reform continues with ongoing capacity-building and organizational change programmes. Both companies have restructured their boards and inducted professional, independent directors, and introduced performance-linked incentive schemes. It is of course too early to declare success. The key challenges now are to sustain the reform momentum, find managerial talent in an era of increased competition, and undertake the ultimate reform: extend access of electricity services to poor and rural households.

Table 3.1 Employee Productivity

Year	2004–5	2005–6	2006–7	2007–8
No. of employees	29,100	27,031	26,136	21,737
No. of consumers served (in million)	5.18	5.682	6.345	6.835
No. of consumers served per employee	178	210	243	315

Source: Data provided to author by the Department of Power.

Looking back at the process of public sector and power reform, we see four clear drivers: first, the state's dire fiscal situation; second, the zeitgeist of the Centre's liberalizing paradigm with its accompanying incentives, and the demonstration effects of other reforming states; third, the political salience of the urban middle class and industrial investors; and finally, the CPI (M)'s political need to deal with public sector employees with kid gloves, an imperative that led to a series of tactical innovations. These, in retrospect, added up to an effective, self-reinforcing change management strategy that was positively framed, paid attention to institutional design, was consultative, carefully sequenced, and incrementally timed. As noted, during the critical years, West Bengal's reformers did not have to contend with the complications of coherent external political opposition, or implacable resistance from powerful lobbies (such as the large farmers in other states). This, however, only provides another theoretical insight: reform has to be opportunistic, and West Bengal seized its opportunity.

ELEMENTARY EDUCATION: A LONG WAY TO GO

Overview

We now move from the description in the preceding section of a dynamic process of reform to an analysis of a static situation of lack of reform.

It is not my case that the West Bengal government has been inactive in the education sector. Rapid rises in enrolment ratios and literacy rates indicate that something is happening. The state leadership has seriously attempted to discipline wayward teachers. My interviews with the policymakers in charge of primary education in the state indicated a great deal of commitment and energy. As Amartya Sen expresses it: 'The problem is not one of cranking up a stationary vehicle, but of making it go better and faster' (Pratichi 2002: 4).

The point is that all the schemes that are driving up enrolment and literacy rates—Sarva Shiksha Abhiyan (SSA, the National Education for All programme),[49] non-formal schools, the mid-day meal scheme, and other incentives like making school education free, supplying free textbooks at the primary level, and free uniforms to needy girl students—have so far had a visible impact in getting more children into school. There is, however, no evident agenda in West Bengal of politically owned, coherent reform to improve outcomes by addressing structural questions relating to budgetary allocations; teacher-related issues such as recruitment, accountability, professional empowerment, absenteeism, and the private tuition racket; strengthening parent participation and voice; and addressing substantive issues such as education quality, student retention, restoring the system of school inspections, and decentralizing appropriate functions.

In short, West Bengal has followed a typical pattern seen in the education sector all over the developing world: a proclivity for quantitative expansion thanks to its political and bureaucratic pay-offs, but little appetite for more complicated, but also more meaningful, qualitative reforms, especially those concerned with tackling powerful teacher unions.

According to the Census of 2001, West Bengal's literacy rate is above the all-India average at 69.2 per cent, an improvement from 57.7 per cent in 1991 and 48.6 per cent in 1981. Rural literacy is lower, but has been improving. For example, literacy among rural females has risen by nearly 16 percentage points between 1991 and 2001. West Bengal has also made good progress in increasing school enrolment: in the 6–10 age group, enrolment rose from 69.5 per cent in 1992–3 to 82.9 per cent in 1998–9 (World Bank 2005: 7). These overall averages can, however, be deceptive. The *West Bengal Human Development Report*[50] candidly observes (Government of West Bengal 2004: 145–63):

1. As many as 27 per cent of households in rural areas and 12 per cent of those in urban areas did not have any literate adult in 1999–2000.

The proportion of households without any female literate adult was 51 per cent (rural) and 31 per cent (urban) respectively.

2. Among the literate population, around 17 per cent is only literate at 'below primary' level.
3. The literacy status of Scheduled Castes, Scheduled Tribes,[51] and Muslim households is significantly worse than for other households, especially in rural areas. (According to the 2001 Census, the literacy rates for these groups are respectively 59 per cent, 43.4 per cent, and 57.5 per cent.)
4. More than half of agricultural labour households are non-literate. In urban areas, casual labour households are the worst off.
5. Gender gaps remain substantial at overall 17.4 per cent. These were significantly more for Scheduled Castes and Scheduled Tribes at 23.6 per cent and 28.2 per cent, respectively.
6. Never-enrolled children tend to be more concentrated among the lower income groups, and the Scheduled Tribe and minority populations.
7. There are serious and continuing concerns about the quality of primary education in both urban and rural areas, including poor infrastructure and inadequate equipment in schools; sporadic and irregular attendance of 'some' teachers; lack of accountability of teachers; and inadequate school inspection.
8. The relative importance of elementary education as a proportion of total general education expenditure fluctuated around 36 per cent during 1980–1 to 1987–8, and fell to around 33 per cent by the late 1990s. Salaries have been the largest single element of this expenditure.

The Report says (p. 169):

> The reasons for the relatively low ratio of attendance at schools in rural West Bengal include the sheer physical lack of schools in the vicinity of children. Lack of basic infrastructural facilities continues to be a serious concern. The number of schools with no room is depressingly high, and amounts to nearly one-fifth of all schools. Schools with only one room amounted to nearly another one-fifth. While the average number of teachers per school is three, this is still below the number of classes. In addition, there are major inadequacies with respect to the physical condition of schools, and the absence of necessary fittings and fixtures, toilets and basic equipment, and teaching materials.

The quality of education is poor with low examination pass-rates and learning outcomes, and a high level of student absenteeism and dropouts: from the cohort of students who enrol in Class I, only 29.5

per cent go on to complete elementary school, only 13 per cent complete secondary school, and only 6 per cent complete higher secondary school (World Bank 2005). Dropout rates are even higher for Scheduled Caste and Scheduled Tribe students. In 1997–8, the dropout rate in primary schools in 10 DPEP districts was 38.4 per cent;[52] while average attendance of enrolled children was 74 per cent in 2005 and 69.5 per cent in 2007 (Pratham 2008).

On the other hand, the rapid increase in enrolments has had an adverse impact on the teacher–student ratio. The average stood at 53 in West Bengal's primary schools in 2002–3, far worse than the all-India average of 42 and better than only Bihar (83), Jharkhand (59), and Uttar Pradesh (55) (NCERT 2005: 166–7, Table 56). The shortage of female teachers is particularly striking. The proportion in West Bengal was just 25, in comparison to the national average of 39 (Ibid.: 140-1, Table 43). These weaknesses are manifested starkly in deprived areas. Rana (2006: 23) reports:

> There is a correlation between the demographic setting of the areas and the failure in providing educational facilities. For example, single-teacher schools form about 6 per cent of the total in West Medinipur district (same as the state average). But Belpahari, a marginal block in the district, had 23 per cent (21 out of 91) single-teacher schools when we visited the area in November 2005. In Gopiballavpur East and West circles of the same district, single-teacher primary schools formed 21 per cent and 16 per cent respectively of the total.

Majumdar (2006: 786) attests:

> There seems to be [an] ironical situation of both acute shortage and surfeit of teachers in the primary school system. In urban and semi-urban areas, some government schools suffer from a shortage of students and surplus of teachers; these are so-called 'uneconomical' schools facing closure. In the disprivileged areas/neighborhoods in contrast, often one or two teachers have to manage single or double-handedly huge classes and all the school-related responsibilities.

A distinct pattern of educational deprivation thus emerges in West Bengal. The problem is regional (the more remote a district, or block within a district, the worse its education provision), social (the Scheduled Castes and Scheduled Tribes, minorities, and females are worst affected), and economic (the lowest income groups are most deprived). These three factors are often coincident: the socially marginal groups will also be the lowest income earners and will be concentrated in the more remote areas. Table 3.2 (using agricultural labour as a proxy for the underprivileged groups) shows the broad correlation of deprivation and low education provision across and within West Bengal's districts.

Table 3.2 Pattern of Education Provision in West Bengal

District	HDI* Rank	Literacy Rate	One-Teacher Schools (%)	No School Building	Agriculture Labour (Percentage of Workforce)
Kolkata	1	80.9	10.0	1	0.1
Haora	2	77.0	0.8	26	10.1
North 24-Parganas	3	78.1	6.4	42	13.5
Darjeeling	4	71.8	20.1	38	11.6
Bardhaman	5	70.2	1.6	34	29.9
Hugli	6	75.2	2.9	27	24.3
W. Medinipur	7	74.9	6.0	44	31.7
E. Medinipur			8.8	29	
South 24-Parganas	8	69.5	11.9	54	26.0
Nadia	9	66.1	4.6	29	23.2
Jalpaiguri	10	62.9	2.6	22	17.6
Koch Behar	11	66.3	0.2	6	29.5
Bankura	11	63.4	7.3	37	35.2
U. Dinajpur	13	47.9	4.3	7	39.6
D. Dinajpur		63.6	3.1	1	36.3
Birbhum	14	61.5	2.6	30	36.9
Murshidabad	15	54.4	1.8	45	28.0
Purulia	16	55.6	21.4	41	36.1
Malda	17	50.3	2.0	68	30.7
West Bengal		68.6	6.1	590	24.9

Source: Compiled from Rana (2006: 25–6).
Note: *Human Development Index.

An important caution here is that geographical remoteness itself is not the key factor: in Table 3.2, Kolkata has a strikingly high ratio of one-teacher schools. A study in metropolitan Kolkata of municipal primary schools found the following problems: high frequency of absenteeism by pupils, low educational achievements, considerable parent dissatisfaction with school performance, considerable irregularity in attendance by teachers and high level of parent dissatisfaction with teachers' performance, non-functioning of parent–teacher committees, extraordinary dependence on private tuition for almost anyone who could afford it, enormous variation between different schools, effective exclusion of children from very poor families, and failure of the inspection system (Pratichi 2006a). Clearly, poor people suffer irrespective of location.

The education situation in West Bengal is thus a classic case of poor delivery of a public service by a government to its most vulnerable citizens. I now analyse this service delivery shortfall by examining the incentives and drivers, or lack of them, along the three axes of the service delivery triangle: the policymaker (that is, the top echelons of the state government); the service provider (schoolteachers, frontline bureaucracy, and panchayats); and the client (households and communities). For specificity, I focus on elementary education.[53]

The Policymaker

No political party in West Bengal has ever made education a priority: neither the Congress prior to 1977 nor the Left Front since then. This is reflected in the state government's budget allocations for education, in which West Bengal trails other major states in education spending both in per capita terms and as a percentage of state GDP. Public expenditure on elementary education as a proportion of state GDP declined in most states during the 1990s, but only in West Bengal (and Uttar Pradesh) did it also decline in absolute terms (Drèze and Sen 2005: 168–9). Between 2000–1 and 2003–4, the share of education in the state's public expenditure declined from 16.6 per cent to 11.7 per cent (Deninger et al. 2009).

West Bengal's poor fiscal situation is often cited as the reason why it has not been able to spend more on health and education.[54] Nevertheless, the question is also of equity and prioritization of spending within the fiscal restraint. We have already seen that there are systemic biases against marginal populations and backward areas in the provision of education services. Further, in West Bengal, the share of elementary education has never exceeded 45 per cent of the total education budget, and has often hovered between 30 and 39 per cent. One study estimates it sunk to 24.9 per cent in 1999–2000.[55] In this study, West Bengal finished last by a long margin in a comparison of the 15 major states, which were assigned scores for their performance in the 1990s on the basis of the following attributes: Real growth of education expenditure; educational expenditure share in state domestic product; educational expenditure as a percentage of the total budget; education plan as a percentage of the total plan; real per capita expenditure on education; real growth of elementary educational expenditure; elementary education's share in total education; elementary education plan share in total education plan; own plan funds for elementary education; and real growth of per pupil expenditure (Bashir 2000: 89).

Key impacts of the state's poor fiscal situation and limited elementary education budget include, first, a growing reliance on federal education schemes; second, recourse to expansion of schooling facilities through non-formal, low-cost arrangements that raise serious questions of quality, equity, and sustainability; and third, cutbacks in infrastructure spending as well as an inability to recruit teachers. (The shortfall of teachers is said to be to the extent of 73,000 if the accepted 1:40 teacher–student ratio is to be met—a situation compounded by the state's generous raising of salaries of existing teachers, which have risen ten-fold since 1977.)[56] Thus, where fiscal stress drove reform in the power and public enterprise sectors, it is a stifling constraint in the case of education.

West Bengal is most conspicuously shown up by Kerala, India's educationally most accomplished state, which has also been ruled for long periods, though not continually, by CPI (M)-led governments. In fact, West Bengal suffers in comparison with even the tiny state of Tripura, the CPI (M)'s third base in the country (Table 3.3). According to one estimate, 31 per cent of West Bengal's illiterate population is in the 15–31 age group; that is, this cohort has lived its entire life under Left Front rule (Pratichi 2002: 14). Therefore, the question often asked is, why has the CPI (M) in West Bengal not experienced the same impulses as its branches in these other two states? However, that may not be a fair question.

Table 3.3 Expenditure on Elementary Education

State	2004–5		2005–6 (BE)		2006–7 (BE)	
	A	B	A	B	A	B
West Bengal	37.68	218.72	37.84	243.95	37.97	282.64
Kerala	43.10	458.67	40.68	456.25	40.32	574.53
Tripura	54.05	764.71	55.81	910.90	52.72	867.60

Source: Ministry of Human Resource Development, India.

Notes: A: Elementary education expenditure as a percentage of total education expenditure.

B: Per capita elementary education expenditure (Rs).

BE: Budget estimates.

Kerala was already on the path to achieving near universal literacy when its first communist government took office in 1957. The advancement in human development indicators in Kerala is generally attributed to its strands of social and land reform in the nineteenth and early twentieth centuries. Along with other factors such as a tradition of progressive local governments and competing missionary activity, this led to empowerment of lower castes and other marginal groups, birth of a class of peasant proprietors, growth of professions, and strong public demand for education.[57] This has been complemented, since the 1970s, by social mobility occasioned by migration to, and remittances from, the Gulf. Tripura's ethnic composition and political history have led to relatively greater mobilization and politicization of its tribal populations (Chadha, 2005: 354–76). Therefore, in these states, the political–bureaucratic–intellectual power structure is more representative of the different social groups, and provision for services like education has historically been more ingrained in the fabric of public policy.

West Bengal has not experienced such empowering and transformational social reform movements. The traditionally privileged upper castes (Brahmin, Baidya, Kayastha) continue to dominate the power structures at local, district, and state levels.[58] One indicator is that though Scheduled Castes, Scheduled Tribes, and Muslims together comprise over half of West Bengal's population, no member of these groups has held a pivotal leadership position in any party or the government, in contrast to Kerala and Tripura, and there is no emerging leader even in the second ranks.[59] Thus, in the absence of a coordinated demand for social transformation from within rural society, West Bengal's elite policymakers have historically not felt pressured to focus on human development.

A question that can be asked is whether socialist ideology should not have impelled the Left Front in West Bengal to do more. However, when it came to office in 1977, the coalition was focused on the tactical challenge of entrenching itself in the countryside. As explained in the section 'The Two West Bengals', it made more political sense at the time for the coalition to advance a limited form of land reform and decentralization. This enabled it to lock in a bedrock of support—a critical factor in its unbroken hold on power, as will be explained later—giving the party no pressing political imperative to focus on (except in a limited way) human development outcomes.[60]

The Service Provider

Formal primary education services in West Bengal are delivered through a state-level body, the West Bengal Board of Primary Education, empowered by the West Bengal Primary Education Act, 1973. This board performs all the major functions, ranging from curriculum design to quality control. District Primary School Councils (DPSCs) under the board handle district-level operations such as teacher recruitment, salary disbursement, and procurement. The board and DPSCs also implement the SSA programme in the state.

The West Bengal Panchayat Act of 1973 leaves it to the state government to assign functions relating to primary education to the three-tier panchayat system. So far, the latter institutions have been given no role other than enrolments and maintenance of school buildings, reflecting West Bengal's limited devolution of functions, funds, and functionaries to local governments.[61] This means the formal education system is very centralized, bureaucratic, top-down, remote from local communities, and as we shall see, prone to political capture and unaccountable.

Partly to get around its fiscal constraint, the state government set up (in 1997–8) a non-formal mechanism to expand education access, called the Shishu Shiksha Karmasuchi. This is a demand-driven and community-managed scheme, under which a community with over 20 children in the 5–9 age group can move the panchayat to open a primary school (Shishu Shiksha Kendra or SSK) if there is no government school within 1 km. Teachers are local women with the same minimum qualifications as those for formal schools, and schools have the same curriculum, books, and teaching hours. They are paid an honorarium which is a fraction of a government teacher's salary. By 2004–5, there were as many as 16,100 SSKs with 1.25 million students, and the programme has now been extended to middle schools or Madhyamik Shiksha Kendras (MSKs) (see http://darpg.nic.in/arpg-website/bestpracticesingovt/SSK.ppt).

These schools are covered by incentives, such as the mid-day meal scheme. Teachers and communities are highly motivated in these schools, but suffer from poor infrastructure and irregular flow of funds (Pratichi 2002). The *Human Development Report* cautions (Government of West Bengal 2004: 162–3):

> There are problems with making this the basic way forward ... In many areas where such education is really required, it is difficult to find a woman who is able to teach primary children. More importantly, the basic assumptions that anyone can teach children and that pedagogy is unimportant at elementary school level must be faulted. The lower salaries, the lack of infrastructure, and the absence of proper facilities all point to the creation of an inferior level of education ... Therefore it is necessary to avoid the possibility of this parallel system becoming another means of class differentiation. It is necessary to devise ways of making the formal system more responsive to local needs and to the specific requirements of children from disadvantaged groups, perhaps by increasing community participation in the supervision of such education. There is therefore a strong case for increasing the control of panchayats over the formal school system.

Our focus then must remain on the formal system. The frontline service provider in the case of education is, of course, the teacher. We have already referred to the problems of teacher absenteeism and performance, and the non-functional inspection system.[62] The key observation about government teachers in West Bengal is that they are politicized, not in a transformational sense but in a partisan fashion. Some 115,000 out of West Bengal's 150,000 primary schoolteachers belong to the CPI (M)-affiliated All Bengal Primary Teachers Association (ABPTA). The teachers' associations, like the party's numerous other 'frontal' organizations, provide it cadres, supporters, electoral manpower, and campaigners.[63]

The schoolteacher, in particular, had a pivotal role in the CPI (M)'s striking such intricate root in West Bengal rural society. Bhattacharyya (2001) explains that back in the 1970s and 1980s, most rural teachers were first-generation literates with limited vested interest in land, who were held in high respect by all sections of the village. Driven by ideology and regional pride, they joined the party in numbers. Being 'articulate in the language of the peasant and the party' and able to practice both 'low and high politics', they played an important conciliatory and leadership role while the Left Front was implementing its land reform programme:

> It is difficult to overplay the teachers' contribution in the CPI(M)'s politics ... The predominant popular perception was that only the village schoolteachers had the intent and ability to reach a commonly acceptable solution to a local dispute. The CPI (M) saw good political sense in utilizing their special position for its own penetration; particularly in the unorganized stretches of West Bengal's political society[[64]] ... The party spread its wings largely by turning the trustees of social capital into managers of political society. (Bhattacharyya 2001: 677)

In 1978, when it revived the panchayats, the CPI (M) had a total membership of around 30,000 in West Bengal, concentrated in the Kolkata metropolis and a few other industrial centres. It had to put up around 80,000 candidates for the panchayats (Bandyopadhyay 2003). The party opened its doors, and members of the two most influential sections in rural society—middle-level peasants and schoolteachers—came to dominate the panchayat system, especially its upper tiers. Now, as land reform proceeded, revenue officials were compelled to sit with this new class of political leaders to register tenants, identify surplus land, verify claims, confirm beneficiaries, and resolve disputes, confirming them as the new loci of power.

Beyond land reform, the panchayats grew into the interface between the bureaucracy and the political society, dispensing developmental resources, holding consultations on local issues, breaking barriers between caste localities, and meddling in all manner of disputes (Bhattacharyya 2001, 2006). Thus, schoolteachers became overtly important social–political players within village communities as mediators, counsellors, guides, and intermediaries with the state. Teaching was relegated to a subsidiary preoccupation. Associations like ABPTA became powerful and were able to negotiate frequent salary hikes and promotions for their members,[65] while weakening existing accountability mechanisms such as the inspection system (which had often been a source of corruption and harassment, and has now virtually collapsed). Sen (Pratichi 2006a: Foreword) delicately observes:

> We need the cooperation of the teachers' unions for doing their duty not only to the interests of their membership (obviously an important function), but also to do what they can to reduce the negligence of some teachers which bring the entire community to some disrepute.

He recently elaborated:[66]

> The lives of nearly all the people in the country are affected in one way or another by the activities of unionized workers, especially in the public services ... Consider the working of state-run elementary schools. Even though a great many primary school-teachers are extremely devoted to their work and to their students, we [Pratichi Trust] observed a shocking incidence of absenteeism and delayed arrival on the part of many teachers ... The neglect of teaching responsibilities is particularly strong, we were distressed to find, when the students come mostly from underprivileged classes.

The landmark Pratichi report on West Bengal explicitly speaks of the politicization of teachers (Pratichi 2002: 17, 31). It quotes a panchayat leader saying that 'no political leader dares touch them as they play a decisive role in elections'. A CPI (M) functionary is quoted as saying that 40 of the 60 party zonal committee members are teachers. A primary schoolteacher in Medinipur says he misses school at least four days a month when on panchayat duties, and 72 per cent of teachers spent one to seven days in the month prior to the Pratichi visit engaged in election duties, union meetings, and panchayat and administrative tasks.

Even teachers who come to school do not necessarily take classes: 31 per cent of the children Pratichi met said no teaching had taken place the previous day. One of the great vested interests that teachers developed was the practice of giving private tuitions. If they are serious about learning, children have to take paid assistance outside the school, a practice heavily biased against the poor. So alarming is the quality of teaching that only 7 per cent of Classes III and IV children who are not privately tutored can write their own names correctly (Pratichi 2002: 31). Sen (Pratichi 2006a: Foreword) continues:

> The complete denial of the right to free basic education that is reflected in the need for private tuition has to be overcome by raising the quality of schools, but it is immediately important to recognize that there is an enormously uncouth problem here... primary school children do not suffer from the need for substantial private tuition in almost any other country in the world.

There is evidence that widening economic and social distance between teachers and children from less privileged families is impairing the delivery of school education. For example, in schools with a majority of children from the Scheduled Castes and Scheduled Tribes, teacher absenteeism was as high as 75 per cent, and teaching days and hours were arbitrarily reduced (Pratichi 2002: 6–7). Sen, in his 'Introduction' to Pratichi (2002), remarks in this context: 'There is clearly less fear of effective censure when the children come from a disadvantaged background... those who need most that their "voice" be heard lack that power fairly comprehensively... the overall picture of the oppressive role of class divisions in school education is quite appalling.' This asymmetry of power and influence between teachers and underprivileged parents is 'a crucial feature of the political economy of schooling in India' (Drèze and Sen 2005: 174).

Partisan politicization of elementary education in West Bengal has become manifest in two other institutions: the DPSCs and village education committees (VECs).[67] Schoolteachers elect DPSC members, and the chairperson, a political appointee of the government, wields most of the authority. According to researchers, DPSCs are virtually schoolteachers' tool, and their effectiveness as governance mechanisms is almost entirely dependent on the personality of the chairperson. Rana (2006) is acutely critical of DPSC failures, especially in the matter of posting teachers to neglected blocks and neighbourhoods. In their study of VECs, Wankhede and Sengupta (2005: 573) report:

> A parent/guardian opined that membership in the committee remained restricted to the followers of the ruling political party only. Even if we ignore the accusation... one must admit the presence of micro politics in the entire selection procedure.

It is, however, possible that the immense power that CPI (M)-affiliated schoolteachers have grown to wield in the West Bengal countryside and in the party is beginning to wane. It is argued that with their growing power and wealth (high salaries and private tuition fees go a long way in rural settings), teachers have lost that very trust and synergy with their communities which in the first place made them so important to the party. On this account, the party has resisted (not always successfully) nominating teachers as its candidates for panchayat posts since the mid-1990s: for example, by asking them to take leave if they wished to contest.[68] Bhattacharyya (2001: 678) says:

> As the left-wing teachers increasingly adopted partisan roles as members of the state institutions at various levels... their managerial role in the organized political sphere came in direct conflict with their role as trustees of social capital in the village political society. The more they got identified with particular groups, the more they lost their ability to act as a credible mediator—and the more they lost their capacity to mediate, the less attractive they were in the field of organized politics... Salary increases over the years saw them become the new elite, removed from the community.

Having used teachers as political agents, the state leadership is now desperate to rein them in, but then has done little to strengthen them professionally. For all their political influence, teachers actually have little autonomy within the education structure. They have a negligible role in such matters as curriculum design, textbook selection, paper setting, and student evaluation, and little space for innovation in the classroom. Because teachers have not been adequately motivated and challenged, it is said that 'they themselves are resigned to play the role of a mere (and rather unenthusiastic and unthinking) implementer of a top-down package' (Majumdar 2006: 787). An important impact of this is loose accountability: parents cannot hold teachers responsible for things beyond the teachers' control.[69]

The accountability tangle of rural India depicted in Figure 3.2 becomes all too clear. Here again we have a stark contrast. Where, in the power and PSE case, politically powerful unions were gradually made partners in the reform process, there appears to be no strategy or even intention to do the same in education.

The Client

The account so far possibly conveys an impression of a passive and helpless client. However, studies of rural West Bengal reveal a high level of aspiration for education even among the poorest communities. In its study of the three rural districts of Birbhum, Medinipur, and Purulia, Pratichi (2002) found that 96 per cent of respondents believed that boys should acquire elementary education, 82 per cent believed that girls should do so, and as many as 84 per cent wanted it to be made compulsory. Further, only 3 per cent of children in the 6–11 age groups had never been enrolled. The rapid expansion of SSKs throughout the state is evidence of this pent-up demand. The bottleneck appears entirely on the supply side, and parents are frustrated. Nearly a quarter of parents in the Pratichi study expressed strong dissatisfaction with the performance of teachers. The 'dissatisfaction rate' with government primary teachers was thrice that of the community-controlled SSK teachers.

The reality is that poor people enrol their children but they are not taught. A 'shocking finding' is that many Scheduled Caste and Scheduled Tribe children are given step-motherly treatment in school, and even excluded from private tuition because of their background, leading to a 'treble advantage' for children from privileged homes: assistance at home (because of literate parents), attention in school, and private tuition (Pratichi 2002: 32).

Another problem for many poor households is their inability to get their children to attend school regularly. Pratichi researchers, during their visits to schools, found only half the registered students present (Pratichi 2002: 5, 30). Livelihood pressure—children's involvement in domestic and agriculture-related work—was the apparent reason, but at least 16 per cent of parents blamed teachers' absence, a hostile atmosphere, and lack of children's interest in what is taught. These factors have been termed the 'discouragement effect' (Drèze and Sen 2005: 158–9). This concept posits that aspiration for education is not the problem, but accessibility, affordability, and quality are. Issues such as dependence of poor families on child labour or weak parental motivation are 'further' reinforcements of the discouragement effect. The issue then is not lack of demand, but lack of client power. Wankhede and Sengupta (2005: 575) observe, for example:

> Schoolteachers... receive respect from the local community [and are] the most educated people in the locality. Questioning such people becomes more or less impracticable. At the same time, caste, class, and other power factors influence the process of monitoring in favour of the school-teachers. As a result, what may happen in the name of monitoring and supervision by VEC [village education committee] members is nothing [but] listening to the problems faced by the teachers.

Where communities do try and assert themselves, the system strikes back. Wankhede and Sengupta (2005: 576) report: 'In some cases, the community has emerged as a rival site of authority, and the state authority... has resorted to a strategy of ignoring and sidelining it.' This study also points to a lack of community participation in village meetings mandated by schemes like DPEP: 'It is necessary to make common people more responsive and vocal in these meetings. This can happen only through reconstruction of local power structures. In this regard, political parties need to play a more responsible role' (Ibid.: 577).

Why has decentralization not helped communities to assert their voice? We have already seen that panchayats in West Bengal have little actual executive power or even planning role devolved to them. Moreover, decentralization has not yet led to democratization, as Table 3.4 on participation in village assemblies (gram sabhas) shows. Bhattacharyya (2006: 108–9) observes:

> While important first steps in local participation were indeed taken ... doubts were raised on how far the panchayat, where the middle peasants and the school teachers continued to play a dominant role, was a representative body ... Decentralization has been partial.

Table 3.4 Gram Sabha Attendance and Participation*
(percentage of households)

Agricultural Land Ownership	Attend Gram Sabha	Participate in Gram Sabha
Landless	33	6.5
0–1.5 acres	44	13.8
1.5–2.5 acres	50	19.8
2.5–5 acres	38	18.7
5–10 acres	35	15.5
10 acres and above	44	37.9
All	37	11.3

Source: Bardhan et al. (2009).
Note: *Participation defined as standing up to speak or ask questions.

Similarly, the land reform programme, while bringing undoubted benefits, has not led to empowerment. For poor sharecroppers, it greatly improved their security and status. This new tranquillity induced cultivators to invest in productivity improvements, and agricultural production surged in West Bengal during the 1980s.[70] However, informal, usurious credit through moneylenders remains a major factor in rural West Bengal. Real wages for agricultural labour have remained very low despite the improved productivity. Indeed now, three decades later, the impact of the reforms has tapered off, and agriculture productivity growth has stalled since the 1990s.[71]

In other words, the rural poor have benefited in some important ways from West Bengal's flagship land reform and decentralization programmes, but not in a transformational sense. West Bengal's underprivileged sections continue to find it difficult to breach or hold accountable its elite, upper caste power structure.

My analysis of the elementary education sector reveals a historically indifferent policymaking class; a set of service-providers tangled in a mass of diffused accountability relationships, and a frustrated, discouraged client. Specific manifestations of this situation include lack of political pressure on the ruling coalition, a tactical alliance between the ruling party and schoolteachers in the countryside, and a remote, centralized, bureaucratic education delivery system with little power delegated to local governments. All the accountability relationships—compact, management, client power, and voice—are in disarray and there has been no incentive for reform.

ADDRESSING THE PUZZLE

Political Accountability

Table 3.5 provides a summary comparison of our two cases. In the PSE and power sector case, will at the political level drove bureaucratic resourcefulness to overcome apparently intractable constraints and convert them into opportunities. The answer to why West Bengal has not applied the same energies and creativity to education is evident. In the first case, external stimuli combined with a powerful set of clients to give policymakers a strong incentive to reform. Client power was so strong that the political leadership even got its affiliated unions to bend. In the second, the external factors acted as a bail-out, and with a weak client unable to apply pressure, policymakers and service-providers have not been pressured to reform. The party remains abject before the interest groups it relies upon, and has, at least till recently, not felt a political need to address the accountability tangle.

Particularly stark is the contrast in behaviour of the policymaking elite: animated by market logic in the first case, it was active and opportunistic; but content with its power of patronage in the second, it was passive and indifferent. That is, the agent of success in the first case is a key factor in the failure in the second.

This, however, raises the question: if poor people are not being adequately served by the elite, and lack institutional platforms to

Table 3.5 Political Economy of PSE, Power, and Elementary Education Sectors

Driver/Actor	Impact on Public Sector Enterprise/Power Sector	Impact on Elementary Education
Externality: Federal actions	Overall liberalization paradigm, Accelerated Power Development and Reform Programme, and Electricity Act are incentives to restructure	Sarva Shiksha Abhiyan, mid-day meal scheme are incentives to expand services, but not to reform delivery
Externality: State's fiscal deficit	With no options, becomes an opportunity for reform	Constraint on services; bailed out by federal schemes
Policymaker: State's political leadership	Proactive, reformist response to above factors	Passive; feels no pressure to act
Policymaker: State's ruling party	Resists; then reconciles; now sees political advantage in reform	Passive; sees benefit in status quo
Policymaker: Departmental leadership	Empowered and given autonomy to act	No such mandate
Service-providers	Employees and politically powerful trade unions are engaged by leadership, allowed to own problem and contribute to solution; after initial resistance, see benefits for themselves; numbers are manageable; clear institutional accountabilities are established	Politically powerful teachers and their associations have not been engaged by leadership, other than rhetorical exhortations to perform; no incentives to improve; numbers are large; institutional accountabilities stay tangled
Clients	Industrial and business investors, urban middle class: Concentrated, vocal, powerful. See benefit in reform; give policymakers incentive to proceed (rural and poor are largely absent)	Rural and urban poor, marginal sections: Dispersed and voiceless. Unable to articulate frustration or apply pressure. (Urban and rich are largely absent)
Public sphere	Big city media backs reform as improvement precedes tariff hikes	Scattered efforts by NGOs; little media traction

express their voice, why has the Left Front been repeatedly rewarded in elections? In trying to explain the Left Front's durability, Bardhan et al. (2009) find:

1. There is a significant statistical relationship between voting for the Left and having less land, less education, belonging to the Scheduled Castes and Tribes, and otherwise being poor.
2. There is no bias in relation to caste or land-ownership in the distribution of benefits within a village. It is political loyalty that counts: on average, households which regularly attend the political meetings of the dominant party receive greater benefits.[72] There are also positive correlations between voting Left and receiving *recurring* benefits, such as agriculture mini-kits, employment, and relief.
3. Attendance at gram sabhas (village assemblies) and help provided by gram panchayats in matters relating to personal occupation and emergencies are positively correlated with voting for the Left.
4. Improvement in agricultural incomes during 1978–2004 is significantly associated with voting for the Left.

The results indicate that the political success of the Left Front reflects a combination of clientelism and voters' 'gratitude' for intangibles (resulting from the land reform and decentralization), such as 'a kind of dignity which was unknown to them before'.[73]

Another study, based on 'life histories', holds that though the average amount of land secured by land reform beneficiaries was modest, it provided 'a durable foundation on which poor households could plan for the future', especially those with better initial social and family conditions (Deninger et al. 2009: 286–347). For many movers (out of poverty), entry into the 'political club' was a turning point, with the political connection becoming, initial conditions permitting, a route out of poverty.

From this, we can see that the Left Front in West Bengal has so far followed a politically successful strategy of balanced land reform, controlled decentralization, and incremental development, which has created a base of grateful supporters and dependent political clients. This situation appears to have led to a suppression of any political demands for services such as health-care and education. We can conclude that poor people reward (or punish) their politicians for performance in channelling benefits from various livelihood and poverty alleviation schemes, and providing protection, opportunity, and security. They do not, however, hold their politicians accountable for inadequate health and education services, for which they are unsure whom to blame.

Clash of the Two West Bengals

The story is not quite over. We have seen how West Bengal straddles two distinct political economies: urban–industrial and rural–agrarian. For the most part, as our two cases showed, the state's policymaking and political elite has managed these constituencies in parallel: placating the first, patronizing the other, and maintaining stability between them. However, a stage appears to have been reached where the lines are beginning to intersect, posing a new set of challenges, including the assumptions underpinning the politically rational strategy just described.

This is illustrated by a recent serious setback to West Bengal's ongoing efforts to attract industrial investors. Two big ticket projects,[74] avidly backed by the state leadership, ran into prolonged political controversy during 2006–8 due to strong local resistance to the acquisition of agricultural land. The contested acquisition process, activism of the political opposition,[75] and strong administrative counter-measures combined to beget a situation of violence and sustained unrest. This led, in October 2008, to the Tata Group withdrawing its globally watched Nano car project from the state, a major blow to West Bengal's image with investors and aspirations of its elite.[76]

Following these controversies, the Left Front has suffered significant election setbacks, losing considerable ground to the Trinamool Congress in the 2008 panchayat elections, the 2009 federal general elections, and a set of bye-elections in November 2009. In the panchayat elections, its share of gram panchayats plummeted from 71 to 49 per cent. In the federal elections, it failed to win a majority of parliamentary seats from the state for the first time since 1977. In the bye-elections, it was able to win just one of 10 seats while the Trinamool Congress swept eight. The Left Front's dramatic losses in rural areas, if they harden into a new trend, foretell an unravelling of its hitherto loyal constituencies. The next state election, due in 2011, will be worth watching. This experience encapsulates the non-sustainability of the Left Front's strategy of clientelism without adequate investments in human development.

From the data provided in Government of West Bengal 2004 (pp. 34–5, 39–40), it is clear that the flip side of a land reform that attempted to politically maximize the number of beneficiaries is that landholdings are very small (the average holding of recipients of redistributed land is 0.39 acres), giving West Bengal one of the highest proportions of marginal farmers.[77] More significantly, given further fragmentation and other factors, nearly half (49.8 per cent) of rural households were landless by the year 2000, up from 39.6 per cent in 1987–8. About 13 per cent of land recipients and recorded bargadars had been alienated from their land by 2001. Reverse-leasing is an increasing trend, so the situation a generation after the land reform programme is that a large number of unemployed and underemployed landless, small, and marginal cultivators can no longer subsist on their parcels of land, but are too poorly educated and unskilled to find jobs off it.[78] That is why they are unable to give up their land, especially to modern industries which create skilled jobs for which they are not qualified. Besides, in India's most densely populated state, the government cannot find any other land to offer industry. (In most districts, the net cropped area is close to 100 per cent of the cultivable land.)

The consequent controversies have been damaging politically for the West Bengal government: besides undermining its credibility, they have clearly provoked anger among the ruling coalition's traditional rural supporters, affected the Left Front rank and file's appetite for policies friendly to industrial investment, and discouraged other potential investors. An anti-industry policy is not tenable either because it keeps tied to the land the very people who need and seek opportunities off it.

The lesson for policymakers is clear. The state's only logical strategy now is to equip its population with the skills to participate in the modern economy. That is, it is politically rational now, where it possibly may not have been earlier, to invest in human development, and this entails reform of the service-delivery system.

We can now square the circle: To learn how to meet this daunting challenge, West Bengal needs to look no further than its own success in reforming its PSEs and power sector. Notwithstanding the different logics driving those sectors, there are lessons of strategy, process, and tactics to be learnt about how to summon up the political will, develop a pragmatic programme, identify entry points, and bring the key stakeholders on board.

CONCLUDING REMARKS

We began with a question, asking what drives reform of public services in the context of a puzzle in West Bengal: its energetic push to improve industrial investment services while relatively neglecting human development outcomes. Applying the policymaker–provider–client service delivery framework to the state's public enterprise/power and elementary education sectors, we found that in the first case it had executed a flawless reform programme, with important theoretical insights; in the second, a host of unresolved, perverse incentives and tangled accountability relationships had resulted in poor outcomes. An examination of political economy factors revealed that the Centre's liberalization paradigm, the state's own fiscal distress, and the needs of its dominant elites had pushed it on to a path of industrialization. This forced it to reform the relevant sectors through a series of impressive tactical innovations. In the countryside, however, the ruling coalition was content with its so far successful strategy of limited land reform and decentralization, and had no incentive to focus on human development.

However, the tactical treadmill in the first case and inaction in the second have culminated in a damaging clash between the state's industrial and agricultural constituencies. This indicates that it is now rational for the political elite to rectify its past neglect of public services and pursue an integrated growth strategy which links industry with skilled manpower through reform of the human development delivery system. In how it must do this lies a challenge for development scholars: to develop a politically feasible and locally owned reform agenda even in an apparently intractable political scenario, lessons must be drawn from examples of what is working within that system, conditions, and context. Those endogenous lessons are potentially far more replicable than any ideal type, exogenous reform design.

NOTES

1. Institutions, in this context, may be taken to include decision-making organizations, bureaucratic agencies, and formal and informal rules.
2. The second-tier political–administrative units in federal India are called states. I use the qualifier 'regional' here to distinguish these entities from the broader concept of state. Later in the chapter, where the context is clear, I will drop this qualifier.
3. This is another reason why West Bengal is a particularly well-suited 'laboratory' for the comparative analysis attempted here. It allows control for another variable: internal political variation over time.
4. Grindle (2004: 536) contends: 'While it is important to ask what's missing in a country's governance profile, questions about improvements that are occurring and the conditions under which they are doing so can provide important insights into the kinds of interventions that produce changes that are good enough for improved performance.'
5. In this respect, the two sectors are living examples of Hirschman's (1970) classic thesis on exit, voice, and loyalty.
6. For an elaboration of this 'journalistic' method, see Lal (2008).
7. The *WDR* defines 'accountability' as a set of relationships among the service delivery actors with five features: delegating (explicit or implicit understanding that a service, or goods embodying the service, will be supplied), financing (providing the resources to enable the service to be provided, or paying for

it), performing (supplying the actual service), information (obtaining relevant information and evaluating performance against expectations and formal or informal norms), and enforcing (being able to impose sanctions for inappropriate performance or provide rewards when performance is appropriate).

8. In India, the federal government is referred to as the Centre.

9. For spellings of district names, I follow the usage in West Bengal (2004).

10. I am unable to do justice to the rich history of this class here. This paragraph is my interpretation of Chatterjee (1997: pp. 22–5, 67, 81–3, 189).

11. West Bengal, under the Left Front, has proportionately distributed more surplus land and recorded the rights of more sharecroppers than any other state. It accounts for 47 per cent of all-India beneficiaries of redistributive land reform (Government of West Bengal 2004).

12. The panchayat or local government system has three tiers: the zilla parishad (district council), panchayat samiti (block or district subdivision committee), and gram (village) panchayat. I use the word 'panchayat' to denote the entire structure.

13. As expressed by a West Bengal opposition leader in an interview, June 2008.

14. For a detailed account, see Sinha (2004, 2005).

15. Another factor that has moderated anti-Centre sentiment is the Left Front's increased role in federal coalition politics since the mid-1990s.

16. Interview, June 2008.

17. The Census of India defines main workers as those whose main activity was participation in economically productive work for 183 days or more in the previous year. Marginal workers are those whose main activity was participation in economically productive work for less than 183 days.

18. For an earlier identification of 'ownership of the problem' as a necessary strategy of political economy (in the context of stalled power reform in other Indian states), see Lal (2006).

19. An important implication of this is: Do not go in with a preconceived reform solution.

20. That is, the principal beneficiaries of reform—consumers of public services in our context—are best served at a second stage, only after the internal house has been put in order.

21. This account draws largely from my interviews in June 2008 with key political and bureaucratic functionaries who were involved in the process. I also rely on Masty (2008).

22. An important reminder here is that India's federal government had begun liberalization reforms in 1991, a paradigm that increasingly forced state governments to economically compete and fend for themselves.

23. Industrial workers and government employees form a core base of the CPI (M). As mentioned earlier, in the 1960s and early 1970s, it had encouraged a militant brand of trade unionism.

24. As phrased by a senior bureaucrat in an interview. The key theoretical learning here is the importance of bringing the wielders of actual power to the table. In other situations, where power might be wielded less obviously but just as really—such as by big farmers in the case of agriculture subsidies—this crucial political pre-condition is often overlooked by reform designers.

25. One such political functionary told me: 'I started talking to unions of the PSEs: managers and workers, together and separately. Using the Centre's liberalization as a shield, I said we have no recourse but to change.' Personal contacts played a big role. He said: 'My own assistant was the secretary of one of the associations. He agreed to make only a proforma protest.'

26. The chief minister is head of government at the state level, a counterpart of the prime minister at the Centre.

27. This number includes public sector companies under the control of other departments, besides the 23 overseen directly by the PSE department.

28. The Left Front's huge legislative majorities notwithstanding, opposition parties have succeeded in retaining a nearly two-fifth vote share in the state. The CPI (M) has maintained the Left Front coalition despite its own dominance to ensure that all pro-left votes get pooled in each voting district in order to outnumber the opposition. During the late 1990s, federal political compulsions pushed the Congress and Left Front closer, undermining the Congress's ability to act as an effective opposition in West Bengal. In consequence, the Congress split in the state in 1998, when a faction called Trinamool Congress broke away. The latter, running on an aggressively anti-Left Front, populist, pro-poor platform, has since emerged as the principal opposition in the state.

29. This only underscores the importance of having a strategic approach to communication: the plan in this case was to go low key externally and be proactive internally.

30. Essentially, the packages comprised monetary compensation, medical and accident/disability insurance, and retraining for employees or, in lieu, dependent children. One person involved in the process described them as 'possibly the best conceived and most generous of their kind in the country'. A description of the restructuring programme is available at http://www.peir.in.

31. In December 2009, the site http://www.peir.in was reporting that eight of these companies will be partially privatized, 14 will be retained by the government after restructuring, one will be shut down, and decisions were pending for the rest.

32. SEBs were vertically integrated organizations that handled generation, transmission, and distribution.

33. By now, a considerable body of literature has developed on India's power reform efforts. For a political economy view, see Lal (2006). Dubash and Rajan (2001) provide an insightful early account of process challenges. For this section, I am particularly grateful to Ashish Khanna, Rohit Mittal, and a group of key informants in Kolkata.

34. Electricity is a concurrent subject under the Indian Constitution, which means that both Centre and the states can set policy in the sector, the Centre with overriding powers. This Act consolidated existing laws on generation, transmission, and distribution; superseded conflicting state legislations; introduced legislation to govern new concepts such as trading and open access; liberalized and de-licensed generation (except hydro); expanded the definition and activities of captive plants; and allowed competition in distribution.

35. Earlier known as the Calcutta Electric Supply Corporation.

36. The Indian Administrative Service (IAS) is India's elite bureaucratic cadre.

37. WBSEB had 14 worker unions and officer associations affiliated to various political parties.

38. My understanding is that in many of these cases, the party's consent would be obtained ahead of the action.

39. One pitch was around variations of the line: 'We are a monopoly. How can we be making losses?' and 'We are not earning our salaries, while outside people are starving.'

40. A positive feature of West Bengal, stemming from its political stability, is stability of tenure for senior bureaucrats. A major problem in many other Indian states is frequent, politically motivated transfers. Thus, reform champions have been allowed to have their run. For example, the West Bengal power reform was subsequently managed by Sunil Mitra (who moved from the PSE to the power department) and another bureaucrat champion, Moloy De (Gautama's successor at WBSEB), without interruption. In 2009, when Mitra moved to the Centre, the reformist Gautama returned to take his place.

41. From a reform management point of view, West Bengal has the 'advantage' of low agricultural consumption of electricity. Politics involving farm sector subsidies has been a complicating factor in power reform in many other states. See Lal (2006).

42. For example, an electronic metering project was begun in 2002, after which meter-based auditing was used to hold local managers accountable for revenue leakages. This was balanced with performance-linked incentives.

43. We must bear in mind that states across India were reforming their power sectors, which had been identified as a major constraint to growth and investment. West Bengal was not immune to this zeitgeist.

44. Under this programme, states agree to achieve time-bound reform milestones in exchange for access to federal soft-funding facilities. In addition, an incentive component provides cash grants against reduction in the financial losses of utilities.

45. For a variety of technical and commercial reasons, unbundling is now accepted as the preferred route for restructuring the Indian power sector. Along with WBSEB, two other state-owned power generation companies, West Bengal Power Development Corporation and Durgapur Projects Ltd, formed part of this programme. The central focus was on WBSEB.

46. Mitra's minister at the PSE department, the late Mrinal Banerjee, a former trade unionist, had also moved to the power department. The latter's role had been to stay out of the way of his reforming bureaucrats while pushing the reform message in political and trade union circles.

47. I do not go into commercial and technical details here. A comprehensive account of West Bengal's power reform can be found in PricewaterhouseCoopers (2009).

48. Power reform programmes in states like Andhra Pradesh, Karnataka, and Delhi have all suffered because of weaknesses in these three areas.

49. SSA is India's flagship national elementary education programme in which the Centre partners with state governments and provides the bulk of the funds. (Education is a concurrent subject in the Indian Constitution.) It is, indeed, premised on institutional reforms aimed at improving the efficiency of the delivery system. States have to assess their prevalent education system, including educational administration, achievement levels in schools, financial issues, decentralization and community ownership, legislation, teacher deployment and recruitment, monitoring and evaluation, status of education of girls and disadvantaged groups, policy relating to private schools, and the like. However, as its primary motivation is to universalize elementary education by 2010 in the wake of India making education a fundamental right (86th Amendment to the Constitution, 2002), the focus of implementation appears to be on numerical targets, and it is unclear how the reform component is being monitored. For details of the programme, see http://education.nic.in/ssa/ssa_1.asp#1.0.

50. A product of the Government of West Bengal with the participation of the United Nations Development Program and the federal Planning Commission.

51. Scheduled Castes and Scheduled Tribes refer to a set of historically marginalized and underprivileged groups who have been listed in a schedule of the Indian Constitution.

52. The *Annual Report 2000–2001*, Department of School Education, Government of West Bengal, cited in Pratichi (2002). DPEP refers to the donor-funded, multi-state District Primary Education Project.

53. Classes I to V. Some sources I cite refer to primary education, that is, Classes I to VIII. My focus is on the government education provision. For an interesting study on private schools in West Bengal, see Pratichi (2006b).

54. A minister in the present government told me in an interview: 'In the past, our fiscal problems and equations with the Centre meant we were not capable of spending as much as other states.'

55. Not that the greater proportional allocations to higher education have resulted in better outcomes at that level. A representative of a leading business association in Kolkata told me: 'The neglect of vocational and higher education is beginning to tell. Industry finds the graduates unsuitable.'

56. The recruitment problem has been further complicated by a court case that has, at the time of writing, resulted in a stay on fresh appointments since 2005.

57. A useful historical account of the spread of education in Kerala is Gopinathan Nair (1983), and for its developmental achievements Ramachandran (1997).

58. Some change is now possibly filtering through the system following the 73rd and 74th Amendments to the Constitution in 1993, which made it mandatory for Scheduled Caste and Scheduled Tribe and female representation in panchayats.

59. Kerala has had chief ministers from the backward Ezhava caste, for example. The Tripura CPI (M) has prominent tribal leaders, and the state has purely tribal-based political organizations. West Bengal's top political leaders, both leftist and that in opposition, all belong to the traditional upper castes.

60. A prominent former CPI (M) parliamentarian from West Bengal told me: 'Political stability has become the biggest impediment to development in West Bengal.' In contrast, in Kerala and Tripura, the Congress and Left Front have alternated in office.

61. World Bank (2008: 39, 41, 51, 55, 58–9).

62. NGO Pratham's *Annual Status of Education Report 2007* reported average teacher attendance in primary schools in West Bengal at 72.5 per cent in 2005 and 90.2 per cent in 2007 (Pratham 2008: 100). Pratichi (2002: 31) reported teacher absenteeism at 20 per cent in primary schools and 14 per cent in SSKs.

63. One reason for the CPI (M)'s continued political success is its deep penetration of West Bengal's civil society, and its usurpation of the space for collective action, through its numerous affiliated or 'frontal' associations for virtually every group that can be organized, from teachers, lab technicians, and librarians to bus conductors, street hawkers, and shopkeepers.

64. Bhattacharyya borrows the term 'political society' from Chatterjee (1997), who used it to denote the manner in which traditional societies mobilize politically to press demands and extract rights and entitlements from the state in exchange for their vote, in contrast to the lobbying and campaigning methods of 'civil society', which is more typical of modern Western societies. Subsequently, Bhattacharyya (2009) has argued that 'party-society' is a better description than 'political society' for the situation in rural West Bengal.

65. Given the low starting base, salary increases were, in themselves, not unjustified. Criticism stems from the poor services provided in return. Several bureaucrats I spoke to used phrases like 'teachers worked only for their self-interest' and 'the education budget is for the teachers, by the teachers'.

66. In the first Hiren Mukherjee Memorial Lecture to the Indian Parliament, 11 August 2008. Media reports of this speech are widely available on the Internet.

67. Parent committees that are supposed to monitor schools under the donor-funded District Primary Education Programme. Actually, partisanship manifests itself at all, even the pettiest, levels. Rana (2006: 12) narrates, in the context of the mid-day meal scheme: 'In many areas, the programme was seen to

have faced difficulties arising out of inter-party and intra-party fighting regarding the appointment of cooks.'

68. In recent years, the Left Front leadership has also strongly criticized and attempted to ban the practice of private tuition.

69. In this description of a structural problem concerning primary schoolteachers, it has not been my intention to paint either ABPTA or all teachers in West Bengal in a negative way. In his Parliament lecture, Sen said: 'I am very encouraged by the fact that the leadership of ABPTA and also that of the smaller unions of primary teachers have been remarkably cooperative in trying to change the culture of work in the delivery of school education.' In Pratichi (2002: 4), Sen says: 'We encountered ... a great many teachers who were clearly committed to their work and very concerned to find ways and means of improving the performance of schools.'

70. Estimates of the exact rate of agriculture growth in West Bengal in the 1980s vary from 4.3 to 6.9 per cent (Bandyopadhyay 2003), but even the low case is impressive. Some scholars believe this was a belated Green Revolution effect. However, as the measured input growth could not explain the entire output growth, scholars agree that institutional factors such as land and panchayat reforms played a role by encouraging greater labour intensity and private investments in technology (Bhattacharyya and Bhattacharyya 2007). The high rate of food grain output growth was primarily the result of yield expansion (Government of West Bengal 2004). Today, West Bengal is the largest rice producer, accounting for over 15 per cent of national production. The introduction of high-yielding *boro* (winter) rice, enabled by the spread of minor irrigation, played a substantial part in this.

71. Bhattacharyya and Bhattacharyya (2007) detect a sharp break after 1992–3. All their eight variables—area, production, yield, consumption of fertilizer, proportion of high yielding varieties, cropping intensity, institutional credit, and land reform—show a decline in growth between the periods 1980–1 to 1991–2, and 1992–3 to 2002–3. The decline is described as significant for all the variables except area and land reform, and especially for production, yield, and fertilizer use. They attribute the decline to the adverse effects of liberalization and depletion of groundwater. Bandyopadhyay (2003) argues that lack of title to sharecroppers (which diminishes their creditworthiness), fragmentation of holdings, and the failure to expand institutional credit are major factors. Another analysis (Government of West Bengal 2004) says that in the 1990s, cultivators in West Bengal were hit by adverse features of greater market orientation and external liberalization—such as input costs, volatile farm-gate prices, decline in access to formal credit and extension services, and inadequate investment in physical infrastructure and irrigation.

72. In contrast, a higher form of political loyalty—campaigning for the party—showed a significant negative correlation with getting benefits. The authors speculate that party campaigners received fewer benefits in order to project a

clean image, but in all likelihood received more lucrative, hidden rewards such as contracts, jobs, and boosts to political careers. Further, political campaigners were more likely to be from the upper strata, indicating the elitist skew of local politics.

73. The study ruled out electoral malpractice as a factor in overall voting trends, a charge that has often been levelled by opposition parties in West Bengal.

74. A Tata Motors project in Singur (Hugli district) and a Selim Group project in Nandigram (East Medinipur district).

75. In contrast to its disarray during the initial years of the PSE and power reform, the political opposition in West Bengal had by now begun to get its act in concert. The Trinamool Congress, a West Bengal-specific breakaway faction of the Congress (note 28), has been able to build a populist, pro-poor platform, and apparently struck a popular chord with poor and marginal farmers—a hitherto core Left Front constituency—with its activist objection to the land acquisition process.

76. The controversies around the two projects have been extensively reported in the Indian media. For an analysis of the land-related factors, see Bose (2007). A detailed timeline for the Tata project can be found at http://development-dialogues.blogspot.com/2008/02/singur-timeline-with-corroborative.html, accessed December 2008.

77. Small and marginal farmers own 84 per cent of total agricultural land in West Bengal, compared to 43 per cent in the rest of India. About 80 per cent of the agriculture-dependent population has an average landholding of 0.64 ha (CII-KPMG 2007).

78. It was telling that in a state with such a high level of unemployment, representatives of industry with whom I spoke repeatedly complained of the shortage of low-cost skilled labour.

BIBLIOGRAPHY

Bandyopadhyay, D. (2001), 'Tebhaga Movement in Bengal: A Retrospect', *Economic and Political Weekly*, 36(41): 3901–7.

_________ (2003), 'Land Reforms and Agriculture: The West Bengal Experience', *Economic and Political Weekly*, 38(9): 879–84.

Bardhan, Pranab, Sandip Mitra, Dilip Mookherjee, and Abhirup Sarkar (2009), 'Political Stability, Local Democracy and Clientelism in Rural West Bengal', *Economic and Political Weekly*, 42(9): 46–58.

Bashir, Sajitha (2000), *Government Expenditure on Elementary Education in the Nineties*, Report prepared for the European Commission, New Delhi.

Bhattacharyya, Dwaipayan (1994), 'Limits to Legal Radicalism: Land Reforms and the Left Front in West Bengal', *Calcutta Historical Review*, 16(1): 57–100.

_________ (2001), '"Civic Community" and Its Margins: School Teachers in Rural West Bengal', *Economic and Political Weekly*, 36(8): 673–83.

_________ (2006), 'Writers' Building and the Reality of Decentralized Rural Power: Some Paradoxes and Reversals in West Bengal', in Niraja Gopal

Jayal, Amit Prakash, and Pradeep Sharma (eds), *Local Governance in India: Decentralisation and Beyond*, pp. 65–71. New Delhi: Oxford University Press.

Bhattacharyya, Dwaipayan (2009), 'Of Control and Factions: The Changing "Party-Society" in Rural West Bengal', *Economic and Political Weekly*, 42(52): 65–71.

Bhattacharyya, Maumita and Sudipta Bhattacharyya (2007), 'Agrarian Impasse in West Bengal in the Liberalization Era', *Economic and Political Weekly*, 42(52): 65–71.

Bose, Deb Kumar (2007), 'Land Acquisition in West Bengal', *Economic and Political Weekly*, 42(17): 1574–5.

Centre for Studies in Social Sciences (CSSS) (2006), *SRD Programme: Design of Purpose-level Indicators and Baseline Measurement in West Bengal Districts*. Kolkata: CSSS.

Chadha, Vivek (2005), *Low Intensity Conflicts in India: An Analysis*. New Delhi: Sage.

Chatterjee, Partha (1997), *The Present History of West Bengal: Essays in Political Criticism*. Delhi: Oxford University Press.

CII-KPMG (2007), *Sustainable Economic Development in West Bengal: A Perspective*. Kolkata: Confederation of Indian Industry, KPMG.

Deninger, Klaus, Deepa Narayan, and Binayak Sen (2009), 'Politics of the Middle Path: Agrarian Reform and Poverty Dynamics in West Bengal', in Deepa Narayan (ed.), *Moving Out of Poverty: The Promise of Empowerment and Democracy in India*, pp. 286–347. New York/Washington D.C.: Palgrave Macmillan/World Bank.

Drèze, Jean and Amartya Sen (2005), 'Basic Education as a Political Issue', in *India: Development and Participation*, pp. 143–88. New Delhi: Oxford University Press.

Dubash, N.K. and S.C. Rajan (2001), 'Power Politics: Process of Power Sector Reform in India', *Economic and Political Weekly*, 36(35): 3367–90.

Gopinathan Nair, P.R. (1983), 'Educational Reforms in India: Universalization of Primary Education in Kerala', Working Paper 181. Trivandrum: Centre for Development Studies, available at http://www.cds.edu, accessed December 2008.

Government of West Bengal (2004), *West Bengal Human Development Report 2004*. Kolkata: Development and Planning Department, Government of West Bengal, available at http://data.undp.org.in/shdr/wb/WBHDR.pdf, accessed December 2008.

__________ (2008), 'Overview of the State Power Sector', presentation by Sunil Mitra, June. Kolkata: Department of Power, Government of West Bengal.

Grindle, Merilee S. (2004), 'Good Enough Governance: Poverty Reduction and Reform in Developing Countries', *Governance: An International Journal of Policy Administration and Institutions*, 17(4): 525–48.

Hirschman, Albert O. (1970), *Exit, Voice, and Loyalty: Responses to Decline in Firms, Organizations, and States*. Cambridge, MA: Harvard University Press.

Lal, Sumir (2006), 'Can Good Economics Ever Be Good Politics? Case Study of India's Power Sector', World Bank Working Paper No. 83. Washington D.C.: World Bank.

_________ (2008), 'The Political Economy of Reform: Role of the Internal "Journalist"', in Sina Odugbemi and Thomas Jacobsen (eds), *Governance Reforms Under Real World Conditions: Citizens, Stakeholders, and Voice*, pp. 75–92. Washington D.C.: World Bank.

Majumdar, Manabi (2006), ' 'Primary Education: Debating Quality and Quantity', *Economic and Political Weekly*, 41(9): 785–8.

Masty, S.J. (2008), 'Communication, Coalition Building, and Development: Public Enterprise Reform in West Bengal and Orissa States, India', in Sina Odugbemi and Thomas Jacobsen (eds), *Governance Reforms Under Real World Conditions: Citizens, Stakeholders, and Voice*, pp. 335–89. Washington D.C.: World Bank.

National Council for Educational Research and Training (2005), *Seventh All India Educational Survey*, Provisional Statistics. New Delhi: NCERT.

Pratham (2008), *Annual Status of Education Report (Rural) 2007*. Mumbai: Pratham Resource Centre.

Pratichi (2002), *Pratichi Education Report: Number 1*. Delhi: Pratichi (India) Trust.

_________ (2006a), *Public Delivery of Primary Education in Kolkata: A Study*. Delhi: Pratichi (India) Trust.

_________ (2006b), *Public–Private Interface in the Primary Schooling System: A Study in West Bengal*. Delhi: Pratichi (India) Trust.

PricewaterhouseCoopers (2009), *West Bengal Power Sector Reforms: Lessons Learnt and Unfinished Agenda*. New Delhi: WB-AusAID Policy Facility for Decentralization, Local Governance and Service Delivery.

Ramachandran, V.K. (1997), 'On Kerala's Development Achievements', in Jean Drèze and Amartya Sen (eds), *Indian Development: Selected Regional Perspectives*. pp. 205–356. New Delhi: Oxford University Press.

Rana, Kumar (2006), 'Midday Meal and Primary Education: Prospects and Challenges in West Bengal', paper presented at the CSSS–CSES seminar on 'Education and Inequality in Andhra Pradesh and West Bengal', Hyderabad, 21–22 September.

Sen, Amartya (2008), 'The Demands of Social Justice', Hiren Mukherjee Lecture, New Delhi, 11 August.

Sinha, Aseema (2004), 'Ideas, Interests, and Institutions in Policy Change: A Comparison of West Bengal and Gujarat', in Rob Jenkins (ed.), *Regional Reflections: Comparing Politics across India's States*, pp. 66–108. New Delhi: Oxford University Press.

_________ (2005), *The Regional Roots of Developmental Politics in India: A Divided Leviathan*. New Delhi: Oxford University Press.

Wankhede, G.G. and Anirban Sengupta (2005), 'Village Education Committees in West Bengal, India: Planned Vision and Beyond', *International Journal of*

Educational Development, 25: 569–79, available at www.elsevier.com/locate/ijedudev, accessed December 2008.

World Bank (2004), *World Development Report 2004: Making Services Work for Poor People*. Washington D.C.: World Bank.

_________ (2005), 'India: West Bengal Policy Note: A Note on Selected Policy Issues', mimeo.

_________ (2008), *India: Rural Governments and Service Delivery*. New Delhi: Oxford University Press, available at http://darpg.nic.in/arpg-website/bestpracticesingovt/SSK.ppt, accessed December 2008.

4

Reforming Public Services in a High Growth State

The Case of Gujarat

ASEEMA SINHA

History is opaque. You see what comes out, not the script that produces events, the generator of history. There is a fundamental incompleteness in your grasp of such events, since you do not see what's inside the box, how the mechanisms work. What I call the generator of historical events is different from the events themselves, much as the mind of the gods cannot be read just by witnessing their deeds. You are very likely to be fooled about their intentions. (Taleb 2007: 83)

Where do developmental reforms[1] come from and what combination of contingent and institutional factors ensures their persistence? The origins and persistence of economic reforms in diverse contexts deserve further scrutiny. It is also important to address a related question: Why and how do policy and institutional reforms work more effectively in some Indian states than in others?[2] I take up an analysis of Gujarat's economic reforms to answer these questions. Can we learn something replicable or generalizable from the analysis of one state within India?

The trajectory of economic reforms in Gujarat, the western Indian state, raises some interesting analytical and empirical issues.[3] Gujarat is an industrially advanced state and is considered to be both a high growth state and a leader in pursuing economic reforms. The state's gross domestic product (GDP) grew at 10.2 per cent per annum between 2002 and 2007, and the Planning Commission set it a target of reaching 11.2 per cent in the next plan period (Government of Gujarat 2008). It is considered to be one of the leaders in attracting domestic investments, even if its record on foreign investment is more indifferent. The transfer of Tata's Nano manufacturing plant, the world's cheapest car wooed by many states, to Sanand in Gujarat was an important achievement (Siddiqui 2009). Similarly, the Vibrant Gujarat summit of 2009, in its newsworthy aggregation of figures, looks impressive and gigantic.[4] Even so, Gujarat, faced with competition from other states, has slipped in its overall competitiveness index to rank three (after Maharashtra and Tamil Nadu), and even in the ranking accorded to administrative and bureaucratic efficiency.[5] What is, however, interesting is that Gujarat has been quite effective in pursuing economic reforms across many sectors: power reforms, fiscal reforms, some limited but notable education reforms, and private sector participation in infrastructural development, to name a few. These specific reforms are crucial in ensuring a sustainable model of public service delivery and are therefore deserving of analysis.

We do not, however, know how these reforms began or unfolded in the state. What combination of factors contributed to their initiation and implementation? Were reforms and effective public service delivery easier in Gujarat than in other states, given Gujarat's historical legacies of state and private sector strengths (Dholakia 2003; Sinha 2005)? State capacity in Gujarat—the ability to translate developmental goals into policy outcomes—has been historically stronger than in many other states, but state performance or capacity may be too blunt a concept to help us fully understand why and how reforms are initiated and implemented. For example, reforms have proceeded in fits and starts notwithstanding strong historical legacies of state strength. The Gujarat case, with its long history of effective state capacity across several policy domains, presents an opportunity for us to unpack and disaggregate those aspects of state capacity that persist across time and across diverse policy domains, and are crucial for the implementation of economic reforms. We also need to know about the institutional and historical *sources* of state capacity both for analytical and policy lessons. What mobilizes state capacity to respond to new challenges and crises? Can other states in India learn any lessons from the economic reform trajectory in Gujarat in order to undertake economic reforms suitable to their problems as well as mobilize their own states to ensure effective implementation? This set of questions makes a case study of Gujarat especially relevant and germane to larger debates on the origins of reforms and state capacity.

Underlying this empirical quest is a set of larger questions: How do institutional arrangements that underlie economic policy regimes, and may be forged in the distant past, 'actually make it to the present' (Thelen 2004: xii)? Alternatively, how do institutions underlying old developmental arrangements transform, decline, or gain power to deal with new challenges and compulsions? What is the balancing weight of historical state capacity, individual initiative, and learning processes in the working out of policy intentions and designs? How do external factors—international agencies or Central rules and institutions—and regional imperatives interact in pursuing developmental agendas at the sub-national level, specifically in Gujarat?

CASES AND METHODOLOGY

I answer these questions through case studies of four diverse yet related policy reforms: fiscal reform and privatization, port development, power reform, and education reform. These four cases are the embodiment of the growth potential in an economy but are also important for public service delivery. One of the salient goals of fiscal reform was to ensure the finances necessary for the development of infrastructure in the state. Port development is conceived as an instrument of regional industrialization, and services not only the private industry but also the people of Saurashtra and Kutch as well as the hinterland of Gujarat. Insofar as it is designed to aid in the larger development of Gujarat, and even the northern and western states of India, it has wider implications worth analysing. Power reform has a clear positive impact on the public good, with both urban and rural consumers benefiting from more stable access to electricity, tariff reform, and the curtailment of transmission and distribution losses. Education of girls has obvious impacts on social welfare and the economic opportunities for all citizens.

I adopt a historical approach to analyse policies and policy outputs as they unfold in time, without biasing our results based on final outcomes, howsoever good and beneficent. This reorientation gets away from the presentism of our conventional analysis and urges us to pay attention to accidental and non-linear factors at work, the contingent element in policy evolution, and the random factors that create success notwithstanding the contrary intentions of many actors. Developmental success has many fathers but the task of policy analysis must be to assess the causal mechanisms precisely and carefully, as they unfold in time, not with hindsight undertaking most of the analytical work. This focus on accidental and non-linear processes does not, however, mean that we cannot replicate good institutions elsewhere, but rather that accidental learning is only possible within a larger frame of smart capacity and innovative institutional features. It is a challenge to 'plan' for innovation and serendipitous learning but one that can be learnt by attending to the mechanisms of success underlying policy innovations in Gujarat (and elsewhere).

How was information gathered for this analysis? Most studies by economists rely on economic data, and some descriptive policy analysis, quite useful but also unsatisfying. I followed a slightly different strategy. I attempt to trace the origins and the evolution of policies and policy change. For this purpose, I followed an intensive strategy of meeting officials, retired and current, of each of the organizations associated with different types of state policy. Retired civil servants or those who had moved to different departments provided valuable and confidential information that was historically specific. I also accessed all relevant economic data as well as the annual reports of all relevant organizations. Careful documentation of data from 12–14 different newspapers yielded detailed and voluminous information that was invaluable in preparing for interviews. At each step, the focus was on comprehensive and accurate information derived from individuals who had taken the initiative or been at the centre of various decisions and events as they unfolded in time.

THE ARGUMENT

Why have reforms succeeded to a significant degree in Gujarat? Four major arguments emerge as salient. First, I suggest that one needs to rethink the timing and periodization of reforms in the state. Most observers focus on the current period of 2002–8 to be an active reform period, where we see crucial achievements. I, however, argue that the foundations of the current successes were laid in crisis and began much earlier in the early to mid-1990s. While many outcomes are visible now, the foundations of these innovations and outcomes were laid over a decade ago, and originated in fiscal and political crisis. Thus, in order to understand recent successes as well as failures, I present a longer time frame of periodization of economic reforms in the state. The story of reforms in the state originated in the early 1990s and can be divided into three stages. The first phase begins with fiscal crisis in 1990–4. The second crucial phase lasted from 1995–2003, and the third phase, where we see some of the outcomes, is 2003–9. Table 4.1 outlines how the reforms unfolded over time across the four policy cases and the rest of the chapter uses this periodization in each of the case studies.

Table 4.1 Timing and Periodization of Reforms in Gujarat

	Fiscal Reform	Privatization	Ports Development	Power Reform	Education Reform
1970–90 (Historical Trajectories)	Ok but Subsidies and Tax Giveaways	Strong	Weak	Weak	Weak
1990–4	Begins	Non-Existent	Begins	Non-Existent	Non-Existent
1995–2003	Continues	Begins	Significant Developments	Limited	Non-Existent
2003–9	Continues	Limited	Continues	Significant Developments	Begins

Second, Gujarat is blessed with advantageous initial structural conditions: a strong industrial base, private sector interest, and basic state capabilities, which are crucial to the trajectory of reform. Without them, the success of reform might, at the very least, have been slower. However, two cautionary variables deserve analysis. At crucial moments, severe crisis (fiscal) and external factors (international aid and Central government initiatives), exogenous to the state, played an important yet indirect role that cannot be underestimated. External factors were quite crucial. Such unpredictable external factors present new opportunities and threats, activating state responses, which may not otherwise have been possible. Second, individuals and leadership vision and initiative emerge as crucial across all policy domains. Even more interestingly, reform proceeds in fits-and-starts and through a trial-and-error process rather than as a blueprint imposed from the top.[6] Neither vision nor structural attributes are sufficient for successful reform, although they may be necessary. Thus, ideological inclinations, which may be termed 'vision', structural factors, and institutional preconditions are *catalysed and mobilized* by key individuals and accidental serendipity creating a powerful momentum in favour of reform despite challenges, some failures, and unpredictable events. Learning is important to the process of reform and can reinforce the more 'structural' variables underpinning reforms. This dynamic between contingent and structural factors suggests a nuanced yet optimistic tale of lessons for other states. Gujarat has learnt from its own history and other states can deploy valuable lessons from Gujarat's experience, but the lessons are not about powerful hubris but about putting key individuals in place and creating the institutions that will work in innovative and unpredictable ways (see the concluding section for lessons for other states).

Specifically, the origins of reforms in Gujarat lay in a fiscal crisis that demanded a local response and home-grown initiative combined with fortuitous external opportunities in the form of a loan from a multilateral development agency. The crisis drove home the necessity for reform of the state's finances in the early 1990s. Fortuitously, the loan to Gujarat created the external conditions for new ideas of reform, such as public–private partnerships (PPPs) for infrastructure or power reform, and created a small but crucial coalition that utilized the loan to compensate losers created by the reform process. It urged the state's leadership to sustain the agenda of politically difficult reforms notwithstanding false starts, delays, and failures.

Third, two primary causal variables working in a complementary tandem are the principal levers of reform success. State capacity and private sector incorporation into the policy process play a major role. Yet, Gujarat's reform experience urges us to think of state capacity in slightly different ways. Bureaucratic autonomy, a variable suggested by the larger theoretical debates on state capacity, while important, is not sufficient and needs a more dynamic and proactive push from political leaders at the top rung of the system. Chief ministers, heads of agencies, and heads of crucial departments such as industry and finance can play crucial leadership roles. When the finance department is proactive, as it was between 1995 and 1999, much can be achieved. There is an indisputable role for cognitive capacity—the ability to see and respond to the problems of the long term—and vision. Yet, institutional variables of monitoring and feedback mechanisms (the creation of overlapping institutions, for example) ensure that a large sprawling bureaucracy works effectively across diverse policy domains (for example, privatization, ports, power, and education). Yet, some dimensions of state capacity are fraying and decaying in Gujarat and new capacities relating to private sector contract negotiation and management need to be created anew to address the next generation challenges and in order to sustain past gains.

The second set of variables having to do with private sector pressure, both implicit and explicit, raise more complex questions and issues. The close historical interaction between private capital and the state in Gujarat ensures that state officials have internalized the requirements of capital in a way that may be impossible in most other states. Gujarat is fortuitous in benefiting from strong path dependence and historical experiences of reform; for example, the joint sector idea that allows it to implement the current model of private sector participation much more easily and without much conflict. Economic reforms give a renewed legitimacy to such interactions and imperatives. Many policies—port and privatization, especially—are shaped and energized by private sector needs and initiatives. This embeddedness or nestedness does raise problems relating to issues of public accountability and public delivery, which demand a more rule-driven rather than discretion-driven framework for the future.

Fourth, which of these variables can be replicated elsewhere? Institutional features make it easier to implement reforms, but strong institutions also face inertia and stasis, and require leaping vision, energetic mobilization, and new institutions that can create a new dynamic for reform. Thus, simple institutional innovations and leaps of effort can make a difference. Monitoring and review of institutions, both formal and informal, emerge as crucial. Many of these institutional features can be replicated in other states even if there is no visionary leadership or crisis at hand.

ECONOMIC REFORM IN GUJARAT: PERIODIZATION, CRISIS, AND SERENDIPITY

The foundations of economic reforms in Gujarat lie in the early to mid-1990s, when fiscal and institutional crises stimulated new thinking as well as new policies that were to have a consequential impact well into the mid-2000s. Internal (within the state) realization coincided with external assistance in the form of an Asian Development Bank (ADB) restructuring loan in 1996, and allowed the state to tie its own hands in favour of reforms and created the conditions for important innovations that followed in the late 1990s and 2000s (Rodrik 1998). In contrast to many Indian states, where crisis creates further crisis, necessity (fiscal and economic crises) and serendipity (the ADB loan) were the mother of important and crucial innovations and inventions in Gujarat.

Historical Legacies: 1960–90

Until recently, Gujarat's population and its leaders have benefited from institutions and policies put into place in the 1970s and 1980s. Gujarat state, since its inception in 1960, has focused on classical industrialization while providing some key support to those sectors that support agriculture, such as fertilizers[7] and irrigation (the early support for the Narmada Dam tribunal award in the late 1970s is one such example).

The national licensing system constrained the choice of policy instruments—backward area development, for example—but also provided specific advantages. State agencies in Gujarat took licences from the Central Ministry of Industry and then invited private parties as joint sector partners, facilitating a hybrid form of capitalist development (Sinha 2005). Interestingly, Central schemes were modified to suit local needs and enhance industrial development.[8]

Paradoxically, state agencies that provided credit, licences, and infrastructure (called industrial estates) gained in strength and vigour as they mediated as well as circumvented the national licensing framework. Some of the powerful and competent state agencies—Gujarat Industrial Development Corporation (GIDC), Gujarat Industrial Investment Corporation (GIIC), IndextB (Industrial Extension Bureau), the Industries Department, among many others—conceived of innovative schemes and implemented them relatively effectively. Equally importantly, many of the public sector units (PSUs) in Gujarat—Gujarat State Fertilizers Corporation, Gujarat Alkalies Chemical Limited, and others—ran efficiently and made profits. Private capital had a mutually synergetic relationship with the government, in which the state both provided for and anticipated its needs: the joint sector concept, where the state shares 26 per cent of equity while handing over managerial control to the private sector, created historical legacies of a complementary state–private capital relationship. Underlying this were also close relationships between key business houses and the state's leadership. Gujarat's state administration embodied a unique model of 'bureaucratic developmentalism' comparable to the East Asian developmental states with strong state capacity and micro-institutions that delivered well and where private capitalists both used the state and contributed to its development in full measure (Sinha 2005).

Fiscal Crisis: 1990–4

The national policy of economic reform in 1991 unleashed tectonic shifts for all states, arising out of the larger national/global context as well as local/regional developments, and generating fascinating changes both in policies and in the institutional structures underlying developmental strategies.[9] In the early 1990s, as path-breaking economic reforms were initiated at the national level, some senior leaders and officials in Gujarat were faced with a fiscal crisis of their own making. Moreover, the dismantling of the national policy framework raised new challenges for the regional states, especially Gujarat, that had derived advantages from the Central rules of the game. As the national policies of licensing and financing were vanishing, the state agencies' relevance and role in mediating Central rules and regulation faced a challenge. Second, Gujarat's finances began deteriorating with a rising revenue imbalance from 1985–6 onwards. The fiscal deficit widened to reach 7.37 per cent of net state domestic product (NSDP) in 1990–1, and to 4.15 per cent in 1996–7 (ADB 2007). In 2001, the fiscal deficit had reached 8.9 per cent and the then finance secretary of the state did not have money to pay salaries of the state employees; by 2002–3 fiscal reform was no longer an option.[10] The fiscal deficit was 5.44 per cent in 2003–4 (ADB 2007).

The aggressive and indiscriminate policy of subsidies and incentives to industry as well as the power subsidy created a fiscal strain on the state exchequer in the 1990s. The major industrial policy instruments used were sales tax deferrals and exemptions. During 1991–5, on an average, Rs 2.10 billion per annum were lost to the Gujarat government as a result of such subsidies; this amount increased manifold between 1998 and 1999 to Rs 13.43 billion, and then to Rs 41.2 billion during 2000–1.[11]

In the early 1990s, the then finance minister together with key state officials set up a State Finance Commission (SFC) to assess the state's financial situation. This committee aimed at re-evaluating the totality of the state's role in the new environment and was an early precursor to fiscal reforms that the Centre would recommend to the states in the late 1990s and early 2000s. The committee came out with its report in 1994 and recommended a serious re-assessment of state's role and urged fiscal reforms. It outlined a crisis situation for the state with its revenue base receding and the state's inability to continue to fulfil its erstwhile roles as an enhancer of Central rules.

Usually, such committee reports collect dust on government shelves but this report serendipitously resonated with a parallel ADB's reorientation of strategy. International developmental banks, such as the ADB, in the early to mid-1990s, were thinking of designing sub-national loan programmes. An ADB team visited a few states and found in the 1994 State Finance Report in Gujarat a sign of internal state commitment in favour of reforms.[12]

After many visits and negotiations with Gujarat state officials, the ADB approved a $250 million loan for public sector restructuring and fiscal reform in Gujarat, with a two-year implementation window. Three broad areas of reform were identified: fiscal reform and consolidation; public enterprise reform or privatization; and, in ADB's words, 'enabling private sector participation in infrastructure' (ADB 2007: 1). The loan was to be released in three stages with specific policy conditionalities associated with each stage, a restrictive and monitoring mechanism. In addition, the ADB authorized 'technical assistance' to build legal and non-legal capacity to implement some of the goals of the loan programme.

Notwithstanding delays in implementation and failure of implementation in certain key respects (power reforms), the ADB loan, by all accounts, played a major role in shaping the state's emergent economic reform strategy. In fact, the origins of many current policies are not purely internally driven but nudged in certain important and even unintended ways by this external loan granted to Gujarat in the late 1990s. To be sure, state officials used and deployed the ADB loan to enhance many of their own reform plans, thereby taking ownership for shaping the ADB loan to their ends. The State Finance Committee report of 1994 reveals that Gujarat had begun to think of reforms in a wide-ranging manner on its own. Many of ADB's suggested actions were the reforms envisaged in the 1994 report (Government of Gujarat 1995). Yet, without the ADB loan, which was supported by the leadership of that time, the trajectory of Gujarat's reform path might have been different.

As reiterated by many respondents, the loan enabled pro-reformers to mobilize political support on behalf of policies that were uncertain and unpopular in the mid-1990s. One civil servant noted:

> The ADB loan was very useful to nudge economic reform, to mobilize political support for ideas which were new even in India. It allowed us to use the money for compensation which was almost impossible otherwise. Remember this was 1996–7, early in the reform process even nationally, and privatization or private sector participation in infrastructure was not on the agenda even at the national level.[13]

The loan was monitored and carefully implemented through the establishment of new institutions and committees; this monitoring and feedback function enhanced pre-existing state capacity. The new institutions included: (i) a policy-level expenditure prioritization committee (chaired by the chief minister); (ii) the Gujarat Infrastructure Development Board (GIDB) (also chaired by the chief minister) to promote privatization of key infrastructure sectors; (iii) the State Public Finance Reform Committee (SPFRC) to provide advice on fiscal reforms, solicit private sector views, and generate public awareness of tax reforms; (iv) three working groups to support the SPFRC on tax reform, expenditure management and control, and computerization and training; (v) a cabinet sub-committee on public sector reform (chaired by the chief minister with the ministers of finance and industry as members) responsible for reviewing and approving details of modality, scope of divestment, pricing, and structuring of state owned enterprises (SOEs); and (vi) a technical secretariat within the finance department to service the SOE reform committee.

Some monitoring mechanisms, such as the SPFRC, set up in the Department of Finance, and an informal group of 'liberalizers' played a more crucial role than others in generating ideas for reform and, most crucially, in maintaining the pressure to undertake difficult reforms. The SPFRC committee prepared a paper entitled, 'Approach to Fiscal Consolidation in Gujarat' (SPFRC 2000), which identified the important fiscal weaknesses in the state and also suggested recommendations for their reform in the medium- and long-term. Many reform ideas—including reform of tax and non-tax administration as well as changes in procedures—were studied and recommended to the government.[14] The reports of the Committee were discussed in the cabinet although many of the recommendations could not be accepted for many years.[15]

Yet, these reports generated new ideas that were subsequently put to use. For example, the Committee reviewed the issue of power reforms and urged reform of the Gujarat Electricity Board (GEB) that was incurring a loss of Rs 1,350 crore at that time. It further recommended that power reforms are not only about agricultural subsidies but must also entail a restructuring of the GEB and induct competition within the power sector.[16] As discussed later in this chapter, restructuring of the GEB preceded any changes in the reform of agricultural subsidies, revealing that this idea found resonance in the sequencing of power reforms pursued by the state in 2003–5. It also reveals a longer time sequence than many of the other reforms in the state.

Another more informal monitoring mechanism was an implicit coalition of a few civil servants with common views on the need for serious fiscal changes, including privatization. They were the chief secretary at that time, the finance secretary, and key officials of Industries Department, among others. This group derived its authority directly from the chief minister and exercised significant autonomous powers to implement reforms and to fulfil the commitments accepted under the ADB loan. Thus, two *overlapping and monitoring institutions* worked to shape the agenda of economic reform in the state. This suggests that monitoring by new, informal institutions can bypass vested interests and mobilize reforms. The experience of privatization exemplifies some of these lessons and merits analysis.

Privatization and Disinvestment

A programme of privatization of state enterprises, envisaged under the ADB loan, was undertaken in the late 1990s. This process is a fascinating case study of state-level privatization with some success but also with notable failures. The Government of Gujarat (GoG) approved a PSU restructuring based on the SFC's recommendations as well as those of the C. Rangarajan Committee on disinvestment. The SFC recommended closure of 11 SOEs and divestment in another 21 PSUs, with only enterprises engaged in 'socially relevant' activities being retained under government ownership. The SFC proposed the establishment of a senior committee under the chief minister to pursue divestment transparently and professionally with a monitoring or feedback mechanism.

The goals of public restructuring were to 'reduce GoG's participation in the commercial sector, and increase private sector participation' and outlined a touchstone test: 'The question is to be asked: (1) whether the undertaking is contributing to the public good through its activities, and whether the same thing cannot be done in a more cost effective manner outside the government and (2) profitability alone of an SOE cannot be considered a justification for the existence of an SOE; such units should also be subjected to the same touch-stone test' (Public Sector Restructuring Programme (PSRP), Annex VI, p. 49; State Public Finance Reforms Committee 2000). This test for privatization was a very demanding criterion, firmly believed by a small group of key members of the Gujarat civil service.[17] In some senses this was one of the first few cases of 'committed privatizations' seen in India, much before the celebrated privatizations that would take place at the national level. It did not fully succeed but the successes and failures are worth documenting.

Five loss-making SOEs—Gujarat State Textile Corporation (1996), Gujarat State Construction Corporation (1997), Gujarat Fisheries Development Corporation (1997), Gujarat Small Industries Corporation (1999), and Gujarat Dairy Development Corporation (1999)—were closed down. The significant impact on the lives of their employees notwithstanding, there was little opposition to the closure of these corporations. The political leadership did not put any obstacles to their closure. Two factors played a role. These enterprises were a clear drag on the state finances, which was apparent for all to see. The decision to privatize and also the design for privatization were managed by a small group authorized to take decisions directly by the chief minister and industry minister. Both the chief minister and the industry minister had been convinced by the civil servants of the need to close these units which were a huge burden on the state budget. The chief minister at that time was regarded as a supreme leader and unlikely to face any protests within the cabinet.

As an illustration, the Gujarat State Textile Corporation was sustaining mounting financial losses of around Rs 611 crore in November 1996.[18] The ADB loan allowed government officials to make a strong case for speedy closure and divestment.[19] While the government made a concerted effort at persuading and building consensus through many meetings with the employees of the various corporations, it was eventually a top-down decision taken by a handful of people and then implemented with authority and speed. As noted by one of the principal actors at the centre of this process: 'The ADB loan allowed us to both provide carrots and a stick. We could argue that there was no option as well as compensate the losers.'[20]

The ADB loan was used to institute a generous voluntary retirement scheme (VRS) for around 14,000 employees, especially those of the Gujarat State Textile Corporation. The ADB loan was used to ensure a relatively pain-free process: the terms of the VRS were so generous that there was no serious protest or challenge to the process of disinvestment. The Gujarat government constituted a 'State Renewal Fund' under the direct control of finance department in September 1996, the principal aim of which was to fund the PSUs for VRS-related expenses. Budgetary procedures were simplified for speedy distribution of VRS funds, a form of discretionary transparency for this specific case. A total of 18,100 employees were affected and the Gujarat government unburdened itself of 17,702 employees at a cost of Rs 324.53 crore. In addition, some state enterprises relieved 3,040 employees at the cost of Rs 96 crore. The government also protected itself by seeking the approval of the Textile Labour Association (TLA) (one of the trade unions at the textile mills) for the VRS and subsequent closure. Some workers did challenge the government decision, but the court found that 90 per cent of the workers had accepted the government settlement and that it was advisable to close down the units in the 'public interest'.[21] Thus, a generous VRS and extensive consultation ensured a relatively smooth and protest-free closure of a large company.

Paradoxically, the role of the private sector during the privatization process was problematic. The government privatized Gujarat Tractor Corporation Ltd (GTCL) by selling its equity to a leading tractor manufacturer in 1999. Fifty-one per cent of the government's shares along with management control were transferred to the company, followed by transfer of 9 per cent at a later date. This, however, proved unviable in the longer term. In September 2004, the company was referred to the Board of Industrial and Financial Reconstruction, which declared GTCL a 'sick' company, its net worth having been completely eroded due to accumulated losses. Overall, the performance of the government in ensuring a just and fair settlement for its employees was far superior to the role of the private sector, which sought to capture government companies at low prices, and in some cases did not fulfil its commitment to reviving the companies concerned, as in the case of the GTCL.

The proposed privatization of Gujarat Communication & Electronics Ltd (GCEL) ran into difficulties. The managing director of the corporation 'fought tooth and nail'[22] to prevent disinvestment, arguing that he could revive the company. The Public Restructuring Committee met with the officials and workers many times, and tried to convince the managing director. Given such opposition, the government made two attempts of privatization but failed. The government eventually closed down GCEL and provided VRS to all its employees.[23] It is interesting that the government chose to close down rather than continue with production operations; this was in line with the strong ideological belief of some key actors who felt that privatization should be undertaken for intrinsic reasons rather than used as a second best option to address fiscal and budgetary problems.[24] This also speaks of the ability of this 'reform coalition' to get its way.

Thus, in the mid- to late-1990s, Gujarat's privatization was relatively successful in that it was implemented with speed and vigour but with some partial but important failures. Commitment at the top levels, an ideological belief shared by a small group of key officials, bureaucratic monitoring capacity, and the ability to use the ADB loan (an external factor) to leverage political support for the disinvestment programme as well as compensate the losers, the workers, played a role in this partial but definite success. Part of the failure to privatize fully and to ensure expected gains for the state arose from the tendency of the private sector to try to capture the offered assets at below market prices. Interestingly, in this case, too much transparency had the negative effect of encouraging capture by the private sector and derailing the process in some instances.

Economic Reform and Governance as Intra-State Power Struggles

Such radical changes both at the Central and regional levels, I suggest, unleashed changes within the state, a form of state re-formation, in the course of which parts of the state faced sudden and precipitous decline while others were renewed and created anew.[25] Policy innovation was undertaken and new institutions were also created. Bureaucratic politics, a struggle not only about the outcomes of policy but also a struggle within the state, was in evidence.[26] As state bureaucrats began thinking about how they should respond to the national policy of economic reforms, they also set in motion crucial power struggles within organizations as well as between state organizations. The attempt to reform or re-tool state agencies, as a response to the incoming policies of liberalization, did not succeed and some agencies suffered a definite death or decline (GIIC, GSFC, IndextB[27]) while new ones were born (GIDB).

The process of privatization was combined with reframing numerous and separate policies for energy, industry, and ports, all in 1995 (Government of Gujarat, Industries and Mines Department 1995). New institutions (GIDB) were set up (1995) and new frameworks articulated between 1995 and 1999: the BOOT (Build, Own, Operate, and Transfer) principles (1997) and a PPP law (1999). This seemed to precede developments at the Central level and in other states; the Central level set up the Expert Group on Commercialization of Infrastructure Projects in October 1994, known as the Rakesh Mohan Committee that submitted its report in 1996. One of the most path-breaking developments of that time was the formulation of a port policy (1995) and the reorganization of the state agency that was to oversee the implementation of port policy: the Gujarat Maritime Board (GMB) (see later for more details on port development in Gujarat). The mid-1990s, thus, represent a constellation of state activism on industrial and development issues. State leaders declared, 'The most distinctive feature of the new industrial policy is that for the first time the industrial policy talks about the industrial development in its totality. So far industrial policy meant just two things: sales tax benefit, and subsidies' (*The Economic Times* 1995a). Economic reform seemed to demand more comprehensive policies, to which the state responded.

However, combined with new policies and institutions, some organizations saw a precipitous decline. Gujarat State Finance Commission (GSFC) virtually died. GIIC, GIDC, and, to a lesser extent, IndextB had to reinvent themselves but lost prestige, power, and functions in the process. As noted by L. Mansingh who was the managing director of GIIC in the mid- and late-1990s, 'GIIC has had to change its role in the post-liberalization era. ... So far our initiative was routed through the central government securing licences and the like. With the relaxation of restrictions, it is time we revived ourselves.'[28] That attempt at the revival of GIIC did not succeed.

Initially, in order to re-invent itself, GIIC was responsible for implementing new infrastructure projects, but lost that authority and power to GIDB over time (*The Economic Times* 1995b). In 1996, GIIC was at the forefront of providing finances for a whole range of industrial activities including infrastructural development and yet, by 1998–9 GIDB had emerged stronger. In 1996, the MD of GIIC said, 'The Corporation is now in the process of tying up a line of credit from the Asian Development Bank for infrastructure-related project-promotion activities. For this purpose, the government had decided, in principle, to privatize GIIC by disinvesting 51 per cent of its equity by December 1997' (*The Economic Times* 1996). Even so, by the late 2000s GIIC was a pale shadow of itself and most of the power had shifted to GIDB. This apparent struggle within the state, a form of bureaucratic politics, suggests that we reframe our understanding of governance as 'governance in motion', which is as much a process of institutional change and reform as it is a matter of institutional struggles and realignment within the state. Economic restructuring, thus, created shifts in power balances between state agencies in Gujarat.

INFRASTRUCTURAL DEVELOPMENT: PORTS AND PPP IN GUJARAT

The Rakesh Mohan Committee on Infrastructure (1996) noted that the principal problem in India was building the right framework for private participation in infrastructure (Rakesh Mohan Committee 1996). Port development in Gujarat has proceeded rapidly with numerous ports and capacity expansion with the potential to divert traffic from ports in Mumbai managed by the Jawaharlal Nehru Port Trust (JNPT). In addition, and strikingly, new policies, laws, and new institutions have been created to facilitate a unique model of PPP for infrastructure. By 2009, Gujarat had implemented competitive bidding for two ports and also undertaken significant port modernization and development based on these frameworks. Underlying these policy changes are crucial reforms in institution creation as well as the creation of new regulatory frameworks for privatization. These developments offer certain important lessons about the processes of policymaking the intimate role of the private sector in shaping policy goals as well as the institutions that govern policy in Gujarat, and insights about how state capacity is mobilized and created in a new policy arena like ports. By starting early, through accidental learning, and random trial and error, Gujarat's model of infrastructural (port) development emerges as a relative success. However, an analysis of the origins and sources of policy development yields fascinating stories of learning, trial and error, and a movement from informal public–private deals to a more stable and a transparent rule-based framework. In addition, external influence in the form of technical inputs from port experts from the Government of the Netherlands had definite consequences for the development of ports in the state.

Port development has proceeded at a remarkable pace in Gujarat.[29] While the Central government visualized 'encouraging private sector investment in select port activities' (Rakesh Mohan Committee 1996), the Gujarat government has given complete control of two ports to the private sector. Forty-one minor (state-run) ports are planned along the 1,600 km coastline to be managed by a state-level autonomous body: the GMB. The state has implemented competitive bidding for ports (Hazira) and jetties, and many port projects are under implementation. A senior official noted, 'GMB is the second largest revenue earner for the state.'[30] Gujarat houses India's only chemical handling port (at Dahej), two of the three liquefied natural gas (LNG) terminals (at Dahej and Mundra), and India's largest private port (at Mundra). Currently, Gujarat handles about 28 per cent of India's cargo traffic and about two-thirds of non-major (minor) port traffic (see Table 4.2).

Table 4.2 Traffic in Ports (million tonnes): India and Gujarat

	1981–2	1994–5	2004–5	2005–6	2006–7	2007–8
Major ports	87.98	195.89	383.60	423.53	463.84	519.24
Gujarat ports	3.18	17.50	97.10	108.26	132.44	147.60
Other non-major ports	3.83	5.13	30.0	37.17	52.56	48.77
Total national cargo	94.99	218.17	510.70	568.96	648.84	715.61
Share of Gujarat in all non-major ports traffic (per cent)	45.36	76.97	76.39	74.44	71.58	75.16

Source: H.K Dash, principal secretary, Ports and Transport Department, Government of Gujarat, 'A Presentation on Gujarat Port Sector to the taskforce of Center–State Relations Commission', 2008. Available with the author.

Notes: 'Major ports' refers to all major port traffic in India, including Kandla in Gujarat (capacity 50 mmt). 'Gujarat ports' refers to all non-major ports in the state; 'other non-major ports' refers to ports in other states.

Even more interestingly, Gujarat has implemented a public–private model with clear examples for such partnership for other states and for the Central government. Many private sector infrastructural companies, such as L&T, Essar group, Haryana-based SRF Limited, DLF, Central Warehousing Corporation, Simplex Infrastructure, Gulf Omkar Petro and Refinery, Gammon India, Zoom Developers, Consortium IL&FS, Sea King Infrastructure, Gremach group, Chennai-based IMC, and Shell, have projects or have shown interest in the port projects in the state. What are the emergent institutional frameworks that make port development so successful in the state? How did port policy evolve in the state?

Port and Infrastructural Policy

Although, Gujarat's industrial infrastructure was historically quite good,[31] by the 1990s the demands of rapid industrialization combined with lack of finances contributed to a decline in its quantity and quality. In 1993, the chief minister at that time proposed setting up an infrastructure development corporation 'to provide basic amenities like roads, water, bridges and drinking water pipeline, which were essential for the development of the state. The idea behind the creation of the corporation was to lessen the burden of expenses on the state as an independent corporation would be able to borrow from the market' (*Hindustan Times* 1993). Interviews reveal that state officials realized then that infrastructure would be very crucial in the liberalized scenario but the state's ability to provide the resources for this was diminishing, thus necessitating different forms of financing or private sector incorporation.[32] This realization emerged not as a faith in markets or the private sector but out of the constraints imposed by the diminishing fiscal basis of the liberalized sub-national state. The chief minister noted that this proposal was:

> part of the overall policy adopted by the state to encourage privatization in various fields, and the idea behind setting up of the corporation in the joint sector was to attract private parties to participate in infrastructure development. He further stated that the response of the private parties was not encouraging and the setting up of an independent corporation with equity participation from the government would hopefully egg them on to invest in this prime sector (*Hindustan Times* 1993).

Analogous with this development, the idea of proposing private ports was mooted in a nascent form in 1993 by Chimanbhai Patel, the then chief minister.[33]

By 1995 these ideas started to coalesce together. Political initiative and vision were quite crucial. The then chief minister Keshubhai Patel played a major role in these developments, as did the bureaucrats associated with the Industries Department. As a study of privatization in ports undertaken in 1994 noted:

Sometimes, however, the innovativeness demonstrated [in ports] has directly come from the political leaders rather than the top management of the GMB. While this lends itself to flexibility in decision-making of sorts, the flipside is that the strategic role of the GMB top management would be in question. Evidence of this often appears in the feeling of non-involvement exhibited by the GMB executives and staff. There is a sense of role erosion in the organization. Often management systems and responsiveness to operational problems are weak. The high traffic growth would seem to have happened in spite of the management of the GMB. For further sustained growth, of which there is ample potential, a top management with a visionary and strategic view and a middle management with a professional outlook would be imperative, even to usher in more privatization (Raguram 1994: Preface; available with the author).

In 1995 the state government took numerous policy and institutional initiatives: that very year a new industrial policy, a new energy policy, and a new IT policy were announced. The GIDB, a nodal agency for infrastructure development, was set up in 1995 through a government resolution. The chief minister stressed the need for the state to focus on ports, and in 1995 took some initiative in appointing two senior Indian Administrative Service (IAS) officials to head the GMB.[34] Till then, the GMB was a small body led by engineers, with a limited scope and no vision for expansion and development. Gujarat ports were tiny, mostly fishing ports with a total volume of mere 2 million tonnes. The two high-level civil servants' task was to generate new ideas for a port policy. The chief minister from Saurashtra himself saw the need to develop the interior districts in Gujarat as well as the potential of the long Gujarat coastline for industrial development and to satisfy the urgent power needs of the state. Power generation required cheap coal, which could to be imported but this required ports.[35]

It is thus clear that the leadership recognized the larger developmental implications of a port policy. The GMB Act of 1981 was modified in 1996 to ensure that a generalist chairman was able to manage the organization (Government of Gujarat 1998). This institutional change was a significant development and highlighted a visionary sense of purpose capable of visualizing both that ports could play a role in overall development of the state and could best be designed by a high-level commitment of a generalist kind. Besides, this institutional change considerably enhanced the power and authority of the organization (GMB).

The port policy of 1995 is remarkable for its vision and ability to see well into the future. It noted that India's external liberalization, entailing both imports and exports, could allow Gujarat to take the Government of India's policy of liberalization 'through a process of globalization' (Government of Gujarat and Ports and Fisheries Department 1995). The policy thus visualized Gujarat to be an important gateway of external openness for the country as a whole. In addition, the notion of ports servicing not only the state but the larger western Indian hinterland, with Rajasthan, Madhya Pradesh, western Uttar Pradesh, Delhi, Haryana, Punjab, Himachal Pradesh, and Jammu and Kashmir as 'potential customers of Gujarat ports', saw port development as an ambitious, far-reaching policy instrument for the overall development of the region. In laying out this second goal, the authors of port policy were leveraging Gujarat's role as an alternative port route to Mumbai ports and competing with Mumbai's unchallenged domination as the gateway to the world. Competition from Mumbai has always been an important feature of developments in Gujarat (Sinha 2005). From the then minuscule traffic of 2 million tonnes, the policy envisaged that by 2000, Gujarat ports would handle 100 mt of cargo. This figure of 100 mt seemed impossible to achieve at that time and had to be justified to the cabinet, but was calculated quite carefully by the authors to be an achievable figure.[36] By 2000, Gujarat's ports were able to reach a figure of around 71 mt, no mean achievement, and 97 mt by 2004–05 (GMB Annual Report, various years).

Simultaneously, the pressure to enhance Gujarat's ports came from a very different quarter, the private sector, and the two impulses (state design and private capital's interests) coalesced. Private investment was seen to be an important route for such development, albeit under the control of the government; the government was conceived as an owner-landlord who would oversee and share rights with the private sector over some parts of the ports. Gujarat's historical strengths in the joint sector led to an easy transition to PPPs in the port sector, even against the then prevailing international practice. For example, the Netherlands, the country that had provided GMB with consultancy in the early years, was surprised at Gujarat's early involvement of the private sector in ports.[37] In the Netherlands, ports were completely controlled by the state, and even now complete privatization of ports remains rare at the international level. The Pipavav port was initiated in 1989 and designated to be a joint sector project in 1992. Later this project ran into serious difficulties and by the mid-2000s, after many changes of ownership, came to be in the private sector.

In the mid- to late-1990s, state administrators had begun to recognize that investments seemed to converge at port sites. As noted by a senior civil servant: 'Once we announced a port, we were amazed at the rapidity with which investments and MoUs [memoranda of understanding] were signed in and around that site; we, then, knew that port development could be a impetus for further investments. The importance of ports was brought home to us by investors themselves. We decided to leverage this further.'[38] The GMB internal study in 1998 confirms this private sector role at the formulation stage:

> Our State is experiencing a phenomenal developmental trend in investment both from mega and industrial sector within the country and also from Multinational companies overseas. An investment of 30 billion US dollars is already in (the) pipeline. Around Rs 1,600 crores investment is taking place at Hazira, Rs 15,000 crores planned in Vagra, Bharuch and Rs 20,000 crores planned around Pipavav and Jamnagar regions, obviously taking advantage of ports in their vicinity. The logic behind locating these industries is very clear that large business houses always wanted an access to national/international market through the sea route, which is the only viable mode of transport. The port infrastructure is the hub of industries without which it cannot survive. (Gujarat Maritime Board 1998)

The private sector played a formative role in port development. Port development initially began when private companies requested that they be given control over some captive jetties in the early to mid-1990s. Many of the early private sector initiatives in the port sector were negotiated through the MoU route without much analysis, supervision, negotiation, or regulatory oversight. This MoU route of privatization was superseded by the passage of the 1999 Gujarat Infrastructure Development Act. The government's environment agency, the Gujarat Ecology Commission, expressed concern about the implications of the pace of port development (*The Economic Times* 2000; *Business Standard* 2000).

Again, the ADB loan negotiated during 1996–7 proved crucial for the emergence of public–private framework in the state, and especially for the development of new institutional mechanisms to facilitate such policies. One of the stated objectives of the ADB loan was to augment private sector participation in the infrastructure sectors, which came to be called PPP.[39] Specifically, the ADB contributed to the specific institutional design that emerged. It gave a technical assistance loan for 'institutional strengthening of GIDB' as part of the fiscal reform loan of 1996 (Asian Development Bank 2007). This included: (a) preparation of BOOT principles and procedures manual completed in 1997, (b) a scheme on sectoral development in Gujarat, (c) preparation of a Model

'Concession Agreement' (an agreement between the government and the private sector party laying out the terms of lease and port development),[40] and (d) a provision for technical training of GMB officials.[41] A senior official of the GMB admitted, 'We did a lot of reforms in infrastructural development under the pretext of ADB.'[42] The ADB consultant to the GIDB recommended that the latter work on a PPP law, and consonant with ADB experience, the Philippine law was used as a model for its Gujarat counterpart passed in 1999, the Gujarat Infrastructure Development (GID) Act (also referred to as the BOT law). A 'PPP Cell' was set up in the GIDB as a monitoring department to develop and monitor project implementation.

The GIDB's role, functions, and powers have changed over time. From a small, irrelevant body that appeared to duplicate the functions of other organizations and was therefore largely bypassed, it became the nodal and pre-eminent agency engaging in policymaking and 'project development', besides monitoring project implementation by other infrastructural agencies such as the GMB and the GIDC.

The passage of the 1999 GID law is an interesting story of how circumstantial factors and individuals play a role in the process of accidental policy formulation. The then industry minister was visiting the US around the time the law was being framed. In a case of pre-emptive policy formulation, the industry department's civil servants accompanying him advised him to announce a law, the GID Act, on US soil as a way of attracting private sector participation.

In 1997–9 the relevant actors concerned had no idea that they were designing what would later be termed a 'path-breaking model of private sector participation in infrastructure'; they had no such grandiose ambitions or plans at the time. They were just hoping to survive and make relevant an organization that seemed to have gone nowhere. Subsequently, institutional power accretion became necessary. As other state agencies resented or failed to see the relevance of GIDB, it was felt that it would have to be made the arbiter of infrastructure decision-making. Thus, in 1999, a separate GID Act was passed to designate GIDB as a nodal agency for infrastructure development. This implied that other agencies, namely, the GIDC, GIIC, and infrastructure departments would have to go through GIDB for approval of major projects. The GIDB also acquired a monitoring or feedback function; in the event of any obstacle or delay, it had the authority to resolve problems. This Act was an attempt to mollify other organizations' fears that they would lose their power by delineating precisely what GIDB could do. However, in an unintended way, by becoming the agency of policy formulation and monitoring, GIDB's power was substantially enhanced.

Evolution of the Port Framework

Prior to 1982, the director of ports, appointed by the Government of Gujarat, dealt mainly with small fishing jetties and shallow draft ports. In the early 1980s, a committee headed by H.M. Trivedi recommended the formation of an autonomous body for the commercialization of ports. The Gujarat Maritime Board was constituted under the Gujarat Maritime Board Act, 1981, which is a replica of the Major Port Trusts Act, 1963, under which the major ports have been notified. GMB built and operated its own ports, called minor ports. In its initial years, it drew its budgetary support from the Government of Gujarat, but by the late 1990s it paid off most of its loans and is perceived to be a pre-eminent revenue earner for the state.[43]

Over time, and not necessarily in a planned manner, but stimulated by ad hoc demands and policy dilemmas, some policies and a legal framework were put in place to regulate the port sector. Initially, the notion of captive jetties was introduced for port-based industries, and these jetties were allotted to some private parties. The port policy of 1995 outlined the basic objectives of growth and expansion, the development of 10 separate port sites, and the possibility of privatization. It became the founding orientation document. In 1998, a more detailed plan vision for GMB and ports was prepared: 'Identification of Infrastructure Requirements for the Year 2010'.[44] Interestingly, an external source provided the formative input for the evolution of port policy, though, as in the past, Gujarat officials deployed the input received in locally specific ways. The Netherlands government provided GMB with technical assistance in the form of a 'Cooperation Agreement', covering transport economics and planning, port planning and development, and institutional strengthening of GMB. The Dutch technical assistance was in the form of two Dutch high-level experts available for regular consultations and advice as members of a joint Gujarat–Netherlands Core Group of experts. There were also two resident experts based in Gujarat for several months.[45] Thus, external impetus has always been a crucial source of local reforms.

Initially, in line with the widespread prevalence of a joint sector in Gujarat, the idea of joint sector ports was mooted as a venture between the GMB and some select private sector parties. In 1989, Pipavav was to be built as a joint sector project, and in the early 1990s, Mundra Port was also conceived as such. In 1997, a set of BOOT principles was set out through a government resolution encouraging competitive bidding and private investment in port projects. Around that time, many of the joint sector ports were further privatized, with GMB selling off its equity. What is striking about the port policies is the implicit guarantee by the state for the facilitation of 'operational freedom' to private parties and the assurance of a commercial and market-driven environment that would encourage competition and efficiency. Even so, the GMB was to be the owner or landlord, leasing out the land around the ports and other assets based on what came to be called a 'Concession Agreement'. Interestingly, tariff flexibility was promised to the developer.[46]

In 1999, with the formulation of the GID Act, a further strengthening of the legal framework was achieved, as well as the formal articulation of a PPP framework. These legal and policy innovations—BOOT principles, the design of a Model 'Concession Agreement', and the PPP framework set out in the GID Act of 1999—were attempts to make transparent the process of port development that had till then proceeded randomly. This institutional architecture was an attempt to impose order over chaos and give legitimacy to deals that were being consummated, but it set into motion a process of expansion of new projects, which may not have fructified if Gujarat had not passed these legal changes.

The process of competitive bidding for infrastructure projects began in early 2000s (Dahej and Hazira), but what is interesting is that the GID 1999 Act was amended in 2006 to incorporate projects awarded through 'Direct Negotiation'. (Section 10A of GID Act was inserted in 2006.)[47] Thus, there are three routes for the selection of projects: (i) competitive bidding through an open competitive bidding process that yields more than one developer; (ii) comparative bidding or what is known as the 'Swiss Challenge Route', when there is only one project developer and for which competitive bids are solicited from other prospective bidders and the original proponents are given an opportunity to match their bids; or (iii) direct negotiation.

In 2007 the government also added the Viability Gap-Funding Scheme (VGF), an enhancement of a similar scheme outlined by the Ministry of Finance, Government of India, which had been proposed to the Thirteenth Finance Commission.[48] Both the 'Swiss Challenge Route' and the 'Direct Negotiation Route' are an attempt to write into law direct, one-to-one deals with the private sector, albeit with some regulatory oversight built in. In addition, captive jetty expansion has also proceeded: Reliance—Sikka and Essar—Hazira, as well as the expansion of the already developed Greenfield ports (Mundra, Pipavav,

Dahej, and Hazira). The GMB also envisaged revival of old ports like Okha, Navalakhi, Porbander, and Magdhalla. By 2009, many such projects with the participation of the private sector have been implemented with a total private investment of Rs 1,86,878 crore (GMB Annual Report, various years).

Notwithstanding an apparent accretion of power and capacity, the process of capacity building in the port sector proceeded through 'incremental change' (Thelen 2000) and was not linear. In contrast, it was marked by crucial failures in the early stages, delays, and random trial-and-error learning. Policies and institutional frameworks were evolved post facto to justify on-the-ground changes and developments; institutions and governance sometimes followed rather than preceded success. Even so, in the second phase, the creation of new institutional frameworks—BOOT principles, the GID Act, and GIDB— had a clear impact. Slowly yet surely, this 'two steps forward, and one step backward process' although marked by some false starts, court cases, and societal challenges, nonetheless led to some notable successes in port development.

Problems and Dilemmas

Notwithstanding these notable successes, is the Gujarat government's port model worth emulating? Alternatively, to express it differently, have these new frameworks and innovations created the requisite capacities not only to initiate but also manage and ensure broader public interest in implementing PPP initiatives? I argue that critical problems and dilemmas have been generated by the implementation of PPP in Gujarat. First, and foremost, PPP requires new state capacities and expertise, such as legal expertise and the skills to manage and monitor private projects. The projects are extremely complex and technical in nature, requiring new skill sets and management techniques. Even at the negotiation stage, many pitfalls could affect how much the state benefits from the project for at least 30 years as many of the 'Concession Agreements' are for that duration. As many officials noted, the private parties come with an army of lawyers, while the government negotiates with one or two bureaucrats with no legal expertise and often very little experience.

In addition to legal expertise, many new sets of skills are required by the state: technical and technological skills relating to the particular sector, the skills to manage and draw up the contracts with private parties, financial accounting, and oversight of the various aspects of managing and implementing the contracts, as well as monitoring skills to ensure that the terms of the contract are fulfilled. Thus, it is clear that state agencies in charge of managing the new environment need to become stronger and more capable. They need to refurbish the basic capabilities of the organization and enhance their legal expertise. In this scenario, the GMB, notwithstanding its notable successes is, in the words of a senior official using an evocative metaphor, 'like an Ambassador [a old somewhat clunky car in India] in Manhattan (New York City)'.[49]

The government has failed to refurbish internal state capacities by re-training or re-skilling its employees[50] or even permitting the hiring of new expertise. Unfortunately, the impetus to liberalize has meant the privatization of the state, as the state tends to outsource even basic functions to private consultants. Therefore, now, many years after the institution of economic reforms, the policies of economic reform have become a real constraint on effective privatization and economic reform. As reiterated by a senior official of the GMB, 'Policies and ideological dogmas about market-oriented reforms—the state shrinking for example—are undermining the real purposes of private–public partnerships, which is [intended] to service the citizens better and more productively.'[51]

Port reform highlights several crucial counter-intuitive insights about the preconditions and origins of effective reform. First, the process of policymaking and policy change can be energized by political vision and leadership at the top of the system. Chief ministers and their individual commitments and abilities, as well as senior bureaucratic functionaries play an indisputable role in energizing states, even those with strong state capacities. Second, the process of policymaking and institutional emergence and consolidation proceeded through an iterative process with failures and ad hoc learning. Also, similar to other policy domains, new monitoring institutions that supersede and coordinate other state agencies emerge as crucial to an effective state. Third, the private sector plays a major role at all stages of policy formulation and implementation in Gujarat and at crucial moments, policy and legal frameworks have merely formalized already existing state–private sector relationships at the ground level. State–capital interactions play a hidden and yet powerful role in Gujarat's port sector.

REFORM OF THE GUJARAT ELECTRICITY BOARD

The unbundling of the state electricity board without privatization in Gujarat is regarded as a case of successful reform.[52] R. Joshi wrote a case study of this turnaround, which was published in *Smart Manager* (February–March 2008), arguing that 'the case study demonstrates how strong commitment at the highest political level in Gujarat led to the transformation of a loss-making utility into one of the best public utilities in the country' (Joshi 2008: 1). This account resonates with the self-projection of the state, which argues that crucial state actors designed and framed an innovative strategy of power reform. My empirical analysis and argument throw up an alternative, more contingency-driven story where different kinds of individuals and external actors matter more, and their actions are stimulated by crisis and accidents. It is a story where, similar to fiscal reform and port development, external actors—in this case the Central government, the ADB, and a regulatory oversight body (Gujarat Electricity Regulatory Commission [GERC])—play a largely unrecognized role.

Between 2003 and 2009, many changes were evident in the power sector in Gujarat. In May 2003, the government passed the Gujarat Electricity Industry Act and subsequently unbundled the Gujarat Electricity Board (GEB) but without privatizing or firing any employees. The GEB was transformed into six corporate entities, but all held by a holding government company, the Gujarat Urja Vikas Nigam Limited (GUVNL), which acts as a nodal planning and coordinating company. From a loss of Rs 1,932 crore in the early 2000s, the GEB showed a profit of Rs 220 crore in 2006–7 and a significant reduction in transmission and distribution losses (Ibid.). How was this achieved? The real story of power reforms in Gujarat is longer-in-the-making, non-linear, and a fascinating story of individuals and chance-specific factors, not visionary 'political will'[53] or state design. It begins in failure and a serious crisis, not in the superhuman vision of its political leaders.

Gujarat thought of reforming its power sector in the mid-1990s. Some reforms were introduced in 1995–6 but not in the right sequence. The government seemed too eager to initiate private power participation and issue policy statements on captive power use and independent power projects by providing state guarantees against demand risks and losses without addressing the internal inefficiencies of the GEB (Dholakia 2003: 309). The state negotiated adverse 'Power Purchase Agreements (PPAs)' with private power producers, with high tariff rates affecting the future viability of the GEB. While the supply of power to the state increased, GEB's financial situation began deteriorating rapidly because it had to buy power at relatively high prices from the private power producers and could neither force tariff revisions nor remove inefficiencies in transmission and distribution, which were as high as 34 per cent. Thus, quick and early privatization added to the woes of the GEB.

The ADB loan had urged power reform of agricultural tariffs in 1996, but this remained a dead letter. Then, in 1998–9 or thereabouts, negotiations commenced with the ADB for a separate power reform loan of $350 million. In 2000, the government at the time committed the state to power reforms to both the Central government and the ADB (Asian Development Bank 2000). In line with national trends, the state had set up a regulatory body, the GERC, in 1999. Simultaneously, the Government of Gujarat signed an MoU with the Government of India in which the former committed itself to time-bound power reforms. Some of the reforms included an energy audit, the reduction of transmission and distribution losses, metering all consumers, as well as the passage of a reform bill in the state legislature. Despite these external pressures, the financial losses of the GEB continued to mount and the government was unable to find any momentum towards reform.

Repeated failures in the power sector in the late 1990s underlined the importance of reform. The involvement of the ADB provided an opportunity to continually keep a discussion of power reforms in the air. Gujarat's officials used the state's failure to implement these provisions as a shaming device. In fact, many internal cost-cutting reforms were begun in 2002–3 when it was clear that the political leadership was unwilling and unable to give the go ahead for a full and thorough reform of power tariffs and reforms. In April 2002, the cabinet discussed the necessity of unbundling of GEB.[54] The reform plan faced hostility and derision from all members of the cabinet and there was no consensus on whether any kind of reforms of the electricity sector should be undertaken.[55] The cabinet merely told the GEB to 'become more efficient'. In actual fact, the GEB was on its own at that time with no political support from the government and no reform agenda in 2003–4. Besides, there was no 'political will at the highest level for power reforms'.[56]

Officials of the GEB were dealing with urgent crises as it was running a huge loss and was unable to pay for many of its day-to-day procurement orders for essential technology or meters. There was no money for coal, the transformers were in trouble, every item or equipment of the GEB was old and inefficient, and staff morale was at its lowest ebb. The GEB in 2002 was completely bankrupt with a huge debt, 'with no money for salaries',[57] creditors at its doors, and with no political backing for reform. In the late 1990s the GEB had signed very high tariff PPAs with private power suppliers and that angered the workers because the corporation was paying large amounts to the private suppliers at a time when there were insufficient resources for salaries. Also, the GEB had taken high interest loans in the mid- to late-1990s. As an erstwhile chairman of GEB put it, 'At that time, we had no time to figure out what to do, or to think or to plan a reform plan; we were dealing with crisis after crisis on a daily basis.'[58]

The GEB decided to start small and address the inefficiencies that were the easiest to cut; no other option was open to them. At this juncture the vast and detailed experience of the then chairperson of the GEB as a member (administration) of the GEB in the late 1980s helped her to design effective cost-cutting measures after 2002. Initially, all procurement procedures were regularized and the GEB began monitoring tender conditions for procurement to prevent corruption, as well as ensure quality in procurement. Tender specifications were made detailed and specific. The Board, under her supervision, insisted on high-quality equipment being procured with a careful testing of meters. Some small changes in the procurement procedures and quality increased some GEB revenues. The GEB also became stringent in collecting the revenues due to it, especially from the high-tension consumers, largely industries and other trading merchants, and ensured that the revenues were paid on time.

In an innovative move, in 2002–3 the GEB approached the various financial institutions and asked that they re-finance the various high-interest loans that were pending payment or in default. In lieu of the waiver of interest and penalty payment with reference to some loans, and some payment, the loans were re-negotiated at much lower interest rates, which began affecting GEB's profitability positively. Loans worth Rs 4,130 crore were restructured, contributing to a savings of about Rs 351 crore for GEB.[59] It immediately freed up resources that could then be used to buy new equipment and thereby plug the transmission and distribution losses.

The GEB also decided to tighten the transmission and distribution losses. Here, the chief minister signalled to the political establishment that no power theft case would be overlooked and strict punishment enforced. In many places, the GEB conducted power raids to check transmission and distribution losses. Since 2001, five police stations under the GEB were set up and the police and GEB engineers conducted raids and monitored power theft. It was a comprehensive effort, the goal of which was to increase revenues. From a loss of Rs 1932 crore in 2003–4, in 2004–5 the losses were reduced to Rs 927 crore in a single year through these various cost-cutting measures.

Then the GEB management addressed the problems on the generation side. The generation of power was handled by the Gujarat State

Electricity Corporation Ltd which incurred a fixed capital cost of Rs 494 crore a year. This notwithstanding, it paid a very high cost for power through PPAs which were bleeding the GEB. The GEB decided to address the variable costs, re-negotiating the supply of gas at a cheaper rate from GAIL to reduce the input costs. In addition, GEB decided to use washed coal, which was cheaper, and also began using imported coal which in some cases proved cheaper. The GEB also negotiated a cheaper price for low sulphur heavy stock (LSHS), a widely used furnace oil, from Indian Oil Corporation, which amounted to a saving of Rs 28 crore.[60]

What was more difficult was the re-negotiation of the PPAs that had onerous power tariffs built into them. The chairperson of GEB knew that unless she was able to re-negotiate the PPAs, she would not be able to make a major dent in the overall lack of profitability of the GEB. A committee was therefore set up to initiate talks with GERC and the private power suppliers with whom the GEB had signed PPAs. This was a very difficult process as it faced strong opposition from the private suppliers and the GERC, which feared that re-negotiating the PPA contracts could set a negative precedent for future privatization of the power sector. The private suppliers argued that the sanctity of the contract would be challenged if this re-negotiation became a reality. The dialogue took almost a year, with the informal GEB committee meeting the GERC and the companies with whom they had signed the PPAs. They consulted their own lawyers in re-negotiating with the private suppliers.

Notwithstanding initial opposition,[61] the GEB made a persistent case that for genuine 'public interest' it was necessary to re-negotiate the PPAs. Moreover, the GEB agreed to pay certain dues (interest penalty) owed to the companies in one go and assured the PPA holders that the GEB would be able to begin paying its outstanding dues to the companies on time. Through this long process of consultation and negotiation, the GEB was able to convince the various suppliers that re-negotiation was necessary for both sides and would also be more profitable for the private companies. This successful negotiation led to a saving of Rs 495 crore towards fixed costs in the first phase and Rs 64 crore in the second. In return, the GEB promised to pay its dues on time and also earned a rebate of Rs 150 crore annually between 2003 and 2006.

A crucial, completely accidental institutional coincidence that made possible such actions on multiple fronts was the fact that the officer driving power reforms held three posts simultaneously: GEB chairperson, the Energy Department's secretary, and chairman of the PSUs of the energy sector (Manjula Subramaniam). This centralization of power in one individual—who happened to be a competent and honest civil servant with great experience of failure in the same organization in the 1980s, when she was a member of the GEB Board, and failed then, as she put it, 'to achieve even a bit of reform within the organization'—was crucial and determinative. It was a case of having the right person (right both in terms of integrity and experience in the power sector) at the right time (when reform could no longer be avoided) and the right place (all three positions held by the same individual), when the state was faced with a large-scale fiscal crisis that extended across all departments.

I thus argue that the eventual reform of GEB was more an unintended outcome of several factors rather than designed or conceived as such. None of the actors in the process knew that they were driving a successful reform model, but they were dealing with a wide-ranging crisis in the Gujarat's power sector as they knew best. The success after 2002 was built on the grave of earlier failures, especially in the mid- to late-1990s; these earlier failures provided crucial learning processes. From the maze of many unintended consequences, individual initiative, and accidental learning processes, as well as incentives and ideas provided by the ADB and the Central government, and effective monitoring by an independent regulatory body (GERC), emerged a 'successful reform model'.

EDUCATION REFORM: ENROLMENT OF GIRL CHILDREN IN GUJARAT

Education of girls is the soft underbelly of an otherwise successful industrial state: the literacy rate of females, and correspondingly the enrolment and retention rates of girls in Gujarat, is much lower than in other states and the gender gap in education is quite stark. Only 58.60 per cent of women are literate in the state compared to 80.50 per cent men (2001 census data). Since 2003–4, the state administration has focused with vigour and commitment on the enrolment of girls, and clear gains are visible as the result of its campaigns.

The Kanya Kelavani Nidhi has been created with a long-term goal that no girl in Gujarat remain illiterate, and the efforts have started yielding results. In 2006–7, the drop-out rate of the girl child dwindled to 3.68 per cent from 20.81 per cent in 2000–1 for Classes I to V, and to 11.64 per cent from as high as 36.30 per cent for Classes I to VII. The dwindling drop-out rates are equally supported by new enrolments through Kanya Kelavani Rath Yatra (girl child enrolment drive), a unique initiative in Gujarat. Since 2003, every year June, the chief minister along with his team travels to remote villages to encourage parents to enrol their children in schools. It is a three-day long state-wide drive covering all the villages and the urban areas in scorching summer heat. An atmosphere of festivity and celebration is created. The young children now wait keenly to get themselves enrolled into schools.[62]

What are the sources and reasons for policy innovation for the education of girls, which was ignored for a number of years, if not decades? Here again similar to the other case studies in this chapter, the focus is on origins and sources of policy change as well as institutional features that make a difference to policy outcomes. Here, we see a state strongly *mobilized* for action. This mobilization of state capacity is possible when new ideas for change—a focus on the girl child—combine with civil society's attention on the theme of the negative situation of girls in Gujarat, and most important, the structure of a Centrally sponsored scheme (Sarva Shikhsha Abhiyan [SSA]). Specifically, SSA's careful and specific guidelines, along with effective implementation and monitoring in Gujarat, are the key to the success of the scheme in the state.[63] The sources of policy innovation in the field of education originated in external sources, acquired momentum through the efforts of Central structures and institutions, and were then reinforced by strong implementation by the state government. Important Gujarat-specific innovations, such as a massive mobilization effort, relied on and utilized the larger Central structure and expectations, thus ensuring a powerful complementarity between a Centrally rooted and funded project and the state's own attempts to improve its education statistics. The SSA structure with the possibility of innovation built in, but closely monitored by the Central and state governments, was the institutional causal mechanism that enabled definite change. These factors, in turn, were combined with the initiative of the education minister and chief minister, who energized the entire state administration into campaign mode.

While Kanya Kelavani Nidhi began in 2003, the International Development Agency (IDA) with financial aid from the Government of the Netherlands had selected the state of Gujarat for the implementation of the District Primary Education Programme (DPEP) much earlier. Gujarat was chosen in Phase II of the programme for the period 1995–2002. The DPEP was a programme consciously targeted at the gender gap in education. The implementation of DPEP Phase II in Gujarat envisaged the selection of the three most backward districts—Banaskantha, Panchmahals, and Dangs—where the female literacy rate was below the national average. The aim of the programme was to support a replicable, sustainable, transparent, and cost-effective means to (i) reduce the differences in enrolment, drop-out, and learning achievement among gender and deprived social groups like Scheduled Castes, Scheduled Tribes, minority children to less than 5 per cent; (ii) reduce the overall primary drop-out rate for all students to less than 10 per cent; (ii) raise achievement levels by 25 per cent above the measured baseline levels, and (v) provide access to all children of primary education or its equivalent. However, gender equity in education was the principal goal as the districts had been selected on the basis of gender disparities.

An internal evaluation of the DPEP noted that Gujarat had witnessed a substantial rise in enrolment from 619,756 to 948,532 between 1996–7 and 2002–3.[64] The average formal school enrolment in three districts increased from 73.25 to 108.04 per cent in Panchmahals and to 114.37 per cent in Banaskantha during the same period. Interestingly, it was the early experience of literacy enhancement in the DPEP programme that brought home the issue of school infrastructure. Due to the enrolment drive and other promotional measures, enrolment in the districts increased dramatically, which led to overcrowding and showed up the paucity of the existing school infrastructure. This led to a demand for the construction of new schools, additional classrooms, toilets for girls, and the provision of drinking water and a strong provision for 'civil works' in the follow-up programme: SSA, launched by the Central government in 2002. It appears that Gujarat was the first state to propose undertaking school repairs through Village Civil Works Committees (VCWC), which was later adopted as a national norm and replicated in other DPEP states. In addition, the repairs by VCWC have been completed satisfactorily in the project districts.[65] In Phase IV of the programme, three more districts in Gujarat were selected: Kutch, Sabarkantha, and Surendernagar; the Government of Gujarat, on its own initiative and funds, added three more: Bhavnagar, Jamnagar, and Junagadh. Interestingly, the basic structure of the DPEP programme relied on strict and clear guidelines about the goals to be achieved with specific goalposts set, but as important was local, or what came to be called, community mobilization or responsibility in fulfilling those goals.

The SSA initiated in 2002 adopted the combination of local monitoring bodies first introduced under the World Bank DPEP Programme, but for all districts in the state. Learning from the DPEP structure, Village Education Committees (VEC), Mother–Teacher Associations (MTA), and Parent–Teacher Associations (PTA) were formed in all districts. In addition, a detailed management structure was evolved, right from the 'State Project Office' in Gandhinagar to VECs at the grassroots levels. There were regular meetings of the various organizational committees, and the focus was on the continual updating of rules and regulations, and approving and monitoring work plans and reviewing outputs. This continual feedback and monitoring yielded results and these ideas and practices were carried over to the state's management of later education programmes. An overarching structure and close monitoring enabled regular diffusion and sharing of knowledge about what was working and what was not. For example, the officials of the new districts in Gujarat observed the actual functioning of the block resource coordinators (BRC) in the three old districts and learnt from positive practices. There were regular meetings both in other states and at the Central level, especially in the SSA. Underlying all this was a huge infusion of human capital: hiring a vast array of new staff to implement the programme and, even more important, capacity-building through the infusion of infrastructure (computers) and training. Capacity building and continual diffusion of knowledge and information sharing were very strong components.

Partly stimulated by the success of DPEP in the backward districts, the national debate also moved towards universalization of education and the expansion of basic education in the late 1990s and early 2000s.[66] The Central government launched the Sarva Shiksha Abhiyan Mission in 2002 along with the 86th Constitutional Amendment that guaranteed as a fundamental right free and compulsory education to children in the 6–14 years age group. SSA was to be implemented in partnership with state governments to cover the entire country and address the needs of 192 million children in 1.1 million habitations. The programme seeks to open new schools in those habitations which do not have schooling facilities and also strengthen existing school infrastructure through provision of additional classrooms, toilets, drinking water, a maintenance grant, and school improvement grants. Existing schools with inadequate teacher strength are provided with additional teachers, while the capacity of existing teachers is being strengthened through extensive training, grants to develop teaching-learning materials, and strengthening the academic support structure at cluster, block, and district levels. SSA seeks to provide quality elementary education including life skills. It has a special focus on girls' education and children with special needs, and also seeks to provide computer education to bridge the digital divide. The SSA was to cover all districts in all states but with a strong continuing focus on gender equality in education.

What is important about this programme is that it has been conceived as a 'convergent framework', not a set of guidelines, and much attention has been devoted to putting into place a delivery system and institutional mechanisms in each district to implement the goals. Central funding was provided to every aspect of the programme, with an explicit monitoring mechanism built in, yet providing significant autonomy in how the targets were to be achieved.

In Gujarat, the initial success of the DPEP project was noted first by the Minister of Education when she visited some of the schools in one of the backward districts in the state in the late 1990s. She was struck by the impact of the mission, especially on girl children.[67] Aware of Gujarat's poor statistics in education, she decided to expand the project and extend state support to it. Thus, in later iterations of the programme, the state provided resources for three additional districts from its own funds. The chief minister in turn made the education of girls part of a broader developmental plank in the state.

Thus, the idea of a focus on girls' education was the contribution of the DPEP and the SSA mission, and was widened by the state government. The Department of Education, Government of Gujarat, began sending bureaucrats to the districts under the Kanya Kelavani Rath Yatra to attract students to the school system and motivate parents of children who had never been to school to enrol their girl children. In 2004, the chief minister harnessed this issue and transformed it into an aggressive political campaign by mobilizing the strength of his government behind it. His enrolment campaign began in 2004 but gathered momentum by 2006 when it was planned for 18,000 villages. In 2004, processions of the Kanya Kelavani Rath Yatra—led by cabinet ministers, the chief secretary, and 268 senior officers—were taken to 2,082 villages with a female literacy rate of under 20 per cent. After 2004, a state-wide drive for greater enrolment occurred during the first day of school. The chief minister, ministers, and civil servants—district collectors, IAS officers, Indian Police Service (IPS) officers—adopted five villages and moved from village to village in the scorching heat of the summer for three days. In accordance with the strategy adopted, every minister and officer visited five such villages a day. Within three days each of them managed to visit 15 villages. In 2006–7, the campaign was planned for each of Gujarat's 18,000 villages.In 2003–4, 75,847 girls were enrolled, and in 2006 the numbers rose to 307,280 as the campaign gradually began attracting greater interest (see Table 4.3).

Table 4.3 State Mobilization in Action: Visits of the State Functionaries for the Enrolment of Children, 2003–8

Year	Ministers on Visit	Officers on Visit	Village Wards Visited
2003	14	All district officers	NA
2004	14	182	7,765
2005	19	291	5,750
2006	27	537	18,113
2007	28	516	20,494
2008*	18	620	20,203

Source: Unpublished government data available with the author.
Note: * Data for 2008 had not been collated by 2009 and is an underestimation of the visits and extent of coverage.

This programme exemplifies the process of mobilization and galvanization of a state. The entire state machinery is mobilized to generate a festive or *mela* atmosphere, which has the effect of attracting all the families living there in a show of solidarity and support, and correspondingly shaming those absenting themselves. It is widely reported that children and parents came dressed up for the occasion, and were greeted by teachers and officials. By 2008 enthusiastic participation was reported from everywhere and the local community even donated funds for the provision of school bags, slates, pens, pencils, textbooks, notebooks, and uniforms. Around Rs 4.63 crore was collected as donations in 2006 as compared to Rs 2.15 crore in 2003 (Saral Communications 2006: 19). Chhotubhai Bamania, officer-in-charge of teacher training in Dahod, said:

> The project is a shot in the arm for girl's education. We celebrate the enrollment of a girl child in primary school as a social function. Earlier, when the parent used to come to admit his or her child, nobody knew. But, now things have changed. Enrolment is celebrated like a marriage, or birth of a child. People are happy that their children's admission is celebrated by the entire village like this. It is due to the impact of gender awareness created by Kanya Kelavani Rath Yatra, that about 50 per cent of mothers are coming to enroll their daughters, now, while earlier only their father used to come for admission. (Ibid.)

Notwithstanding this focus on Kanya Kelavani, without the DPEP and the structure of the SSA, the state-specific programme could not have been conceived or even implemented. This specific state campaign is wholly reliant on the institutional architecture of the SSA, and the mission officials are those who organize the melas, visits of the ministers, and the like. It is thus an example of a rare complementarity between state-level initiatives, benefited by the larger concept provided by DPEP, SSA, and the framework of a Central government scheme. Without these external elements, such improvement in the drop-out results would not have been possible.

Is Gujarat a Developmental South Asian Tiger?

What does this analysis across diverse sectors and policies tell us about the larger comparative model that has emerged in Gujarat? In comparison with the classic developmental states—the economies of East Asia and their miracle growth rates—India was perceived to be a 'failed developmental state' (Herring 1999). From 1960–85, India grew slowly, at 3.5 per cent per annum, which amounted to 1.5 per cent per capita (GoI, *Economic Survey*, various years). The theory of a developmental state argued that states are not hindrances or incidental but necessary for rapid economic growth. States can identify winning sectors and industries as well as facilitate learning and flexible innovations (Johnson 1982; Amsden 1989; Wade 1990), provide a managed financial regime that redirects industrial policy to its best uses, subsidize credit, provide incentives, and deploy technological innovation for the service of the nation-state.

An analysis of Gujarat (and other sub-national states within India) shows that faced with the reality of a restrictive central regime during the license raj, state leaders devised a system that enhanced state objectives and facilitated private (domestic) investment. Thus in India, sub-national developmental states flourished even as the national state floundered in comparison with the East Asian tigers prior to the unleashing of reforms from 1991 onwards (Sinha 2005).

Strikingly, the motivations and elements of a developmental state in Gujarat mirror the dimensions that were crucial in Japan and South Korea. Johnson (1982) argued that the Japanese state was neither socialist nor free market but a 'plan-rational capitalist state' conjoining state guidance with private initiative. He outlined how the Ministry of International Trade and Industry (MITI) exemplified strategic bureaucratic capacity, as it designed and shaped industrial policy with remarkable abilities and technical skill. Interestingly, and I would argue in a manner parallel to Gujarat, Johnson highlights the role of nationalism as a catalyst in fuelling a 'will to develop'. Gujarat's location and proximity to Mumbai, and the implicit competition with the state of Maharashtra together with the rise of linguistic sub-nationalism in the 1950s and 1960s, created a parallel impetus for the rise of Gujarat as a developmental state. The political and bureaucratic leadership was keen to see Gujarat rise as a state that could develop rapidly in competition with Maharashtra (Sinha 2005).

Johnson confirms the high position of the economic bureaucrats in the Japanese government where civil servants in the priority ministries of finance, industry, and trade are selected with care and attention. A similar process of informal selection was practised in Gujarat where the best bureaucrats were chosen for finance, industry, and the various corporations linked to industry. In a similar vein, Amsden (1989), in a now famous study of South Korea, highlights the role of learning and innovation by copying that characterizes late developer countries like South Korea and Taiwan. Gujarat's state agencies display some of these capacities of turning crisis into opportunities and using developmental achievements to mobilize society into a unified agenda for development.

However, Gujarat must also learn from the East Asian tigers. The East Asian tigers combined growth with equity, even using industrial policy as a means of social protection for workers in the small-scale sector, farmers, and declining sectors, and ensuring a system of lifetime employment and systematic insurance of its workers, alongside strong institutions furthering literacy to raise the skill level of the population at large (Chang 2002; Estevez-Abe 2008). Even more interestingly, the South Korean state provided subsides, credits, and regulatory access to big business, the *Chaebol*, but also extracted performance from them. Amsden shows how the state disciplined private capital in the service of development through diverse means such as export targets (1989: 16–18). Gujarat's rush to attract investment has tended to give free rein to the private sector and faces a declining capacity to manage the power of private initiative for sustainable development of the state and its citizens.

Second, when faced with the financial crisis of 1997–8, South Korea expanded the welfare state to larger sections of the population (Kuhnle 2004). Third, developmental states such as Japan and South Korea have faced challenges of renewing the state, and have suffered mixed results in re-tooling the state to respond to the new challenges of the global economy. Gujarat faces similar dilemmas across all three fronts and needs to derive the correct lessons from the developmental states if it is to replicate their successes.

The experience of economic reforms in Gujarat also reveals insights about the role of the private sector in economic development. First, the private sector is clearly seen as a partner in the growth process by the state's political leadership. This pro-private sector orientation goes back to the joint sector concept that prevailed in the 1970s and 1980s. Second, both formal, institutionalized mechanisms of public–private interaction—for example, the presence of private sector actors on the Board of State Public enterprises—and informal consultations with key private sector actors embody this orientation. Formal mechanisms can help nudge state actors to promote greater efficiency and growth in economic policy, while informal channels can contribute to key policy innovations adopted by the state. Other states should adopt and create mechanisms to allow for greater interaction between governments and the private sectors. The state should also incorporate research and policy expertise in its policymaking process, as was done in the case of tax and fiscal reforms in Gujarat. Local universities and research institutions should be used more for such purposes.

Additionally, as the private sector becomes more complex, refurbishing technical capacity to manage contracts and public–private sector partnerships becomes a key priority, and demands new kinds of expertise within the state. State officials should be provided with mid-career training in business schools and in technical subjects related to their fields of operations. It should be noted that key organizations, such as the Gujarat Maritime Board and the Gujarat Infrastructure Development Board, have come a long way in recasting their skill profile to deal with increasingly sophisticated counterparts to address the twin challenges of contracting and monitoring implementation. A challenge for the future is the need to strengthen public oversight to ensure greater accountability and transparency in the working of the private sector more generally in the state.

CONCLUSION: IMPLICATIONS AND LESSONS

Gujarat has given birth to crucial and admirable developmental achievements and instituted crucial changes in governance over the past 10–15 years. The state benefited from a long history of strong state capacity and the innovative and flexible abilities of its leadership to leverage historical strengths. Gujarat succeeded in good governance before that idea became a fashionable slogan. How and why have reforms been at the forefront of developments in Gujarat in the face of enormous internal and external challenges? What can other states learn from Gujarat's successes and failures, and the processes of economic reform in the state? What common lessons can be drawn from the four different case studies of fiscal reform and privatization, ports, power reform, and education enrolment?

First, at each stage, far-sighted vision and plans have paved the way for future developments and helped to transform crises into opportunities. Gujarat's visionary and competent civil servants modelled the state after East and South-East Asia much before those countries had emerged as models on the national stage. In 1994, L. Mansingh, the then managing director of GIIC, noted: 'I want to emphasize that we are not competing with any state. We are now deliberately benchmarking ourselves with the newly industrializing countries so that we know how far we lag behind. ... We believe that we must compare ourselves with the Asian Tigers.'[68] The leadership in recent times also hopes to emulate some of the successes of South Korea and Japan.[69]

This, however, raises the issue of the sustainability of the gains in Gujarat. For Gujarat to become a real Japan or South Korea, the state must make the current rhetoric of social development and social sector infrastructure a concrete reality rather than a mere media campaign and slogan. As an illustration, it must be as ambitious for its social goals as for industrial development, perhaps even more so.

Notwithstanding a state commitment towards the social sector, these goals are not integrated into any of the policies towards infrastructure or industrial development. Vis-à-vis education of the girl child, it must enhance the Centre's initiatives through the SSA and focus on retention, access, equity, and quality of education, and not only on formal enrolment alone. To put a human face to its development is no longer an option but the demand of the new century, and in line with the goals of a new developmental state that every state in India must achieve.

Second, severe economic and political crises have provided the urgency and threats necessary to energize pending reform strategies at crucial moments in the state's history. In fact, crises have been deployed by state officials to create new opportunities for unpopular reforms, which might not have otherwise have been possible. Fiscal crisis in the mid-1990s and in the early 2000s was so utilized. In this deployment, external factors exerted valuable pressure (on power reform and universalization of education) and were also adapted by the state for local and regionally specific goals.

State capacity emerges as a crucial independent variable that enables the state to mediate crisis or external opportunities as well as threats. What specific aspects of state capacity are important? Three elements emerge as crucial. One is accidental learning in the course of policy-making, fiscal reform, and privatization, as well as in port and power policy. Flexible, innovative, and independent officials are the key to such serendipitous learning. Yes-men and status-quo officials are incapable of institutionalizing change and random innovations. Second, it is essential to have institutions to monitor and overlapping ones to coordinate the effective translation of vision and goals into actual outcomes (for example, fiscal reform [informal group, and ADB committee], port reform [GIDB], education reform [SSA], and power reform [GERC]). Similarly, at the governmental level, the weekly meetings of the current chief minister with all the secretaries to review policies, the necessity of reporting how many state officials have visited the villages during the enrolment drive are important monitoring devices. Another key governance reform is the refusal to nominate party members as chairpersons of most economic corporations, which has positively impacted the performance of many government agencies. These mechanisms institute a feedback and cross-checking feature and prevent the growth of inertia and vested interests that could derail reform even in strong states.

Third, the state in Gujarat is energetic and mobilized, and is able to go into a campaign mode at the instance of innovative leadership. Strong complementarity between the Central government and the state initiatives is also exploited for the benefit of citizens of the state (for example, power and education reforms). Yet, this harnessing of the state in a campaign mode can have some deleterious consequences. As an illustration, the current administration has directed all profit-making autonomous corporations to deposit 30 per cent of their tax before profit into a separate state agency; this is harmful to the autonomy and incentives in many state agencies. Two of these three dimensions of state capacity—monitoring mechanisms and an energetic and mobilized state—can be replicated in other states, while flexibility and non-linear innovative ability are more difficult to emulate. Even so, encouraging autonomous civil servants and corporations and rewarding new policy initiatives could facilitate such non-linear accretions of state capacity.

However, a cautionary note needs to be heeded by other states regarding the decay of state capacity. State strengths take a long time to build but can rapidly decay. Notwithstanding historical strengths and crucial innovations, the state institutions in Gujarat are in decline and losing their historical capabilities. New expertise and knowledge are demanded by the new challenges of economic reform, which should be embodied in new and reformed state institutions. Today the industries department has less than half its staff deployed in monitoring and implementation, notwithstanding a political obsession with numbers and aggressive claims about Gujarat's ability to implement MoUs. Since the early 1990s, the industries department has stopped hiring new staff, and as people periodically retire, the size of the state apparatus is declining at a time when Gujarat is attracting more and more investments. The GMB lacks the capacity to effectively negotiate with private partners or to manage and ensure that PPP projects serve the public good without denying the private interest. The SSA, with its strong focus on external infusion of capacity through a Centrally sponsored scheme, provides a counter-example of high capacity. This erosion of technical and non-technical state capacity within the state runs across many departments and sectors, and will affect the ability of the state to respond to new challenges and to oversee the public–private model of development that the state hopes to implement. As noted by a senior civil servant of the industries department, the current challenge is to 'create new professionals of facilitators, and new expertise and knowledge that can make current developments in the state sustainable for many years in the future'.[70]

As an illustration, state governments, including Gujarat, rely heavily on private consultants for simple functions and roles. These consultants are, however, over-used and strain scarce state revenue and further erode its capacity to perform effectively. Most general consultants have become glorified presentation producers; their glossy brochures more in evidence than actual policy expertise. Besides, they seal themselves off from public scrutiny and transparency while recommending transparency to the state. In most states, the problem is not the lack of funds but the courage and vision to think outside the box, to reorient their priorities, and renew their capacities.

Finally, the role of the private sector provides crucial lessons. The political leadership of the state thinks of the interests of private capital to be tied to the progress in the state; at face value there does not seem to be a zero-sum relationship between the state and the private accumulation of wealth. It generates both remarkably conflict-free prosperity and some betrayals of the public interest, as in the case of privatization, and to some degree port development. The challenge for the state is to ensure continuing investment and growth-oriented initiatives while instituting some checks on the unbridled capture of public assets for narrow ends by the private sector. 'Guiding markets',[71] a task that the Gujarat state has done relatively well so far, is as necessary after liberalization as earlier, if not more so. It is a lesson which other states also need to pay heed to.

NOTES

1. Economic reform is an amorphous term with many meanings. I define it as a combination of fiscal, policy, and governance changes that re-allocate the relative weight of state power and market forces in an economy. In this chapter, I study fiscal reforms, disinvestment of public enterprises, public–private partnership in the port sector, and enrolment of girl children.

2. For a sampling of studies that focus on states within India, see Jenkins (1999); Sinha (1999; 2004); Bajpai and Sachs (1999); Paul (2000); and Kennedy (2004). Also, see the special issue devoted to economic reforms in Andhra Pradesh, *Economic and Political Weekly*, 22, 8 March–4 April 2003.

3. While excellent studies on Gujarat exist, none of them analyse the pathways of economic reform in the state, especially for the period 1990–2009. For important studies on Gujarat, see Hirway et al. (2002); Shah et al. (2002); Shinoda (2002); Yagnik and Sheth (2005); and Menon (2009).

4. The 'Vibrant Gujarat' concept is the continuation of a very similar meet organized in March 2001, entitled 'Resurgent Gujarat'. See CII (2001). Also see, *Business Line* (2002).

5. Srinivas (2009). In *Business Today* surveys in the late 1990s, Gujarat would consistently rank second and first on many parameters. See, for the older surveys, 'A Business Today–Gallup-MBA Survey: Best States to Invest In', *Business Today*, 7–21 June, 1996; 'A BT–Gallup Research Project: The Best States to Invest In', *Business Today*, 22 December–6 January 1998; and 'The Best States to Invest In: A Business Today–Gallup Organization Research Project', *Business Today*, 22 December 1999–6 January 2000.

6. For a perspective that stresses contingent factors in the making of policy, see Pierson (2000a) and (2000b).

7. The Gujarat State Fertilizers Corporation was the public sector enterprise set up for that purpose.

8. As an illustration, Gujarat's industry secretary and other officials were required to give a list of backward districts for the central capital subsidy scheme in the early 1980s. The officials realized that even with incentives, no development will be possible in absolutely backward districts where even the basic infrastructure was missing. Thus, they gave a list of second-best backward districts, with some proximity to large metropolitan areas and some infrastructure. Bharuch was designated as a 'backward district' for the purpose of this scheme and developed rapidly in consequence. Interview, retired industry secretary, Ahmedabad, 19 March 2009.

9. For an argument that emphasizes the role of fiscal crisis in sub-national reforms in India, see Howes et al. (2003).

10. A former finance secretary noted that the fiscal situation in Gujarat by 2001–2 was so dire that urgent reforms were not an option any longer.

11. These figures are from Dholakia (2003).

12. ADB (2007). In an interview with some ADB functionaries, they noted that the SFC report of 1995 played a crucial role in their decision as they realized

that the key state officials were thinking along similar lines, and this would ensure internal credibility to the reform process and their loan.

13. Interview with Author, Gandhinagar, 13 February 2009.

14. See 'Institutional Reform: Budgetary Procedures, and Management', in State Public Finance Reforms Committee (2000). Many of these recommendations were never adopted, although an internal report on the extent of the subsidies given by the state, to be kept confidential, was taken up each year.

15. Interviews with author, February–March 2009, Ahmedabad.

16. State Public Finance Reforms Committee (2000). Also see Asian Development Bank (1999); Operations Research Group (1999).

17. Interviews with the concerned officials confirmed this; there was a strong ideological belief that the government should undertake only those activities to which it was best suited. It was a small group of people (names withheld for reasons of confidentiality) who firmly held this view.

18. Judgment on the *Civil Application on Gujarat Trade Union Manch v. Gujarat State Textile Corporation*, available at http://www.vakilno1.com/judgements/companiesact/2000-099compcas0461guj.htm, accessed on 26 March 2010.

19. 'State Government to Partially Privatize GSFC, GMDC', *The Economic Times*, 30 November 1997: 'The Gujarat Government is all set to fully or partially privatize certain public sector units and merge several others in keeping with guidelines laid down by the Asian Development Bank (ADB). This will enable the state to secure the $350 million loan offered by the bank for developing infrastructure in the state.'

20. Confidential interview, Ahmedabad, 26 February 2009.

21. http://www.vakilno1.com/judgements/companiesact/2000-099compcas0461guj.htm, accessed on 26 March 2010.

22. Interview with Author, Ahmedabad, March 2009.

23. Interview with Author, Ahmedabad, March 2009.

24. Interviews with Author. One member of the group that implemented disinvestment told me that initially he also believed that only loss-making PSUs should be privatized; but as the group began discussions, he was gradually convinced that most PSUs should be disinvested.

25. The counter-intuitive result that liberalization demands state formation or regulation, or state-building has been confirmed by empirical evidence from a wide set of cases: Mexico (Snyder 1999); Chile and Britain (Schamis 2002); financial sector reform in UK, USA, and Japan (Moran 1991); and Brazil (Pereira 1999). Also see, Solimano et al. (1994) and Wise (2003).

26. For a perspective that focuses on bureaucratic politics, see Allison and Zelikow (1999).

27. Gujarat Industrial Investment Corporation, Gujarat State Finance Corporation, Industrial Extension Bureau.

28. Interview with L. Mansingh, MD, GIIC, 'BS State Survey on Gujarat', *Business Standard*, 1998.

29. India has 12 major ports and 139 operable minor ports. While the primary responsibility for the development and management of major ports lies with the Central government, the intermediate and minor ports are under the control of the state governments.

30. Interview, Chief Minister's Office, Gandhinagar, 15 March 2009.

31. Gujarat is ranked first in terms of an 'Infrastructure Index' constructed by a study conducted by the National Council of Applied Economic Research (NCAER). See Venkatesan and Varma (1998: 57, Table 31).

32. I interviewed around five to six key officials who were shaping the industrial and infrastructure policies of the state in the early- to mid-1990s.

33. The government began examining the feasibility of establishing a port in Gujarat in line with those in Rotterdam and Singapore. See *The Economic Times* (1993).

34. Kailashanathan and A.D. Desai were given this responsibility.

35. Interview, Keshubhai Patel, Ex-Chief Minister March 2009, Gandhinagar. Interview, Suresh Mehta, Ex-CM and ex-Industry Minister, March 2009.

36. Interview with one of the authors of the port policy, Gandhinagar, March 2009. See, for those calculations, Gujarat Maritime Board (1998).

37. Author's Interview with GMB officials who went to Holland for training.

38. Author's Interview with a retired senior civil servant, New Delhi, February 2009.

39. For the emerging issues in implementing public–private partnerships, see 3i Network (2008: Chapter 2).

40. While the GMB formulated a Model Concession Agreement with the help of ADB, such an initiative stalled at the Centre. While the Prime Minister's Office asked the cabinet secretariat to prepare such an agreement, differences emerged between the Planning Commission and the shipping ministry, with the result that such an agreement is yet to be finalized. See 3i Network, *India Infrastructure Report, 2008*, p. 18.

41. 'Public–Private Partnership Initiatives in the State of Gujarat', A presentation by the Gujarat Infrastructure Development Board, 2 September 2006.

42. Interview with a senior GMB official, Gandhinagar, March 2000.

43. In 2009, it is one of the richest corporations in the state. This has, in turn, led to conflict with the Central government, which wants to tax its earnings, and the state government, which wants to use its revenues for the general functions of the state. This has given rise to an interesting tussle.

44. Gujarat Maritime Board, Internal Document, September 1998 (available with the author).

45. Gujarat Maritime Board, Internal Document, September 1998, pp. 48–9 (available with the author).

46. Government of Gujarat, Ports and Fisheries Department, Resolution No. WKS-1097-G-213-GH, Annexure B. Available with the author.

47. Direct negotiation is for the following projects: (1) a project, which is innovative or involves proprietary technology or franchise, exclusively available globally with the individual; (2) a project in which competitive public bidding, as provided in Section 9, has failed to select the developer; (3) a project to provide social services to the people; and (4) an infrastructure project, which is an essential link for another larger infrastructure project, owned or operated by the same individual. A copy of the Act is available at http://gidb.org/Act_2006_.pdf, accessed on 12 May 2009.

48. The Government of India will defray 15 per cent of project cost as a VGF. It has designated Rs 4,840 crore for providing VGF in infrastructure projects.

49. Interview with Author, Gandhinagar, March 2009.

50. Interestingly, the GEB did re-train its officials, a fact that contributed to its success in restructuring.

51. Author's Interview with GMB's CEO, March 2009.

52. In contrast to the Orissa model, which is considered to be a failure.

53. State agencies as well as journalistic accounts attribute to political will much causal power. I have shown in this chapter that political will is generated by specific features of state capacity, such as monitoring and mobilization. Political support for reformers undertaking difficult reforms is crucial, but that support is made possible by pre-existing state traditions and activated bureaucratic leadership and skills. At crucial moments, political leaders are also found wanting, as in the case of the power reforms, and bureaucratic micro successes precede the stepping stone for larger and macro success without state design from the top. Thus, 'political will' needs to be unpacked and its historical antecedents delineated more carefully than is usually the case in easy celebrations of political will.

54. Interview with Author, March 2009.

55. Interview with Author, March 2009.

56. Political leaders have taken credit for the power reforms in Gujarat after the GEB had already been reformed and achieved success through a very painful process.

57. The GEB in 2001–2 was selling its own scrap and using that money to pay some of the salaries of its employees.

58. Interview with Author, February–March 2009.

59. Author's Interview with ex-GEB Chairman, who re-negotiated these loans.

60. Author's Interview with ex-GEB Chairman, who re-negotiated these agreements.

61. In the first two dialogues with the companies, it seemed impossible to achieve.

62. See: http://www.gujaratindia.com/Initiatives/Initiative2(3).htm, accessed on 15 May 2009.

63. See Rustagi (2009) for an analysis of the central schemes for the universalization of education.

64. This covers the initial three DPEP districts as well as three more added to the programme by the state government.

65. Gujarat Council of Primary Education, DPEP and SSA, Implementation Completion Report. Available with the author.

66. See Rustagi (2009).

67. Author's interviews with the education officers of the state, February–March 2009.

68. *Business Standard* interview with L. Mansingh, MD, GIIC.

69. Author's interview with Narendra Modi, Chief Minister, Gujarat, March 2009.

70. Interview with Author, Gandhinagar, March 2009.

71. Robert Wade (1990) used this concept in his analysis of South Korea and Taiwan.

BIBLIOGRAPHY

Primary Documents

Asian Development Bank (1999), Gujarat Reform of Public Finances (TA No. 2668-IND), *Final Report, Directions of Sales Reform and Proposal for Value Added Tax Introduction*, February. Gandhinagar: Government of Gujarat (GoG).

_________ (2000), *Report and Recommendation of the President to the Board of Directors on the Proposed Loans and Technical Assistance Grants to India for the Gujarat Power Sector Reform*, November. Gandhinagar: GoG.

_________ (2007), *Performance Evaluation Report*, India: Gujarat Public Sector Resource Management Program, July.

Business Line (2002), 'Small is Beautiful for "Resurgent" Gujarat', 7 February.

Business Standard (2000), 'Marine Bounty in Gujarat Coast Facing Extinction', 21 August.

CII (2001), 'Gujarat Annual Day, Session on Resurgent Gujarat', March. Ahmedabad: CII.

Government of Gujarat (1995), *State Finance Commission Report*. Gandhinagar: GoG.

_________ (1998), Gujarat Act. No. 30 of 1981, as modified up to 30 November 1998. Gandhinagar: GoG.

_________ (2008), *Socio-Economic Review: Gujarat State, 2007–2008*. Gandhinagar: GoG Press.

Government of Gujarat and Industries and Mines Department (1995), *Industrial Policy: Gujarat 2000 AD and Beyond*, July.

Government of Gujarat and Ports and Fisheries Department (1995), *Port Policy 1995*. Ahmedabad: GoG.

Government of India (various years), *Economic Survey*. New Delhi: Government of India.

Gujarat Council of Primary Education (2004), DPEP and SSA, *Implementation Completion Report*. Gandhinagar: Department of Education, GoG.

Gujarat Electricity Board (2009), *The Unbundling of Gujarat Electricity Board: A Case Study*, 20 March, GEB Presentation, (unpublished) available with Author.

GIDB (2006), 'Public–Private Partnership Initiatives in the State of Gujarat', A Presentation by the Gujarat Infrastructure Development Board, 2 September, unpublished paper, available with Author.

Gujarat Maritime Board (1998), *Gujarat Internal Study*: '*Identification of Infrastructure Requirements for the Year 2010*', September. Gandhinagar: GMB.

_________ (various years), *Annual Report*. Gandhinagar: GMB.

Hindustan Times (1993), 'Gujarat to Set Up Infrastructure Corporation', 7 May.

Operations Research Group (1999), *Companion Volume to the Report of State Public Finance Reforms Committee (December 2000): Gujarat Finances: Reform of Budgetary Management, Minor Taxes and Non-Tax Revenue*. Gandhinagar: Operations Research Group.

Raguram, G. (1994), *Privatization of Ports Under Gujarat Maritime Board*, Report Submitted to the Gujarat Maritime Board. Ahmedabad: Indian Institute of Management.

Rakesh Mohan Committee (1996), *The India Infrastructure Report: Policy Imperatives for Growth and Welfare*, Expert Group on the Commercialization of Infrastructure Projects, vols 1–3. Published for the Ministry of Finance by NCAER, New Delhi.

Saral Communications (2006), *Efforts for Girl Child Education in Gujarat: A Case Study*. Ahmedabad: Saral Communications.

Siddiqui, Tanvir A. (2009), 'In Gujarat, BJP Rides the Nano', *Indian Express*, 8 April, p. 6.

Srinivas, Srikanth (2009), 'State of our States', *Business World*, 23 February, pp. 30–47.

State Public Finance Reforms Committee (SPFRC) (2000), *Report on the Fiscal Consolidation of Gujarat: A Medium Term Plan*, December. Gandhinagar: Government of Gujarat.

The Economic Times (1993), 'Gujarat to Throw Open Core Industry to Private Sector', 8 May.

_________ (1995a), 'Industrial Policy Document Must Go Beyond Mere Subsidies: MLA', 25 August.

_________ (1995b), 'GIIC to Invest Rs 5000 Crore in Infrastructure', 21 December.

_________ (1996), 'GIIC Chief Calls for Pollution Free Industrial Growth', 2 October.

_________ (2000), 'Marine Bounty Faces Extinction', 1 September.

Secondary Sources

3i Network (2008), *India Infrastructure Report 2008, Business Models of the Future*, 3rd imp. New Delhi: Oxford University Press.

Allison, Graham and Philip Zelikow (1999), *Essence of Decision: Explaining the Cuban Missile Crisis*, 2nd edn. New York: Longman.

Amsden, Alice H. (1989), *Asia's Next Giant: South Korea and Late Industrialization*. New York: Oxford University Press.

Bajpai, Nirupam and Jeffrey D. Sachs (1999), 'The Progress of Policy Reform and Variations in Performance at the Sub-National Level in India', Development Discussion Paper No. 730, November. Cambridge MA: Harvard Institute of International Development, Harvard University.

Chang, Ha-Joon (2002), 'The Role of Social Policy in Economic Development; Some Theoretical Reflections and Lessons for East Asia', paper prepared for the UNRISD Project on Social Policy in a Development Context (UNRISD).

Dholakia, Ravindra (2003), 'The Role of the State Government in Promoting Private Sector Growth', in Stephen Howes, Ashok Lahiri, and Nicholas Stern (eds), *State-Level Reforms in India: Towards a More Effective Government*, pp. 302–19. Delhi: Macmillan.

Estevez-Abe, Margarita (2008), *Welfare and Capitalism in Postwar Japan*. Cambridge: Cambridge University Press.

Herring, Ronald (1999), 'Embedded Particularism: India's Failed Developmental State', in Meredith Woo-Cumings (ed.), *The Developmental State*, pp. 306–34. Ithaca: Cornell University Press.

Hirway, Indira, S.P. Kashyap, and Amita Shah (eds) (2002), *Dynamics of Development in Gujarat*. Ahmedabad: Centre of Development Alternatives.

Howes, Stephen, Ashok K. Lahiri, and Nicholas Stern (eds) (2003), 'Introduction', in Stephen Howes, Ashok Lahiri, and Nicholas Stern (eds), *State-Level Reforms in India: Towards a More Effective Government*, pp. 1–30. Delhi: Macmillan.

Jenkins, Rob (1999), *Democratic Politics and Economic Reform in India*. Cambridge: Cambridge University Press.

Johnson, Chalmers (1982), *MITI and the Japanese Miracle: The Growth of Industrial Policy, 1925–1975*. Stanford: Stanford University Press.

Joshi, Rakesh Mohan (2008), 'Gujarat Electricity Board's Turnaround', *The Smart Manager*, 2 (February–March): 42–57.

Kennedy, Loraine (2004), 'Contrasting Responses to Economic Liberalization in Andhra Pradesh and Tamil Nadu', in Rob Jenkins (ed.), *Regional Reflections: Case Studies of Democracy in Practice*, pp. 29–65. New Delhi: Oxford University Press.

Kuhnle, Stein (2004), 'Productive Welfare in Korea: Moving towards a European Welfare State Type?', in Ramesh Mishra (ed.), *Modernizing the Korean Welfare State: Toward the Productive Welfare Model*, pp. 47–64. New York: Transaction Publishers.

Menon, Sudha (ed.) (2009), *Gujarat Economy: The Way Ahead*. Hyderabad: The ICFAI University Press.

Moran, Michael (1991), *The Politics of the Financial Services Revolution: The USA, UK, and Japan*. New York: St. Martin's Press.

Paul, Samuel (2000), 'Do States have an Enabling Environment for Industrial Growth? Some Evidence from Karnataka', *Economic and Political Weekly* 35(43–44): 3861–9.

Pereira, Luiz C.B. (1999), 'Managerial Public Administration: Strategy and Structure for a New State', in Luiz Carlos Bresser and Peter Spink (eds), *Reforming the State: Managerial Public Administration in Latin America*, pp. 1–14. Boulder/London: Lynne Rienner.

Pierson, Paul (2000a), 'The Limits of Design: Explaining Institutional Origins and Change', *Governance*, 13(4): 475–99.

_________ (2000b), 'Not Just What, but When: Timing and Sequence in Political Process', *Studies in American Political Development*, 1(April): 72–92.

Rodrik, Dani (1998), 'Promises, Promises: Credible Policy Reform via Signaling', in Federico Sturzenegger and Mariano Tommasi (eds), *The Political Economy of Reform*, pp. 307–27. Cambridge, MA: The MIT Press.

Rustagi, Preet (ed.) (2009), *Concerns, Conflicts, and Cohesions: Universalization of Elementary Education in India*. New Delhi: Oxford University Press.

Schamis, Hector (2002), *Re-forming the State: The Politics of Privatization in Latin America and Europe*. Ann Arbor: University of Michigan Press.

Shah, Ghanshyam, Mario Rutten, and Hein Streefkerk (eds) (2002), *Development and Deprivation in Gujarat: In Honour of Jan Breman*. New Delhi: Sage.

Shinoda, Taskashi (ed.) (2002), *The Other Gujarat; Social Transformations Among the Weaker Sections*. Delhi: Popular Prakashan.

Sinha, Aseema (1999), 'From State to Market—via the State Governments: Horizontal Competition after 1991 in India', conference paper presented to Annual Conference on South Asia, Madison, Wisconsin.

_________ (2004), 'Ideas, Interests and Institutions in Policy Change in India: A Comparison of West Bengal and Gujarat', in Rob Jenkins (ed.), *Regional Reflections: Case Studies of Democracy in Practice*, pp. 66–108. New Delhi: Oxford University Press.

_________ (2005), *The Regional Roots of Developmental Politics in India: A Divided Leviathan*. Bloomington: Indiana University Press.

Snyder, Richard (1999), 'After Neoliberalism: The Politics of Re-Regulation in Mexico', *World Politics* 51(January): 173–204.

Solimano, Andrés, Osvaldo Sunkel, Mario I. Blejer (eds) (1994), *Rebuilding Capitalism: Alternative Roads after Socialism and Dirigisme*. Ann Arbor: University of Michigan Press.

Taleb, Nassim (2007), *The Black Swan: The Impact of the Highly Improbable*. New York: Random House.

Thelen, Kathleen (2000), 'Timing and Temporality in the Analysis of Institutional Evolution and Change', *Studies in American Political Development*, 14(Spring): 101–8.

_________ (2004), *How Institutions Evolve: The Political Economy of Skills in Germany, Britain, the United States, and Japan*. Cambridge: Cambridge University Press.

Venkatesan, R. and Sonalika Varma (1998), *Study on Policy Competition among States in India for Attracting Direct Investment*. New Delhi: NCAER.

Wade, Robert (1990), *Governing the Market: Economic Theory and the Role of Government in East Asian Industrialization*. New Jersey: Princeton University Press.

Wise, Carol (2003), *Reinventing the State: Economic Strategy and Institutional Change in Peru*. Ann Arbor: University of Michigan Press.

Yagnik, Achyut and Suchitra Sheth (2005), *The Shaping of Modern Gujarat: Plurality, Hindutva and Beyond*. New Delhi/London: Penguin Books.

5

Regulation and Infrastructure Development in India

Comparing Telecommunications, Ports, and Power

RAHUL MUKHERJI

This chapter analyses the reasons for differential performance in regulation and promotion of competition across three infrastructure sectors in India: telecommunications, ports, and power. Competent regulation in infrastructure was required to create an even playing field for private and public investment in order to promote competition, rationalize user charges, and to facilitate universal access. The challenge to this emanated from the clout of government-owned incumbents unwilling to surrender the privileges arising from their monopolies. This challenge was addressed by the creation of regulatory institutions which were expected to promote competition and fight monopolies. This chapter addresses the issue of why telecommunications, ports, and the power sector met with differential levels of success in regulatory consolidation.

Telecommunications, power, and ports constitute varying levels of success in regulatory consolidation. The regulator serves as a referee between the service provider and the policymaker, ensuring that these roles are kept discrete, and that all service providers enjoy a level playing field. This is a critical function in an economy that wishes to rely on the private sector to attract investment and engender efficiency. This chapter explores the possibility that different levels of success across sectors could lead to learning. Are there causes of regulatory consolidation common to the three sectors?

I chose three critical infrastructural sectors with varying degrees of regulatory success. The telecommunications sector has been the most successful in attracting private investment and in pushing the public sector to become efficient. Growing efficiency has catapulted India to the position of being one of the fastest growing and most efficient telecommunications markets in the world, a fact that has aided its competitiveness in information technology. Indian ports have attracted private investment, but well below the requirements of an emerging trader like India, constituting a middling level of success in utilizing markets to improve service delivery. The power sector has been the least transformed. I compare power sector regulation in Andhra Pradesh with West Bengal. These two states constitute varying degrees of success in power sector regulation.

The chapter points to factors that aided service delivery in telecommunications, power, and ports, especially the rise of more effective regulation. Improved regulation helped propel greater private investment, especially in telecommunications. How did the government carry out the politically daunting task of ushering in competition for its own enterprises? First, the history of policy ideas mattered. Sectors that had a history of home-grown reform ideas succeeded to a greater degree than others. The telecommunication sector was more fortunate in this respect than the ports sector.

Second, regulatory evolution depended on fiscal and financial crises.[1] The telecommunications, ports, and power sectors were opened to private investment because it was felt that the state should withdraw from areas where private investment could successfully provide services at a time when India was running large fiscal deficits and was faced with a balance of payments crisis in 1991. Financial crises helped reform ideas to embed themselves in politics and institutions. Third, political will at the level of the political chief executive and its ability to deal with the incumbents aided regulatory consolidation. Fourth, the nature of consumers of the particular infrastructure service also mattered. Consumers of telecommunications and ports services paid for their services, and lower tariffs led to increased access. These sectors were easier to reform from this perspective. The power sector, on the other hand, was affected by the clout of the rich farmer who could garner substantial votes. Fifth, technological evolution aided private sector consolidation in the telecommunications sector. The private sector had betted on GSM[2] cellular technology at a time when the public sector had not seen much business potential in this area. The success of this technology and the private sector's first mover's advantage in this industry sub-sector helped it survive the competition from the Department of Telecom (DoT).

This chapter describes how the interplay of these factors produced varying degrees of regulatory consolidation in telecommunications, ports, and the power sector in India.

THE TELECOM SECTOR: THE PROMOTION OF COMPETITION

India's telecommunications sector is one of the fastest growing markets in the world, which adds over 8 million new telephone lines every month. The growth has surpassed expectations. The new telecom policy of 1999 had set a tele-density target of 15 telephone lines per 100 people by 2010. In January 2010, India crossed the 580 million telephone mark and its tele-density per hundred people was 49.5 (data available with Telecom Regulatory Authority of India on http://www.trai.gov.in/Default.asp). India was adding more GSM mobile connections every year than China, and the telecommunications gap between India and China was narrowing. Telecommunications sectors have been transformed the world over in recent years, and India's telecommunications revolution is spectacular by global standards. How did India's democracy produce such a phenomenal success story? This is a story of enabling the private sector to compete with the government-owned service providers.

The Legacy of Good Policy Ideas and Practice

While India's telecommunications revolution has its immediate roots in the balance of payments crisis (1991) and the consequent withdrawal of the state from commercially viable sectors, the decade of the 1980s was important. The legacy of thinking within the Prime Minister's Office (PMO) was critical to the telecommunications transformation. There was an evolving conviction within Indira Gandhi's and Rajiv Gandhi's PMO that telecommunications was being neglected because it was being treated as a service for the elite. The Sarin Committee (1981) recommended the segregation of the DoT from the Department of Posts because postal services, which were considered to be friendlier to the common man, were the major concern of the Ministry of Communications. Separation would enable the government to focus attention on telecommunications.

The DoT was separated from the Department of Posts within the Ministry of Communications under the premiership of Rajiv Gandhi. This separation helped the ministry to focus its attention on developing telecommunications services in India. Second, Rajiv Gandhi took the efficiency consideration further by corporatizing[3] the parts of the DoT into the Mahanagar Telephone Nigam Limited (MTNL), which would serve the metropolitan areas of Delhi and Mumbai. Such was the extent of opposition to corporatization that the PMO had to set up a Telecommunications Restructuring Committee in 1989 to decide whether or not MTNL should be merged with the DoT. The DoT was unwilling to let parts of it function as an autonomous corporate entity. Third, Rajiv Gandhi took the initiative and created the Centre for the Development of Telematics (CDoT) for research and development of telecom switches. The Rural Automatic Exchange (RAX) switch developed by the CDoT competed favourably with the existing telecommunications switch jointly produced by the government-owned Indian Telephone Industries and the French company Alcatel. The CDoT switch, which was produced by a government organization, was licensed for private production. This was the first time that private manufacture of telecom switches was allowed in India. These switches serve a majority of the rural networks in India today.

These were important legacies on the eve of the balance of payments crisis because the Telecommunications Restructuring Committee (March 1991), which submitted its report before the crisis became full blown, had provided a clear blueprint for reforms in India's telecommunications sector. It had recommended the need for an independent regulator and separation between the policy and service provision function of the DoT. The report had also recommended that the government allow private entry in a phased manner in domestic, national long-distance, and international long-distance telephony, in that order. The next section will describe how these reforms would be realized after a decade, aided by financial crises.[4]

Financial Crises, Executive Orientation, and Regulation

Policy ideas needed financial crises for their implementation. The latter enabled the PMO and the Ministry of Finance (MoF) to fight the incumbent DoT, which would make token concessions that could have had disastrous consequences for the private sector. The National Telecom Policy (NTP) of 1994 was largely the result of pressure from the PMO and the MoF on the DoT, in the aftermath of the balance of payments crisis of 1991. The NTP 1994 allowed private sector entry in basic fixed telephony and did not recommend a regulator and could be viewed as a success of the PMO and the MoF over the DoT. The telecommunications minister at the time was averse to it.

The first major bidding process initiated in 1995 produced a litigious business environment. The size of the bid was the most important consideration for the award of a licence to the private operator, at a time when government-owned incumbents did not need to make any payments. Second, basic telephony, the area where the private sector had been invited to participate, was the least profitable part of the telecom business. These predatory characteristics of the bidding process, which loaded the dice against private sector participation, made it imperative for the government to create an independent regulator to establish a level playing field between the private and public sectors. The need for an independent regulator was stressed in an important judgment of the Supreme Court. The Telecom Regulatory Authority of India (TRAI) was born, despite political opposition, in 1997. Even though the consequences of the absence of a regulator were clearly spelt out by the Telecommunications Restructuring Committee in 1991, it had taken a financially messy investment situation for the government to implement the idea of independent regulation.

A regulator without substantial powers was born in 1997. The paucity of its legal powers notwithstanding technocratic competence was exposed when MTNL sought a free entry into the GSM cellular area at a time when the DoT's predatory behaviour mentioned earlier had already created a precarious financial situation for the private sector. A New Telecom Policy (NTP) in 1999 saved the day for private investors, aided by the efforts of Prime Minister Atal Bihari Vajpayee. The Vajpayee PMO played a stellar role by creating a technocratic Group on Telecommunications, which laid the basis for the NTP of 1999. Subsequently, the Group of Ministers implemented the ideas articulated in the NTP of 1999. The NTP paved the way for accommodating MTNL while bailing out the private sector by giving concessions on the licence fee requirement.

A strengthened regulatory institution was born in 2000, aided by the NTP and work done by the Group of Ministers. The TRAI was given a greater say in licensing under its new constitution in 2000. It was now mandatory for the government to seek the recommendation of the TRAI, even though the final decision lay with the former. A Telecom Dispute Settlement Appellate Tribunal (TDSAT) was established. The TDSAT was given the status of a high court with the authority to arbitrate disputes between the DoT and service providers. The only higher court of appeal would be the Supreme Court of India.[5]

The interplay of ideas, rationality, and crisis is an integral part of the reform story. Sound policy ideas make gradual and sub-optimal progress within the political economy in normal times. However, when new ideas such as private sector participation in infrastructure lead to a financial crisis resulting from inadequate regulatory institutions, politics opens up the path for institutional change. The PMO played a critical role in disciplining the DoT by strengthening regulation.

It was the promotion of competition between the CDMA and GSM cellular operators, and between the government and the private sector, that unleashed the genie of competition, low tariffs, and booming teledensity in India. The consolidation of the TRAI and the birth of TDSAT were central to this story.[6]

The Role of Technology

Private sector participation in telecommunications was aided by the phenomenal development of GSM cellular technology for two reasons. First, GSM telephony had attracted the attention of the private sector at a time when the DoT thought that it would be a small niche area for a few people. The DoT had not foreseen significant market potential and had not expressed an interest in entering the GSM cellular business till 1998. This provided the private sector with a first mover's advantage. Second, cellular telephony reduced the capital requirements for promoting telecom operations. Laying telephone lines entailed technical, manpower, and administrative costs that could have been prohibitive for the private sector. Therefore, cellular technology saved the day for the private sector by making telecommunications service provision a less capital intensive business activity (Desai 2006: 23–8; Mukherji 2009). This is the area where private sector growth is most significant.

The Role of Foreign Investment

Between 1998 and 2004, regulatory decisions supported the large cellular operators who had betted on the CDMA technology. Cash-rich service providers with investments in CDMA technology did not need foreign investment. The foreign equity limit could not be raised above 49 per cent, and entry barriers such as the long-distance licence fee remained very high during this period.

The regulatory environment changed substantially to support the smaller but efficient telephone operators after 2004. Considerable effort was expended to make the regulatory playing field favourable for the smaller GSM operators. This increased competition orientation in the sector and led to significant export-oriented investments in the manufacture of mobile handsets by companies such as Nokia and Motorola.

Two significant decisions created a favourable regulatory environment for the smaller GSM operators. Between 2004 and 2006, the foreign equity limit was raised from 49 to 74 per cent. This aided telephone operators like Bharti's Airtel, whose ability to compete with the larger operators had depended on the infusion of foreign capital. Second, reduced entry barriers also favoured the smaller operators and increased the competition in the sector. The national long-distance service licence fee was reduced from Rs 1 billion to Rs 25 million and the international long-distance licence fee from Rs 250 million to Rs 25 million. The entry of foreign capital and a reduction in entry barriers increased competition by enhancing the ability of the smaller operators to compete with the bigger ones (Mukherji 2008).

A telecom ministry promoting competition and foreign investment was a significant change from the times when the PMO had to assume the telecom portfolio because telecom ministers were typically averse to competition and the private sector. This signalled the arrival of a new era when competition orientation began characterizing the telecom bureaucracy.

In Sum

India's mobile telephony revolution points to the importance of good policy ideas, rationality, financial crises, technology, and political will as contributors to successful regulatory evolution in telecommunications. First, the engagement with good policy ideas was important. Second, crisis aided the process of converting good ideas into policy and regulatory institutions. Third, this process was aided by significant political will within the PMO and the MoF. As the sector got adjusted to private sector participation and competition, the DoT, which had historically opposed the private sector, became a promoter of private and foreign investment.

Last but not the least, technology played a silent role in promoting the private sector and competition orientation. Cellular technology reduced the capital costs entailed in spreading telecommunications. Cellular technology had the unintended consequence of promoting competition because this was an area for which private operators opted when the government had not realized its potential. This first mover's advantage helped the private operators to deal with the predatory behaviour of the DoT during the initial stages of reform.

This largely successful story faces two serious challenges. The executive has reasons for favouring one set of private operators over others.

A powerful regulatory set-up would guard against monopoly-generating propensities within the government. Such an independent regulatory institution may not yet have evolved in India. Second, the promotion of tele-density has served the rich and the middle class to a greater extent than the poor. The trickle-down effect in rural tele-density is Pareto optimal[7] but it is also contributing to the growing rural–urban divide.

THE PORTS SECTOR[8]

India's trade-dependent globalization is seriously in need of investment in ports. India's trade to gross domestic product (GDP) ratio has grown after 1990. This was also the period of its economic globalization and high economic growth. Whereas the Indian economy grew just over 5 per cent between 1975 and 1990, the growth rate accelerated to over 6 per cent between 1991 and 2004. India has grown at a rate greater than 8.5 per cent between after 2003, making it the second fastest growing economy after China. Even though India's trade dependence is considerably lower than that of China and Korea, its trade dependence has overtaken that of the US and Japan. China's higher trade dependence has sustained a 9–10 per cent growth rate since the early 1980s. India's economic growth driven by trade is a phenomenon that gathered momentum after 1991.

India's trade needed substantial investment in port infrastructure, and the government invited the private sector to participate in this endeavour. This section will discuss how this happened and the substantial challenges for the regulation of investment in Indian ports. This chapter codes regulation in the ports sector as a middling level of success.

India's ports carry 95 per cent of its trade by volume and 70 per cent in terms of value. India has 12 major ports, six each on the west and east coast. It also has 45 private and minor ports. The major ports fall under the governance of the Department of Shipping (DoS) located within the Ministry of Shipping, Road Transport and Highways. The non-major ports are often governed by state governments and are gradually beginning to challenge the jurisdiction of the state governments (Ministry of Shipping, Road Transport and Highways 2006: 1–5; Ghosh and De 2001: 3273–4).

The Committee on Infrastructure (July 2007) within the Planning Commission estimates an investment need of approximately Rs 933.8 billion in the ports sector to keep up with the need for increased capacity of 1,002 million metric tons (mmt) by 2011–12. Approximately 73 per cent of this investment is expected from the private sector. The fiscal constraints on the state and efficiency considerations demand public–private partnership in infrastructure development. The success of the ports sector depends to a great extent on the degree to which private investors are comfortable with the regulatory environment (Planning Commission 2007a: 3–6).

The poor quality of Indian ports is adversely affecting its trade. In 2004–5 three-quarters of India's trade passed through its major ports. The average dwell time[9] of cargo in Indian ports is 1.8 days for imports and 3.78 days for exports. The same figure for imports and exports is 0.85 days in Singapore. While port authorities take three to five hours for their work in India, the rest of the time is consumed by shipping, customs, and transport agents. Large vessels often cannot berth in Indian ports because of the shallow draft. Indian exporters trans-ship their merchandise to Colombo, Singapore, and Dubai for goods to be shipped to other parts of the world. Forty per cent of the total container traffic handled by Colombo is trans-shipped from India. Trans-shipment costs naturally increase the costs for Indian exporters and importers (Ghosh and De 2001: 3279–81; *Economic and Political Weekly* 2004).

Public–private partnership in infrastructure is premised upon a regulatory environment within which private enterprise feels comfortable about the certainty of its investment. It demands a regulatory structure separating the policymaker, regulator, and the service provider. The regulatory evolution in the ports sector is primitive in comparison with that in the telecommunications sector. The DoS is in charge of the bidding process. The Tariff Authority for Major Ports (TAMP), which is a tariff-setting authority with no licensing powers, is guided by the interests of the DoS. TAMP depends on the ministry for its appointments and financial resources. TAMP and its orders can be interfered with and reversed by the DoS. This section will demonstrate that the ports sector in India is in a primitive state of regulatory evolution in comparison with the telecommunications sector.

Ports should be more amenable to efficient market regulation than the power or the telecommunications sector in India. The success of the Indian telecommunications sector, driven by the GSM cellular technology and the promotion of competition, has been brilliant in urban settings where markets work very well given the economies of scale, but to a much lesser extent in rural settings where such economies cannot be easily realized. India's banks and stock markets have been reformed substantially because the markets could be reformed to serve urban middle-class customers. The ports sector serves customers who are willing to pay tariffs and would benefit from competition. This should make it easy for the ports sector reforms to succeed. Why has private sector participation in ports been lukewarm in relation to India's investment needs?

The limited success of India's ports sector in relation to other ports in the region, such as Colombo, Bangkok, Shanghai, Hong Kong, and Singapore, and in relation to other infrastructure sectors requires explanation.[10] The government's provision of 100 per cent foreign equity in the ports sector, a 10-year tax holiday, the absence of Malaysian *bhumiputra*-type policies that favour national investors, and customs duty concessions for the import of capital goods helped to attract foreign and Indian investors in India's port sector.[11] Foreign companies such as the Port of Singapore Authority, Dubai Ports World, and AP Moeller-Maersk are actively involved in the sector. Indian companies such as Larsen & Toubro, Tata Steel, Gammon, Shapoorji Pallonji, and Adani were also involved with the ports sector.

Private Sector Participation and Competitiveness

Private sector participation has pushed the government to become more competitive. The DoS and the World Bank both began drawing attention to port sector reforms and private sector participation in the mid-1980s, at a time when the shipping traffic was seriously beginning to challenge India's port infrastructure.[12] Initially the government wanted to lease out existing public sector assets to the private sector to enable to it to operate the ports more efficiently.

The status quo bias favouring inefficient ports was supported by port trusts, which were largely governed by representatives of the government and trade unions. Cargo stored in a port for a long time earned trust demurrage charges for the port trusts. Surpluses were overestimated due to flawed accounting practices, and profitability was of no concern. Organized labour benefited from overstaffing and was a powerful lobby favouring the status quo. Speed money passing hands to getting work done was a usual practice in connivance with the port authorities. Private participation in the port sector would erode the DoS's control over business in the sector.

The Jawaharlal Nehru Port Trust (JNPT) in Mumbai was chosen as the first site for reforms because it was one of the better managed ports at the time when reforms were initiated. The port was set up in 1989 with funds from various agencies, including the World Bank. It had modern container and bulk-handling facilities and enjoyed superior connectivity to the hinterland. Terminal charges at the port were relatively low and labour was productive because there was no Dock Labour Board to recruit the workforce. A modern port could do away with some legacies of the past like the Dock Labour Board.[13] The evolution of the JNPT in the pre-reform period is evidence of India's willingness to reform the sector even prior to 1991 when it was faced with a severe balance of payments crisis and a fiscal crunch.

Politics ensured that JNPT's existing facilities would not be privatized but a new private container terminal would be permitted. The initial intention was to contract the JNPT container terminal to private operators. The JNPT board, 10 out of 19 of whose members represented the government and the unions, resented the idea of letting a government asset pass into private hands. Instead, private participation was sought for the creation of a new container terminal. JNPT issued a global tender for the construction of a new two-berth container terminal for an estimated investment of Rs 9 billion. P&O Ports, Australia, was granted the tender and the new container terminal was christened Nhava Sheva International Container Terminal (NSICT). This was quite an achievement considering that bidding in India is marred by delays and deliberate ambiguities favouring incumbents and to garner rents.

NSICT was to follow the globally practised landlord port model. JNPT as the landlord port would be responsible for the overall activities, such as scheduling entry, dredging, navigation safety, supply of electricity and water, while the NSICT would build, operate, and maintain equipment in the new terminal. The landlord port would earn a royalty from the tenant, which would form part of its revenues. It would also obtain the facilities free of cost at the end of the concession period.

Competition between the JNPT and the NSICT was a healthy development. The NSICT set new standards in performance and began diverting traffic from the Jawaharlal Nehru Port Container Terminal (JNPCT). JNPCT responded by capacity expansion: obtaining new cranes, creating a new shallow draft berth, and by converting idle tracks into operational container tracks. Two leading public sector oil companies were invited to develop a liquid cargo handling facility capable of dealing with 5.5 million tons of cargo. Capital restructuring was initiated, as were official incentive schemes for workers. These practices replaced unethical ones such as obtaining speed money for the performance of ordinary jobs. A scheme was initiated to ensure that there would not be any break between the shifts. These reforms were supported by the JNPT authority because it had to respond to the superior performance of the NSICT.[14]

Flawed Bidding Procedure

The port sector in India is facing a challenge today that is reminiscent of that faced by the telecommunications sector prior to the consolidation of TRAI in 2000. Before the consolidation of TRAI, telecommunications bids were weighted excessively towards the highest bidder. Operational experience and service criteria were not the principal considerations for award of a bid. In addition, there is the problem of lack of transparency in the bidding procedure and allegations of rent-seeking. This scenario led to a major crisis of investment by 1998. The private sector had bid unreasonable amounts, which was a tax that the government did not have to pay. Moreover, the government-owned MTNL was granted a free licence to enter GSM cellular telephony at a time when the private sector's finances were somewhat precarious, and the Delhi High Court ruled that the regulator's (TRAI's) intervention was not justified. At this stage, the Industrial Credit and Investment Corporation of India (ICICI) and the Bureau of Industrial Costs and Prices were of the view that it was the faulty bidding procedure rather than operational inefficiency that had led to the crisis. ICICI, a government-owned financial organization, would know because it was involved in financing private sector telecommunications operators in India. The consequence of the faulty bidding procedure was that the private sector had to be bailed out of the crisis via the New Telecom Policy of 1999 and the regulatory institution had to be strengthened. New telecommunications licences would now need regulatory consultation.[15]

The ports sector is in a primitive stage of regulatory evolution in comparison with its telecommunications counterpart. The bidding process in the ports sector today is reminiscent of that in the telecommunications sector in the mid-1990s, which created a crisis for private sector organizations by 1998. As the bidding process is entirely in its hands, the DoS—like the DoT of the mid-1990s—has an interest in earning high royalty payments for the Port Trust, which are largely controlled by the DoS. The higher the bid, the greater is the tax on the new private operators, which the government-owned terminals do not have to pay, and the greater is the earning potential of the port trusts. The highest royalty bid rule is encouraging private sector operators to make unreasonably high bids, and to agree to share 35–50 per cent of revenues as royalty with the landlord port. Although it is difficult to report the precise financial details of the major shipping companies in India, there is little doubt that the bidding procedure is seriously hurting the financial position of the private operators.[16]

There is an easy solution to this problem, of using royalty as a tool to maximize port productivity rather than maximizing the revenue of the port trust. Royalty could be pegged at a certain fixed level, depending on the quality of infrastructure available to the terminal operators. The lowest royalty could be paid by an operator who was given a water body for development. Royalty payment to the port trusts could increase depending upon whether the water body also came with land, and the extent to which this land was developed for terminal operations.

Shipping companies were making bids, notwithstanding the faulty bidding incentives, for two reasons. The first is that the operators were convinced that the growth in the Indian economy and its trade would remain a reasonably sustainable phenomenon and that India would evolve as a major market for the shipping business. Second, there is the hope that there will be a bail-out when the financial crisis spirals out of proportion. The assumption is that the ports sector will enjoy the same consideration from the government in the event of a financial crisis as was the case with the telecommunications and insurance sectors.

Tariff-setting Procedures

There are a number of problems with the tariff-setting procedures followed by the TAMP, which create the wrong incentives for private investment in Indian ports. Tariff-setting, like bidding procedures, can be used to curb the profitability of the private sector. The regulator has to tread the thin line between initiating competition and reducing tariffs, while at the same time ensuring that terminal operators remain profitable. This section details a number of ways in which excessive curbs are being placed on the profitability of the private sector as a consequence of the rule governing the tariff-setting procedure.

First, the most serious problem is that of not viewing royalty payment to the landlord port, pledged in the bid document, as a cost for the calculation of tariff. If royalty were treated as cost, this would lead to a rise in the permissible tariff level stipulated by TAMP. Private operators would welcome a more generous tariff ceiling if the DoS allowed royalty to be treated as a part of cost in assessing tariffs.[17]

There is a contradiction in the approach of the DoS, which encourages high bids but does not allow royalty payments to be treated as part of the cost for determination of the tariff. If the department was really concerned about low tariffs, it would award a bid based on service expectations rather than the value of a bid. This would help keep the bidder's costs at a reasonable level, especially because royalty payment is a regular payment made to the landlord port, representing a proportion of revenues collected by the terminal operator. Encouraging private operators to bid a high royalty figure by designing bidding rules that award a terminal to the highest bidder, and then ruling that royalty is not a part of cost is a predatory stipulation. This would make it tough for private operators to survive and discourage them from making the kind of financial commitments that are the stated goals of the National Maritime Development Programme.

Second, port tariffs are determined by TAMP by evaluating actual costs, which recognize capital and operating costs and a 16 per cent rate of return on capital employed. This leads to a second problem of incentives.[18] The terminal operator has an incentive to inflate the costs of handling cargo at a terminal. High cost and declaration of low commercial traffic would yield a high tariff calculation by TAMP. This tariff-setting procedure can lead to over-investment. There is no incentive to realize economies of scale because the rate of return on capital is fixed, no matter what the volume of business might be.

Current tariff-setting stipulations have led to a scenario where different terminals within the jurisdiction of the same landlord port are often stipulated to charge differential maximum tariffs by TAMP, none of which comprehensively cover costs. Let us conceive of an Indian port with three terminals, I, II and III, which are permitted to charge Rs 3,000 per TEU,[19] Rs 3,500 per TEU, and Rs 4,000 per TEU, respectively. The double tragedy of low and differential tariffs is that terminal I may have to exit business because Rs 3,000 per TEU does not cover its costs. On the other hand, terminals II and III will lose business to terminal I and may also be forced out of business.

Third, the Report of the National Working Group on Normative Cost-Based Tariff for Container Related Charges (see Prabhakaran 2005) suggests that while normative cost-based tariff may be difficult to calculate, normative capacity is not. A suggestion made by the Indian Private Ports and Terminals Association worth considering is that a methodology for determining a floor and ceiling level for tariffs can be worked out based on the normative capacity 113,100 TEU per quay crane.[20] The floor tariff could constitute costs plus a reasonable rate of return on capital at 100 per cent of normative capacity; and the ceiling tariff could equal costs plus the rate of return on capital at 60 per cent normative capacity. The ceiling tariff will both protect the consumers from monopolistic propensities and service providers in times of low business. Also, the floor tariff will guard the consumers against the emergence of predatory pricing.

There is a need to evolve a methodology for the determination of tariffs that is favourable for investment, consumers, and producers. It is possible that with optimal investment, economies of scale, the inclusion of royalty as cost, and allowance for a higher rate of return on capital, tariffs may fall and revenues and royalty payments may become more buoyant. This is an area that requires serious investigation as it has implications for a firm's profitability, investible resources, and tariffs. Ultimately, it is the efficiency and availability of Indian container terminals that will draw traffic away from ports such as Colombo towards Indian ports.

The telecom sector tariffs have fallen as the revenue share amount has progressively decreased. The boom in the telecom sector has ensured that the growth of business in the sector has more than compensated for the loss due to reduction in revenue share.

Fourth, even though India has one of the lowest cargo charges in the world, it suffers from one of the highest vessel-related charges. Vessel-related charges are levied by port trusts that govern the landlord port. While the competitive tariff regime could push down cargo charges through the promotion of competition discussed earlier, the landlord port should submit itself to internationally competitive vessel-related charges. These charges can easily be benchmarked against those prevalent in busier ports like Colombo, Bangkok, or Singapore. Reasonable vessel-related charges will bring more trade to India.

There is no reason to push competition differentially in the cargo-handling area and in the area of vessel-related charges because the former is operated by the private sector while the latter is governed by port trusts under the control of the DoS, which are not easily amenable to corporatization. Corporatization of port trusts would free them from government control and enable them to work profitably. If vessel-related charges in Colombo are lower than those in the neighbouring ports of Tuticorin and Cochin, this would naturally divert valuable traffic to Colombo. India needs to move towards internationally competitive vessel-related charges in all its ports.

Corporatization and Minor Ports

Corporatization of port trusts is central to the evolution of good governance within them, and this would imply a transition from a government agency to a public company based on sound management principles. This would imply that ports are governed by independent directors rather than by those largely representing the interests of the DoS. Better management of the landlord port will improve port infrastructure and lead to a reduction in vessel-related charges that are debilitating the business today. Ennore is today the only major port in India that has been corporatized. It needs to be examined why this single port could be corporatized and whether corporatization has occurred both in letter and spirit.

Competitive pressures to improve port infrastructure and efficiency have arisen not only from the ports of neighbouring countries but also from minor ports being developed by state governments in India. State-level port development is aided by the fact that ports are a subject in the Concurrent List of the Indian Constitution, which gives them powers to develop ports within their territorial jurisdiction. This has enabled the governments of states like Gujarat and Maharashtra to take the initiative in this area and develop their maritime ports. These state governments attract investors by providing them better incentives than those provided by the Central government. The Mundra Port in Gujarat developed by the Adanis is regarded as a success story.

The strategy of developing minor ports by the states could increase fragmentation and debilitate a coherent national-level vision for developing Indian ports. Ports demand physical and financial infrastructure and logistics. Centre–state cooperation would be in the best interest of developing ports on the east and west coasts of India, and to link them to the hinterland with adequate road and rail networks. A situation that empowers state governments, because of the flaws in the bidding, tariff-setting, and governance mechanisms of the major ports under the jurisdiction of the DoS, could lead to fragmented port development driven by exigencies and state capacities to attract investment.

In Sum

The DoS continues to be more predatory towards private investment than the DoT. This is evident from the bidding procedures and royalty payments pledged by private terminal operators. Second, this is reflected in the predatory nature of tariff-setting procedures. Third, port trusts representing the DoS in the governance of the landlord port are unwilling to accept competition. They successfully avoid corporatization and refuse to be disciplined by considerations of efficiency. While India's telecom sector is among the most efficient in the world, India's major ports are challenged by other ports in Asia and by minor ports controlled by the state governments.

How can one explain this difference? First, there seemed to be a relative lack of reform ideas and attempts in the ports sector, when compared with the initiatives pursued by Rajiv Gandhi in the telecom sector. The reforms of JNPT were important, but these were also supported to a greater extent by the World Bank and were not an entirely home-grown effort.

Second, one did not find in the ports sector the kind of involvement of the PMO which pushed the telecommunications sector towards reform. While the prime minister took over direct charge of the telecom portfolio during critical phases of the reform, this was not the case in the ports sector.

Third, the predatory behaviour of the DoT resulted in a series of financial crises for the private sector, which aided regulatory consolidation of the telecom sector. The story described points to the genesis of a crisis in the ports sector. It remains to be seen whether this crisis will muster sufficient political will to direct regulatory consolidation of the sector.

Telecommunications services were critical to India's service and IT trade. The manufacturing sector needed ports as acutely as the service sector needed telecommunications. If India's growth is to become more inclusive, port-dependant labour-intensive manufacturing growth will be critical to its success. Public–private partnerships are essential to reduce the transaction costs for Indian exporters and importers. The port sector perhaps requires greater involvement of the PMO to discipline the DoS into accepting competition by promoting regulatory consolidation.

THE POWER SECTOR

The power sector was served largely by government-owned utilities prior to 1991. The Central public sector undertakings were actively involved with the generation of electricity, and the state electricity boards were involved with the generation, transmission, and distribution of electricity on the eve of the reforms, which began in the mid-1990s. State-level governance has been critical for this sector. Fiscal populism in the 1980s, which encouraged free electricity to farmers and permitted theft of electricity, contributed substantially to India's fiscal crisis and had an impact on the balance of payments crisis in 1991. The fiscal crisis, negative creditor sentiment, and the balance of payments crisis made the sector an ideal candidate for reforms. Why could India's power sector, which enjoyed a great deal of attention from the Government of India and multilateral agencies such as the World Bank, not be reformed substantially? What factors impeded regulatory consolidation in the power sector?

This chapter seeks to answer these questions by analysing two Indian states: Andhra Pradesh (AP) and West Bengal (WB). AP has consistently been rated as a top reformer. These cases reveal that structural reforms in

India are path-dependent. AP was committed to reform ideas even prior to the involvement of the World Bank, and this might have promoted synergies between the Bank and the Government of Andhra Pradesh (GoAP). The reforms have been aided by an excellent track record in generation and governance of the power sector. The challenge for reforms in AP lies with the political economy of Indian agriculture. Being a drought-prone state, and the first that offered free electricity to farmers in the early 1980s, it continues to offer free but poor-quality electricity, even though there is clinching evidence that free electricity largely benefits the rich and the middle farmers to the detriment of the small and marginal farmers. Power generated by the private generating companies is more expensive than that of the public utilities. The expensive power purchase agreements contribute to the subsidy burden of the government. Good governance of the state-owned utilities has lured industrial consumers towards electricity generated by the government, a factor that has helped cross-subsidize free electricity to farmers. Civil society organizations are quite vigilant in AP.

The WB case is a study in contrast. Regulation and restructuring occurred much later in WB. Being sufficiently rain-fed, free power for irrigation was less of a political issue and agricultural subsidy less of a problem in the state. In WB, the state-owned generation companies were quite inefficient and the government was averse to the idea of independent power producers in the private sector. WB had a positive legacy of competition given the presence of the Calcutta Electric Supply Corporation (CESC), which had been an efficient private sector operator in urban areas since colonial times. The state also benefited from the power being generated by the centrally owned Damodar Valley Corporation (DVC). WB was not hungry for power because of low agricultural and industrial demand. The state was able to garner resources by selling power to the central grid at a high price, notwithstanding inefficient generation by the state-owned generating companies (gencos). There was a relative lack of coordination and engagement between the state utilities, the regulator, and civil society organizations in WB, in contrast to AP. Private sector generation was much less significant in WB, if one excludes the CESC.

Andhra Pradesh

This section is divided into three parts: (1) the positive ideational legacies that contributed to AP's relatively stellar performance in the power sector; (2) achievements and challenges; and (3) the lessons learnt about the political economy of reforms.

Reform Ideas

In April 1995, the *Report of the High Level Committee: Guidelines on Restructuring and Privatisation of Power Sector and Power Tariff* was a significant development to thinking on power sector reforms. The committee, chaired by a former secretary of the Central Electricity Authority, reflected the technocratic competence within the GoAP in the mid-1990s. The report was aided by the expertise available at the Administrative Staff College of India, Hyderabad.[21] This report's penetrating insights came a year after the *Report of the National Development Council Committee on Power* sponsored by the Planning Commission.[22] The report highlighted (1) the problem of agriculture tariffs; (2) the need for captive generation and private independent power producers in the light of the fiscal crunch; (3) the need to unbundle the utilities; (4) the need for a regulator, especially to rationalize the tariff-setting process; and (5) the need for newer technology and improved governance to reduce electricity theft. AP was fortunate to have sophisticated thinking on power sector reforms before entering into an agreement with the World Bank in 1996. Sophisticated policy ideas within the GoAP contributed towards averting some of the blunders that occurred in Orissa. While the report would support many aspects of the World Bank agenda, its views were quite independent of the Bank.

One of the positive pre-reform legacies was the superior performance of the AP State Electricity Board's thermal power plants. These plants enjoyed a higher plant load factor[23] over the national average of similar power plants. Private participation would not replace inefficient generation in AP. This legacy endures, as AP's state-owned generating and transmission companies maintain their reputation of being India's pre-eminent performers (Bhaya 1995: 16–23).

The report's prescriptions were ahead of their time in their view of the role of the private sector. It encouraged private sector participation in generation but cautioned against the higher costs of private generation. It was of the view that higher costs would result from foreign collaboration, technical fees, and imported equipment.[24] The private sector was to ease the financial strain of greater investment and was to promote competition. Even though the AP State Electricity Board would buy power from the private generator, the committee was against a guarantee of any kind.

The latter also wanted private gencos to get involved with the transmission and distribution process. It was opined that linking the distribution licence with generation could make it more attractive for the private sector rather than the offer of an exclusive distribution licence, and also relieve the government of its obligations. Policies proved to be different from this prescription. The high cost of power purchase agreements with the private sector continue to exacerbate the fiscal strain on the state (Bhaya 1995: chapter 4).

The report spoke about the virtues of the High Voltage Distribution System (HVDS) and recommended it as being better suited to Indian conditions than the Low Voltage Distribution System (LVDS). The HVDS was a system of distributing electricity that could technically reduce theft in urban areas. It was argued that HVDS, based on North American practice, was more appropriate for scattered loads, which was characteristic of the Indian environment. HVDS could reduce energy losses, distribution transformer failure, electricity theft, and voltage fluctuation, and increase the reliability of supply by reducing the incidence of motor burnout. The HVDS has been initiated in AP as part of its reform policies (Bhaya 1995: 54–9).

The report had noted the importance of industry cross-subsidizing agriculture. Industrial consumption (32 per cent) was cross-subsidizing agriculture and domestic consumption (57 per cent). The agricultural sector paid Rs 0.06 per unit out of an actual cost of Rs 1.26 per unit. The sector was receiving a subsidy of Rs 10 billion (Bhaya 1995: 51–2). AP's agricultural tariff was among the lowest in India. The report pointed out the need for a strategy for either increasing industrial consumption or increasing tariffs on agriculture (Bhaya 1995: chapter 8). One of the successes of AP has been its ability to retain industrial users, which is useful for cross-subsidizing electricity to agriculture.

The committee had a detailed plan for unbundling the AP State Electricity Board into AP Power Corporation, AP Transmission Corporation, and regional distribution companies. Distribution had to be divided into smaller and manageable units. The committee opined that the regulator needed to take an objective view of the level of burden-sharing by each category of customer. It also pointed out the dilemma of regulation in the sector that 40–5 per cent of the customers who did not contribute to the revenues could not be cross-subsidized forever (Bhaya 1995: chapters 7 and 9). The report had thus pointed out to one of the limits of regulating tariffs, as tariffs were a highly politicized issue. This challenge of free electricity to farmers is the single most important challenge facing

AP, notwithstanding a high level of regulatory competence within the AP Electricity Regulatory Commission.

Achievements and Challenges

Andhra Pradesh followed a remarkable reform time-table. The relationship with the World Bank was born in the mid-1990s. The AP Electricity Reform Act came into force in 1998; the AP State Electricity Board was unbundled into APGENCO and APTRANSCO (Transmission Corporation of Andhra Pradesh Limited) in 1999; the Andhra Pradesh Electricity Regulatory Commission (APERC) was formed in 1999, with public hearings initiated that very year; and the first tariff order of the APERC was issued in 2000. The tariff order, which hiked domestic charges, led to violent protest. APTRANSCO was further unbundled into four distribution companies in 2000.[25]

Statesmanship and Regulation The chief minister of AP from 1995 to 2004, Chandra Babu Naidu, had a strong interest in power sector reform.[26] He afforded a reasonable degree of independence to the utilities and the regulator. Naidu saw the benefit of a relationship with the World Bank in pushing the domestic reform agenda. Unbundling and regulation were as much a part of the Hiten Bhaya Report (see Bhaya 1995) as they were a part of the World Bank agenda. Even though agriculture tariffs remained a political issue, farmers paid a subsidized tariff and enjoyed electricity supply of some quality till 2004.[27]

G.P. Rao was the fiercely independent first chairman of the APERC. He had served the Central government with distinction in areas such as commerce, defence, and rural development before accepting the chairmanship of the newly found APERC. Rao had engineered a financial turnaround in Singareni Collieries during his tenure within the state as an AP cadre Indian Administrative Service (IAS) officer. There was mutual respect in the relationship between the regulator and the chief minister. Having retired as a senior civil servant, the regulator had a reasonable understanding of the extent to which the theoretical aspects of regulation, such as open access and rational tariffs, could be embedded in the political reality of vote-bank politics.[28]

It was at the regulator's insistence that the BPL[29] power purchase agreement did not come through during the Naidu tenure because the profit margin quoted was too high. A rent-seeking propensity is rampant in India's political system and is often manifested in power purchase agreements. However, if the chief minister is willing to put up with checks and balances, these propensities can be curbed to some degree, and ways of curbing them deserve serious policy attention.

The regulator was positive about the relationship between the World Bank and the GoAP. World Bank funds were liberally used to build regulatory competence, and this has been extensively discussed in the literature.[30] The APERC developed a fair degree of tariff-setting competence. Second, World Bank funds were used for improving systems that curbed transmission and distribution losses. These systems aided the process of reducing transmission losses.

The regulator succeeded remarkably in allowing a diversity of civil society groups into the process of consultation. Critical left-wing newspapers, such as *Prajashakti*, were actively involved in criticizing the rent-seeking propensities that marred the process of agreements with private generating companies. A non-governmental organization (at the time), *Lok Satta*, was involved with improved governance of power supply to agricultural households in villages.[31] This is the kind of grassroots level work that holds out the promise of metering electricity consumption. Metering consumption is the first step towards charging a progressive tariff on agricultural consumption. The Communist Party of India's Farmer's Federation and the Federation of Farmers Association were also involved in discussions about the costs and benefits of free electricity to agriculture.

A competent regulator as a civil servant opens up possibilities of gradual reform within the constraints posed by the political system. Independence is derived from competence and the autonomy that the chief minister is willing to grant in return for systemic reforms. However, both the chief minister and a retired civil servant as a regulator accepted the larger political constraints, which can only be gradually tweaked. Two politically charged areas discussed later, which demanded substantial policy attention, were (1) the rationalization of agriculture tariffs, and (2) greater oversight over power purchase agreements between private generators and the GoAP.

The telecom experience demonstrates the importance of the first regulator's personality in embedding institutional values. The first telecom regulator Justice S.S. Sodhi and his vice-chair Ambassador B.K. Zutshi were deeply committed to promoting private sector competition. They challenged the DoT in matters which the courts opined were beyond their regulatory jurisdiction (Mukherji 2007b: 310–11). A committed regulator without licensing and adjudicatory powers may have lent a competition-promoting personality to the institution, which may have had an impact on the performance of regulators who followed the Sodhi–Zutshi team (Mukherji 2009). The regulatory team at the APERC was one that was independent within its limited political and legal mandate. The political circumstances allowed some rationality in tariff setting within the political boundaries set by the government. It also allowed the regulator to intervene to a limited degree in power purchase agreements and encouraged stakeholder consultations.

APGENCO and Independent Power Producers: An Uneven Playing Field The history of efficient governance of the AP State Electricity Board was useful in sustaining good governance in post-reform AP. The tariff order of March 2008 noted that APGENCO, the unbundled government-owned generating company, continued to maintain a high level of efficiency with a plant load factor of 84 per cent (April 2007–January 2008) (APERC 2008: 64–5; figures provided to author by APTRANSCO and APGENCO in December 2007). From 2000–1 to 2006–7 APGENCO maintained a plant load factor greater than 85 per cent in all the years except in 2005–6. This was substantially higher than the national average, and APGENCO was ranked first among all the government utilities in three out of the seven years.[32] The per unit cost of power from the APGENCO between 1998–9 and 2005–6 at Rs 1.44 was much lower than the cost of purchasing power from the independent power producers.[33] The best practices of APGENCO included its ability to acquire high quality coal, energy auditing, access to captive mines, setting up coal washeries, and attention to creating green belts to curb greenhouse gases.

Private sector participation is not an end in itself. Rather, it is a means to generate resources and engender efficiency. Reforms seem to have been a spoiler for the relatively efficient generation within the APGENCO. Electricity generation by the government sector grew by 13.57 per cent between 1980–1 and 1990–1. The growth figures for state government-owned utility declined substantially to 6.94 per cent and –9.2 per cent during the period 1991–2 to 1999–2000 and 2000–1 to 2005–6, respectively (Pani et al., 2007: 24).

There is reason to be concerned about the decline of a healthy low-cost producer in the government sector. There are several reasons for APGENCO's relatively slower growth in recent years. APGENCO enjoys less favourable purchase and payment options from the APTRANSCO in comparison with those that independent power producers receive. APGENCO is not allowed a minimum rate of return on equity whereas the private sector is allowed an assured 16 per cent rate on equity. Incentives were added to APGENCOs variable costs, whereas they were shown separately for the independent power producers (IPPs).

APGENCO suffered financially at the time of unbundling. In order to make the distribution companies attractive for privatization, all the debts of the AP State Electricity Board arising from the terminal benefits of retiring employees were shifted to APGENCO. This occurred even though these employees were moved to different unbundled units such as APGENCO, APTRANSCO, and the distribution companies. An efficient government sector undertaking was thus pushed towards an uneven financial playing field (Pani et al. 2007: 24).

The higher costs of the private generators were taking a toll on the state's finances. The inflated capital costs of the private generation companies were a major problem. To give one example, the Andhra Pradesh Gas Power Corporation Limited (APGPCL), which is a joint sector company involving the government and the private sector, was generating power at the rate of Rs 24.1 million per megawatt (MW) whereas the private sector-owned Spectrum project quoted Rs 31.3 million per MW during the same period. Second, GoAP had agreed to an incentive of additional Rs 0.25 per unit if a private generating company operated at a plant load factor exceeding 68.5 per cent. This was a rather generous provision considering that APGENCO was consistently operating at an efficiency level of greater than 85 per cent plant load factor.[34]

Third, many of the private generating companies were gas-based plants, which came up at a time when gas was both expensive and in short supply. This was driven by the fact that private producers were given the choice of deciding the type of fuel they considered appropriate. Inadequate supplies of gas from the Gas Authority of India Ltd could escalate costs and reduce the efficiency level (or plant load factor). Gas-based plants, alternative fuel-based plants working with an expensive fuel such as naphtha and non-conventional sources of energy,[35] all produced a syndrome of escalated fuel costs. APTRANSCO, which purchased power from these plants, was involved in litigation at various levels with the private generating companies. The high court judgments have so far been less favourable than those of the Appellate Tribunal for Electricity based in New Delhi (M.V. Rao 2007a: 311–18).

Given the superior performance and lack of policy and regulatory attention to the uneven and adverse playing field for APGENCO, there was need for greater policy and regulatory attention towards scrutinizing prudent deals with private power purchasers. The Enron deal was an example of a less than successful deal that occurred in the absence of a state regulator and a low level of public consultation.[36] Even though such deals have been avoided in the context of regulation in Andhra Pradesh, regulation and public scrutiny of the regulator are important for pre-empting such undesirable outcomes.

Measuring Transmission and Distribution Losses and Agricultural Consumption The reduction in transmission and distribution losses from about 37.9 per cent in 2000–1 to 19.06 per cent in December 2007 was a good achievement for APTRANSCO.[37] This achievement, which is worthy of applause, must take a couple of factors into consideration. First, the transmission and distribution losses, which amount to system losses plus electricity theft, rose from 26.19 per cent in 1980–1 to 38.95 per cent in 1999–2000. They climbed from 19 per cent in 1996–7 to 33.33 per cent the following year, to an all time high of 38.95 per cent in 1999–2000, just before the reform brakes needed to be applied (Pani et al. 2007: 30–2). Do such wide fluctuations in theft reflect an ability of the government to play around with figures? While improved technology and governance have clearly led to a reduction in theft and an increase in revenue, its precise extent is difficult to judge.

It is difficult to ascertain whether or not reduction in losses resulted from adding theft figures to agricultural consumption because the latter was not metered in AP. During the period between 1999–2000 and 2005–6, the extent of metering rose from 37 to 55.21 per cent (Pani et al. 2007: 32. Approximately 55 per cent of consumption in AP was metered in December 2007. While urban consumption was metered, non-metered agricultural consumption resulted in an inaccurate estimate of agricultural sales. The government utilities argued that once metering was given up in the early 1980s, farmers got used unmetered agriculture consumption. They feared that metering would be the prelude to an agriculture tariff, which farmers oppose quite vehemently. The APERC was unsuccessful in metering agricultural consumption because the GoAP thought it unwise to expend political resources towards metering agricultural consumption.

The Indian Statistical Institute (ISI) in Kolkata was commissioned to gauge agricultural consumption through a sampling method. Sampling would be the second best to full metering. While there were rumours about the ISI's interim report at the time of interviews in December 2007, the report was not publicly available (interviews conducted by the author). A recent tariff order affirms the view that there is no firm methodology and information to assess the precise extent of agricultural consumption (APERC 2008: 70–1).

Interviews with farmers' groups in AP across the spectrum revealed that it should not be difficult to meter agricultural consumption up to the feeder level.[38] Farmers understood quite well that such metering is not tantamount to an agriculture tariff. They were concerned that transmission and distribution losses were being understated and agricultural consumption was being overstated. This view is corroborated by a systematic study of the agricultural sector in AP and Haryana conducted by the World Bank in 2001 (see World Bank 2001).

The Impact of Free Electricity There is evidence to suggest that free electricity to farmers since 2004 was harmful for the small and marginal farmers. This view was substantiated by independent studies of AP based on systematic data conducted by the World Bank (2001) and by Dossani and Ranganathan (2005a). These studies report data before 2004, when electricity was supplied for nine hours and at a subsidized price in AP. The quality of supply has deteriorated after the announcement of free electricity in 2004. The effects mentioned in the following should be more pronounced after the announcement of free electricity from 2004. Free electricity is a way of forcing the regulator to acquiesce to an increase in the loss making potential of the state utilities. It politicizes tariffs and erodes the impact of a regulation.

Free poor-quality power was more expensive for the small farmer because it did not enjoy economies of scale. The costs relating to low-quality free power due to frequent motor burnouts could be viewed as a tariff that would be the same for the small and the large farmers. Such a notional common tariff would adversely affect the smaller farmer to a greater degree.

Second, the poorer farmers depended on pumps to a lesser degree than the richer farmers. In AP, the gross annual incomes of electric pump owners was the highest (Rs 112,000) followed by diesel pump owners (Rs 91,000) according to the World Bank (2001).[39] Poor farmers in AP have historically depended on tanks and water conservation measures.[40] The large farmer enjoying economies of scale, on the other hand, might use the benefit of free electricity to cultivate areas that might not be economical in the absence of subsidy. Therefore, while cheap power is a windfall for the middle and rich farmers, it has little significance for the poor farmer for whom the costs of cheap, poor-quality power are quite exorbitant.

Third, quality of supply, which is related to the extent of subsidy,[41] is inversely proportional to the frequency of motor burnout. This is because free electricity leads to poor quality of supply. Also, the less a government earns in revenues from the farmer, the lower is its incentive to service clients. Free electricity is accompanied by poor service at the distribution end. The incidence of motor burnout raises the cost to the farmer. Often the farmer has to spend his resources to repair and maintain the electricity infrastructure at the distribution end.

There was a higher incidence of transformer burnouts in AP than in Haryana but AP was able to replace transformers faster than Haryana prior to 2004 when electricity was subsidized but not available for free. These burnouts occurred as a result of using too many pumps and more powerful pumps than those that had been registered (Dossani and Ranganathan 2005b: 51–65).

The woes of the small and marginal farmers have increased after the announcement of free electricity in May 2004. Farmers' voices opposed to free power could be heard from expected and unexpected quarters in December 2007. Even those who were opposed to privatization agreed that free power was harmful. A prominent leader of the Communist Party of India (Marxist) [CPI (M)]-backed All India Kisan Sabha described the woes of free power consistent with the analysis suggested earlier. Key functionaries of The Federation of Farmers Association and Lok Satta also expressed similar opinions. Views about the poor quality of electricity and consequent misery for farmers were also aired by a senior representative of the India's pre-eminent non-governmental organization (NGO) dedicated to the power sector, Prayas.[42] What was interesting was that organizations that do not necessarily see eye to eye were expressing largely similar opinions about the plight of AP farmers in the aftermath of free electricity in May 2004. A dominant view that emerged was that the nine hours of subsidized electricity that was supplied earlier was more beneficial for farmers than the seven hours of free electricity provided later.

The views of farmers' organizations deserve attention because they could lead to the articulation of the need for an optimal subsidized and progressive tariff that works better for small and marginal farmers who are least dependent on electrified pump sets. First, the seven hours of free electricity that was promised by the GoAP was being provided only for three to four hours in many places in December 2007. This power was delivered to farmers at a late hour in the night when it is not easy to cultivate the fields. Farmers preferred electricity during non-peak hour slots such as late evening or early morning than very late past midnight. Clearly, the state utilities that dispensed with free power also wished to keep its consumption at a low level by delivering it late at night. The paradox is that electricity delivered in this way could lead farmers to keep their pump sets on, which would lead to wastage of subsidized electricity.

Second, the quality of free electricity being delivered to farmers was very poor in comparison to the subsidized electricity being delivered prior to 2004.[43] This led to a higher incidence of motor burnouts. Even capacitors certified by the Bureau of Indian Standards did not help. As motor burnout is a cost for all farmers, whose impact on profitability increases with economies of scale, one can conjecture that increased pump-motor burnout is like a regressive tax. Better quality subsidized power delivered at different prices, depending on farm size, could work better for small and marginal farmers.

Third, the poor quality of free electricity being delivered at night has increased the number of human and animal electrocutions. Distribution companies did invest in a market that did not produce financial returns and transformer burnouts became more commonplace. Till 2004, AP not only had a higher rate of transformer burnout but also a faster replacement rate. The transformer replacement rate slowed down after free electricity was offered in 2004. With a dismal commitment to the maintenance of the system arising out of low financial returns from free electricity, farmers cannot afford to wait for the utilities to attend to transformer burnouts and they try to repair the transformers themselves. Poor earthing and unbalanced loads too have led to an increasing number of people and farm animals being electrocuted at night.[44]

The preceding discussion suggests that improving the quality and timing of electricity delivered and the performance of the maintenance system will reduce the human and financial costs, especially for the small and marginal farmers. The paradox is that the state wants to provide free electricity and reduce the subsidy provided by the government to the agriculture sector. These goals are inherently incompatible and are likely to be more harmful for the poorer farmers.

This problem can be handled in three discrete ways. First, a greater amount of emphasis needs to be placed on investing in small public irrigation works such as canals and tanks that can be accessed by poorer farmers. At the time of formation of AP in 1956, the amount of cultivable land served by public irrigation works was 3.7 times that under well irrigation. Recent estimates suggest that the area under wells is 1.5 times the area under small public irrigation projects. Small public irrigation projects could be encouraged to reduce the dependence of small farmers on tube-well irrigation.[45]

Second, there needs to be a political strategy for pricing electricity for agriculture. My fieldwork suggests that a large political constituency of small and marginal farmers exists, which is being hurt by free electricity. One hypothesis that found support during the interviews was that the well-endowed farmers' group in AP could capture policy and rally votes behind their interests, even though such policies did not serve the majority of the population. Concentrated interest groups continue to be a paradox in liberal democracies. These groups can be countered by mobilizing larger numbers through effective communication strategies. It is worth exploring whether political parties and non-governmental organizations could take up the cause of mobilizing the small and marginal farmers hurt by free electricity. Groups like Lok Satta have taken up such causes and would currently be faced with formidable political opposition.

An important step towards pricing electricity would be to install meters at the feeder level that would not measure electricity consumption of the household but would be able to measure electricity consumption by agriculture in AP. Interviews in December 2007 suggested that such a policy with proper communication can be implemented.[46] Raising the metering of electricity from the current low level of 55 to 100 per cent will provide a clear picture of agricultural consumption and subsidy. Once the subsidy to agriculture is measured accurately, this can be compared with the costs involved with the free delivery of electricity. Better quality electricity delivered at a subsidized cost would work out cheaper for poorer farmers considering the costs associated with hazardous late-night agriculture, frequent transformer and motor burnouts, and human and animal electrocutions. Priced power of superior quality would also reduce wastage of electricity and would have a positive impact on the extent of cross subsidy. There is credible evidence of over 350,000 unauthorized pump sets at work that add to consumption and subsidy to the richer farmers.

Third, there needs to be better service delivery on the part of the distribution companies who serve customers beyond the sub-station. One approach to reducing costs and improving service delivery is to empower the panchayats.[47] This would work along the principle that those who use the system could serve it better if resources were made available for this purpose. This strategy found some support among the farmers interviewed. Whether panchayats would deliver and under what circumstances needs further analysis. Distribution companies will not easily cede their powers to the panchayats.

Management of electricity distribution at the local level can also be improved by involving a franchisee[48] to oversee the maintenance of operations, which was originally supposed to be tasked to distribution companies. There is evidence to suggest that a franchisee selected and monitored by Lok Satta performed quite creditably in Takidalapudi sub-station in AP, reducing transmission and distribution losses from 27 to 9.19 per cent during a period of three years. Consumer cooperation was quite substantial and metering at the feeder level was acceptable to consumers. A report by a United Nations expert affirms substantial improvement in performance in four sub-stations in Kollur, Pellerilamjdi, Tadikalapudi, and Rajanagaram through the involvement of a franchisee. Improvements were documented in addressing fuse complaints, street light failure, low voltage problem, and fast running and dead meters; noting complaints; and in the general behaviour towards consumers. Repairing transformers and lines required human and financial contribution from the villagers before an official from the distribution company could attend to problems. In the post-franchisee world, local people saved much time and money. If franchisees could deliver more efficiently than a distribution company, this could reduce costs and improve service delivery. Franchisees would need to be chosen carefully with a clear commitment to serving the local people by involving them.[49]

Government Utilities Perform despite Handicaps The good news is that the utilities and the regulator have performed quite admirably on issues that enjoyed greater political commitment. Industry subsidizes agriculture but needs low tariffs to remain competitive. The industrial tariff has steadily declined from Rs 4.25 per unit in 2000–1 to Rs 3.70 per unit in 2005–6. Reduced tariffs coupled with high quality supply of electricity to industrial consumers have led to an increase in industrial consumption. Industrial revenues have consequently risen from Rs 39.02 billion to Rs 80.27 billion during the same period (APTRANSCO and Distribution Companies 2006b: 33–4).

The revenue subsidy burden of the GoAP owing to agriculture has fallen substantially over the years, from Rs 29.36 billion in 2000–1 to Rs 15.13 billion in 2003–4. Thereafter, free electricity to farmers increased the revenue burden to Rs 17.15 billion in 2004–5. The figures for 2006–7 were Rs 13.51 billion. Given the increase in industrial consumption driven by tariff reduction, the cross-subsidization of agriculture by industry increased by Rs 4.47 billion between 2001–2 and 2004–5. This means that reduction in losses driven by demand-side measures[50] and rising industrial consumption were able to reduce the GoAP's subsidy burden, despite free electricity to farmers. This was a significant achievement of the government utilities.

Lessons

Sound technocratic knowledge of the strengths and weaknesses of the power sector in the pre-reform period was a great plus for AP. The challenge posed by agriculture and the need to cultivate industrial consumers for subsidizing agricultural consumption were well known. Unbundling and regulation were priorities of the GoAP. Technocratic knowledge was backed by political commitment, and the combination of these two facilitated a positive relationship between the AP and the World Bank, enabling the latter to play an important role in enhancing regulatory competence and funding the purchase of equipment that would aid the reduction of losses.

One of the challenges for the political class and the regulator is to ensure an even playing field for the efficient APGENCO. Power purchase agreements favouring private generating companies require greater regulatory oversight over rent-seeking propensities. Regulatory capacity is largely a function of the degree to which the political class is willing to discipline itself in the larger interest of development. Ways of strengthening regulatory oversight in this area would make the sector more efficient.

The most serious challenge for the power sector and for AP's development is the financial burden of free electricity on the GoAP. Policies such as that of free power expose the limits of regulation in India. Free power hurts poor farmers and encourages waste. It locks in negative outcomes when a politics of optimal subsidies and prices, which will discourage waste and be more beneficial for the poor and marginal farmers, can exist. There is also need to spur public irrigation works that are both used more extensively by small farmers and can reduce the need for electric pump sets. There is a need to work out political strategies for mobilizing larger numbers of farmers who are suffering at the hands of the rich who can better afford electric pump sets. Finally, the distribution end requires greater local-level involvement in the form of franchisees or panchayati raj institutions.

Driven by efficient generating and transmission utilities and tariff-setting competence within the regulatory institution, AP has been able to perform despite the handicap of agricultural subsidy. It has been able to reduce losses and increase industrial consumption, which subsidizes agricultural consumption. All this has had the positive impact of lowering the level of government support for free electricity.

Regulation, no matter how competent, is unable to adequately deal with politically charged issues such as agricultural tariff or the propriety of power purchase agreements. The good news is that there is substantial civil society involvement in power sector issues aided by a good regulatory legacy in AP. This should aid the construction of a politics that both drives the sector towards lower losses and brings comfort to the small and marginal farmers.

West Bengal

West Bengal and AP are a study in contrast. Being a rain-fed state, the problem of agricultural tariff and subsidy was not a major political issue in WB. Agricultural subsidy was under control and consumption was almost perfectly metered. Moreover, the state did not enjoy the legacy of sophisticated thinking on power sector reforms that had given AP the ability to chart out and consolidate a reform path by 2000. There was much greater political opposition to unbundling and building regulatory capacity. The good news was that there was considerable political will at the highest level to reform the sector, and major executive decisions to corporatize and build regulatory capacity had been taken in 2007. There seemed greater interest in making the government utilities efficient than in encouraging private sector participation in WB.

Historical Legacy: Gradual Evolution of Reform Ideas

The Government of West Bengal (GoWB) thought very differently from the GoAP in the 1990s. This reflected both a difference in thinking and politics in the state. The first significant post-reform policy document was the *Final Report of the State Level Reorganization Committee* (1998) which came three years after the *Hiten Bhaya Committee Report* (1995). The 1998 report noted high transmission losses (19.1 per cent) and even higher distribution losses. The WB State Electricity Board (WBSEB) was making losses, and interest payments were becoming a financial constraint. The gaps between tariffs and the average cost of supply were to the order of 20 per cent. Agriculture and domestic consumption were highly subsidized. The declining debt–service ratio led to a situation in which the state electricity board (SEB) was unable to internally generate resources, having defaulted in meeting its capital liabilities. The SEB had 18.6

employees per consumer when the national average was 11.2. The fiscal crisis in WB was driven largely by poor governance in that state (Department of Power 1998: 1–4).

This fiscal crisis had occurred despite the fact that free agricultural consumption in West Bengal was not the problem.[51] The move towards governance reforms was far more gradual in WB than in AP, no clear unbundling of generation, transmission, and the distribution functions of the WBSEB being proposed. Rather, it was proposed that all thermal generation be brought under the WB Power Development Corporation Ltd (WBPDCL), which should enter into a power purchase agreement with the WBSEB transmission and distribution remaining with the latter. Hydroelectric power generation would stay with the WBSEB with no mention of independent power purchasers. A tariff authority rather than an independent regulator was proposed in the *Final Report of the State Level Reorganization Committee* (Department of Power 1998: 6–8).

The next major development was the *Report of the State Level Committee on Restructuring of Distribution System in the Power Sector* (2003). This report was a response to the direction given by the Electricity Act (2003) to the GoWB. Whereas the GoAP had already undertaken much of the restructuring consistent with the Act by 2003, much work remained for the GoWB to complete. This report spoke about the need to separate distribution from transmission under different companies.While there was no mention of independent power purchasers, the report spoke of captive generation. This was an acknowledgement of the GoWB's incapacity to serve industrial consumers efficiently. The need to reduce cross-subsidy, charge cost of supply, and to improve metering were also stressed (Department of Power 2003: chapters 1, 5, and 7).

The state of the WBSEB was critically analysed in the report. The rising figures of transmission and distribution losses were reported, which reflected poor governance of the utilities. High industrial tariffs and poor quality of supply were forcing the industrial sector to move towards captive generation. Poor management of human resources affected the work culture negatively. The threat of competition from captive generation and from the central public sector undertakings was noted (Department of Power 2003: chapters 2 and 3).

The strengths of the sector noted in the report were a professionally qualified workforce, an extensive transmission and distribution network, and a strong information technology (IT) network for billing. What was most significant was extensive metering at the 11 KV and higher voltage level,[52] which is critical for energy accounting. In this, WB was ahead of AP.

Achievements and Challenges

WB has low agricultural consumption and subsidy, and enjoys extensive metering of electricity consumption. Low agricultural consumption is due to low usage of electric pump sets in a rain-fed state. Water for irrigation is easily available in numerous ponds. Measures have been taken to reduce the extent of theft, and these have borne tangible results. Power trading has helped improve the financial condition of state utilities, aided by WB's power surplus during off-peak hours.

Inefficient generation poses a real threat, and this continues despite competition from CESC and DVC. Inefficiencies of the state-owned generating companies had inspired a plan to restructure the utilities, which had been approved by the GoWB in 2007. Whether or not restructuring with the same level of competition in the absence of independent power producers will produce the desired results remained to be seen. Regulatory capacity in WB seemed to lag behind that in AP, even though there was interest in augmenting such capacity. The pro-competition and private sector pressures emanated from the office of the chief minister, whilst the department of power was in favour of the status quo. The department had successfully opposed privatization of government assets and the entry of independent power purchasers.

Low Agricultural Consumption and the Metering of Agriculture A lower level of agricultural consumption in WB reduces a major reform challenge faced by drought-prone states like AP. In AP, a relatively efficient power sector gets saddled with cross-subsidy because it is politically difficult to charge agriculture tariffs, even at a subsidized rate. Aided by abundant ground water availability and fewer pumps, WB has been able to keep agricultural consumption under control. In 1993–4, whereas WB had approximately 581,000 pump sets, the same figure for AP was 1.48 million. Whereas subsidy due to agriculture for the WBSEB ranged from Rs 1.04 billion to Rs 4.05 billion between 1992–3 and 2001–2, the same figures for AP were 7.26 billion and 41.76 billion.[53]

WB, unlike AP, does not have a powerful farmers' lobby. Interviews suggested that fragmented landholdings in WB could have kept the power of the rich rural elite at bay. Successful land reform and small landholdings impeded the growth of a powerful farmers' lobby in WB. Those in need of rural electrification were not a political force, and rural electrification has progressed slowly.[54] Annual growth of rural electrification fell from 1,185 per cent between 1977 and 1991, to 78 per cent between 1996 and 2001. The same figures for pump-set energization were 5,146 and 1,912.[55] Low levels of rural consumption have resulted in a reduction in the subsidy burden.

WB has an ambitious plan for 100 per cent rural electrification, which draws extensively from Central government funds. It is to be seen whether metering and cost realization will keep the subsidy burden in WB within control (Department of Power 2007b: slides 24–5). There was an easier politics within the state to work with, and agricultural power consumption would be less due to better ground water availability and fewer rich farmers.

Second, WB has achieved significantly more extensive metering of agricultural consumption than AP. The lack of opposition to metering from farmers has helped in this context. The GoWB has taken the initiative to meter nearly 100 per cent of power consumption. This will provide accurate information about the extent of theft, since it will be difficult to show agricultural consumption as theft with 100 per cent metering of agriculture (Department of Power 2007b: slide 7).

Theft Control Theft control measures have yielded results: losses reduced from 31.22 per cent in 2003–4 to 19.47 per cent in 2007–8 (Guha 2009). While transmission and distribution losses in WB are probably greater than in AP, in former the loss figures are more accurate due to extensive metering of the agriculture and non-agriculture sectors. A legislation in 2001 reduced the extent of energy loss by 6 per cent between 2001 and 2002. Transmission and distribution losses had fallen from 28 to 24 per cent between 2002–3 and 2006–7. If we added commercial losses, the same figures would be 45 and 32 per cent, respectively. Theft control is a governance area where substantial progress has been made in WB (Guha 2005: 12–13; Department of Power 2007b: slide 15).

Power Trading Third, the WBSEB has been aided by the Electricity Act of 2003 as it was able to sell the off-peak surplus power to other states at a remunerative price of Rs 5 per unit, which is higher than the cost of supply. Low levels of current domestic consumption aid the ability of the state to export power at high cost. The WBSEB earned additional revenue of Rs 6.3 billion via this route, and its operating surplus increased from Rs 380 million to Rs 5 billion between 2003 and 2004. The profits of Durgapur Project Ltd jumped from Rs 189 million to Rs 400 million between 2003 and 2004. The WBPDCL's profit jumped from Rs 91.3 million in 2002 to Rs 113.7 million during the same period (Guha 2005: 17–18).

Given its potential for exporting power for some time into the future and the revenue potential of this, WB would like to enter into long-term agreements with different states and power trading companies. The state could think of a dedicated export corridor to the northern grid to ensure that this earning route remains viable.

Inefficient Generating Companies and Need for Restructuring Unlike AP, WB's generating companies are largely inefficient. Whereas AP's state-owned generating companies maintained a plant load factor greater than 80 per cent between 2000 and 2006, the average figures for thermal power plants in WB improved from 55.6 to 65 per cent between 2001 and 2006. Of the thermal power plants in WB, the oldest privately owned power supplier in India, the CESC, fared the best with a plant load factor of almost 80 per cent in 2004. WB's state-owned utilities, such as WBPDCL and the power generated by Durgapur Projects Ltd, enjoyed a plant load factor under 60 per cent (Guha 2005: 16). The cost of producing power by the public sector in West Bengal was higher than the prices quoted by the expensive private power producers in AP, and considerably higher than the cost of power being produced in the joint sector by APGPCL. The low productivity of the gencos is hurting their profitability.

The low level of productivity of the state-owned enterprises is a cause for concern, especially because there is competition from the central public sector undertakings, the privately owned CESC, and the captive power producers who generate power for their own industries. The central public sector undertakings, such as the National Thermal Power Corporation and the DVC served approximately 36 per cent of the state's requirements in 2007. The state utilities, such as the WB State Electricity Board and the WBPDCL generated about 43 per cent of the state's power. Independent power producers, unlike AP, were unable to find their feet in WB. The private producer CESC supplied about 16 per cent of the power,[56] the balance coming from captive generation, which served an increasingly large proportion of the industrial consumers. Competition from CESC, captive generation, and the central public sector undertakings was posing a real threat to the inefficiently run gencos. CESC was the most efficient genco followed by the central public sector undertakings.

Captive generation posed a threat to the government-owned gencos because industrial consumers typically subsidize rural and domestic households in India. Maintaining efficient, low-cost supply to industrial customers was one of the components of AP's success. In WB, captive power generation was on the rise, and the state-run utilities were losing customers to CESC and the central public sector undertakings. These organizations were accused of cherry-picking customers without having to share the rural service burden.

The paradox is that planned generation by the state utilities in WB was on the rise even when its efficiency levels were precariously low. The state had planned capacity addition to the extent of 8,131 MW and was considering retiring old plants with a combined capacity of 1,233 MW (Department of Power 2006: chapter 1). Low levels of efficiency were blamed on low quality of coal rather than management inefficiencies by the politically powerful incumbents in the Department of Power. Trade unions in WB were powerful and they seemed to be averse to the idea of external involvement.[57] The critical question was why WB received poor quality coal when AP was able to access coal of high quality. The question was one of efficiently managing inputs.

The issue of restructuring government utilities was central to balanced state-led development of the power sector in WB. Increased capacity and the inefficiency of the state power utilities would serve as a toxin for the power sector in WB. In 2007, the GoWB had undertaken an elaborate plan to restructure and corporatize the WBSEB into two separate corporations. These would be the WB State Electricity Transmission Company (WBSETC) and the WB State Electricity Distribution Company (WBSEDC). The WBSETC would undertake the transmission and state load dispatch functions and the WBSEDC would undertake the distribution and hydel generation functions. Rs 70.8 billion of the debts of the WBSEB would be written off, and Rs 27.25 billion of the debts of the WBPDCL would be written off in the process. The new entities would have 50 per cent non-executive directors and 33 per cent independent directors. Even though the state was neither privatizing assets nor encouraging the private sector beyond captive generation, the policy was to push corporate governance within the government utilities. The successor entities of the WBSEB, Durgapur Projects Ltd, and the WBPDCL were being empowered to recruit and monitor performance along commercial lines (Department of Power 2007a; 2007b: slides 9–13).

Pressure from the chief minister's office was the critical element in promoting the unbundling of power sector assets in WB, notwithstanding some opposition from the Department of Power. This is an admirable move. Given the paucity of home-grown reform ideas, restructuring had taken a much longer time in WB. It remains to be seen how the restructuring of the GoWB's assets into separate generation, transmission, and distribution companies will evolve over time. The reform process in West Bengal whas taken more time, partly because of a longer consultation process. Ideas like private sector participation and unbundling have taken more time to become internalized. Indeed, West Bengal focused more on improving the financial health and management of the power sector, including curbing power theft before moving to address the issue of unbundling.

Regulatory Capacity The website of the WB Electricity Regulatory Commission (WBERC) is quite opaque in comparison to that of the APERC. The WBERC follows the average cost model of tariff-setting rather than the cost to serve model. The cost to serve model is more demanding and could lead to politically unsustainable tariff hikes. The privately owned CESC and the state-owned gencos have an excellent relationship with the WBERC. The WBERC has issued tariff orders, but these were not posted on its website. There was little interaction between civil society groups and the WBERC. In AP, civil society groups, however adversarial, make their voice heard and have begun to develop a healthy respect for the utilities and the regulatory staff.

INSIGHTS FROM A COMPARISON OF TELECOM, PORTS, AND POWER

Regulatory evolution was critical for successful infrastructure service delivery in the telecommunications, ports, and the power sectors in India. Regulatory evolution and efficient service delivery were affected by fiscal and financial crises, the legacy of reform ideas, political will, the nature of consumers, and technology. The telecommunications sector had evolved to a greater extent towards regulation, private sector participation, and economical tariffs in comparison with the ports and the power sectors in India.

First, fiscal and financial crises were crucial to spurring the reform agenda in India. Even though Rajiv Gandhi was deeply engaged with the project of making Indian telecommunications more efficient, it was only after the balance of payments crisis of 1991 that private service providers were allowed entry in the telecom sector. The institution of a regulator in 1997 and the further consolidation of the office in 2000 were preceded by crises faced by private investors. Ports and power sector reforms were also spurred by the fiscal crisis of the state, which required serious attention at the time of the balance of payments crisis in 1991. It remains to be seen how the government will manage an impending crisis for private investors in India's ports sector.

Second, prior existence and engagement with home-grown reform ideas was important to ensure that crisis situations could be converted into opportunities to invite private investment and consolidate regulation. The telecom sector benefited from technocratic and policy engagement with reform in the 1980s more than the ports and the power sectors. Even though the reform of JNPT had occurred prior to the balance of payments crisis of 1991, reform efforts in this area had fewer home-grown inputs and were less intensive in comparison to Rajiv Gandhi's engagement with telecom reforms in the 1980s.

The major issues facing power sector reform remained unaddressed till 1991. AP's success in building regulatory capacity, creating efficient generating companies, unbundling the SEB, and in reducing the fiscal burden notwithstanding unmetered free electricity to farmers, owes a great deal to the existence of reform ideas before its engagement with the World Bank. Ideas for the reform of the power sector in WB, on the other hand, evolved much more slowly.

Third, political will was essential to consolidate regulation in India. The telecom sector evolved as a result of serious attempts made by the PMO to even the regulatory playing field for private investment. Former prime minister Atal Bihari Vajpayee had to take direct control over the telecom portfolio during crucial moments of regulatory consolidation. The ports sector, on the other hand, did not witness a similar intervention from the PMO for regulatory oversight of the powers of the DoS in the management of port trusts, in bidding, and in tariff setting. While the DoT was promoting competition, the DoS was still seeking to protect its monopoly position.

Political will was necessary for the reform of the power sector. Former chief minister Chandra Babu Naidu's statesmanship in AP provided autonomy for the regulator and the CEOs of the unbundled state utilities. This autonomy enjoyed by civil servants from the political class was essential for the success of the government-owned utilities and the regulator. The state utilities were able to compete with the independent power purchasers. Chief Minister Buddhadeb Bhattacharjee of WB was engaged in a similar struggle with the Department of Power in the state. The capacity of the chief minister's office to deal with the incumbent will play a decisive role in consolidating regulation and in making WB's gencos more efficient.

Fourth, regulatory consolidation was affected by the political power of consumers. The regulator in a well-governed state like AP was unable to make much headway with metering or charging electricity used for farm consumption. The political power of the rich farmers won them a subsidy for electric pump-set consumption. The telecom and the ports sector were more fortunate in this context because consumers were willing to pay tariffs.

Political strategies to deal with the dilemma of free electricity, which benefits rich farmers using electric pump sets, are critical for the reform of the power sector in many states. This is a paradox of collective action, where a minority of powerful, rich farmers with their ability to stall reforms were able to win benefits that did not accrue to the poorer sections of the farming community. Research is necessary in the area of mobilizing the majority who do not benefit from free electricity to arrive at a progressive tariff with better quality of supply, which would be a win–win situation for all.

Fifth, technology affected the reform process in peculiar ways. Cellular technology aided the private sector because it foresaw its future and opted for it when the government and some large Indian companies had not. This gave smaller private sector companies an advantage in cellular telephony, which became the growth area in Indian telecommunications. A first mover's advantage in cellular telephony helped these companies to compete with the government, which owned the entire telephone network in India at the time of the reforms.

Why did the different sectors succeed in varying degrees in promoting competition and service delivery? First, telecommunications was aided by prior home-grown policy ideas, financial crises, resolute political will favouring reform, the emergence of cellular technology that aided private sector participation, and consumers who never reneged on their telephone bills. Second, while the ports sector had disciplined consumers, it lacked prior policy ideas and extent of political will favoring reform that was evident in the power sector. This explains the lack of any spectacular success in reforming the sector. Finally, the relative success of the power sector in AP was guided largely by excellent home-grown ideas prior to the involvement of the World Bank and Chief Minister Chandra Babu Naidu's clear inclination to reform the sector by restructuring the utilities and consolidating the regulatory institution. What has held back this star performer in the power sector is the politically powerful constituency of rich farmers who successfully garnered the free electricity benefit for farm consumption in the state.

This study of India's telecommunications, ports, and the power sectors reveals that while fiscal and financial crises are tipping points for reforms, there are at least four other separate factors that determine how far the reforms will proceed as a result of these crises. These other factors that intervene between a crisis and reform are availability and engagement with good reform ideas; political will to convert the crisis and reform ideas into regulatory consolidation; the political opposition to reforms from consumers of infrastructure services and the political implications of that opposition; and the impact of technology on the regulatory process.

ACKNOWLEDGEMENTS

The author would like to thank Vikram Chand (World Bank), Dipak Dasgupta (World Bank), Montek S. Ahluwalia (Planning Commission, New Delhi), Ashish Khanna (World Bank), Sri Kumar Tadimalla (World Bank), Amit Kapur (JSA Associates & Solicitors, New Delhi), Gyanesh Kudaisya (National University of Singapore), and Anjali Mukherji for discussions. A number of people provided inputs that were critical for this chapter. They included: V.S. Ailawadi (ex-Haryana ERC, New Delhi), Suresh N. Amirapu (Port of Singapore Authority, Chennai), Mrinal Bannerjee (Minister of Power, Kolkata), Ashok Basu (Planning Board, Kolkata), Utpal Bhattacharya (Calcutta Electric Supply Corporation, Kolkata), Rachel Chatterjee (Transmission Corporation of AP, Hyderabad), P.V. Subbaiah Choudhury (Federation of Farmers Association, Hyderabad), Kevin D'Souza (Dubai Ports World, Mumbai), Malay K. Dey (WB State Electricity Distribution Co. Ltd.), Sujit Dasgupta (Department of Power, Kolkata), Anita George (International Finance Corp., New Delhi), S.N. Ghosh (WBERC, Kolkata), Geeta Gouri (APERC, Hyderabad), Anirban Guha (WBERC, Kolkata), T.K. Gupta (Damodar Valley Corporation, Kolkata), Gajendra Haldea (Planning Commission, New Delhi), Ajai Jain (AP Power Generating Co. Ltd., Hyderabad), Amit Kapur (JSA Associates & Solicitors, New Delhi), Ashok Lavasa (Department of Power, Haryana, Chandigarh), Sanjay Mitra (PMO, New Delhi), Sunil Mitra (Department of Power, Kolkata), Y. Harish Chandra Prasad (Malaxmi Infrastructures India Pvt. Ltd., Hyderabad), B.N. Puri (Planning Commission, New Delhi), M. Venugopal Rao (Prajasakti, Hyderabad), P. Madan Mohana Rao (Energy Conservation Mission, Hyderabad), Balarama Reddy (Federation of Farmers Association, Hyderabad), P. Chengal Reddy (Federation of Farmers Association, Hyderabad), Ramakrishna Reddy (Federation of Farmers Association, Hyderabad), Sarampally Malla Reddy

(AP Rytu Sangam, Hyderabad), Y.S. Rajasekhar Reddy (late Chief Minister, AP Secretariat, Hyderabad), G.P. Rao (ex-APERC, Hyderabad), K. Rosaiah (former finance minister, AP Secretariat, Hyderabad), T.L. Sankar (Administrative Staff College of India, Hyderabad), Sankar Sen (ex-minister of power, GoWB), Subimal Sen (WB State Council of Higher Education, Kolkata), N. Sreekumar (Prayas, Hyderabad), Rakesh Srivastava (Ministry of Shipping, Road Transport and Highways, New Delhi), K. Swaminathan (APERC, Hyderabad), and Ashok Verma (Pricewaterhouse Coopers Pvt. Ltd., Kolkata). The presentation and interpretation of data in this chapter solely reflect my views.

The research support provided by Siddharth Pathak and Taberez Ahmed Neyazi is gratefully acknowledged.

NOTES

1. On the role of the fiscal crisis in generating the reform momentum after 1991, see Mukherji (2007a: 117–45).

2. GSM stands for Global System for Mobile (originally from Groupe Speciale Mobile) and is the European standard, while CDMA stands for Code Division Multiple Access technology, which is an American technology. Over 80 per cent of the global mobile market uses the GSM standard.

3. Corporatization is a strategy of making government-owned corporations more autonomous from the government to enable them to run like private companies without the obstruction of political considerations.

4. See Desai (2006: 37–47); Mukherji (2007b: 302–4).

5. However, a Supreme Court judgement of 17 December 2002 in Cellular *Operators Association of India* v. *Union of India* ruled that all decisions of the TDSAT were amenable to the writ jurisdiction of a high court.

6. See Mukherji (2006: 66–81).

7. A situation is Pareto optimal when one individual can be better off without making any one else worse off. The middle class and the rich in India benefited to a greater extent from India's telecommunications revolution without making the poor worse off. The growing rural–urban divide and low rural tele-density are causes for concern. Poorer areas with fewer subscribers need to be subsidized as there can be no profit margin there.

8. Much of the material included in this and subsequent sections is referenced and the inputs of key persons have been acknowledged. The interpretation from the referenced documents is entirely mine. I did not footnote these documents or interviews in order to preserve the anonymity of those who generously shared their views and relevant documents.

9. Dwell time is the duration for which a vessel stays in the port for service and reflects the efficiency of a port.

10. On the performance of other ports, see Ghosh and De (2001: 3274).

11. E-mail exchange with Suresh Amirapu, Port of Singapore Authority, in June 2007.

12. See World Bank (1995).

13. The creation of a Dock Labour Board was left to the discretion of the various port trusts, and there was no stipulation in the Dock Workers Act (1948) that a certain number of labourers needed to be employed. The Dock Labour Act protected the job security of all the workers.

14. On the evolution of the NSICT and the positive effect this had on JNPT, see Ray (2005).

15. See Mukherji (2006: 69–79). ICICI has become a private sector bank since 2007.

16. The terminal authors who reported this situation would like to remain anonymous and were unwilling to reveal the precise company figures.

17. The tariff ceiling could equal costs and a certain return on capital when 60 per cent of normative capacity is realized, and the tariff floor could be the lowest tariff charged when 100 per cent normative capacity is realized.

18. See Tariff Authority for Major Ports (28 February 2008). See also, Planning Commission (28 August 2007).

19. A TEU or a 20-ft equivalent unit is an inexact unit of cargo capacity, often used to describe the capacity of container ships at container terminals.

20. A gantry crane is a crane with a hoist, which is fitted in a trolley for horizontal movement. See Prabhakaran (2005: 2–4).

21. See Bhaya (1995). I am grateful to T.L. Sankar for having introduced me to reform thinking in AP in December 2007.

22. See Planning Commission (1994).

23. The plant load factor measures the efficiency of a generating plant. A high plant load factor in thermal plants implies greater usage of coal, which pollutes the environment.

24. Rent-seeking possibilities in private power purchase agreements and lenient conditions added to the generation costs of private producers.

25. For a quick overview, see Pani et al. (2007: 11); Tongia (2007: 147–8).

26. On Chandra Babu's iconization as a reformer, see Rudolph and Rudolph (2007) and Mooij (2007).

27. Free power from 2004 was a Congress election pledge after it came to power in May 2004.

28. Open access relates to a situation where private producers can access the distribution network owned by the government. This view is based on a personal interview with G.P. Rao in Hyderabad on 14 December 2007 and other interviews in Hyderabad in December 2007.

29. BPL stands for British Physical Laboratories.

30. I am referring especially to Dubash and Rao (2007: chapter 1).

31. Lok Satta has since become a political party.

32. Figures are from APGENCO, Profile of APGENCO, a power point presentation shared by Ajai Jain, managing director of AP Power Generation Corporation on 14 December 2007.

33. The private sector producers charged an average rate of Rs 2.58 per unit during this period. Power generated by the Central government-owned utilities

was charged Rs 1.59 per unit from the same. See Pani et al. (2007: 11–25). I am grateful to N. Sreekumar for sharing this excellent paper. See also M.V. Rao (2007a: 311–18).

34. On inflated capital costs of independent power producers, see Mahalingam (2005: 206–20). On Andhra Pradesh, see Pani et al. (2007: 16–23); M.V. Rao (2007a: 311–18). The figure of 68.5 per cent was calculated on the assumption of coal-based plants of vintage technology. The private producers, on the other hand, used the combined cycle gas technology, which was capable of performing at full capacity.

35. Bagasse plants could deliver at an investment cost of Rs 30 million per MW, wind at Rs 40 million per MW, and waste to energy plants at Rs 60 million per MW. Pani et al. (2007: 19).

36. The World Bank and the Central Electricity Authority had cautioned against this deal but there was little public awareness about it till its consequences worked themselves out in the form of astronomical and unsustainable tariffs. Mukherji (2007b: 315–16).

37. See APERC (2008: 64); APTRANSCO and Distribution Companies (2006b: 8).

38. Agricultural consumption was metered till 1983. Meters were removed under the chief ministership of N.T. Rama Rao. For a brief overview of agricultural electricity consumption in India, see Tongia (2007: 125–7).

39. See World Bank (2001: 15–17, 25); Reddy (2007).

40. According to some reports, GoAP policies have led to a decline in drip irrigation, which benefits small and marginal farmers. Free electricity has encouraged well irrigation.

41. There was a unanimous view that the quality of free power being supplied to farmers was inferior to the quality of priced power prior to 2004.

42. This view is based on an interview with N. Sreekumar of Prayas on 16 December 2007 and farmers' leaders in December 2007. See Sreekumar et al. (2007: 26–7).

43. This is evident from a number of interviews with T.L. Shanker (Administrative Staff College, Hyderabad, 13 December 2007); Chengal Reddy (Federation of Farmers Association, Hyderabad, 15 December 2007); M. Sreekumar (Prayas, Hyderabad, 16 December 2007); and Malla Reddy (All India Kisan Sabha, 15 December 2007).

44. This view is based on a number of interviews. See also Sreekumar (2007: 27).

45. For the importance of public irrigation works, see Reddy (2007). See also Bhaya (1995: 51–3).

46. Some farmers' leaders even took the extreme view that farmers would not oppose the metering of electricity.

47. Panchayats are local governments at the village level.

48. A franchisee is a local organization that is tasked to look after a small territory at the distribution end of the power sector.

49. On the franchisee model, I benefited from discussions with Madan Mohana Rao who worked for Lok Satta. He now runs the Energy Conservation Mission in Hyderabad. See also, Bhavanulu (2004).

50. Demand-side measures such as the high voltage distribution system are used for energy conservation. See APTRANSCO (2007: 3–8).

51. In 1998, the subsidy for agriculture in AP was Rs 27 billion when the same figure for WB was Rs 3.3 billion. These figures were provided by S.M. Reddy in Hyderabad who represents AP Rythu Sangham.

52. Department of Power (2003: chapter 3, pp. 9–10). There was 98.5 per cent metering at this level in December 2007.

53. These figures were provided by S.M. Reddy in Hyderabad in December 2007 from the office of the AP Rythu Sangam.

54. According to a knowledgeable source who did not wish to be named, WB had the lowest level of rural electrification in India in 2001–2. *Mouza* level electrification was 80.16 per cent and the quality of electrification was not documented properly. *Mouza* is the lowest revenue unit, which is larger than a village. In Mughal times, *mouzas*, rather than the gram or village, was the common usage, and *mouza* is a term that continues to be commonly used in WB for a revenue unit.

55. See Guha (2002: 129, 136). Department of Power and Non-Conventional Energy Resources (2006: chapter 4, pp. 5–12). Department of Power (2007b: slide 25).

56. Department of Power (2007b: slide 4). The only independent power producer in WB was the HPL Cogeneration Ltd. of Haldia.

57. One found that the left and the trade unions in AP were very open to the idea of consultations with an independent consultant of the Bank. In WB, while access was possible at the highest political level representing the incumbent, the trade unions were quite averse to the idea of sharing their views about the pitfalls in the path to restructuring.

BIBLIOGRAPHY

Administrative Staff College of India (1997), *Restructuring the Regulatory System: Report Submitted to the Ministry of Power*, Hyderabad.

Andhra Pradesh Electricity Regulatory Commission (APERC) (2008), *Tariff Order on Retail Supply Business for FY 2008/09 of Central Power Distribution Company of AP Ltd, Eastern Power Distribution Company of AP Ltd., Northern Power Distribution Company of AP Ltd., and Southern Power Distribution Company of AP Ltd.* Hyderabad: Government of Andhra Pradesh, 20 March.

Banerjee, Mrinal (2006), 'Restructuring of State-Owned Power Utilities', Statement in West Bengal Legislative Assembly, Kolkata: Government of West Bengal, 4 December.

Bhattacharya, Sougata and Urjit R. Patel (2005), 'New Regulatory Institutions in India', in Devesh Kapur and Pratap B. Mehta (eds), *Public Institutions in India*, pp. 406–56. New Delhi: Oxford University Press.

Bhavanulu, P.S. (2004), *Executive Summary on [of] Survey to Ascertain the Consumer Satisfaction and Public Opinion in the Areas Managed by the Franchisee in Place of APEDDCL/APSDDCL*. Hyderabad: Lok Satta.

Bhaya, Hiten (chair) (1995), *The Report of the High Level Committee: Guidelines on Restructuring and Privatisation of Power Sector and Power Tariff*. Hyderabad: Government of Andhra Pradesh.

Department of Power (1998), *Final Report of the State Level Reorganization Committee in the Power Sector*. Kolkata: Government of West Bengal.

_________ (2003), *Report of the State Level Committee on Restructuring of Distribution System in the Power Sector, Vol. 1*, December. Kolkata: Government of West Bengal.

_________ (2006), *Perspective Plan of West Bengal Power Sector 2006–2030*, June. Kolkata: Government of West Bengal.

_________ (2007a), *Restructuring of the West Bengal State Electricity Board, Key Documents: 2005–07*. Kolkata: Government of West Bengal.

_________ (2007b), *Restructuring of the State Power Sector: A Power Point Presentation*, August. Kolkata: Government of West Bengal.

Department of Telecommunications (2008), *Annual Report 2007/08*. New Delhi: Government of India.

Desai, Ashok V. (2006), *India's Telecommunications Industry*. New Delhi: Sage.

Dossani, Rafiq and V.R. Ranganathan (2005a), 'Management of Power Supply to Agriculture', in Joel Ruet (ed.), *Against the Current, Vol. II*, pp. 51–65. New Delhi: Manohar.

_________ (2005b), 'Farmer's Willingness to Pay for Power in India', in Joel Ruet (ed.), *Against the Current, Vol. III*, pp. 51–65. New Delhi: Manohar.

Dubash, Navroz and Sudhir C. Rajan (2001), 'Power Politics', *Economic and Political Weekly* 36(35): 3367–90.

Dubash, Navzroz K. and D. Narasimha Rao (2007), *The Practice and Politics of Regulation*. New Delhi: Macmillan.

Economic and Political Weekly (2004), 'More Berthing Space', 39(1): 1360.

Ghosh, Buddhadeb and Prabir De (2001), 'Indian Ports and Globalization', *Economic and Political Weekly*, 36(34): 3271–83.

Guha, Anirban (2002), 'A Planning Perspective of Power in West Bengal', *Indian Journal of Power*, July–August, 126–45.

_________ (2005), 'Power Sector on the Trunk Road to Self-reliance', *West Bengal* (December): 9–19.

_________ (2009), data on West Bengal Electricity Regulatory Commission (30 December 2009).

Indian Private Ports and Terminals Association (2007a), *Tariff Policy and Sustainable PPPs in the Port Sector: Presentation to the Planning Commission*, New Delhi, 1 February.

_________ (2007b), *Tariff Policy and Sustainable PPPs in the Port Sector: Presentation to the Tariff Commission*, 12 September.

Indian Private Ports and Terminals Association (2007c), *Correspondence with Director (Ports Development)*. Mumbai: Department of Shipping, 19 November.

_________ (2007d), *Correspondence with Secretary Shipping (Ports Wing)*. Mumbai: Ministry of Shipping, Road Transport and Highways, 26 November.

Mahalingam, Sudha (2005), 'Economic Reforms, the Power Sector and Corruption', in Jos Mooij (ed.), *The Politics of Economic Reforms in India*, pp. 196–226. New Delhi: Sage.

Ministry of Shipping, Road Transport and Highways, Department of Shipping (2006), *National Maritime Development Programme: Ports Development*, March. New Delhi: Government of India.

Mooij, Jos (2007), 'Hype, Skill and Class: The Politics of Reform in Andhra Pradesh, India,' *Commonwealth and Comparative Politics*, 45(1): 34–56.

Mukherji, Rahul (2006), 'Promoting Competition in India's Telecom Sector', in Vikram Chand (ed.), *Reinventing Public Service Delivery in India*, pp. 57–94. Washington D.C./New Delhi: World Bank/Sage.

_________ (2007a), 'Economic Transition in a Plural Polity', in Rahul Mukherji (ed.), *India's Economic Transition: The Politics of Reforms*, pp. 117–45. New Delhi: Oxford University Press.

_________ (2007b), 'Managing Competition', in Rahul Mukherji (ed.), *India's Economic Transition, The Politics of Reforms*, pp. 300–27. New Delhi: Oxford University Press.

_________ (2008), 'The Politics of Telecommunications Regulation', *Journal of Development Studies*, 44(10): 1405–23.

_________ (2009), 'Interests, Wireless Technology and Institutional Change: From Government Monopoly to Regulated Competition in Indian Telecommunications', *Journal of Asian Studies* 68(2): 491–517.

Mukhopadhyay, Partha S. (2008), 'Falling Through the Cracks: India's Failing Infrastructure Policies', *India in Transition*. Philadelphia: Centre for the Advanced Study of India, University of Pennsylvania, 19 May, available at http://casi.ssc.upenn.edu/iit/mukhopadhyay, accessed on 2 July 2010.

Nayar, Baldev R. (2006), *India's Globalization*. Washington: East-West Center.

Noronha, Ernesto (2001), 'Bombay Dock Labour Board 1948–1994', *Economic and Political Weekly*, 36(52): 4851–8.

Panagariya, Arvind (2008), *India: The Emerging Giant*. New York: Oxford University Press.

Pani, B. Saranga, N. Sreekumar, and M. Thimma Reddy (2007), 'Power Sector Reforms in Andhra Pradesh', *Governance and Policy Spaces*, Working Paper 11. Hyderabad: Centre for Economic and Social Studies.

Planning Commission (1994), *Report of the NDC Committee on Power*, September. New Delhi: Government of India.

_________ (2006), *Public Private Partnerships in Ports: Model Concession Agreements*, October. New Delhi: Government of India.

Planning Commission (2007a), *Report of the Task Force: Financing Plan for Ports*, July. New Delhi: Government of India.

_________ (2007b), *Report of the Task Force: Tariff Setting and Bidding Parameters for PPP Projects in Major Ports*, 28 August. New Delhi: Government of India.

Prabhakaran S. (chair) (2005), *Report of the Working Group on Normative Cost Based Tariffs for Container Related Charges*. Delhi: Government of India.

Raghavan, Vikram (2007), *Communications Law in India*. New Delhi: Lexis Nexis Butterworths.

Rao, M. Venugopal (2007a), 'Power Purchase Agreements and Legal Litigation', in R.S. Rao, V. Hanumantha Rao, and N. Venugopal (eds), *Fifty Years of Andhra Pradesh 1956–2006*, pp. 311–18. Hyderabad: Centre for Documentation, Research and Communication.

_________ (2007b), 'Supply of Power to Domestic and Agricultural Consumers in Andhra Pradesh', unpublished MS.

Rao, P. Madan Mohana (2005), *Organization Structures, Roles and Responsibilities: What Works in Indian Environments? Case Studies*, 28 August, All India Seminar on Power Distribution Issues, Hyderabad.

Ray, Amit S. (2005), 'Managing Port Reforms in India: Case Study of Jawaharlal Nehru Port Trust', New Delhi, background paper for *World Development Report 2005*.

Reddy, Sarampally M. (2007), 'Status of Minor Irrigation in Andhra Pradesh', in R.S. Rao, V. Hanumantha Rao, and N. Venugopal (eds), *Fifty Years of Andhra Pradesh 1956–2006*, pp. 199–211. Hyderabad: Centre for Documentation, Research and Communication.

Rudolph, Lloyd I. and Susanne H. Rudolph (2007), 'Iconization of Chandrababu: Sharing Sovereignty in India's Federal Market Economy', in Rahul Mukherji (ed.), *India's Economic Transition: The Politics of Reforms*, pp. 231–64. New Delhi: Oxford University Press.

Sankar, T.L. (2002), 'Towards a People's Plan for Power Sector Reform', *Economic and Political Weekly*, 37(40): 4143–51.

Sreekumar, N., M. Thimma Reddy, and K. Raghu (2007), 'Strengths and Challenges of Andhra Pradesh Power Sector', *Economic and Political Weekly*, 36(52): 24–7.

Tariff Authority for Major Ports (2008), *Guidelines for Upfront Tariff Setting for PPP projects at Major Port Trusts*, Mumbai, 26 February.

Tongia, Rahul (2007), 'The Political Economy of Indian Power Sector Reforms', in David G. Victor and Thomas C. Heller (eds), *The Political Economy of Power Sector Reform*, pp. 109–74. Cambridge: Cambridge University Press.

Transmission Corporation of Andhra Pradesh Limited (APTRANSCO) and Distribution Companies (2006a), *Performance Improvement Initiatives: Power Sector in Andhra Pradesh*. Hyderabad: Government of Andhra Pradesh.

Transmission Corporation of Andhra Pradesh Limited (APTRANSCO) and Distribution Companies (2006b), Correspondence between Chief Engineer/ RAC and Reforms and Indian Institute of Public Administration, Hyderabad: Government of Andhra Pradesh, 6 July.

_________ (2007), Overview of AP Power Sector: Presentation to Nirupam Bajpai (Columbia University). Hyderabad: Government of Andhra Pradesh.

World Bank (1995), *India: Port Sector: Strategy Report*, 3 March. Washington: Infrastructure Operations Division South Asia Country Department II: South Asia Regional Office.

_________ (2001), *India: Power Supply to Agriculture*. Washington D.C.: World Bank, Energy Sector Unit, South Asia Regional Office.

6

Urban Reforms in Three Cities

Bangalore, Ahmedabad, and Patna

DARSHINI MAHADEVIA

URBAN CONTEXT AND CHALLENGES

The image of the Indian city today is quite Dickensian in its contours with its ubiquitous slums and squatter settlements; regular inundation in parts during the monsoons; open sewerage and storm-water drains, sometimes with water supply pipelines running through them; potholed roads and chaotic traffic; haphazard building construction in apparent violation of all planning norms and legislation; waste-pickers, children, and animals foraging amidst mounds of garbage; and the like. Over the past decade or so, public and private investments have begun changing parts of city landscapes, accompanied by higher awareness and representation of urban issues within the government and other forums. At the policy level, the first major urban development initiative, the Jawaharlal Nehru National Urban Renewal Mission (JNNURM), introduced in December 2005 by the central government, is an attempt to change this Dickensian image of the Indian city through, infusion of public investment on the one hand, and improvement of urban governance, on the other. The JNNURM has two dimensions: project-based funding and reforms; the former tied to progress on the latter.

India's level of urbanization is relatively low. According to the 2001 population census, 27.5 per cent of the country's population (285 million) lived in urban areas in 5,131 urban settlements. In 2005, the urban population was estimated to be 320 million or 30 per cent of the national population. Of this, 36 per cent or 115 million lived in 38 million-plus (metropolitan) cities.[1] The overall rate of urbanization in India has been slow: just 2.73 per cent per annum in the decade of the 1990s (Sivaramakrishnan et al. 2005: 27). However, there are variations across the country, with western and southern states registering higher levels and rates of urbanization in comparison to the northern, eastern, and north-eastern states.

Urban development falls under the jurisdiction of the respective state governments under the Indian Constitution. Therefore, legislation governing various aspects of urban development and the implementation of various development programmes, implementation of the 74th Constitutional Amendment Act (CAA) promulgated in 1992, urban reforms in general, and now the JNNURM reforms in particular, vary across states. The 74th CAA is briefly discussed later for its implications for urban governance.

Urban systems are dynamic. The boundaries of entities called 'urban centres' change continually with increases in population. Any legislation or a programme for urban areas should respond to this dynamic process. However, urban development programmes and urban governance reforms, more often than not, tend to have a unitary view, with policies generally leaning towards the 'one size fits all' approach. In other words, policies are the same for a mega city like Mumbai with a population of around 18 million and a small urban centre with a population of 50,000. This profoundly affects the success of policies, programmes, and schemes, and influences systems and styles of governance. Finally, each state in India has its historic trajectory of development and development paradigms, which also influence implementation of national-level policies and programmes. This chapter, therefore, contextualizes the implementation of the Central government programme—JNNURM—within the state-specific diversities of levels of development, the paradigms of development, and historic trajectories of the cities selected for investigation of the implementation of the reforms.

Service Deficiencies

There is an acute water shortage in urban areas: over 60 per cent of the urban population did not have access to water for their own individual use; and an estimated 17.73 million[2] or 26 per cent of the urban households did not have access to tap water (NSSO 2004). Urban sanitation is in an even more parlous state: 60 per cent of urban households do not have proper drainage (NSSO 2004); only 41.7 per cent (or 28.11 million) urban households are connected to closed drains; 18.5 per cent (or 12.47 million) of households do not have any access to a drainage network, and another 39.8 per cent (or 26.83 million) of households are connected to open drains; 12.04 million (7.87 per cent) of urban households do not have access to a latrine; another 5.48 million (8.13 per cent) use community latrines, and 13.14 million (19.49 per cent) use shared latrines. The urban households living under such deprivation are very large in actual numbers. The problem is focused at the bottom end of consumption expenditure; only 37 per cent of the households in the bottom half of the urban population had access to all three basic facilities: water supply, sanitation, and electricity; the comparative figure for the top half was 80 per cent (based on NSSO 2004). The urban housing shortage has been estimated to be at 24.7 million dwelling units,[3] and of this, 90 per cent of the deficit is among the urban poor.

Financial Inadequacy

'The infrastructure bottlenecks in urban centres are likely to pose serious impediments in enhancing productivity' (Expert Group on Commercialization of Infrastructure 1996: 27). The Expert Group arrived at a figure of Rs 800–940 billion as the requirement in fresh investment/operational maintenance costs for the period 1996–2001. The requirement for water supply and toilet facilities alone was estimated to be Rs 210 billion for the period 2001–11 and Rs 228 billion for the 2011–21 (Expert Group on Commercialization of Infrastructure 1996: 27). The expert group recommended that commercial sources of funds be tapped for the construction and renewal of urban infrastructure. Since then, the urban local bodies (ULBs), with sound resource bases and good credit rating, have been raising resources from financial institutions and bonds in the capital markets. However, the problem of expanding the revenue base of the cities to meet these financial obligations remains.

The revenue sources of the ULBs are limited with property tax as the principal self-generated income.[4] Besides, the ULBs are constrained by legislation that forbids them from deficit budgeting. They also require the permission of the respective state governments to resort to debt-financing. Property tax is inadequate and the fiscal gap is managed from the transfers recommended by the Central Finance Commissions (CFCs) and State Finance Commissions (SFCs), and allocations made by the Planning Commission, Planning Boards of the respective states, and centrally sponsored and state plan schemes. Thus, ULBs have to depend largely on grants from higher bodies to run efficiently (Mohanty et al. 2007). The 74th CAA mandates that the states set up SFCs[5] for the purpose of systematic tax sharing between the state government and the local governments, including the ULBs. There is mixed progress in the functioning of SFCs across states. In fact, the 12th CFC has criticized the states for delays in the constitution of SFCs, or constituting them in a phased manner, their frequent reconstitution, and generally for their lacklustre performance in most states. ULBs continue to receive ad hoc grants from the respective state governments, which seriously compromises their ability to function as the third tier of government as mandated under the 74th CAA.

Institutional Deficiencies

Deficiencies here span a range of areas. The key institutional problems are: (i) the multiplicity of organizations engaged in governing and service delivery; (ii) lack of coordination among them in relation to territorial functions; (iii) ever-expanding boundaries and often boundaries demarcated in an ad hoc manner creating further confusion in defining the jurisdictions and functions of existing institutions; (iv) lack of functional and financial powers of the ULB for it to function as a true third tier of government, for example, state governments holding on to functional powers through parastatals and state-level departments; (v) lack of adequate decentralization, for example by not forming ward committees as mandated by the 74th CAA, and dysfunctional ward committees wherever formed; (vi) lack of public participation and stakeholder involvement in key city/local-level decisions; (vii) inadequate monitoring of service delivery; (viii) lack of an enabling legislative framework to fill in institutional lacunae; and (ix) lack of transparency in the utilization of funds and negotiating contracts relating to public–private participation (PPP) agreements.

A multiplicity of organizations is a problem largely in the metropolitan cities, Mumbai, Delhi, Kolkata, and Chennai, where there is more than one local government directing the functioning of the city. For example, the Mumbai Metropolitan City (also called Mumbai Urban Agglomeration [MUA]) has the Brihan Mumbai Mahanagar Palike (BMMP), Thane Municipal Corporation, Kalyan–Dombivali Municipal Corporation, and five other local governments under its demarcated area. Delhi has the Municipal Corporation of Delhi (MCD), New Delhi Municipal Committee (NDMC), and Cantonment Board. The Cantonment Boards, whenever they fall within the cities, are under the overall control of the defence ministry.

Thus, there is no one entity called a city government controlling all the city-level functions, rather there are separate planning and service delivery institutions. In many cities, planning is undertaken by the designated development authorities, whereas service delivery is undertaken either through the ULB or the designated parastatals. Over and above this, there are industrial development corporations for the development of industrial estates. A classic case of dysfunction arises when the development authority hands over the developed areas (through infrastructure provision, sub-plotting, and sale of developed plots to households) to the ULB and the latter may refuse to take the responsibility of managing them. The ULBs also refuse to manage the areas developed by the Housing Boards or Slum Clearance Boards. Examples of this abound. The problem of coordination among these agencies is immense, and the 74th CAA mandates that all the service delivery and planning functions be brought under a single institution, the ULB. The integration of the peri-urban areas within an urban jurisdiction is entirely up to the state government, and this decision is taken without consultation with the concerned ULB and the peripheral local governments. In this way, the multiplicity of institutions gets carried forward to the new urban jurisdiction.

The ULBs are governed through legislation framed by the state government. These take the form of Municipal Acts which define the functional and financial powers of the ULBs. They have been so framed that the state governments continue to hold powers relating to the sanction of the Master Plan, zonal plans, and all other plans prepared for the city. The state governments decide the source of revenue and rates of taxation of the cities. They may directly engage themselves in service delivery through parastatals or state government departments. In the past, some of the ULBs were superseded by the state governments; for example, in Chennai from 1973[6] onwards for almost 25 years, and in Hyderabad too for an equal number of years, till the 74th CAA was promulgated. Patna Municipal Corporation (PMC) was also superseded by the state government till municipal elections were held in 2002. The third tier of government in the urban areas has, therefore, been weak in terms of powers and functions, something that the 74th CAA had sought to amend, and the JNNURM now seeks to alter. Lastly, the ULB's administration and management are controlled by the state government through the appointment of municipal commissioners (in the municipal corporations) and chief executive officers (in the municipalities). The city mayor has limited powers, unless there is mayor-in-council (MIC) system where the mayor has the power to form a council of ministers and take financial decisions. The mayor is directly elected in some states, such as in Madhya Pradesh; but in other states the mayor is elected by the councillors. Nonetheless, wherever an MIC has been formed, the mayor has greater powers than the city's municipal commissioner or the CEO (Expert Committee 2008: 62–4).

Decentralization, through the formation of ward committees as mandated by the 74th CAA has seen uneven implementation across the states. Kolkata has the longest history of decentralization since 1983 (when the Kolkata Municipal Corporation (KMC) Act 1980 was passed), with three important elements, namely: an MIC, Borough Committees, and enlarged obligatory responsibilities for the local government (Kehle, Mahadevia and Wolfe 2008). The borough is a unit between the ULB and the ward. With exceptions, formation of ward committees has been slow because many states did not amend their respective municipal acts to include the provision for ward committees (for example, Gujarat). Some states did amend the act but the ward committees were not formed. In some cities, ward committees were formed that lacked the spirit of the 74th CAA. For example, in Mumbai, one ward committee represents a population of a million. Lastly, there is a general lack of a consultative process for urban decision-making, either at the ward level or the city level, with a few exceptions. The institutional challenges are, therefore, huge.

Equity

This is a cross-cutting concern within each of the urban challenges discussed earlier. The extent of poverty is high, with 25.9 per cent of the urban population (about 80 million people) living below the poverty line in 2004–5, a decline from 32.6 per cent in 1993–4 (Himanshu 2007), but there was also an increase in inequalities; the Gini coefficient increasing from 34.4 (in 1993–4) to 37.6 (in 2004–5) (Himanshu 2007: 498). Besides this, the cities have also observed exclusionary processes with regard to land access, shelter, and basic services provisions, particularly in the context of the segmented city structures.[7] The service deficiencies are largely among the low-income settlements. Housing deficiencies are also prevalent among the urban poor. Urban planning does not incorporate participatory mechanisms, existing structures for participation in city development processes being restricted largely to the middle class. For example, the Resident Welfare Associations (RWAs), active in many metropolitan cities, are largely middle-class organizations (Kundu 2009). Some of the innovative governance systems have also been criticized for being elitist (Ghosh 2005; Nair 2005). The solid waste management (SWM) cases studies in Mahadevia and Wolfe (2008) also find that the participatory structures are limited to middle-class residential areas (see Mahadevia and Pharate [2008] for Mumbai; Kehle, Mahadevia and Parasher [2008] for Bangalore; Acharya and Parashar [2008] for Vejalpur Municipality, now merged with the Ahmedabad Municipal Corporation [AMC]).

Where the ULBs have moved towards institutional or capital market borrowings or have sought private sector participation in the delivery of basic services, there is a real question of a section of the urban population being priced out. The assessment of affordability for basic services is quite low. For example, the Bangalore Water Supply and Sewerage Board (BWSSB) assessed 2 per cent of the household income to represent affordability of water supply and sanitation among the slum dwellers.[8] A sound urban policy would mainstream the equity concerns within the overall development and reforms process.

RESEARCH FRAMEWORK, QUESTIONS, AND SCOPE

This chapter assesses the immediate impact of the JNNURM reforms on the four major urban development challenges discussed earlier. It needs to be mentioned that the four challenges discussed are not independent of one another. For example, service deficiencies can be improved by increasing financial allocations as well as by improving the institutional setting.

It needs to be mentioned at the outset that urban reforms in India began much before the JNNURM reforms. The latter are an extension of prior national-level attempts at urban reform as well as to mainstream the knowledge gleaned from successful city-level experiences of reforms. Therefore, they form part of the continuum of previous efforts at urban reforms. It is also relevant to mention that JNNURM is a three-year-old effort; this chapter looks at the immediate impact of this major urban development initiative on just three cities. JNNURM consists of both projects and wider reforms, with project funding linked to progress on reform milestones established under the programme. The cities are expected to benefit both from project funding and the implementation of reforms. This chapter focuses on the reform side of the story in the three cities under consideration rather than the projects undertaken as part of JNNURM.

In order to understand the specific unfolding of the JNNURM reforms in particular urban contexts, three cities—Ahmedabad, Bangalore, and Patna—have been selected.[9] Their experience has also been evaluated against the ongoing process of urban reform in the three states. It must be noted that the experiences of the three cities, and of the three states in which these are located, cannot be generalized for India as a whole. This case study does, however, allow one to extract lessons on the intersection of JNNURM and the specific urban challenges of these three cities to better understand processes of change in complex urban environments. The JNNURM reforms have been assessed against the historical background of each city, including its own history of reforms, and specific institutional context.

This chapter also seeks to evaluate reform outcomes in terms of mega-goals. In the urban context, John Friedmann (1998: 20) regards inspired political leadership, public accountability, inclusiveness, responsiveness, and non-violent conflict resolution as key dimensions of 'good city' governance. In his view, accessibility, transparency and responsiveness, effectiveness, efficiency, and honesty are the key dimensions of 'good city' management. UN Habitat (UNCHS 2000) has provided a practical mega-framework for moving towards an inclusive and well-governed city. This mega-framework also provides a basis for an evaluation of the achievements of reforms pursued in the three cities under consideration here (see Table 6.1).

Table 6.1 Normative Goals, Operational Components, and Mechanisms for the Inclusive City

Normative Goals	Operational Components	Mechanisms
Decentralization and participatory democracy	Local autonomy	• Delegation of authority to the competent level closest to the citizens (decentralization, subsidiary and proximity)
	Leadership for public participation and stakeholder involvement	• City referenda • Public hearings and town hall meetings • City consultation and participatory planning • Citizens' fora and other mechanisms for negotiation • Processes for conflict mediation
	Building democratic culture	• Enabling legislative framework to protect the rights and entitlements of all groups in society • Women's participation

(*contd.*)

Table 6.1 (*contd.*)

Normative Goals	Operational Components	Mechanisms
	Enablement	• Affirmative actions for marginalized groups • Procedures for public petitioning
Efficiency	Transparent financial management	• Participatory planning and budgeting • Transparent contracting and procurement systems
	Administration and service delivery	• Popularization of service standards and complaint procedures • Codes of conduct for leaders and officials • 'Best value' approaches to target-setting
	Efficient investment in infrastructure	• Participatory strategic planning to address the needs of all groups in society • Public–private partnerships for service provision
Equity	Resource allocation	• Investment incentives for targeted sectors and geographic areas • Social pacts and fair and predictable regulatory frameworks
	Empowerment	• Rules governing freedom of access to local authority information • Civic education • Enabling legislative framework for traditional economic and social institutions and informal sector operators
Security	Environmental management	• Environmental planning and management methodologies based on stakeholder involvement
	Disaster preparedness	• Partnership disaster prevention strategies
	Crime control and prevention	• Conflict mediation mechanisms, taking into account local and ethnic democratic traditions • Safety audits (especially for women) • Partnership crime-prevention strategies

Source: UNCHS (2000).

The key research questions addressed in this chapter include the following:

1. Have the objectives of the JNNURM reforms been met in the three cities?
2. Do JNNURM reforms address the four urban challenges of poor service delivery, financial inadequacy, institutional weaknesses, and equity in the three cities?
3. Do JNNURM reforms have the potential to take the three cities closer to a larger mega-goal or benchmark for inclusive governance? This question could be broken into number of sub-questions: Will the reforms bring about the autonomy of the ULB? Will they introduce decentralized democracy? Will they result in full operational transparency of all the public agencies in the cities? Will they bring about financial sustainability within the cities or create conditions for a move towards financial sustainability? Lastly, and importantly, will these reforms bring about a more equitable distribution of urban resources than is now the case?
4. Conversely, would the three cities studied have met their development challenges or moved towards an idea of an 'inclusive city' in the absence of the JNNURM reforms?

Approach to Assessing Reforms

Reforms have been assessed at two levels: one, at the overall level, looking at the progress the states have made in implementing them; two, at individual city level. At the city level, there is, first, a narrative of the historical background of the city, urban reforms initiatives (or otherwise) at the city level, identification of development challenges in the city, and then implementation of the reforms themselves. To the degree possible, an attempt is also made to match the claims made with the actual results of reforms. Thus, if the city states that property tax reform has been implemented, then actual collections have been examined to test this claim. The second aspect examined is whether the stated objectives of the JNNURM reforms have been fulfilled for the particular city. Finally, I assess whether or not implementation of reform is likely to lead to the realization of the mega-goal of the 'inclusive city'.

While there are an array of JNNURM reforms, only a few of them, have been picked up for discussion at the city level, at my discretion (based on my experience of researching urban issues). For example, for Bangalore, my assessment of the issues of utmost importance is local autonomy, building a democratic culture, and equitable resource allocation. For Ahmedabad, financial sustainability, building a democratic culture, equitable resource allocation, and now the emerging problem of erosion of local autonomy are important. For Patna, the most important dimensions for good governance or moving towards an 'inclusive city' are an enabling policy framework, local autonomy, enhancement of the financial base, improvement of service delivery, and building a democratic culture. In fact, Patna almost begins with a clean slate in urban reforms as a consequence of the JNNURM reforms and any progress is a good beginning for the city.

HISTORY OF URBAN REFORMS

Urban reforms in India have a history of about two decades. The most important events are briefly discussed below.

74th Constitutional Amendment Act

This is the first important step of urban reform introduced through the amendment of the Constitution in 1992. Known as the 74th CAA, this legislation assigned powers of self-governance to the ULBs. The contents of the legislation are: (i) giving the ULBs stability by recognizing them as the third tier of the government and holding mandatory elections at the ULB level;[10] (ii) one-third reservations for women in the elected wing of the ULB together with reservations for the Scheduled Castes (SCs) and Scheduled Tribes (STs); (iii) formation of Metropolitan Planning Committees (MPCs) for all urban agglomerations with a population of over a million and District Planning Committees (DPCs) for each administrative district; (iv) two-thirds of the MPC members and four-fifths of DPC members to be made up of elected officials to give these committees political decision-making powers; (v) converging 18 major functions listed in the 12th Schedule of the legislation at the ULB level (See Annexure I for the list of functions); these functions include planning, service delivery, and poverty alleviation; (vi) formation of a ward/wards committee, one committee for a population of up to 300,000; (vi) mandatory constitution of the SFC to ensure adequate local government finance so that the functional devolution can match financial capabilities; and (vii) eventually all local policy decisions to be taken by the elected council of the ULB. Provisions of the 74th CAA had mechanisms to meet three of the goals referred to in Table 6.1, including decentralization and participatory democracy, efficiency, and equity.

The states did not move at any speed on implementing the 74th CAA. Apart from the first two provisions of the legislation—regular elections to the ULB council and reservations for women, Scheduled Castes and Scheduled Tribes—the other provisions were virtually ignored by the state governments. Hence, on the eve of the JNNURM reforms, most of the provisions of the 74th CAA had not been implemented by the states.

Urban Reform Incentive Fund

The precursor to the JNNURM reforms was the Urban Reform Incentive Fund (URIF), which was announced in the 2002–3 budget with an allocation of Rs 5,000 million (Rs 500 crore), to provide reform-linked central assistance to states and approved in June 2003. The reforms proposed were[11] to do with (i) enabling the housing and land markets through repeal of the Urban Land Ceiling and Regulation Act (ULCRA) at the state level, rationalization of stamp duty and bringing it down to 5 per cent by the end of the Tenth Five Year Plan, reforming the rent control laws and computerized land registration; and (ii) increasing the financial base of the ULBs through property tax reform, increasing collection efficiency of property tax to 85 per cent, the levy of user charges on certain services to achieve full cost recovery of operation and maintenance costs, and the introduction of a double-entry system of accounting in the ULBs.

The Central funds were to be released to the ULBs as Additional Central Assistance (ACA) based on their achieving the prescribed reform milestones. The Central government committed just Rs 500 crore for the URIF (just 1 per cent of the amount under the JNNURM). The funds committed were too small to interest the states and the ULBs, thus the reforms agenda did not gather steam.

Individual City-level Efforts

Individual cities went ahead with their own indigenous efforts at urban reforms. For expanding their financial base, the cities first went ahead to obtain a credit rating and then borrowed from financial institutions, besides raising bonds from the capital market. The latter is a cheaper source of finance compared to borrowing from financial institutions. Ahmedabad, Bangalore, Hyderabad, Nasik, Nagpur, Ludhiana, and Madurai, among other cities, have issued one or more issues of municipal bonds. States such as Tamil Nadu and Karnataka have set up pooled finance mechanisms. Bangalore moved on to a fund-based accounting system and then to a double-entry one. The self-assessment system (SAS) in property tax was first introduced in 1994 in Patna and then in other cities, namely, Bangalore, Mangalore, and Hyderabad, and others.

Kolkata, as already mentioned, introduced decentralization in 1980, introducing a concept of a borough committee under the municipal corporation to stimulate participation. Bangalore experimented with the Bangalore Agenda Task Force (BATF) in 1999, aimed at coordinating multiple agencies in order to upgrade city infrastructure. Ahmedabad has a participatory slum development programme—the Slum Networking Programme (SNP), introduced in 1997, which won the Habitat Award of Best Practice. SNP was also implemented in Indore city in a few slums. SWM has seen an abundance of indigenous efforts at participation, bringing in the private and community sectors into the SWM system. Examples include Mumbai (through Advanced Locality Management [ALM] schemes), Ranchi (NGO-initiated SWM system), Hyderabad and Ahmedabad (contracting waste collection to women's Self Help Groups [SHGs]), Bangalore (contracting waste collection and disposal to the private sector), and Exnoras (a community-based institution) in Chennai and Hyderabad. Bangalore has experience of community networking through Janaagraha, NGO supporting participatory governance.

Bangalore and now some other cities have undertaken service delivery monitoring through Citizen's Report Cards (CRCs) (Paul 2002, 2006; Centre for Youth and Social Development and Public Affairs Centre 2005; Sekhar and Shah 2006). CRCs are intended to bring in accountability and reduce corruption amongst public services providers, streamline public service delivery, increase interaction between service providers and citizens,[12] improve grievance redressal, encourage and strengthen community participation, promote innovative measures, and, in the final analysis, bring about change (Sekhar and Shah 2006).

Mahadevia (2001), Mahadevia et al. (2008), and Mahadevia and Wolfe (2008) find that most of the innovative practices have, at best, remained independent standing practices and have not been replicated in different contexts or up-scaled. At worst, the overall structure of governance remaining unchanged, these practices have lost steam after a few years. One could argue that there has been an attempt to replicate and upscale 'innovative practices' or 'best practices' through the JNNURM reforms while ensuring that the previous reforms, as of the 74th CAA and devised under URIF, are carried forward but the path adopted for this is through the conditionalities attached to JNNURM funds.

JNNURM

The first major national urban renewal mission, JNNURM, was introduced in December 2005 by the Government of India. It has two major goals: improving urban infrastructure, and urban governance. Reforms are an essential component of the entire mission, and the reforms are a pre-condition for funding the project.

It is called a mission and not a programme, because:

> cities and towns in India ... contribute over 50 per cent of the country's GDP ... are central to economic growth. For the cities to realize their full potential and become effective engines of growth, it is necessary that focused attention be given to the improvement of infrastructure.[13]

Besides the objective of growth, the Mission addressed the Common Minimum Programme[14] agenda of the Central government led by the first United Progressive Alliance and also meeting the Millennium Development Goals (MDGs). [15]

The Mission has two components: (i) Urban Infrastructure and Governance (UIG), for projects relating to water supply and sanitation, sewerage, solid waste management, road network, urban transport, and re-development of old city areas; and (ii) Basic Services for the Urban Poor (BSUP), for integrated development of slums through projects to provide shelter, basic services, and other related civic amenities to the urban poor.

The Mission is being implemented through the following process:

1. Preparation of a city development plan (CDP), which indicates the city's development strategy,[16] prioritizing projects, and preparing financing plans for the latter.
2. Preparing detailed project reports (DPRs) for each project in such a way as to take the life-cycle cost[17] of each of the projects into consideration.
3. Appraisal of the CDPs and then the DPRs by the technical wings of the ministry; or, if necessary, by specialized/technical agencies before placing such proposals for sanction before the Central Sanctioning and Monitoring Committee (CSMC). The CSMCs can use their own discretion in prioritizing projects.[18]
4. Releasing Central funds in such a way that these are used to leverage other sources of funds. The funds are released to the State Level Nodal Agency (SLNA), which is responsible for leveraging other funds. A

Project Monitoring Unit (PMU) is set up within the SLNA. The PMUs in the states can be internal to the SLNA or part of a consultancy firm appointed by it. The funds are released in instalments to ensure their appropriate utilization in conjunction with the institution of urban reforms.

5. While the CDP and DPRs are prepared and approved, the states and the cities/parastatals enter into a memorandum of agreement (MoA) with the Government of India (GoI), indicating their commitment to implementing identified reforms by spelling out specific milestones. Signing the MoA is necessary to access Central assistance.
6. Anticipation of private sector participation through the mechanism of using Central funds to leverage additional resources for the projects.
7. Quarterly monitoring of the projects and the reforms process. (These aspects of the JNNURM have not been reviewed in this chapter.)

The Mission covers 63 cities: seven cities with a million plus population, 28 with a population between 1 million and 4 million, and 28 that are either state capitals or cities of religious, historic, and tourist significance.[19] However, cities are periodically added as mission cities, depending upon the interest of the state governments concerned.

The objectives of the Mission are:[20]

1. Establishing modern and transparent budgeting, accounting, financial management systems designed and adopted for all urban service and governance functions.
2. Establishing and then operationalizing a city-wide framework for planning and governance.
3. Universalizing access to all basic levels of urban services.
4. Establishing financial sustainability of ULBs and other urban service delivery agencies by enhancing revenue instruments.
5. Conducting local service delivery and governance in a transparent and accountable manner.
6. Introducing e-governance applications in core functions of ULBs/parastatal (other service delivery agencies), resulting in reduced cost and time of service delivery processes.

The national government was expected to contribute Rs 50,000 crore over a seven-year period (up to 2012 when the JNNURM would end), an amount that has since been enhanced, to leverage funds at the state and local government levels to the extent of Rs 120,000 crore.

Funds are released as ACA (100 per cent Central grant) to the state government or its designated SLNA, which in turn disburses the ACA to the ULBs or parastatal agencies (as the case may be) as a soft loan or grant-cum-loan, or a grant. It is suggested that the grant-cum-loan should be so sanctioned that 25 per cent of the Central and state grant put together is recovered and ploughed into a revolving fund to leverage market funds for infrastructure projects. At the end of the Mission period, this revolving fund may be transmuted into a State Urban Infrastructure Fund.[21]

The first instalment of 25 per cent is released on signing of the MoA by the state government/ULB/parastatal for implementation of the JNNURM projects. The balance amount of assistance is released in three instalments when the utilization certificates are received, and subject to the achievement of milestones agreed for the reforms implementation in the MoA.[22] The SLNA sends quarterly progress reports (QPRs) to the mission directorate (in the two ministries)[23] on the projects and reforms. Thus, reforms are key to receiving Central grants.

Reforms

The JNNURM reforms fall into three categories: (i) mandatory at the state level, (ii) mandatory at the ULB and parastatal levels, and (iii) optional at the state and ULB/parastatal levels. Two optional reforms are required to be achieved every year; in this way, all the optional reforms have to be accomplished by the end of the mission period. The classification of reforms, their nature, and progress at the state and city levels are shown in Annexure II. Evidently, the reforms have progressed at an uneven rate across India. Some states have done comparatively well while others have just begun the process. At the top of the table of reforms accomplished are Andhra Pradesh, Tamil Nadu, Gujarat, and Karnataka; at the bottom are the north-east states, Punjab, Haryana, Uttar Pradesh, and Bihar. The ranking of cities by achievement of the reforms is shown in Annexure III.

Table 6.2 lists the reforms under the following broad categories: nature of the reform, normative goal addressed, and urban challenge addressed by each. There can be a contention about the goals fulfilled by each reform. For example, the neo-liberal framework could interpret financial sustainability as a pre-condition for decentralization and equity. Some scholars in India have viewed decentralization as an expansion of a neo-liberal agenda. Therefore, experiments such as that of BATF have been viewed as an expansion of an elitist model of governance through legitimized institutional means (Ghosh 2005; Nair 2005). Kundu (2009) has viewed the RWAs and the Bhagidari system in Delhi as elitist capture of urban governance. Many JNNURM reforms are a reiteration of the provisions of the 74th CAA, coming as conditionalities of the Mission, as has been discussed earlier. Reforms for e-governance are new, as is a mechanism for implementating the Right to Information (RTI) Act, and reforms for introducing environmental sustainability.

Table 6.2 Reforms Checklist by Category, Nature, Goal Fulfilled, and Challenge Addressed

Checklist of Reforms	Nature	Goal	Challenge
Financial Sustainability			
Shift to Double-Entry Municipal Accounting	Mandatory: ULB	Efficiency*	Financial deficiencies
Property tax coverage: 85 per cent	Mandatory: ULB		
Property tax collection efficiency: 90 per cent	Mandatory: ULB		
User charges for 100 per cent cost recovery for (operation and maintenance (O&M) in water supply	Mandatory: ULB		
User charges for 100 per cent cost recovery for O&M in solid waste management	Mandatory: ULB		
Encouraging PPP	Optional		
Efficiency Enhancement			
Administrative reforms	Optional	Efficiency	Institutional deficiencies
Structural reforms	Optional		
Transparency and Accountability			
Revision of building by-laws—streamlining the approval process	Optional	Efficiency	Institutional deficiencies
Simplification of legal and procedural framework for conversion of agricultural land for non-agricultural purpose	Optional		
Introduction of computerized process of land and property registration	Optional		
Introduction of Property Title Certification System in ULBs	Optional		
Devolution of Powers to the ULBs from the State Governments			
Implementation of 74th Constitutional Amendment Act—Transfer of 12 Schedule Functions	Mandatory: state	Decentralization & participatory democracy	Institutional deficiencies

(*contd.*)

Table 6.2 (*contd.*)

Checklist of Reforms	Nature	Goal	Challenge
City planning functions to be transferred to cities	Mandatory: state		
Water and sanitation functions to be transferred to cities	Mandatory: state		
Institutional Coordination			
Implementation of 74th Constitutional Amendment Act—Constitution of DPC	Mandatory: state	Decentralization & participatory democracy	Institutional deficiencies
Implementation of 74th Constitutional Amendment Act—Constitution of MPC	Mandatory: state		
Deepening Participation			
E-Governance to be set up	Mandatory: ULB	Decentralization & participatory democracy	Institutional deficiencies
Enactment of public disclosure law	Mandatory: state		
Community participation law*	Mandatory: state		
Equity			
Internal earmarking for basic services for poor	Mandatory: ULB	Equity	Equity
Earmarking 25% developed land in all housing projects for EWS/LIG	Optional		
Environmental Sustainability			
Rainwater harvesting in all buildings—Revision of building by-laws	Optional	Security	-
By-laws on reuse of recycled water	Optional		
Land Market Promotion			
Rationalization of stamp duty to 5%	Mandatory: state	Efficiency	Institutional deficiencies
Rent control	Mandatory: state		
Repeal of Urban Land Ceiling and Regulation Act (ULCRA)	Mandatory: state		

Source: http://jnnurm.nic/, accessed 20 December 2008.

Notes: *Also fulfils the goal of decentralization by creating conditions for the financial sustainability of the cities. It may also be argued that if the cities have resources on hand, they may be able to deploy these to targeted sectors and geographic areas, and thereby address the question of equity.

Given that the implementation of reforms requires substantial changes in the way the states and the cities are functioning, and the lack of enthusiasm shown by the states in implementing the 74th CAA and the URIF, progress on the JNNURM reforms has been slow (see Annexure II). The progress is slowest in implementing reforms that would devolve powers to the ULBs, deepen democracy, and usher in institutional coordination. The cities are floundering in implementing administrative and structural reforms. Progress is also slow with regard to the cost recovery of O&M (operations and maintenance) charges for water supply and SWM. Many cities have, however, taken to promoting PPP for certain services. It is heartening to see that a number of cities have earmarked funds in their budgets for deployment towards services for the poor, but the progress in earmarking land for low-income housing programmes is deficient. Finally, many cities have begun reforms on e-governance, but case studies highlight that setting up an e-governance portal is as difficult as undertaking other reforms.

Annexure III, which lists the status of reforms achieved by the cities, shows that Vishakhapatnam alone has accomplished all the mandatory reforms and is on the way to accomplishing optional ones. Of the 10 optional reforms, the city has accomplished seven. Among the top 10 cities in terms of completion of reforms, three are from Andhra Pradesh, three from Tamil Nadu, three from Gujarat, and one from Rajasthan. Ahmedabad is in the top 10 in the overall implementation of the reforms. Haridwar, Panaji, Patna, and Nainital have implemented only one reform each. By and large, the cities in the hill states, the North-East, and some special category cities have not moved ahead on the reforms. A detailed study of Patna indicates why this is so.

MONITORING THE REFORMS

As the reforms are mandatory for accessing Central government funds, their implementation is being tightly monitored. To enable the states and cities to complete one reform, the Central government has broken up each component into sub-components. The state government has to commit itself to a timeframe to complete each sub-component of the reform. For example, to complete the reform relating to property tax, the ULBs have to act on 25 items (Annexure IV) and set a date for completing action on each item. The monitoring formats for the reforms are extensive. This approach, it seems, has been taken to assist the state governments to carry out the reforms, on the one hand, and to categorically ensure that the reforms are carried out, on the other. Two opinions have been expressed about this tight monitoring of the reforms by the Central government: (i) that such top-down enforcement of the reforms violates the federal structure and spirit of Indian state; and (ii) whether top-down or bottom-up, the reforms need to be viewed from the perspective of whether or not the direction of change expected is acceptable. The outcomes will have to be monitored in the long run.

IMPLEMENTATION OF REFORMS

Selection of Cities

Three cities—Bangalore, Ahmedabad, and Patna—have been selected for somewhat detailed analysis of the extent of the JNNURM reforms' implementation and to understand the conditions under which these reforms were successful or otherwise. All three are metropolitan cities and, therefore, share certain common problems of institutional complexities, decentralization, and coordination.

The three cities were selected because each of them had a different institutional context: Ahmedabad has a powerful ULB with a convergence of all functions at the ULB level. Bangalore has a weak ULB and all its services have been delivered by parastatals, the service delivery of which has, according to some studies, improved in recent years. Patna has poor service delivery and suffers from a lack of institutional development at the ULB level. The three cities selected broadly represent three different types of institutional arrangements prevalent in most states in India. Each type has different implications for the goals of decentralization and democracy. While the ULB is the third tier of government and has elected representatives, parastatals, however efficient, may not be directly answerable to the city residents unless special efforts are made to ensure such accountability. The state government departments are not by any means at a level close to the residents of the city.

The three cities were also chosen based on a combination of two JNNURM criteria: (i) progress of reforms, and (ii) the extent of project implementation. Annexure V provides the data on the percentage of ACA released of the total committed amount.[24] This indicator has been used because the percentage of ACA released depends upon the progress of the reforms, on the one hand, and the city's capacity to utilize funds, on the other. Annexure VI sets out the ranking of cities in completing the reforms and in the percentage of ACA received by them. The combined ranking of both the parameters, rank in reforms and rank in ACA released, puts Rajkot at the top, followed by Hyderabad, Vijayawada, Vadodara, and Jaipur. Ahmedabad is at the 12th position in the combined index, Bangalore at the 23rd position, and Patna at the 44th. In the reforms ranking, Ahmedabad is at number eight, Bangalore at number 15, and Patna at number 47.

Case of the Parastatal Model and Indigenous Reforms: Bangalore

This is a case of a parastatal-dominated service delivery system, state government control over the affairs of the city; it also has a long history of indigenous reforms at city level. Bangalore, India's fifth largest metropolis, is the capital of Karnataka state, and is known as the 'Silicon Valley of India' with most major information and technology companies based here. In January 2007, the seven city municipal councils (CMCs), one town municipal council (TMC), and 111 villages were merged with the Bangalore Mahanagar Palike (BMP) to form the Bruhat Bengaluru Mahanagar Palike (BBMP) (Greater Bangalore Municipal Corporation) (Expert Committee 2008) with an area of 800 sq km and a population of 6.8 million.[25] The total number of wards in the city has increased from 100 to 147. The BBMP, with a size 3.5 times the erstwhile ULB, was created to improve and coordinate infrastructure development in urban and peri-urban areas.[26] This expansion of the city was effected by issuing a notification through the Urban Development Department of the Government of Karnataka (GoK). This change in the ULB boundaries meant changing the jurisdiction of all the parastatals functioning within the city.

Water supply deficiencies were and continue to occur in the peripheral areas of Bangalore (in the former CMCs and TMCs) in accordance with the now outdated CDP prepared in 2006.[27] The old ULB, the BMP, had 100 per cent water supply coverage, 40 per cent drainage coverage, and 100 per cent SWM coverage. The data of services coverage in the peripheral areas is not available. About 10 per cent, 4.3 lakh population of the BMP, lived in slums according to the population census of 2001 (Office of the Registrar General & Census Commissioner, India 2005: 22).

Public utilities in Bangalore are provided by parastatals (see Figure 6.1). Besides the institutions mentioned in Figure 6.1, there is Bangalore International Airport Area Planning Authority (BIAAPA), which also owns large chunks of land. The state has an apex infrastructure finance institution, like the State Urban Infrastructure Fund recommended under the JNNURM, called Karnataka Urban Infrastructure Development and Finance Corporation (KUIDFC), which is the SLNA for the JNNURM.

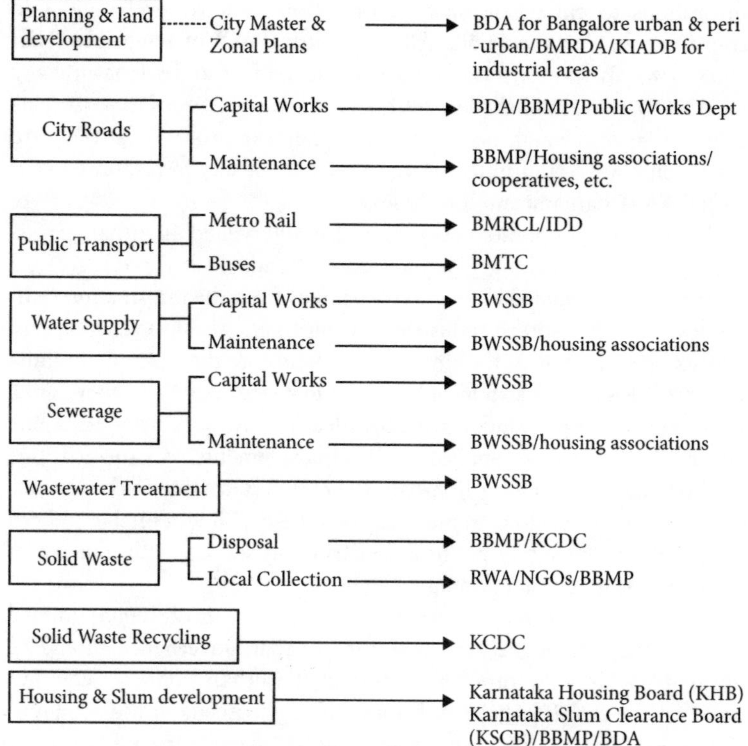

Figure 6.1 Institutional Structure, Bangalore

Source: Author's construction.
Notes: BDA = Bangalore Development Authority; BMRDA = Bangalore Metropolitan Regional Development Authority; KIADB = Karnataka Industrial Area Development Board; BMRCL = Bengaluru Metropolitan Rail Corporation Limited; IDD = Infrastructure Development Department; BMTC = Bangalore Metropolitan Transport Corporation; KCDC = Karnataka Composting Development Corporation; KSCB = Karnataka Slum Clearance Board.

Bangalore has a long history of civil society participation in urban governance, with the philosophy of 'citizens of Bangalore taking ownership of the city'. In response to the 74th CAA, a forum called Citizen's Voluntary Initiative for the City (CIVIC) was set up. CIVIC focused on participatory budgeting and holding public hearings on proposed development projects in the city. In the mid-1990s, a state-sponsored initiative, 'Swabhimana', was established to develop new non-governmental institutions to enhance citizen participation in ward-level politics in coordination with the Public Affairs Centre (PAC) of Bangalore (Nair 2005: 318). In the spirit of the new 'ownership' attitude, Janaagraha, a local NGO, was established in 2001, and urged the citizens to participate in governance through neighbourhood planning processes at the ward level. Some ward committees were formed in the city in response to the 74th CAA (Chamaraj and Rao 2006).

The private corporate sector has also intervened in urban governance and policymaking. The Bangalore Agenda Task Force (BATF), a 15-member nominated body of professionals from the information technology (IT) and biotech industries, management and financial experts, was set up in 1999 with the aim to make Bangalore the 'best city in India by 2004'.[28] BATF was also meant to serve to coordinate the activities of a large number of parastatals, with the idea that the success of corporate governance should be applied to city management. As expected, this initiative did not last long. The Bangalore CDP states that in the absence of space for elected local representatives, the BATF was unable to keep pace with the changing political scenario and subsequently ran out of steam and stopped functioning.

There have, however, been critics of this effort. Ghosh (2005) pointed out that the role of the private sector in urban governance should be evaluated within the broader context of the urban political economy, and that the BATF policies did not address the needs of the economically poor. Ghosh (2005) also pointed out that while the BATF survey highlighted environmental degradation as the overwhelming problem,[29] the organization prioritized other infrastructure such as flyovers, power, telecom, and public transportation (essentially the Metro). This criticism of BATF is in line with the argument about the increasing elitism in urban governance in the name of citizen participation.

Given that there are so many parastatals at the city level, there is a need to coordinate their activities. A new entity named ABIDE (Agenda for Bengaluru Infrastructure Development) was set up in 2008 as a task force by B.S. Yeddyurappa, the current chief minister of the state. ABIDE, chaired by the CM, coordinates the activities of the 15 public agencies functioning in the city. ABIDE has 23 other members: heads of the 15 public agencies working in Bangalore, politicians, representatives from NGOs, private sector representatives, and some well-known residents of the city.[30] The structure, objectives, and approach are very similar to those of the BATF, and some individuals who were part of the BATF are now with ABIDE. The chief minister being the chair of the initiative gives it greater teeth than the BATF, but as it is not a statutory authority, there is a possibility of it being wound up in the event of a change of government in the state.

The GoK has decided to continue with the existing institutional structure for service delivery because efforts have been made over time to bring about their accountability. Also, it is administratively difficult to merge parastatals with the ULBs because it requires transfer of staff from the former to the latter together with a transfer of functions. Both might have different pay structures and it might be virtually impossible to bring about pay parity between different public organizations.

For accountability of the parastatals, which are not elected bodies, civil society has played very important role in Bangalore. Efforts to monitor public services delivery in the city began in 1993 through the CRCs by the PAC. Since then, three CRCs have been conducted, first in 1994, then in 1999, and the last in 2003. The results of the CRCs are shared with the public service providers, who are then encouraged to improve their services and make their functioning more citizen friendly. The CRCs, given media pressure, have yielded results. General households have reported an improvement in overall satisfaction with regard to performance of the various public agencies from 9 per cent in 1994 to 49 per cent in 2003 (Balakrishnan 2006). Service delivery has thus noticeably improved in Bangalore over time.

The then BMP (renamed BBMP in 2007) was the first organization to adopt the double-entry accounting system and has also introduced the accrual-based accounting system. The city moved to a fund-based budget system (FBS) from 2001 onwards. The state is among only a few with a state-level urban infrastructure fund, the KUIDFC. Besides, the then BMP and now the BBMP has a self-assessment system (SAS) for property tax. The BBMP has also decentralized the property tax collection system to eight zonal offices, and the city portal assists taxpayers to calculate the tax on their own and guides them to where this tax is payable. BBMP changed the property tax assessment from a capital value-based system to a unit area value-based system from 31 January 2009.[31] The draft of this notification was pending with the BBMP for a year, almost since the beginning of 2008, and therefore no property tax collection could take place for the financial years 2007–8 and 2008–9. After the announcement of this notification, BBMP has begun collecting the property tax for both these years. Because of the expansion of the city limits and change in the property tax assessment system, the BBMP's finances were in a parlous situation in February 2009.

Limited Impact of the JNNURM Reforms

As discussed earlier, the JNNURM reforms in Bangalore are being implemented on the prior base of governance innovations. Given that the city has developed a long tradition of consultations, however narrow-based or middle-class oriented these may be, this has led to consultations in the city regarding the JNNURM. The JNNURM reforms guidelines suggest that the states and cities commit to reforms after effective consultations with agencies, institutions, and civil society.[32]

With regard to local autonomy, the GoK has decided not to converge all urban functions at the ULB level and will continue with the existing model of parastatal-based service delivery. The Bangalore Supply and Sewerage Corporation (BWSSB), for example, was relatively healthy financially and its improved performance was captured by report cards conducted by the PAC. The GoK did not want to destabilize the situation by dismantling an institution that was a relatively well functioning public utility by handing it over to the BMP. Doing so would also have raised complex questions of how best to allocate staff to the ULB without seriously disrupting existing seniority, promotion, and salary structures. This fitted in with a national pattern of resisting decentralization in water supply and sanitation with few exceptions.

Two important changes have, however, been introduced in the powers of the ULB: (i) representative of the BBMP will sit on the boards of the BDA, BWSSB, and BMTC for integration of the functions, and (ii) the ULB will have a contractual or direct relationship with the parastatals for delivering services listed in the 12th Schedule of the 74th CAA. The latter will mean that the BBMP will enter into a contractual arrangement with the BWSSB for the delivery of water supply and sanitation services. The detailed contents and the modalities of the contract are not yet known. Besides, the urban planning function were to be transferred from the BDA to the BBMP by the end of 2009. At the time of my field visit in early 2009, from the discussions I had with the BDA officials, it was not clear whether that would happen or not; and that the BDA officials were unaware of any such possibility. For integration of the functions of numerous parastatals, ABIDE has been created, as discussed earlier. The DPCs were constituted by a GoK circular on 12 April 2001, and the MPC will be set up in accordance with the recommendations of the Expert Committee, also called the Kasturirangan Committee (Expert Committee 2008). Finally, the autonomy of the ULB will not be possible in any real sense as all the powers relating to legislation concerned with city functioning and decisions on local tax rates will continue to remain with the state government, a universal phenomenon in India.

For the goal of participatory democracy, the creation of institutions at the grassroots is extremely important. The 74th CAA recommended setting up ward committees. The JNNURM reforms mandate the enactment of community participation law, making ward committees mandatory: there are currently 33 ward committees in the city. The community participation law has been drafted but remains with legal experts for finalization. Interestingly, the Karnataka Local Fund Authorities Fiscal Responsibility Act, 2003, provides for two rounds of consultations with local organizations during budget preparation. I have yet to see any evidence of the implementation of this Act.

The accounting reforms for the municipal budgets which have been included in the JNNURM reforms have antecedents in Bangalore's experience. Therefore, all these reforms were carried out by the city much before these became mandatory under the JNNURM. The city has been regularly applying for a credit rating and the BBMP has published its balance sheet for 2006–7 on its website. However, more important analysis would be of the financial sustainability elements built into the city budgets. The BBMP finances have not been scrutinized for this because of the difficult current situation with which the ULB is faced. However, one aspect of cost recovery of SWM has been examined. In the current property tax regime, there is no separate tax or charge for the SWM. The property tax has three additional cesses tagged on to it: (i) health cess (15 per cent over the assessed property tax), (ii) library cess (6 per cent), and (iii) beggary cess (3 per cent). There is an idea of introducing an SWM cess to cover the cost of this service.[33] In the absence of any existing revenue from SWM, it is not possible to assess the impact of this reform on the city.

Another important reform for the financial autonomy of the ULBs is the establishment of the SFC. Currently, Karnataka is implementing the recommendations of the 2nd SFC, whose operational period was 2003–4 to 2007–8. The 2nd SFC provides for 40 per cent of the Non-Loan Gross Own Revenue Receipt (NLGORR) to be devolved to the local governments—the panchayats and the ULBs—of which 20 per cent is to be for the ULBs and 80 per cent for the panchayats.[34] There is a need to undertake a study of whether the SFC devolution of grants is adequate for the ULB.

As explained earlier, the parastatals have been performing relatively well in Bangalore city. The BWSSB has been able to coordinate with the local government in Bangalore to expand its functional areas with the expansion in the area of the BBMP. Because the BWSSB works as a special purpose vehicle (SPV), it has been able to introduce a cost recovery mechanism in its functioning. The water supply is metered and the BWSSB is able to recover the revenue (recurring expenditures), and the operating ratios (ratio of revenue to expenditure) have been over one for the years 2005–6 (1.07), 2006–7 (1.00), and 2007–8 (1.01).[35] Similarly, the BMTC has been a profit-making corporation; its profit for 2007–8 was Rs 140 crore, albeit down from Rs 224 crore in 2006–7, according to a news report of May 2008. Indeed, the BMTC has been posting profits since 1998–9 (Shastry 2008).

The goal of equity is cross-cutting and could be analysed in the processes of participation, financial resource allocation, and land resource allocation. A study by RoyChowdhury (2008) of the Bangalore slums indicated that even though basic amenities were highly inadequate in the slums, the principal problem articulated by the slum dwellers as well as leaders related to land rights. As a large number of slums were on private land, the land rights issue could be resolved only if the private landowners, whose land had been squatted upon, transferred land rights to the slum-dwellers. RoyChowdhury (2008) argues that the public agencies had been woefully dragging their feet in finding a solution to this widespread problem.

If the land tenure question is not addressed, then the other options of land supply to low-income groups must be ensured. ULCRA has been repealed in the state since 1999 but that has not resolved the problem. The BDA could have increased the small lots in their layouts. A draft bill has been enacted for the purpose, but is yet to be accepted.[36] Research by Solomon Benjamin and his collaborators in Bangalore indicates that these layouts have in the main been purchased by the middle-income groups and above, and these are beyond the affordability of the urban poor (Benjamin 2008; Benjamin et al. 2008).

The Karnataka Slum Clearance Board (KSCB) is implementing the BSUP component. The KSCB has estimated 542 slum pockets in the city, housing 198,600 households.[37] Of these, 311 slum pockets have not been notified and therefore do not qualify for any basic services extension. Under the BSUP, the KSCB is going to construct only 10,551 dwelling units (DUs) (just 5.3 per cent of its estimated households living in slums in Bangalore). There is no way the demand for housing from among the slum households is going to be met by the BSUP. However, interestingly, all the BSUP housing being constructed by the KSCB is in situ upgradation, which does not entail displacement of the slum-dwellers to the city periphery, as is the case with new housing projects. However, these schemes are only on the land owned by the KSCB and, therefore, the city does not have any mechanism to increase land access to the slum-dwellers.

The last aspect relating to equity is service delivery in slums. Although the PAC studies mentioned improvement in satisfaction among the slum-dwellers with regard to service delivery (Sekhar 2009), the Bangalore CDP (p. 20) states that just 17 per cent of the slums have a water supply and sanitation network. Thus, the subsidized BWSSB activities are yet to reach the slums to any substantial degree. The most important problem in Bangalore is that the city does not have a comprehensive listing of slums, and that three public organizations—BBMP, BDA, and KSCB—are responsible for slum development, resulting in a multiplicity of institutions and lack of coordination among them.

Case of an Inclusive City Regressing: Ahmedabad

Ahmedabad's case is that of an inclusive city regressing over time. The city already had convergence of all the municipal functions listed under the 12th Schedule of the 74th CAA, and did not have to do much in this area. This made the city complacent about moving ahead with other reforms, such as creating structures of participation and accountability, on one hand, and withdrawal of the state government's grip on ULB functioning, on the other.

Ahmedabad currently has a population of 4.5 million and an area of 466 sq km. In February 2006, it covered an area of 198 sq km and had a population of 3.5 million. Seven municipalities and contiguous areas were merged with the former Ahmedabad Municipal Corporation (AMC) limits (*The Times of India*, Ahmedabad, 15 February 2006). Ahmedabad is India's seventh largest metropolis and is the commercial capital of Gujarat. The expansion of its city limits has meant an increase in the number of its wards from 43 to 58.

Unlike Bangalore, the AMC is the sole public authority in charge of providing all collective services. The AMC has also been fulfilling its non-obligatory functions, such as health care and education, through its own funds. The city has a remarkable presence and participation of civil society groups, working either as charity or developmental organizations. The latter have their antecedents in the Gandhian movement and philosophy of voluntary work, while the former are attributable to the philosophy of philanthropy[38] that emerges from capitalism. Indeed, the early capitalism of Ahmedabad was entirely indigenous and the capitalist class was forward looking. The city's first drainage line was laid in the late nineteenth century (Vashi and Mehta 2009). Unlike Bangalore, whose early institutional development could be attributed first to the British and then the public sector entities (Nair 2005), Ahmedabad's is attributed to the indigenous capitalist class, Gandhian philosophy, and decisions taken by the leaders of the Indian National Congress (INC) prior to independence. Spodek (2002), tracing the contemporary institutional history of Ahmedabad, states that Sardar Patel accepted the proposition of the Gandhian trade union, the Textile Labour Association (TLA), to field one industrial worker for municipal elections, and this worker, by caste a Harijan (SC), won the seat unopposed. Spodek (2002) states that representation of the TLA in the municipality increased steadily to five by 1936 (citing Banker 1965: 218) and to 17 in the late 1940s (citing Lakha 1988: 116). Ahmedabad was a textile city, with a predominantly industrial working class. The decline of the textile mills brought about the city's transformation to a service city, on the one hand, and a decline in the philanthropy of the capitalist class, on the other.

The city also has other firsts. The first example of a private utility company, Ahmedabad Electricity Company (AEC), was a product of Ahmedabad. It was subsequently brought under the public sector and has once again been privatized as a corollary of economic reforms. Under both, the public sector and then under the private sector, the utility's functioning has been considered to be efficient. This is the first city that issued municipal bonds worth Rs 100 crore in 1998, which were not tax free. Up to now, the city has issued four bond issues and a fifth issue was expected in June 2009.[39] The city has another first, a partnership-based slum improvement programme called SNP (see Acharya and Parikh 2002; Dutta 2002; Joshi 2002). The city has introduced property tax in the slums since 2001 and now nearly all the slums, with pucca or semi-pucca[40] structures have been assessed for property tax. After Delhi, this is the only city where a bus rapid transit system (BRTS) project is under implementation.

On the institutional front, the state-level agencies have not been very successful in their functioning. For example, the Gujarat Housing Board (GHB) and the now defunct Gujarat Slum Clearance Board (GSCB) were never very active in the city. AMC runs public health facilities on its own with some contribution from the state government (Mahadevia 2002a). It has its own schools, whose number and student enrolment have declined over time (Mahadevia 2002a). Even the BSUP component of the JNNURM is being implemented by the ULB and not the state government. The state government passed a resolution in the financial year 2008–9 to transfer all the housing estates belonging to the GHB and GSCB to the AMC for better maintenance.[41]

An interesting institutional feature of the city is that the ULB has created special purpose vehicles or corporations under its control to provide specialized public services. For example, public buses are run by Ahmedabad Municipal Transport Services (AMTS), a corporation that receives a grant contribution from the AMC each year. The AMTS has been mandated to run bus services even in the peri-urban areas so that the people living in these areas contiguous to the AMC boundary are not subjected to hardship. It has also authorized the AMTS to have variable ticket prices for such services. Therefore, in a way, the AMTS is a metropolitan transit agency under the management of the AMC. BRTS is being implemented by an SPV called Ahmedabad Jal Marg, which is also under the AMC.

While there are many good governance practices in the AMC, it still has a powerful municipal commissioner heading it and the mayor has limited financial powers. The city had not set up ward committees till the JNNURM reforms mandated it, because the state government, which had to amend the municipal act, was not very enthusiastic about it and it was not demanded by civil society. Paradoxically, a city with relatively large number of NGOs and charity institutions did not have structures for civil society participation in urban governance. As discussed earlier, the former were established as service delivery institutions and the latter as welfare organizations, and none were intended for participatory decision-making processes. The only participatory organization, the TLA, set up by M.K. Gandhi in 1918 to mediate between the industrialists and the striking workers, declined in influence and then membership after the demise of the textile industry in the city in the early 1990s (Spodek 2002), leading to a decline in associational interactions important for the control of ethnic violence (Varshney 2002) and to influence the city's politics and policies. Another paradox is that the welfare orientation of the city has not been sufficient to make it violence-free. These paradoxes in the city's development path need to be examined more closely, but elsewhere.

A nascent experiment of setting up Urban Resource Centres (URCs) by an NGO named Saath began in 2008. A URC has been set up as a platform to effectively link the service users with the service providers at the bottom of the pyramid and also to bring various stakeholders together for sustainable growth and development. Four URCs had been set up within the slum and low-income localities till April 2009, as per the discussions with Saath.

In past few years, decision-making in the state has become centralized and an erosion of local autonomy is visible. The octroi tax was abolished in 2006 from all the municipal corporations of the state by the state government, a move that had been resisted in the past by the municipal commissioners. Octroi tax was abolished from the municipalities in 2001, and resistance from the municipal commissioners stalled this decision in the municipal corporations. The state does not have a state planning board and no input from any quarter was taken before the octroi tax was abolished. Although this is a regressive tax, the state has not worked out any alternative to it, thus far, settling instead for devolution of an ad hoc grant in lieu of octroi. The second instance of erosion of local autonomy is the decision to expand the city's boundaries by 2.5 times without consulting the ULB. Local autonomy has also been eroded with the emergence of a strong right-wing political ideology which has, on the one hand, led to a division of the city on religious lines (Mahadevia 2007) and, on the other hand, led to a reduction in space for development discussions.

The city's limits were extended just when its principal source of revenue was withdrawn, both at the behest of the state government. The SFC is not functional and municipal grants are distributed through the Gujarat Municipal Finance Board (GMFB). Thus, from a self-sufficient and revenue-surplus ULB, the city has become dependent on disbursal of ad hoc grants. Octroi constituted half the revenue income of the city (Kundu 2002, Mahadevia 2002a; Mahadevia and Brar 2008). The same proportion of the city's income comes from the ad hoc grants from the state government.[42] In the current year's (2009–10) proposed budget, property tax is estimated to contribute just 18.43 per cent of the total revenue income of the AMC.[43] Thus, for the time being, this city and the state of Gujarat present a picture of 'lost opportunity' so far as the SFC mechanism is concerned.

The planning function was vested with the ULB. For the planning and development of peri-urban areas, the Ahmedabad Urban Development Authority (AUDA) was created in 1976. However, the current development plan of the city for the period 1996–2011 was prepared by AUDA for both the peri-urban and AMC limits. In so doing, planning powers have been passed on from the ULB to AUDA, which is a state-level parastatal, yet another instance of the erosion of the ULB's power.

It needs to be mentioned that the AMC had moved to a double-entry accounting system from the 1996–7 budgets and had already developed its own accounting manual in 1996. The AMC has also maintained its credit rating since 1996–7 for raising municipal bonds.

While the population census of 2001 estimates that 13.46 per cent of the population live in slums (Office of the Registrar General & Census Commissioner, India 2005: 22), the AMC's own estimate is 25.77 per cent,[44] according to a survey carried out by an NGO, Mahila Housing Trust (MHT), for the Corporation.

Reforms' Achievements

The city's first CDP was prepared with just token consultations. It began its JNNURM reforms on a strong base of an autonomous ULB, but with somewhat eroding powers and increased interference of the state government in the city's affairs. The city did not have to adjust its institutional structure to implement the JNNURM reforms. The state implemented some of the state-level mandatory reforms such as constitution of the DPCs in 2006[45] and constitution of an MPC for Ahmedabad in 2008,[46] which is not yet functional. However, the MPC has been placed under the authority of AUDA, a state-level parastatal.

As argued earlier, the most important reform Ahmedabad requires is the creation of participatory structures for development and governance, and encouraging the population to in fact participate in these. JNNURM reforms have helped here to a degree. The state enacted a community participation law in June 2007 and consequently constituted ward committees. This is, however, an inadequate law, which requires closer scrutiny. The 2007–8 budget was prepared on the basis of demands made by the ward committees. The ward committee structure, according to the community participation law, does not include provision for the inclusion of experts. Also, the AMC finds that it is not necessary to constitute an area sabha and hold elections to it at the current stage, arguing that this would result in too many elections.

On e-governance, the city has made good progress. AMC's website has modules on property tax, building plan approval, birth and death certificate issuance, complaints registration, hawkers' licence issuance, city transport concession pass, vehicle tax collection, and the right to information. It has established 20 civic centres through which it provides several electronic services. Of these, six civic centres are based on a PPP model. The city plans to introduce e-procurement in the near future.

Progress on property tax collection is noticeable. The AMC has completed the assessment of properties merged with the city in 2006, with property tax coverage of 99 per cent. One per cent is a safety margin to account for exclusions of properties that might have inadvertently been overlooked. The slum households are also receiving a property tax demand, irrespective of their tenurial legality. The city has tagged water and conservancy tax along with the property tax, both pegged at 30 per cent of the property tax.[47] The SWM charges are part of the conservancy tax and, therefore, it is not possible to assess the SWM user charge collection. The principal revenue source for AMC is the property tax, which still does not represent a significant proportion of the total revenue income (see Table 6.3). In the table, the revenue grant is that which is transferred through the GMFB. Non-tax revenues are incomes from the AMC properties and investments.

Table 6.3 Revenue Composition of the AMC (percentage)

Revenue Item	2008–9 (Revised Estimates)	2009–10 (Proposed Budget)
Grant in lieu of octroi	50.5	49.6
Property tax	18.3	18.4
Water tax	2.9	4.1
Conservancy tax	3.4	4.6
Vacant land tax	0.3	0.2
Professional tax	3.4	3.2
Non-tax	6.7	6.6
Revenue grant	9.2	8.3
Other income	5.3	5.0
Revenue income	100.0	100.0

Source: AMC Budget, source: www.egovamc.com (accessed on 10 March 2009).
Note: Revised estimates are based on those made mid-term in a budget regarding the actual expenditures made/income accrued.

The property tax collection falls far short of the demand from the AMC for the last three years. If the arrears are included in the demand, then the property tax collection has been below 40 per cent of the total demand (Table 6.4). However, going by the current year's demand, AMC has been able to increase its collection to about 60 to 70 per cent of this. The city has devised a scheme to give a rebate to those willing to pay arrears in property tax. The current year's collection has not risen to 90 per cent, as mandated by the JNNURM reforms, because of the properties of the closed textile mills, which continue to receive the demand but do not pay property tax. A considerable percentage of the property tax arrears can also be attributed to industries that have shut down.

Table 6.4 Property Tax Demand and Collection: AMC

Year	Demand (Rs lakh)	Collection (Rs lakh)	Percentage Collection to Demand
	Arrears + Current		
2006–7	45,942	14,969	32.58
2007–8	44,515	16,887	37.94
2008–9	50,810	15,353	30.22
	Only Current Year's		
2006–7	15,332	8,819	57.52
2007–8	15,622	11,220	71.82
2008–9	19,706	11,845	60.11

Source: From the AMC, Finance Department.

In 2008–9, the water tax collected was Rs 5,100 lakh and the O&M cost of water was Rs 8,169.98 lakh (AMC 2009). The operating ratio is, therefore, 0.62. For the proposed budget for 2009–10, the water tax collection is expected to be Rs 7,000 lakh and the O&M cost of water supply is expected to be Rs 8,819.93 lakh, improving the operating ratio to 0.79. AMC has assessed that it will not be able to recover 100 per cent costs of the O&M in water supply as yet.

The past two decades of the development processes in Ahmedabad City have posed many challenges on the equity front. Mahadevia (2002a, 2002b, 2005) has argued that the city has moved from an inclusive to exclusive approach, particularly since the beginning of the decade of 2000. Besides, the city has divisions not across class lines alone, but also across religious lines (Mahadevia 2007). Given that slum dwellers in Ahmedabad too have rated access to land as a key issue concerning them (Mahadevia et al. 2009b), as in the case of Bangalore, access to land is reviewed here.

As discussed earlier, the city has been implementing SNP and has upgraded 13,000 dwelling units (3.6 per cent of the total slum-dwelling households) in 60 slums through partnership with MHT and Saath (Mahadevia 2009a). The AMC has taken to implementing BSUP projects with great zeal. It has allotted about 100 hectares of land for BSUP to construct 110,000 DUs, to reach about 31 per cent of the current estimate of slum households. Of these, 50,000 DUs have already been sanctioned and construction work is underway (Ahmedabad Municipal Corporation 2009). Of the total DUs under construction, about 19,000 (Guatam 2009) are to be located within the city. These units are spread across the city and are not concentrated in any particular segment of it. However, as in many cities, the BSUP units are going to be used to rehabilitate the slums evicted under the various other infrastructure projects.

A Case of Beginning from Scratch: Patna

Patna's case is interesting as the city is initiating urban reforms from scratch, in line with the state government's initiatives to reform the administration over the past three and half years. Patna, the only metropolitan city of Bihar, had a population of 16.98 lakh within the Patna Urban Agglomeration[48] (PUA) area, while Patna Municipal Corporation (PMC) had a population of 13.66 lakh, according to the 2001 population census. The PUA consists of the PMC and its outgrowths: Phulwari Sharif (population of 53,166), Danapur (population of 285,338), Khagaul (population of 48,330), and Danapur Cantonment Area. All the three municipalities are covered by the JNNURM along with the PMC and, therefore, reforms are being monitored in the three municipalities as well.

It is estimated that 63.5 per cent of the PUA population resides in slums (Central Statistical Organization 1997). The population census puts this figure at only 0.3 per cent (Office of the Registrar General & Census Commissioner, India 2005: 22), which is absurdly low. Water availability is not a problem given that groundwater is used and its level is high because the city is situated along the river Ganga. Sanitation is a problem because only 20 per cent of the total households in the urban agglomeration area are covered by the underground sewerage system. In slums, 52 per cent households depend on municipal supply and the rest on tube wells and hand pumps; about 52 per cent of the slum-dwellers defecate in the open; and there is no SWM in the slums, leading to garbage disposal in the streets adjoining slums (Infrastructure Professionals Enterprise (P) Ltd and Intercontinental Consultants and Technocrats Pvt. Ltd. (2006). Thus, on the whole, the level of basic services in the city is very poor and the living conditions in the slum far worse than that of the city as a whole.

The city's institutional development has been very weak, as Figure 6.2 shows. No institutions exist to deliver many of the public services. Planning and land development were undertaken by the Patna Regional Development Authority (PRDA), which is now in the process of being wound up and its functions being transferred to the PMC. There is, however, a District Urban Development Authority (DUDA) that continues to hold responsibility for constructing roads. There are multiple organizations for planning and land development. Water supply is by the Bihar Rajya Jal Parishad (BRJP), a state-level parastatal. The sewerage and waste management was previously undertaken by the Public Health and Engineering Department (PHED), but these functions have now been transferred to the ULBs, namely the PMC, Khagaul Municipality, and others. There is the Bihar Housing Board (BHB), which does not have any capacity to implement housing projects. Therefore the Housing and Urban Development Corporation's (HUDCO's) Patna office has been drawn in to implement the BSUP component through an agreement drawn up between the Government of Bihar (GoB) and HUDCO's Delhi office.

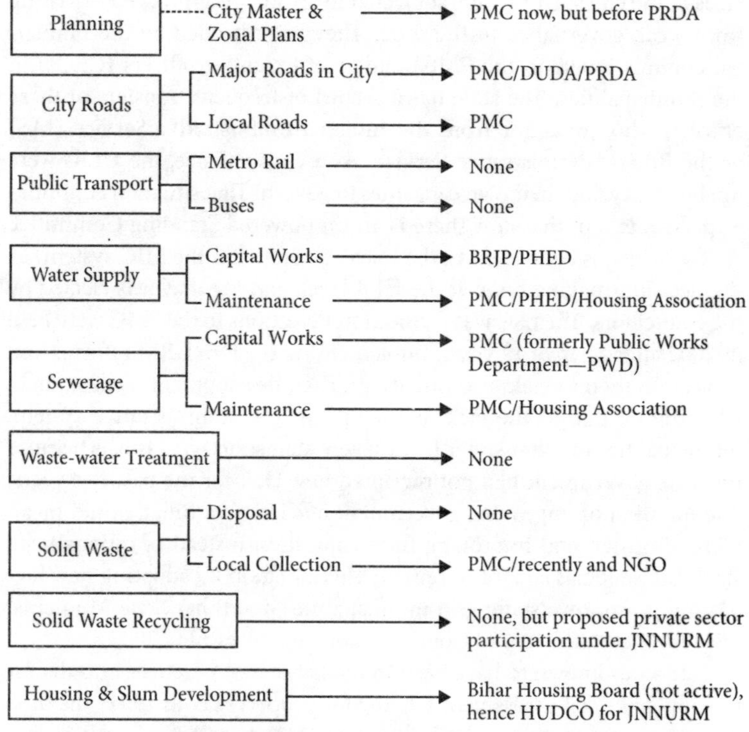

Figure 6.2 Urban Planning and Infrastructure Provision, Patna

Source: Author's construction.

Other participants in the urban space are few and weak. For example, the state does not have much private sector presence. There are thus no bidders for the JNNURM works' tenders. Civil society organizations are also non-existent, barring one, Nidan, which is engaged in door-to-door solid waste collection in a few wards in Patna and in Phulwari Sharif municipality. It takes Re 1 a day as collection charges and then sorts garbage and sells recyclables in the market to generate additional income. In short, public agencies are non-existent, the private sector is weak, and the NGO sector is minuscule. Thus, all the three pillars of urban governance are weak.

One important explanation for such poor capacities of the ULBs and poor institutional development is the low level of both economic development and particularly urbanization (just 10 per cent in 2001) in the state. Thus, state-level departments stepped in to deliver public services in the cities. ULBs were subjected to an ad hoc approach emanating from weak governance in the state. They were headed by the municipal commissioner (in the PMC) and chief executive officers (CEOs) in the municipalities. The state has a record of frequent transfers of these officers, who are either from the Indian Administrative Service (IAS) or the Bihar Administrative Service. As a consequence, the ULBs were unable to develop their own capacities to govern. That situation continues to persist, except that now there is an Empowered Standing Committee (ESC) (which is equivalent to the mayor's council in the MIC system) as the decision-making body at the ULB level; and the mayor is elected by the councillors. The ESC was formed after elections to the PMC were held in 2002 after a gap of 17 years. Implementing the JNNURM reforms and projects is therefore akin to initiating urban development from scratch. In addition, due to the lack of stability in the administrative system, municipalities in Bihar suffer from severe staff shortages. This is because the state government had not recruited new staff for the past five years. The question of improving government efficiency in Bihar would mean increasing staff and improving their capacities, instead of rationalizing staff. The state has sought to remedy this situation by adopting new legislation to improve staffing in municipalities, the Bihar State Municipal Officers (Recruitment and Conditions of Services) Rules, 2008.

Patna was known to have been in the list of best practices in India for introducing a self-assessment scheme for property tax in 1994. The then municipal commissioner also reduced property tax rates to curb evasion. The tax rates have, however, remained unaltered since then. In January 2007, the PMC's financial condition was quite bad and in consequence the city had not paid salaries to the staff for six months. The total budget of PMC in the 2008–9 fiscal year was Rs 161.43 crore[49] (which is much lesser than a ULB of the same size in developed states such as Gujarat). Of this, Rs 69.12 crore were balance funds from the previous year. In other words, on one hand, the ULB could not utilize available funds, as these had been received for specific programmes and, on the other, it was unable to pay staff salaries. Property tax comprised 31 per cent of the revenue income of the ULB in 2008–9.

The size of Khagaul's 2008–9 budget was Rs 2.86 crore, of which the property tax collection amounted to only 8 per cent of the total revenue.[50] The bulk of this ULB's income came and continues to come as grants from the state government. The financial situation in other ULBs was no different.

Reforms Introducing Urban Agenda in State

Bihar state's and Patna city's progress on urban reforms has been quite slow. The city has up to now received only 25 per cent of the approved ACA because of its inability to implement JNNURM projects, and also the state's and the city's relative inability to progress with reforms.[51]

An important change that has come about in Patna and other municipalities around it is that the state has begun devolving the 12th Schedule functions to the ULBs. To this end, the PRDA had transferred planning functions to the PMC, and the staff of the former was absorbed by the latter. The problem, however, remained of bringing about parity between the pay scales of the PRDA and PMC staff. The BRJP's role has been restricted to only implementing capital projects whereas the O&M functions for water supply were transferred to the PMC and other ULBs. The PHED has also transferred its functions to the ULBs, barring some areas in Patna. For this purpose the Bihar Municipal Act was amended in 2007.[52] The fire-fighting and forestry functions are still retained by the state government, because fire-fighting is a highly specialized function which a ULB is not equipped to perform.

DPCs have been constituted by the Department of Rural Development. The draft of the MPC is ready along with the rules. However, the MPC has yet to be constituted. The draft states that the chairman of the Patna MPC will be the minister of urban development of the GoB, and to that extent, the MPC will not be independent of the state government. The process of delineating the jurisdiction of the MPC is also underway.

The state did not have the capacity to implement Urban Infrastructure and Governance (UIG) projects related to JNNURM and, therefore, the

National Building Construction Corporation (NBCC) was brought in for the purpose. To overcome this limitation, the state has recently set up an Urban Infrastructure Development Corporation (UIDC), with equity of Rs 50 crore from the state government.

The PMC has not yet formed any ward committees. The community participation law—the Bihar Municipal Ward Committee (Community Participation) Rules, 2008—has been prepared and vetted by the law department but has not yet been accepted because the chief minister had asked for further discussions on it over a year ago.

For transparency, the PMC has a website, but the data available on it is still inadequate and considerable data needs to be collected. For example, 25 per cent of the plots in the city have been covered under the Geographic Information System (GIS), which requires 'ground-truthing' surveys to be superimposed on the satellite images. Another example is that the PMC does not have a list of slums. Similarly, for all other information that could be put on the website, data has yet to be collected. A public sector agency has been appointed for the purpose. In municipalities in the PUA, websites are being constructed by the National Informatics Centre (NIC). However, the ULBs were barely able to locate a room to house this facility and get an electricity connection. The Bihar Municipality Disclosure Act, 2008, has been enacted by the state government, but data has to be made available for this law to become effective.

On the financial reforms side, the ULBs currently do not have the capacity to move to a double-entry accounting system. For Patna, the Bihar Urban Development and Housing Department has engaged the All India Institute of Local Self Government, Lucknow centre, to assist in this. Other ULBs in the PMC do not have the staff to move to this new system, and the PMC itself has not yet done so.

In the PMC, the total property tax is 3.25 per cent of the annual rateable value (ARV) of property.[53] Another 2.5 per cent of the ARV is deducted as education cess, 1.25 per cent as health cess, and 2 per cent as water tax. There is no separate SWM charge in the city, as is the case in other cities. In 2008–9, the property (holding) tax collection was about 39 per cent of the demand. There has been no significant improvement in the property tax collection in the PMC. Also, the PMC is nowhere near meeting the mandatory reform of recovering 100 per cent of the O&M costs. For example, in 2007–8 the expected water tax collection[54] was to be Rs 249.25 lakh and the O&M expenditure on water supply was Rs 387.47 lakh. This means that expenditure on water supply was 154 per cent of the revenue from water tax.

For the two other ULBs in the PUA, close monitoring of the property tax collection has shown positive results. The Phulwari Sharif ULB improved its collection in 2008–9 by delegating property tax collection to 14 tax collectors whose daily collections were monitored by the ULB. Table 6.5 shows this improvement; data for 2008–9 showing a remarkable effort to raise the demand and then to collect the tax. Therefore, the property tax collection efficiency (percentage of total demand/total collection) has increased from 47 per cent in 2006–7 to 54 per cent in 2007–8, and reached 75 per cent in 2008–9. At the same time, the property tax coverage has also increased, shown by a nearly 4.5 times increase in the property tax demand in 2008–9 in comparison to the previous year.

Table 6.5 Property Tax Demand and Collection in Phulwari Sharif[55]

(Rs lakh)

Year	Demand			Collection			Outstanding		
	Out-standing	Current	Total	Out-standing	Current	Total	Out-standing	Current	Total
2006–7	5.70	5.51	11.22	2.42	2.84	5.26	3.29	2.67	5.96
2007–8	5.96	5.54	11.50	3.50	2.71	6.21	2.45	2.83	5.29
2008–9	5.29	25.01	30.30	2.43	20.44	22.87	2.86	4.56	7.43

In Khagaul, the total collection for 2007–8 was Rs 4.36 lakh, which was just 26 per cent of the total demand. In 2008–9, the collections increased to Rs 17.82 lakh, a four-fold increase.[56] The issue now remains of institutionalizing this to move towards the targets set by the JNNURM reforms and arrive at a situation of financial sustainability. My own assessment is that both Phulwari Sharif and Khagaul have shown improvement in the property tax collection as a result of the efforts of their respective CEOs.

In this city, only one dimension of equity has been examined, which is implementation of the BSUP projects. The state was unable to find a public agency at the state level to prepare DPRs and then implement the BSUP projects, which is why HUDCO's Patna office was contacted. The progress of work on the BSUP is very slow. There are four major problems that HUDCO is facing. The first is that there has been very poor response to the tenders of BSUP projects obliging HUDCO to enter into repeated tendering. Second, neither the state government nor the PMC is allocating land. Third, if the land allocation has been made, then the state government has not provided clearance on land transfers to HUDCO, without which the contractors are unwilling to go ahead with work. Last, the schedule of rates (SORs) specified by the DPRs are so low that HUDCO had to seek revised approvals from the CSMC at the Central level for each project, thereby delaying the entire project implementation.[57]

CONCLUDING REMARKS

On the whole, the JNNURM reforms could be viewed as part of a continuum of an ongoing urban reform process at the city, state, and national levels. This chapter has only looked at one of the two components of the JNNURM, that is, the reforms and not the projects, although both are linked because progress on reforms is necessary for the release of project funds.

Learning from Three Cities

This chapter selected three different cities in three different states with different urban institutional structures to analyse the progress of urban reforms in the context of JNNURM. The key observation that emerged from this study was that historical trajectories matter and that the success of reforms depends upon the development paradigm, capabilities created by the state institutions, and the activism of civil society. Historical institutional development and ideologies reflect on the relationship between the state, market, and civil society, and also on the success of the partnerships of this triad of urban governance. However, the reforms have not changed and may not significantly change city-level practices of development and governance in the short term.

The three cities selected are very different from one another. Ahmedabad is an industrial city that has declined but which in the past had a predominance of the working class. The loss of industrial employment and ensuing casualization of workers (Mahadevia 2002c) created a number of vulnerabilities. The period of economic growth in the state saw manufacturing activities moving farther away from the city and it became primarily a service city with a very large presence of the informal sector and slums. To some degree, the NGO sector stepped in to address these vulnerabilities through service delivery and to an extent the ULB continued to pursue an 'inclusive growth' strategy. For a long period of time, the city was left without any identifiable leadership, unlike the city up to the 1970s when the leadership was provided by the industrial elite (Spodek 2001). Then for a brief period, the NGOs gained centre stage. The city, however, did not create, apart from the TLA of the past, strong institutions for participation in urban governance and development discussions.

Bangalore was a city dominated by the public sector that transited to a new economy city based on information technology and other sunrise industries. Middle class-based organizations are very strong, and these have networked through formalized structures, such as Janaagraha now and CIVIC and other organizations in the past. There is, therefore, a long history of participatory institutions, however limited these may be. Mechanisms for monitoring service delivery by parastatals have also been set up. Besides, the emergence of new economy entities such as IT firms have brought in new players in the urban field, many seeking to transfer their experience of private sector professionalism to city governance, and many corporate leaders of the new economy stepped in to assume leadership on city issues.

Patna is a case of a city where the state, the private sector, and the civil society are all very weak and inactive. None hold any leadership position. The state's economic and social development is low, with Bihar forming part of what are called the *Bimaru*[58] states of India. The pre-eminent concern in the state and the city was 'law and order' and the security of its residents. Patna is an administrative city with residual employment in informal service sector. Education is a big industry, and the state exports educated labour. The condition of Patna is poor and the city was not in a position to even pay the salaries of the ULB staff. To overcome the weak nature of the ULB, the state has been engaged in service delivery through the ULBs. The ULBs in Bihar suffered from a legacy of poor governance, although this is now beginning to change.

Bangalore's case illustrates that the city had gradually implemented reforms on its own within the structural constraint of a state government-dominated institutional structure. The state has decided not to undo this structure and, therefore, the ULBs, and in particular, the BBMP, will continue to remain weak institutions. The city has, however, experimented with multi-stakeholdership with regard to provision of services, in particular SWM (Sekher 2001, 2005). Multi-stakeholdership has been experimented too through the activities of Janaagraha. The city is ranked in the middle with regard to JNNURM reforms because a convergence of planning and service delivery functions at ULB level has not taken place and also because certain legislation, such as the Community Participation Law and Public Disclosure Law, have not been enacted. The city is, however, strong in relation to financial reforms but not in a position to meet the conditionality of 100 per cent cost recovery from the

O&M of SWM. Interestingly, however, the parastatals, in particular the BWSSB whose finances were analysed, have been able to recover their O&M costs. Finally, the city's innovative governance structure has been viewed as elitist while progress on addressing the slum land question has been slow. The reforms initiated by the city are indigenous and it appears that the JNNURM reforms have not been of much concern to it.

Ahmedabad's case illustrates that the city did not have to do much to implement JNNURM reforms: all the urban functions listed in the 12th Schedule of the 74th CAA have been performed by the ULB. However, the tragedy of the city is that from a financially sustainable situation, it has moved to a condition of dependency on the state government. This has happened because of the abolition of octroi tax. This transition could have been better managed than it has been through the SFC, which has not happened and the city and the state have lost an opportunity to further strengthen the financial capability of the former. Also, the state government could have invited the city government's opinion rather than taking a unilateral decision on the matter. Thus, although it has a structure that could have brought about a higher order of autonomy, the city has regressed somewhat with increasing state government intervention in its affairs. In this the JNNURM reforms were unable to help, as this chapter illustrates.

The city also had a strong welfare orientation, originating from all the three pillars of urban governance—the state, the private sector, and civil society. Notwithstanding that, the city has witnessed a decline in spaces for participation and discussion at the city level, which is indeed an area that requires further investigation and research. The key challenge in the city is to create lasting structures (and a spirit) of participation in decision-making. This is indeed a daunting task given the informal nature of the economy and difficulties that impede participation. The JNNURM reforms have, therefore, created conditions to move in the direction of increased participation, with the setting up of ward committees. The task is to ensure that the latter do indeed become more active over time. The city has been able to achieve property tax reform to the degree possible, with property tax now covering even slum dwellings. However, the industries that have shut down have defaulted and continue to default on property tax payment. The city has also moved ahead in enacting a Community Participation Law and Public Disclosure Law, besides setting up the MPC. The JNNURM reforms have thus had some effect on the city. But these need to be accompanied by a change in attitude on the part of the state government towards the city governments, and also a change in the political outlook at the city level, ushering in a congenial atmosphere for participation in and ownership of the city by its residents.

In the context of Bihar, it can be argued that the agenda of urban development has been pushed ahead by the JNNURM projects as well as reforms. Mandatory reforms, although pushed from above, have achieved results to the degree that a new policy framework has been set up for urban reforms. The state has begun to pass on the planning and service delivery functions to the city and has also become conscious of the need to raise local financial resources.

This brings us to the question of accounting reforms. The budgets of all the four cities, the PMC and the three municipalities (Phulwari Sharif, Danapur, and Khagaul) in the PUA, are not yet in place and have not yet moved to the double-entry accounting system because they did not have qualified technical staff to do so. A way out was to outsource this work. Given that the state also did not have a private sector, they had to locate firms from outside the state. Khagaul municipality contacted a private firm to assist them in setting up software for accounting but the idea was then dropped because the firm quoted Rs 1 crore as charges, which far exceeded the ULB's budget. Eventually, the ULB located an IT-trained person from Patna at a cost of Rs 70,000 to set up the accounting software. This experience brings to the fore the question of pushing too hard for certain technical reforms, such as accounting reforms, in a situation where it is difficult to locate local capacities to undertake it. The same issue arose with regard to setting up and managing an e-governance portal; public sector IT companies were contacted and awarded contracts. The smaller ULBs were hard-pressed to make the physical space available for e-governance and then arrange to obtain electricity. An option for such states and ULBs could have been to introduce a process of hand-holding to develop internal capacity for such technical reforms, which requires greater time and cannot be accomplished in the timeframe set by the JNNURM.

The Bihar administration, in general, is unstable and the tenures of the chief officers are very short. To top it all, there is an inadequacy of staff. The JNNURM reforms, or any other urban reforms for that matter, depend on the overall reforms in administration, which have begun (through administrative staff recruitment, for example), but the JNNURM reforms may not in themselves bring about administrative reforms.

Increased financial allocation from the Central government to the state for development purposes does not mean that the state will be able to deliver the projects. Public and private sector institutions have to be in place to implement projects. Realizing the lacunae on the institutional front, the state has also begun setting up institutions such as UIDC, for which the credit goes to the JNNURM.

The state government continues to play an active role in the affairs of the cities because of the lack of capabilities at the ULB level. There is gradual progress towards making the ULBs somewhat autonomous in their functioning. However, the involvement of state government in the ULB's affairs can translate into a lack of consultation. Agreements affecting ULBs can sometimes be concluded without involving them directly. The lack of capacity thus remains a challenge for ULBs in Bihar.

In case of Patna's governance, individuals matter, and this begins from the state government leadership down to that of the ULB. Certain reforms, such as property tax collection and e-governance portals have been successful where the CEOs have taken interest (as in case of Khagaul and Phulwari Sharif). Finally, Patna and the other ULBs have not been able to implement the BSUP projects because the necessary land has not been allocated for the purpose.

Cross-cutting issues that have emerged are that the state governments continue to play a dominant role in the affairs of the cities. The reforms would have been more successful had they been indigenously developed rather than imposed from the Centre, accompanied by conditionalities, as has been the case with the JNNURM. The historical trajectories of the cities matter in urban reforms. In some less developed states such as Bihar, individuals matter in pushing the case for reforms. Certain technical reforms such as accounting and e-governance portals require massive local capacities and resources at the disposal of the ULBs. Thus, developed states and their developed cities have shown a superior capacity to implement these reforms than the less developed states and cities. Local political ideologies do matter in sustaining reforms and good practices.

Another important cross-cutting issue that emerged from the study of the three cities was with regard to monitoring the JNNURM reforms. These are being monitored by ticking off long checklists, with the cities being required to accomplish a long list of mandatory reforms in a very short period of time. There is also no prospect of the cities prioritizing their reforms, and, therefore, the cities and the state SLNAs have been expending a lot of their time and energy in the process. The BSUP component's implementation is very weak in two cities, Bangalore and Patna. In the former, the reason is its multiplicity of institutions and in the latter because public agencies are not providing land for the purpose.

Finally, urban data availability is a big bottleneck in setting up e-governance portals and facilitating the monitoring of service delivery. Urban data systems are very poor. Property tax data on a GIS base is essential but requires large surveys for 'ground-truthing', for which considerable time and resources are required. Also, the efforts have to be continuing and cannot be tied to a Central programme. Besides, there is no mechanism as of today to link the available data, say from the population census to the property tax and services data. Cities such as Bangalore and Patna do not even have a list of slums, leave alone data on the level of services. The CDPs of all the three cities fall far short on the quantity and quality of data. There are no data on social indicators—the infant mortality rates, death rates, birth rates, enrolment rates, etc.—at either the city or ward level. This is a very serious issue of urban development and governance, and cannot be addressed in short period of time. However, an effort to build e-governance portals has brought the data lacunae to the fore very strongly.

On Reforms and Centralization

States in India have become autonomous over the past few decades and have responded to Central reforms and programmes in a way that suits them, and this is furthering the case of federalism. In the case of urban areas, the 74th CAA was tardily implemented across India, and thus, while the states cherish autonomy, they have not instituted processes to make cities autonomous to the necessary degree. ULCRA's repeal was suggested by the Central government in 1999, but its implementation could be accomplished across all the states only after the JNNURM reforms were made mandatory. This has been the case not just with the JNNURM reforms and urban development but also with regard to other Centrally assisted programmes. We may, therefore, veer to the argument that conditionalities can assist the reform process in states under certain circumstances. Another example of this is the Fiscal Responsibility and Budget Management (FRBM) Act, which helped control fiscal profligacy on the part of the states.

On the other hand, there has been an increasing erosion of state autonomy in matters of public finance. Alagh (2009) writes that the Normal Central Assistance, which gives states autonomy of decisions on financial matters, has declined whereas there is increasing fund transfer to the states through Centrally sponsored schemes (CSS) and ACA. The CSS and ACA come in with attached conditionalities, leaving very little leeway on the expenditure side at the state and local levels. The JNNURM reforms and its predecessor, the URIF, too are a continuation of this change in Centre–state fiscal relations.

The key question, therefore, is: do conditionalities work? Experience of the JNNURM reforms shows that there would be a healthier and therefore more sustainable practice on reforms if these emerged indigenously to suit local needs. The Central government could indicate the contents of the reforms, much in the same way as the economic reforms were pursued. Many states, such as Gujarat, came with their own economic reforms package as well as industrial policies, adopting from the Central government reforms packages and policies. That a centralized approach does not work can be gauged from the fact that 25 of the 64 cities alone picked up a quarter or less of what the ACA had committed.

Meeting the Objectives of the Mission?

Some of the Mission's objectives have been achieved and some not. First, the move towards modern and transparent budgeting, accounting, financial management systems, designed and adopted for all urban service and governance functions has been achieved, with some difficulties faced by the ULBs and parastatals in the cities in which the case studies were conducted. Less developed states in particular have faced a great many difficulties in implementing these reforms but they will eventually be achieved. Second, the object of establishing and operationalizing a city-wide framework for planning and governance is being evolved, but it is easier said than done. It entails evolving new institutional arrangements for planning and service delivery and for this either new public institutions have to be created or the old ones merged. Both require changes in legislation and the question of staff being addressed. Patna's example of merging PRDA with PMC illustrates this. Looking at the enormity of the task and the futility of doing away with existing well-functioning institutions, Bangalore is evolving its own structure of coordinating planning and service delivery functions. This objective can be met if flexibility is maintained.

The third objective, that of enabling all urban residents to access a basic level of urban services, is still a distant goal and will depend not just on the reforms but also on the development dynamics within a city. The fourth objective was to achieve financially self-sustaining agencies for urban governance and service delivery through reforms of revenue instruments. This goal will also take time to achieve because the appropriate costing mechanisms have yet to be achieved. Cost recovery mechanisms for various services have to evolve also, keeping equity concerns central to revenue-raising instruments. The fifth objective is that the local services and governance are so conducted that they are transparent and accountable to citizens. The sixth is to establish e-governance applications to reduce the cost and time of service delivery, and this, as already discussed, would require an improvement in data systems.

Reforms a Path to Inclusive Cities?

The success of the JNNURM reforms is dependent on the historical capabilities of the states and the cities. Better performing states are likely to continue to perform well, regardless of the JNNURM. The JNNURM has, however, given them additional funds to increase urban investments in infrastructure and low-income housing. It also needs to be understood that a move towards good governance or inclusive cities requires far more than just the JNNURM reforms.

Financial problems will remain unless the fiscal system is reworked to give the cities their dues. This would require an equitable tax sharing formula to be worked out between the Central, state, and local governments, and ensuring that the taxes are shared as a right of the cities and not as charity transfers or as transfers attached to conditionalities. This would require a change in legislation as well as institutions. The cities do not have the powers to decide their own tax sources and tax rates.

There is a massive informal sector in the cities. These properties and activities are not within the local tax net. Sometimes, the slum-dwellers want to pay property tax as this provides them with some assurance of security of tenure. The city governments do not, however, wish to do that, primarily stemming from the fear that land rights will have to be surrendered to the slum-dwellers. The local government officials need to change their attitude towards informal sector households and enterprises. A good example is that of AMC, which has begun taxing these enterprises and households since 2001 to expand property tax collection.

Autonomy of the cities from the state government remains a sensitive question. The state governments have kept the powers to themselves through a variety of mechanisms, notwithstanding the 74th CAA:

1. By not making the SFCs functional, the ULBs are still dependent on the state government for finances. This has indeed been a case of lost opportunity.
2. The state government decides the boundaries of the city government and also declares a settlement to be urban. The considerations vary from state to state and are ad hoc. Neither in decisions concerning

tax rates and sources nor in those relating to the city's boundaries (amalgamation of the local governments or separation of local governments), are the concerned bodies consulted. In some countries, referendums are held for taking such decisions and yet this important aspect has not even been brought on the agenda by the JNNURM reforms.

3. The state governments continue to hold the power to sanction the development plans and master plans and thereby the control of land allocations, activities, and development within the city.
4. The cities are to a substantial degree dependent on the state governments for the executive heads. The JNNURM reforms do not address this aspect of local autonomy.
5. Indeed, in order to give the cities complete autonomy, wholesale restructuring of the national governance system is necessary. The cities have been passed on all the responsibilities and are expected to perform these with a very low financial base and little ability to raise finance. It is beyond the powers of the JNNURM to move towards the full functional autonomy of the cities.

The JNNURM reforms provide only limited mechanisms to achieve the goals of an inclusive city. For example, they do not set out mechanisms for public participation and stakeholder involvement beyond stating that ward committees should be formed and there should be stakeholder consultations for the CDP. The reforms do not provide mechanisms to operationalize the construction of a democratic culture, institutionalize participatory planning processes, improve service levels by setting service standards, codes of conduct for the leaders and officials, generate empowerment; further they do not ensure equitable resource allocation. In a sense, the JNNURM reforms are inadequate in meeting the larger goal of inclusive cities. The reforms can, however, serve as a starting point for the purpose and should encourage the cities to set their own goals of inclusiveness and sustainability.

Policy Recommendations

The first recommendation emerging from the experience of the three cities is that the states and the cities should be given greater flexibility in implementing the reforms. The Central government could ask the states and cities to prioritize reforms based on their own assessment of the issues that confront them and ask them to set their own deadlines for achieving the reforms. For example, Patna or Khagaul may first focus on strengthening its financial base rather than setting up an e-governance portal. In other words, the cities are being asked, in the name of reforms, to do far in excess of what they are capable of doing or what they would wish to do.

Second, a reform such as repeal of the ULCRA has been introduced without a thought about how the cities would be able to make land available to the poor. This reform should have been accompanied by an urban land policy and housing and slum policy at the state level. Thus, reforms have to be seen in consonance with other development processes observed within the cities. In other words, a reform such as the repeal of ULCRA should have been viewed against the political economy of the cities. In addition, cities should have been encouraged to find land for housing the urban poor. One of the approaches could have been to encourage them to prepare an inventory of public land and present it in the city CDPs. As the BSUP funds are not going to meet the currently assessed housing shortage, alternative methods such as giving land tenure to the existing slum-dwellers could have been thought of and the proposal included in the CDP. Carrying out mandatory reform does not absolve the local governments of their obligation to the low-income groups in the city.

The financial sustainability of the cities can become a reality only when the cities receive their due share of public finances and not in the way in which the JNNURM reforms have been framed. In all probability, the JNNURM reforms are a small step in that direction but the long-term requirement is for a new paradigm of governance in India.

More thought now needs to be devoted to the relationship between the cities and state governments. The latter need to pass on greater powers to the cities, while the functions have been devolved through the 74th CAA and now mandatory JNNURM reforms.

Sound and robust urban data systems, which give spatial as well as temporal data, are important, and any reform process should enable that to happen. For this, time and financial resources are necessary. Financial resources are required to collect data and deploy trained human resources for the purpose. Identifying data needs and collecting data cannot be outsourced to consultancy firms and will require the competence of research institutions set up for the purpose. The Ministry of Urban Development and Ministry of Housing and Urban Poverty Alleviation have now set up national resource centres and also centre of excellence, whose services should be harnessed to make the urban data system more robust and dynamic.

ACKNOWLEDGEMENTS

In writing this chapter I have benefitted from numerous discussions with a large number of individuals. Writing it would not have been possible without information provided by the following, to whom I am deeply indebted.

In Ahmedabad, Vijay Anadkat of Gujarat Urban Development Mission (GUDM), and U.C. Padia, Deputy Municipal Commissioner, Ahmedabad Municipal Corporation (AMC).

In Bangalore, D. Thangaraj, Principal Secretary, Department of Urban Development, Government of Karnataka; C.V. Prasad, Financial Advisor, and M. Suresh Babu, Assistant Executive Engineer of Bangalore Water Supply and Sewerage Board (BWSSB); J.V. Nandana Kumar, General Manager, Arvind Srivastava, Managing Director, V. Chandra Mohan, Executive Director, and Ashathnarayana Shastri of Karnataka Urban Infrastructure Development and Finance Company (KUIDFC); Vasantha Rao, Finance Officer and N. Vani, Assistant Controller (finance) of Bruhat Bengaluru Mahanagar Palike (BBMP); Madhuranatha, Assistant Engineer of Bangalore Development Authority (BDA); Narayan Shastri, Joint Director, Statistics, and Zafarullah, Engineer of Karnataka Slum Clearance Board (KSCB); Ramesh Ramnathan, Co-founder, Janaagraha and member of the Technical Advisory Group, JNNURM; and Anurima Mukherjee, Project Management Unit (PMU), KUIDFC.

In Bihar, Deepak Kumar, Principal Secretary, D.K. Shukla, Special Secretary, B. Ojha, Deputy Secretary of Department of Urban Development and Housing, Government of Bihar (GoB); Chand Rehmani, PMU, Bihar Urban Development Authority (BUDA); B.N. Singh, Municipal Commissioner, Arvind Prasad, Executive Engineer and Nodal Officer, P.K. Singh, Chief Accounts Officer, B.N. Das, Additional Commissioner, Revenue & Planning, Brahmi Ram, Additional Commissioner, public health, of Patna Municipal Corporation (PMC); Satish Kumar Sinha, Project Appraisal Office, HUDCO Regional Office, Patna.

Additionally, for the Patna study, I had the support of O.P. Mathur, Nilesh Rajadhyaksha, and Harpreet from the National Institute of Public Finance and Policy (NIPFP).

Roshan Toshniwal and Kuldeep Singh, students of the Faculty of Planning and Public Policy, CEPT University assisted me in assembling the data on the progress of reforms and funds disbursement by cities and states.

Finally, the comments and suggestions of the reviewers, O.P. Mathur (NIPFP) and Chetan Vaidya, director, National Institute of Urban Affairs (NIUA), have been very valuable in finalizing the chapter, and I am extremely indebted to them for their valuable time to this. The lacunae in this chapter and the opinions expressed are entirely mine and I own full responsibility for them.

NOTES

1. http://www.censusindia.gov.in/Census_Data_Online/Population/List_of_Million_Plus_Cities.aspx, accessed on 12 December 2008.

2. The National Urban Housing and Habitat Policy (NUHHP) 2007 has estimated 67.4 million as constituting total urban households in 2007, when the Eleventh Five Year Plan began. Based on this, 26 per cent would come to 17.73 million households without access to tap water. In this and the next paragraph, the percentage figures are from National Sample Survey Organisation (2004), applied on the total estimated households of 67.4 million when the Eleventh Five Year Plan began.

3. From NUHHP 2007 of the Ministry of Housing and Urban Poverty Alleviation, Government of India, New Delhi. Source: http://mhupa.gov.in/policies/duepa/HousingPolicy2007.pdf, accessed 2 January 2008.

4. Some states had octroi tax, which was quite a large source of own revenue. In Ahmedabad, for example, before the removal of the octroi tax, it constituted about 50–60 per cent of the city's own revenue (Kundu 2002; Mahadevia 2002a; Mahadevia and Brar 2008).

5. Article 243I of the 74th CAA.

6. http://chennai-online.in/Profile/History/milestone.asp, accessed on 8 March 2009.

7. See articles in Kundu and Mahadevia (2002) and Mahadevia (2008).

8. According to a discussion with the financial advisor, Bangalore Water Supply and Sewerage Board.

9. These cities were visited in February 2009 and therefore the data relates to that period. The JNNURM reforms have progressed since then.

10. This was done to overcome the problem of supersession of the ULBs by the state governments.

11. The URIF details are from http://www.niua.org/Publications/newsletter/urb_fin_dec04.pdf, accessed on 5 February 2009.

12. I would tend to use the term residents and not citizens, given that the latter assumes a very narrow definition bound by the legalities. A discussion on processes of de-ligitimization of urban poor, in particular new migrants in Mumbai, is in Mahadevia and Narayanan (2008).

13. http://jnnurm.nic.in/nurmudweb/toolkit/Overview.pdf (p. 4), accessed on 8 March 2009.

14. A programme of action for the incumbent Central government formed of a centre to centre-left coalition that came to power in May 2004.

15. http://jnnurm.nic.in/nurmudweb/toolkit/Overview.pdf, accessed on 8 March 2009.

16. Once the first CDPs were formed, the city governments were made to understand that these had to be within the framework of their existing master plans or development plans.

17. The lifecycle cost of a project must cover the capital outlays and the attendant O&M costs to ensure that assets are in good working condition. Source: http://jnnurm.nic.in/nurmudweb/toolkit/Overview.pdf (p. 6), accessed on 8 March 2009.

18. From http://jnnurm.nic.in/nurmudweb/toolkit/guidelines_jnnurm-English.pdf (p. 9), accessed on 14 March 2008.

19. http://jnnurm.nic.in/nurmudweb/toolkit/Overview.pdf (p. 10), accessed on 8 March 2009.

20. http://jnnurm.nic.in/nurmudweb/toolkit/Overview.pdf (p. 7), accessed on 8 March 2009.

21. From http://jnnurm.nic.in/nurmudweb/toolkit/guidelines_jnnurm-English.pdf (p. 13), accessed on 14 March 2008.

22. From http://jnnurm.nic.in/nurmudweb/toolkit/guidelines_jnnurm-English.pdf (p. 13), accessed on 14 March 2008.

23. The Ministry of Urban Development (MoUD) and Ministry of Housing and Urban Poverty Alleviation (MoHUPA).

24. Twenty-five of the 64 cities have been released only a quarter of the ACA committed, which could be on account of non-implementation of the reforms. Puri and Delhi have received none. Thirty-three of the 64 cities that have either not received any ACA or have received a quarter or less of the amount committed, have not progressed with the reforms.

25. http://www.bmponline.org/, accessed on 8 March 2009.

26. http://www.bmponline.org/account-dept/Greater_Notification1.PDF, accessed on 16 March 2009.

27. See http://www.bmponline.org/Bruhat%20Bangalore/Vol-1%20Bangalore%20CDP.pdf, accessed on 16 March 2009.

28. BATF webpage, http://www.batf.org accessed on 1 September 2005.

29. The BATF's inaugural sampling survey revealed five problems that required immediate attention. In order, these were: the condition of the roads, garbage, mosquitoes, pollution, and public toilets (Nair 2005: 335).

30. http://abidebengaluru.in/attachments/1/original/plan_bengaluru_2020_agenda.pdf, accessed on 16 March 2009.

31. http://www.bmponline.org/propertytax/recent%20amendments.shtml, accessed on 16 March 2009.

32. On 15 March 2006, the first consultation meeting with the implementing agencies was held by the KUIDFC. Thereafter, on 7 April 2006, a consultation with the NGOs was held. Consultations with the local area MLAs, councillors, and RWA members within the eight ULBs in the BUA were held between 21 and 28 April 2006. One consultation each with the citizens in 30 places covering 100 wards was held on 6 May 2006, with elected representatives of Bangalore on 9 May 2006, and finally with the NGOs and slum organizations for the BSUP was held on 27 May 2006.

33. Based on a discussion with N. Vani, assistant controller of finance, BBMP, on 12 March 2009.

34. V.N. Alok, 'A Capsule of Major State Finance Commissions Reports'. Source: http://www.solutionexchange-un.net.in/decn/cr/res12060605.pdf, accessed on 25 March 2009, pp. 20–1.

35. Data from the Financial Advisor, Bangalore Water Supply and Sewerage Board, provided on 11 March 2009.

36. Based on discussions with Madhuranatha, assistant engineer, BDA, held on 13 March 2009.

37. The KSCB data collected from the organization. The officers concerned, Narayan Swamy (joint director, Statistics) and Zafarullah (assistant engineer), were interviewed for the information required on 13 March 2009.

38. Now reworded corporate social responsibility (CSR).

39. http://timesofindia.indiatimes.com/Ahmedabad/AMC-to-issue-Rs-150-cr-tax-free-bonds-in-June-/articleshow/4581600.cms, accessed on 19 June 2009.

40. A pucca structure is one constructed with permanent materials and a semi-pucca structure is one with mix of permanent and temporary construction materials.

41. From the AMC budget 2009–10, see http://www.egovamc.com/amc_budget/Budget_2009-2010.pdf, accessed on 16 March 2009.

42. Budget data from AMC's 2009–10 budget, see http://www.egovamc.com/amc_budget, 2009-2010.pdf, accessed on 16 March 2009.

43. http://www.egovamc.com/amc_budget, 2009-2010.pdf, accessed on 16 March 2009.

44. Based on data collected from the MHT.

45. See Government Rule (GR) dated 19 July 2006.

46. See GR dated 27 March 2008.

47. The state government amended the Bombay Provincial Municipal Corporation (BPMC) Act in 2007 with effect from 1999 to levy water and conservancy charges based on the carpet area of property.

48. An urban agglomeration is an entity defined by the population census and which means the main city together with all the contiguous area, which may include other ULBs and their outgrowths, panchayats, and outgrowth of the main city. This is in contrast to an entity called a metropolitan area, whose jurisdiction is decided by the state planning authority or state urban development department.

49. The PMC budget data in this chapter are from the PMC finance office.

50. Khagaul budget data provided by the Chief Executive Officer of Khagaul on 9 February 2009.

51. A visit was made to Khagaul municipality, where the chief executive officers (CEOs) of the two other municipalities had come to discuss the progress of the JNNURM reforms.

52. Section 290 of the New Municipal Act provides for the preparation of a master plan for Greater Patna with a jurisdiction over 1,000 sq km.

53. In 1995, the then municipal commissioner of Patna, S.K. Singh, brought it down from 42 to 9 per cent. This remains the same today.

54. Expected figure is mentioned because the half-yearly collection for the year was Rs 124.63 lakh. The water tax collection figure for the entire year was not available.

55. Budget data of Phulwari Sharif in Table 6.5 and the text was provided by the CEO of the municipality on 20 February 2009.

56. According to data provided by the executive officer of Khagaul on 20 February 2009.

57. According to discussions with Satish Kumar Singh, senior project appraisal officer, HUDCO, Patna. The discussions were held on 20 February 2009.

58. BIMARU means sick in Hindi. BIMARU stands for Bihar, Madhya Pradesh, Rajasthan, and Uttar Pradesh—the four least developed states from economic and social perspectives.

BIBLIOGRAPHY

Acharya, S.K. and A. Parashar (2008), 'Managing Waste in a Peri-Urban Locality: Vejalpur', in D. Mahadevia and J. Wolfe (eds), *Solid Waste Management in Indian Cities: Status and Emerging Practices*, pp. 312–28. New Delhi: Concept.

Acharya, S.K. and S. Parikh (2002), 'Slum Networking in Ahmedabad: An Alternate Approach', in A. Kundu and D. Mahadevia (eds), *Poverty and Vulnerability in a Globalising Metropolis: Ahmedabad*, pp. 349–72. Delhi: Manak Publishers.

Ahmedabad Municipal Corporation (2009), 'Options for Land Tenure in Slums of Ahmedabad', a unpublished paper presented at the National Workshop on Approaches to the Lands for the Urban Poor, organized by CEPT University and Ministry of Housing and Urban Poverty Alleviation, Ahmedabad, 17 April.

——— (2009): *Budget 2009–10*. Ahmedabad: AMC, available at www.egovamc.com, accessed on 10 March 2009

Alagh, Y.K. (2009), 'Fixing Formula', *Financial Express*, Ahmedabad, 20 March.

Balakrishnan, Suresh (2006), 'Making Service Delivery Reforms Work: The Bangalore Experience', in Vikram K. Chand (ed.), *Reinventing Public Service Delivery in India*, pp. 157–85. New Delhi and London: Sage and Thousand Oaks.

Bangalore Bruhad Mahanagar Palike (2009), *Budget Estimates 2009–10*. Bangalore: BBMP.

Banker, S. (1965), *Gandhiji ane Majuuropravrutti* [Gujarati: Gandhi and Labour Activities]. Ahmedabad: Navajivan Press.

Benjamin, S. (2008), 'Inclusive or Contested: Conceptualizing a Globalized Bangalore', in D. Mahadevia (ed.), *Inside the Transforming Urban Asia: Processes, Policies and Public Actions*, pp. 170–93. New Delhi: Concept.

Benjamin, S., R. Bhuvaneswari, P. Rajan, and Manjunath (2008), 'Fractured Terrain, Spaces Left Over or Contested: A Closer Look at the IT-Dominated

Territories in East and South Bangalore', in D. Mahadevia (ed.), *Inside the Transforming Urban Asia: Processes, Policies and Public Actions*, pp. 94–131. New Delhi: Concept.

BWSSB (2008), *Annual Accounts and Audit Report for the Year 2006–07*. Bangalore: BWSSB.

Central Statistical Organization (1997), *Compendium of Environment Statistics*. New Delhi: Ministry of Planning and Programme Implementation, Government of India.

Centre for Youth and Social Development and Public Affairs Centre (2005), *Setting a Benchmark: Citizen Report Card on Public Services in Bhubaneshwar*. Bhubaneshwar: CYSD, and Bangalore: PAC.

Chamaraj, Kathyayini and Prasanna Rao (2006), 'Functioning of Wards Committees in Bangalore: A Case Study', in K.C. Sivaramakrishnan (ed.), *People's Participation in Urban Governance: A Comparative Study of Working of Wards Committees in Karnataka, Kerala, Maharashtra and West Bengal*, pp. 57–137. New Delhi: Concept, for Institute of Social Sciences.

Dutta, S. (2002), 'Partnerships for Urban Poverty Reduction: A Review Experience', in A. Kundu and D. Mahadevia (eds), *Poverty and Vulnerability in a Globalising Metropolis: Ahmedabad*, pp. 237–67. Delhi: Manak Publishers.

Expert Committee (2008), *Governance in the Bangalore Metropolitan Region and Bruhat Bangalore Mahanagara Palike*. Bangalore: Government of Karnataka.

Expert Group on the Commercialization of Infrastructure (1996), *The India Infrastructure Report: Policy Imperatives for Growth and Welfare*. New Delhi: Ministry of Finance, Government of India.

Friedmann, J. (1998), 'The Common Good: Assessing the Performance of Cities', in H.C. Dandekar (ed.), *City Space & Globalization: An International Perspective*, pp. 15–22. Ann Arbor: University of Michigan.

Ghosh, Asha (2005), 'Public–Private or Private–Public? Promised Partnership of the Bangalore Agenda Task Force', *Economic and Political Weekly*, 40(47): 4914–22.

Government of India (2001), *Good Governance Campaign*, Ministry of Urban Development and Poverty Alleviation. New Delhi: Government of India.

Guatam, I.P. (2009), Presentation by I.P. Guatam, the municipal commissioner of the AMC at a workshop 'Shelter Security and Social Protection for the Urban Poor and the Migrants in Asia', organized by CEPT University and MHT SEWA in Ahmedabad, 11–13 September 2009.

Himanshu (2007), 'Recent Trends in Poverty and Inequality: Some Preliminary Results', *Economic and Political Weekly*, 42(6): 497–508.

Infrastructure Professionals Enterprise (P) Ltd and Intercontinental Consultants And Technocrats Pvt. Ltd (2006), *City Development Plan for Patna Under JNNURM*, Bihar Urban Development Agency, Urban Development Department. Patna: Government of Bihar, November, available at http://jnnurm.nic.in/nurmudweb/toolkit/PatnaCdp/Final_Report.pdf, accessed on 10 March 2009.

Joshi, R. (2002), 'Integrated Slum Development: Case of Pravinnagar–Guptanagar', in A. Kundu and D. Mahadevia (eds), *Poverty and Vulnerability in a Globalising Metropolis: Ahmedabad*, pp. 268–308. Delhi: Manak Publishers.

Kehle, N.D. Mahadevia, and A. Parasher (2008), 'Centralized and Decentralized Solid Waste Management Practices in Bangalore', in D. Mahadevia and J. Wolfe (eds), *Solid Waste Management in Indian Cities: Status and Emerging Practices*, pp. 85–132. New Delhi: Concept.

Kehle, N., D. Mahadevia, and J. Wolfe (2008), 'Modernizing Municipal Management: Kolkata', in D. Mahadevia and J. Wolfe (eds), *Solid Waste Management in Indian Cities: Status and Emerging Practices*, pp. 170–211. New Delhi: Concept.

Klink, J. (2002): *Recent Perspectives on Metropolitan Organization, Functions and Governance*. Washington D.C.: InterAmerican Development Bank.

Kundu, A. and D. Mahadevia (eds) (2002): *Poverty and Vulnerability in a Globalising Metropolis: Ahmedabad*. New Delhi: Manak Publications.

Kundu, D. (2002), 'Provision of Infrastructure and Basic Amenities: Analysing Institutional Vulnerability', in A. Kundu and D. Mahadevia (eds), *Poverty and Vulnerability in a Globalising Metropolis: Ahmedabad*, pp. 133–78. New Delhi: Manak Publications.

_________ (2009), 'Elite Capture and Marginalization of the Poor in Participatory Urban Governance: A Case of Resident Welfare Associations in Metro Cities', in Ministry of Housing and Urban Poverty Alleviation, Government of India (ed.), *India: Urban Poverty Report 2009*, pp. 271–84. New Delhi: Oxford University Press.

Lakha, S. (1988), *Capitalism and Class in Colonial India: The Case of Ahmedabad*. New Delhi: Sterling Publishers.

Mahadevia, D. (2001), 'Sustainable Urban Development in India: An Inclusive Perspective', *Development in Practice*, 11(2 & 3): 242–59.

_________ (2002a), 'Interventions in Development: A Shift towards a Model of Exclusion', in A. Kundu and D. Mahadevia (eds), *Poverty and Vulnerability in a Globalising Metropolis: Ahmedabad*, pp. 80–132. New Delhi: Manak Publications.

_________ (2002b), 'Communal Space Over Life Space: Saga of Increasing Vulnerability in Ahmedabad', *Economic and Political Weekly*, 37(48): 4850–8.

_________ (2002c), 'Changing Economic Scenario: Informalisation and Increased Vulnerability', in A. Kundu and D. Mahadevia (eds), *Poverty and Vulnerability in a Globalising Metropolis: Ahmedabad*, pp. 30–79. New Delhi: Manak Publications.

_________ (2005), 'The Megacity Should Work on Rational Projects', *The Times of India*, Ahmedabad, 12 December.

_________ (2007), 'A City with Many Borders: Beyond Ghettoisation in Ahmedabad', in A. Shaw (ed.), *Indian Cities in Transition*, pp. 315–40. Hyderabad: Orient Longman.

Mahadevia, D. (ed.) (2008), *Inside the Transforming Urban Asia: Processes, Policies and Public Actions*. New Delhi: Concept.

_________ (2009a), 'Deprivations, Vulnerabilities and Shelter Security: Linkages in Urban India', draft, SPA Working Paper, http://www.socialprotectionasia.org/pdf/CEPT-SPA-W-draft26.05.09_7.pdf (accessed on 18 June 2009).

_________ (2009b), 'Urban Land Market and Access of the Poor', in Ministry of Housing and Urban Poverty Alleviation, Government of India, *India: Urban Poverty Report 2009*, pp. 199–221. New Delhi: Oxford University Press.

Mahadevia, D. and H.S. Brar (2008), 'Changes and Continuities in Development Priorities', in D. Mahadevia (ed.), *Inside the Transforming Urban Asia: Processes, Policies and Public Actions*, pp. 132–67. New Delhi: Concept.

Mahadevia, D., R. Joshi, and R. Sharma (2009), 'Options for Land Tenure in Slums of Ahmedabad', unpublished paper presented at the National Workshop on Approaches to the Lands for the Urban Poor, organized by CEPT University and Ministry of Housing and Urban Poverty Alleviation, Ahmedabad, 17 April.

Mahadevia, D. and H. Narayanan (2008), 'Slumbay to Shanghai: Envisioning Renewal or Take Over?', in D. Mahadevia (ed.), *Inside the Transforming Urban Asia: Processes, Policies and Public Actions*, pp. 94–131. New Delhi: Concept.

Mahadevia, D. and B. Pharate (2008), 'Multiple Partnerships: Mumbai', in D. Mahadevia and J. Wolfe (eds), *Solid Waste Management in Indian Cities: Status and Emerging Practices*, pp. 212–56. New Delhi: Concept.

Mahadevia, D. and J. Wolfe (2008), 'Introduction', in D. Mahadevia and J. Wolfe (eds), *Solid Waste Management in Indian Cities: Status and Emerging Practices*, pp. 1–23. New Delhi: Concept.

Mahadevia, D., J. Wolfe, and A. Parashar (2008), 'Solid Waste Management in Indian Cities: An Overview', in D. Mahadevia and J. Wolfe (eds), *Solid Waste Management in Indian Cities: Status and Emerging Practices*, pp. 24–84. New Delhi: Concept.

Mohanty, P.K., B.M. Misra, R. Goyal, and P.D. Gerome (2007), *Municipal Finance in India: An Assessment*. Mumbai: Development Research Group, RBI Study no. 26.

Nair, J. (2005), *The Promise of the Metropolis: Bangalore's Twentieth Century*. New Delhi: Oxford University Press.

National Sample Survey Organisation (2003), *Condition of Urban Slums, 2002: Salient Features*, NSS 58th Round, July 2002–December 2002, Report no. 486(58/0.21/1). New Delhi: Ministry of Statistics and Programme Implementation, Government of India, December.

_________ (2004), *Housing Condition in India: Housing Stock and Constructions*, NSS 58th Round (July 2002–December 2002), Report no. 488(58/1.2/1). New Delhi: Ministry of Statistics and Programme Implementation, Government of India. March.

Office of the Registrar General & Census Commissioner, India (2005), *Slum Population, Series 1, Census of India, 2001*. New Delhi: Office of the Registrar General & Census Commissioner, India.

Paul, S. (2002), *Holding the State to Account*. Bangalore: Books for Change.

_________ (2006), 'Citizen Report Cards on Urban Services: An Aid to Public Accountability', in P.S.N. Rao (ed.), *Urban Governance and Management: Indian Initiatives*, pp. 451–73. New Delhi: Indian Institute of Public Administration/ Kanishka Publishers.

RoyChowdury, S. (2008), 'Slums and Civil Society: The Limits of Urban Activism', in D. Mahadevia (ed.), *Inside the Transforming Urban Asia: Processes, Policies and Public Actions*, pp. 601–18. New Delhi: Concept.

Sekhar, S. (2009), 'Urban Poverty and Service Delivery in Bangalore', unpublished presentation in the workshop on 'Integrating the Urban Poor in Urban Planning and Governance', organized by the CEPT University and the Ministry of Housing and Urban Poverty Alleviation, GoI, 10 April.

Sekhar, S. and M. Shah (2006), *Benchmarking Bangalore's Public Services: What the Third Citizen's Report Card Reveals*. Bangalore: Public Affairs Centre.

Sekher, M. (2001), 'Tackling Society's Detritus: Stakeholder's Partnerships and Urban Service Delivery', *Asian Journal of Political Science*, 9(2): 54–77.

_________ (2005), 'Ward Committees and Urban Governance: A Comparison of the Post 74th Constitutional Amendment Scenario in South India', Paper presented at the Seminar on New Forms of Urban Governance in Indian Mega-Cities, New Delhi, Jawaharlal Nehru University.

Shastry, A.K. (2008), 'BMTC posts Rs. 140 cr profit', *The Hindu*, 20 May. Available at: http://www.hindu.com/2008/05/20/stories/2008052061450400.htm, accessed on 25 March 2009.

Sivaramakrishnan, K.C., A. Kundu, and B.N. Singh (2005), *Handbook of Urbanization in India*. New Delhi: Oxford University Press.

de Soto, H. (2000), *The Mystery of Capital: Why Capitalism Triumphs in the West and Fails Everywhere Else*. London: Black Swan.

Spodek, H. (2001), 'Crises and Response: Ahmedabad 2000', *Economic and Political Weekly*, 36(19): 1627–38.

_________ (2002), 'Struggle and Development: A History of Coping with Poverty', in A. Kundu and D. Mahadevia (eds), *Poverty and Vulnerability in a Globalising Metropolis: Ahmedabad*, pp. 207–36. New Delhi: Manak Publications.

UNCHS (2000), 'The Global Campaign for Good Urban Governance', *Environment & Urbanization*, 12(1): 197–203.

Varshney, A. (2002), *Ethnic Conflict and Civic Life: Hindus and Muslims in India*. New Delhi: Oxford University Press.

Vashi, A. and A. Mehta (2009), 'Nightingale Hailed A'bad's Hygienic Life', *The Times of India*, Ahmedabad, 17 June. See http://timesofindia.indiatimes.com/Cities/Ahmedabad/Nightingale-hailed-Abads-hygienic-life/articleshow/4664990.cms, accessed on 19 June 2009.

Annexure I
The Functions Listed in the 12th Schedule

1. Urban planning, including town planning
2. Regulation of land-use and construction of buildings
3. Planning for social and economic development
4. Roads and bridges
5. Water supply for domestic, industrial, and commercial purposes
6. Public health, sanitation, sanitation conservancy, and solid waste management
7. Fire services
8. Urban forestry, protection of the environment and promotion of ecological aspects
9. Safeguarding the interests of weaker sections of society, including the handicapped and the mentally retarded
10. Slum improvement and upgradation
11. Urban poverty alleviation
12. Provision of urban amenities and facilities such as parks, gardens, playgrounds
13. Promotion of cultural, educational, and aesthetic aspects
14. Burials and burial grounds, cremations, cremation ghats/grounds, and electric crematoria
15. Cattle pounds, prevention of cruelty to animals
16. Vital statistics, including registration of births and deaths
17. Public amenities, including street lighting, parking lots, bus stops, and public conveniences
18. Regulation of slaughter-houses and tanneries

Annexure II
Reforms Implemented by States and Cities

Checklist of reforms	States and cities which have implemented
Financial Sustainability	
Shift to double-entry municipal accounting	Hyderabad, Vijayawada, Surat, Kolkata, Vishakhapatnam, Kochi, Ahmedabad, Mysore, Chennai, Rajkot, Nagpur, Bhubaneshwar, Shimla, Bangalore, Madurai, Thiruvananthapuram, Ujjain, Bhopal, Jaipur, Greater Mumbai, Coimbatore, Allahabad, Indore
Property tax coverage: 85 per cent	Hyderabad, Allahabad, Madurai, Vijayawada, Vishakhapatnam, Pune, Rajkot, Vadodara, Agra, Coimbatore, Chennai
Property-tax collection efficiency: 90 per cent	Hyderabad, Allahabad, Vijayawada, Coimbatore, Vishakhapatnam, Lucknow, Chandigarh, Pune, Asansol
User charges to be 100 per cent cost recovery for O&M in water supply	Vishakhapatnam, Nashik, Pune, Greater Mumbai, Chennai, Madurai
User charges to be 100 per cent cost recovery for O & M in solid waste management	Hyderabad, Vijayawada, Surat, Kolkata, Vishakhapatnam, Kochi, Ahmedabad, Mysore, Chennai, Rajkot, Nagpur, Bhubaneshwar, Shimla, Bangalore, Madurai, Thiruvananthapuram, Ujjain, Bhopal, Jaipur, Greater Mumbai, Coimbatore, Allahabad, Indore
Encouraging PPP	Vishakhapatnam, Nashik, Greater Mumbai
Efficiency enhancement	
Administrative reforms	Nashik, Madurai, Coimbatore, Chennai
Structural reforms	Mysore, Madurai, Coimbatore, Chennai
Transparency and accountability	
Revision of building by-laws—streamlining the approval process	Hyderabad, Vijayawada, Surat, Vishakhapatnam, Ahmedabad, Guwahati, Amritsar, Jaipur, Pune, Ludhiana, Ajmer, Bhopal, Rajkot, Vadodara, Indore, Nagpur, Nashik, Asansol, Kolkata
Simplification of legal and procedural framework for conversion of agricultural land to non-agricultural purpose	Hyderabad, Vijayawada, Jaipur, Vishakhapatnam, Bhopal, Bangalore, Ahmedabad, Rajkot, Surat, Vadodara, Kochi, Indore, Coimbatore, Ujjain, Ajmer, Madurai, Asansol, Mysore, Thiruvananthapuram, Indore, Jabalpur, Ujjain, Chennai, Kolkata

(contd.)

Annexure II (*contd.*)

Introduction of computerized process of land & property registration	Hyderabad, Vijayawada, Rajkot, Vishakhapatnam, Ahmedabad, Vadodara, Surat, Shimla, Bangalore, Mysore, Nagpur, Nanded, Greater Mumbai, Jaipur, Coimbatore, Madurai, Chennai
Introduction of Property title certification system in ULBs	Chandigarh, Rajkot
Devolution of powers to the ULBs from the state governments	
Implementation of 74th Constitutional Amendment Act (CAA): Transfer of 12 Schedule Functions	Andhra Pradesh, Bihar, Chhattisgarh, Gujarat, Kerala, Madhya Pradesh, Maharashtra, Tamil Nadu, Tripura, West Bengal
City planning functions to be transferred to cities	Andhra Pradesh, Assam, Chhattisgarh, Gujarat, Himachal Pradesh, Kerala, Madhya Pradesh, Maharashtra, Tamil Nadu, West Bengal
Water and sanitation functions to be transferred to cities	Andhra Pradesh, Bihar, Tamil Nadu, Chandigarh, Chhattisgarh,Gujarat, Haryana, Himachal Pradesh, Kerala, Madhya Pradesh, Maharashtra, West Bengal
Institutional Co-ordination	
Implementation of 74th Constitutional Amendment Act (CAA): Constitution of DPC	Andhra Pradesh, Assam, Bihar, Chhattisgarh, Goa, Gujarat, Haryana, Orissa, Himachal Pradesh, West Bengal, Kerala, Madhya Pradesh, Karnataka, Maharashtra, Orissa, Rajasthan, Tamil Nadu, Uttar Pradesh
Implementation of 74th Constitutional Amendment Act (CAA): Constitution of MPC	Andhra Pradesh, Gujarat, West Bengal
Deepening participation	
E-governance to be set-up	Hyderabad, Vijayawada, Rajkot, Vishakhapatnam, Ahmedabad, Greater Mumbai, Coimbatore, Kolkata, Madurai, Chennai, Surat,
Enactment of public disclosure law	Andhra Pradesh, Assam, Gujarat, Maharashtra, Tripura, Uttar Pradesh
Community participation law	Andhra Pradesh, Assam, Gujarat

(*contd.*)

Annexure II (*contd.*)

Checklist of reforms	States and cities which have implemented
Equity	
Internal earmarking of basic services for the poor	Hyderabad, Vijayawada, Ajmer, Vishakhapatnam, Raipur, Kochi, Chandigarh, Ahmedabad, Puri, Rajkot, Surat, Vadodara, Jaipur, Faridabad, Meerut, Bangalore, Thiruvananthapuram, Indore, Mysore, Bhopal, Jabalpur, Agra, Ujjain, Nagpur, Nanded, Nashik, Pune, Greater Mumbai, Kohima, Kolkata, Amritsar, Kanpur, Bhubaneshwar, Coimbatore, Madurai, Chennai, Dehradun, Haridwar, Nainital, Allahabad, Lucknow, Mathura, Varanasi, Asansol,
Earmarking 25 per cent developed land in all housing projects for EWS/LIG	Chandigarh, Ahmedabad, Rajkot, Surat, Vadodara, Jabalpur, Amritsar, Ludhiana, Jaipur, Ajmer
Environmental sustainability	
Rain-water harvesting in all buildings: revision of building by-laws	Hyderabad, Vijayawada, Delhi, Vishakhapatnam, Patna, Rajkot, Ahmedabad, Agra, Surat, Vadodara, Faridabad, Simla, Bangalore, Kochi, Dehradun, Thiruvananthapuram, Mysore, Indore, Ujjain, Nagpur, Jaipur, Ajmer, Coimbatore, Madurai, Chennai, Kolkata, Kanpur, Allahabad, Lucknow, Mathura, Meerut, Agra, Varanasi, Pune, Asansol
By-laws on reuse of recycled water	Hyderabad, Vijayawada, Pune, Vishakhapatnam, Delhi, Kolkata, Chandigarh, Coimbatore, Bangalore, Mysore, Chennai, Asansol, Kolkata, Madurai
Land market promotion	
Rationalization of stamp duty to 5 per cent	Chandigarh, Goa, Gujarat, Jharkhand, Maharashtra, Puducherry, Sikkim, Tripura
Rent control	Karnataka, Manipur, Mizoram, Nagaland, Orissa, Rajasthan, West Bengal
Repeal of Urban Land Ceiling & Regulation Act (ULCRA)	Andhra Pradesh, Bihar, Assam, Arunachal Pradesh, Chandigarh, Goa, Chhattisgarh, Gujarat, Haryana, Himachal Pradesh, Jammu & Kashmir, Kerala, Madhya Pradesh, Karnataka, Maharashtra, Manipur, Orissa, Meghalaya, Mizoram, Nagaland, Puducherry, Punjab, Sikkim, Rajasthan, Tamil Nadu, Tripura, Uttarakhand, Uttar Pradesh

Annexure III
Number of Reforms Implemented by the Mission Cities

Cities	Mandatory reforms	Optional reforms	Total reforms
Vishakhapatnam	7	6	13
Chennai	5	7	12
Coimbatore	5	7	12
Madurai	5	7	12
Hyderabad	5	6	11
Rajkot	4	7	11
Vijaywada	5	6	11
Ahmedabad	3	6	9
Surat	3	6	9
Jaipur	2	6	8
Kolkatta	3	5	8
Mysore	2	6	8
Pune	4	4	8
Vadodara	2	6	8
Asansol	2	5	7
Bangalore	2	5	7
Greater Mumbai	5	2	7
Ajmer-Pushkar	1	5	6
Allahabad	4	2	6
Indore	2	4	6
Nagpur	2	4	6
Nashik	3	3	6
Bhopal	2	3	5
Chandigarh (UT)	2	3	5
Kochi	2	3	5
Thiruvananthapuram	2	3	5
Ujjain	2	3	5
Agra	2	2	4
Amritsar	1	3	4
Jabalpur	1	3	4
Lucknow	2	2	4
Bhubaneshwar	2	1	3
Kanpur	1	2	3
Mathura	1	2	3
Meerut	1	2	3
Nanded	1	2	3
Shimla	1	2	3
Varanasi	1	2	3

(contd.)

Annexure III (*contd.*)

Cities	Mandatory reforms	Optional reforms	Total reforms
Dehradun	1	1	2
Delhi	0	2	2
Faridabad	1	1	2
Guwahati	0	2	2
Kohima	1	1	2
Ludhiana	0	2	2
Puri	1	1	2
Raipur	1	1	2
Haridwar	1	0	1
Nainital	1	0	1
Panaji	0	1	1
Patna	0	1	1
Agartala	0	0	0
Aizwal	0	0	0
Bodhgaya	0	0	0
Dhanbad	0	0	0
Gangtok	0	0	0
Imphal	0	0	0
Itanagar	0	0	0
Jammu	0	0	0
Jamshedpur	0	0	0
Puducherry (UT)		0	0
Ranchi	0	0	0
Shillong		0	0
Srinagar	0	0	0
Cochin			
Total reforms required	7	11	18

Source: (1) http://jnnurm.nic.in/nurmudweb/cityuser/reform_data/overall_status.pdf, accessed on 20 December 2008.
(2) http://jnnurm.nic.in/nurmudweb/cityuser/reform_agenda.aspx, accessed during 20–25 December 2008.

Annexure IV
Components of Property Tax Reform

a. Extension of property tax regime to all properties
b. Elimination of exemptions
c. Migration to Self-assessment system of property taxation
    i. Setting up a committee/team to draft/amend legislation
    ii. Stakeholder consultations
    iii. Preparation of draft legislation
    iv. Approval of the cabinet/ government
    v. Final enactment of the legislation by legislature
    vi. Notification
    vii. Preparation and notification of appropriate subordinate legislation
    viii. Implementation by municipality(ies)
d. Setting up a non-discretionary method for determination of property tax (for example unit area, etc.)
e. Use of GIS-based property tax system
    i. Selection of appropriate consultant
    ii. Preparation of digital property maps for municipality
    iii. Verification of digital maps and preparation of complete database of properties
    iv. Full migration to GIS system
f. Next revision of guidance values
g. Fix periodicity for revision of guidance values
    i. Periodicity to be adopted
    ii. Deadline for adoption
h. Establish taxpayer education programme
    i. Local camps for clarification of doubts and assistance in filling out forms
    ii. Setting up a website for property tax issues/FAQs, etc.
i. Establish dispute resolution mechanism
j. Rewarding and acknowledging honest and prompt taxpayers
k. Achievement of 85 per cent Coverage Ratio
l. Achievement of 90 per cent collection ratio
m. Any other reform steps being undertaken

Annexure V
City-wise Funds Released upto 31 December 2008

City	No. of projects	ACA committed (in Rs lakh)	Funds released (in Rs Lakhs)	Percentage of ACA released
Nanded	10	54,963.56	29,550.23	53.76
Faridabad	3	10,550.85	5,616.57	53.23
Rajkot	5	15,225.87	8,048.33	52.86
Hyderabad	21	79,026.13	39,967.88	50.58
Ajmer-Pushkar	4	36,684.84	16,720.41	45.58
Amritsar	3	18,286.50	8,308.89	45.44
Allahabad	2	6,005.24	2,622.44	43.67
Lucknow	4	46,496.19	19,434.55	41.80
Vadodara	6	17,838.52	7,313.40	41.00
Jaipur	8	23,153.69	9,455.96	40.84
Asansol	5	10,649.12	4,289.71	40.28
Pune	17	132,532.22	51,738.02	39.04
Vijayawada	11	28,266.00	10,500.39	37.15
Agra	2	2,623.00	926.00	35.30
Surat	24	81,725.37	28,428.58	34.79
Chandigarh	2	4,558.88	1,544.92	33.89
Greater Mumbai	21	156,357.38	51,496.58	32.94
Ahmedabad	24	76,913.18	25,255.83	32.84
Indore	8	28,958.50	9,435.54	32.58
Nashik	4	28,464.12	9,247.23	32.49
Vishakhapatnam	10	57,961.50	17,460.13	30.12
Nagpur	15	40,996.82	12,198.44	29.75
Madurai	7	31,855.09	9,422.82	29.58
Gangtok	1	2,152.81	613.20	28.48
Bangalore	39	89,826.99	25,219.80	28.08
Bhopal	6	30,780.08	8,548.62	27.77
Kolkata	25	72,438.98	19,911.35	27.49
Coimbatore	3	29,369.09	8,066.09	27.46
Meerut	2	14,779.70	3,977.49	26.91
Varanasi	5	37,326.87	9,946.47	26.65
Aizwal	1	1,513.62	378.41	25.00
Patna	1	1,847.70	461.93	25.00
Itanagar	2	8,027.73	2,006.94	25.00
Jammu	1	11,630.70	2,907.68	25.00
Srinagar	2	25,316.10	6,329.03	25.00
Shillong	3	21,938.79	5,484.70	25.00

(contd.)

Annexure V (*contd.*)

Kanpur	4	30,953.67	7,738.42	25.00
Imphal	1	2,322.64	580.66	25.00
Guwahati	2	28,449.64	7,112.41	25.00
Agartala	1	7,043.40	1,760.85	25.00
Dehradun	2	7,570.16	1,892.54	25.00
Kohima	1	2,273.04	568.26	25.00
Nainital	1	437.60	109.40	25.00
Puducherry	1	16,272.00	4,068.00	25.00
Raipur	1	24,291.20	6,072.80	25.00
Ranchi	1	23,071.32	5,767.83	25.00
Thiruvananthapuram	3	26,170.40	6,542.60	25.00
Bhubaneshwar	2	40,394.13	10,098.53	25.00
Ludhiana	1	12,069.50	3,017.37	25.00
Shimla	2	2,090.45	522.61	25.00
Ujjain	1	5,349.15	1,337.28	25.00
Haridwar	1	3,827.54	956.77	25.00
Jabalpur	2	7,441.00	1,860.00	25.00
Cochin	4	18,874.00	4,673.53	24.76
Chennai	22	70,809.14	17,357.12	24.51
Mathura	2	7,769.28	1,593.32	20.51
Mysore	6	59,009.35	9,976.43	16.91
Dhanbad	1	18,292.65	914.63	5.00
Delhi	1	8,882.30	0.00	0.00
Puri	1	13,352.00	0.00	0.00
Bodhgaya	ND	ND	ND	ND
Jamshedpur	ND	ND	ND	ND
Kochi	ND	ND	ND	ND
Panaji	ND	ND	ND	ND

Source: From http://jnnurm.nic.in/nurmudweb/Project/list-of-project.pdf, accessed on 20 January 2009.

Notes: ACA = Additional Central Assistance
ND = No Data available.

Annexure VI
Ranking of Cities by Reforms Achieved and Percentage ACA (to total ACA) Funds Released

Reforms		% ACA released		Combined (Reforms & ACA released)*	
Cities	Rank	Cities	Rank	Cities	Rank
Vishakhapatnam	1	Nanded	1	Rajkot	1
Chennai	2	Faridabad	2	Hyderabad	2
Coimbatore	2	Rajkot	3	Vijayawada	3
Madurai	2	Hyderabad	4	Vadodara	4
Hyderabad	5	Ajmer-Pushkar	5	Jaipur	5
Rajkot	5	Amritsar	6	Pune	6
Vijayawada	5	Allahabad	7	Vishakhapatnam	6
Ahmedabad	8	Lucknow	8	Ajmer-Pushkar	8
Surat	8	Vadodara	9	Surat	8
Jaipur	10	Jaipur	10	Allahabad	10
Kolkata	10	Asansol	11	Madurai	10
Mysore	10	Pune	12	Ahmedabad	12
Pune	10	Vijayawada	13	Asansol	12
Vadodara	10	Agra	14	Coimbatore	14
Asansol	15	Surat	15	Greater Mumbai	15
Bangalore	15	Chandigarh	16	Nanded	16
Greater Mumbai	15	Greater Mumbai	17	Amritsar	17
Ajmer-Pushkar	18	Ahmedabad	18	Lucknow	18
Allahabad	18	Indore	19	Indore	19
Indore	18	Nashik	20	Kolkata	19
Nagpur	18	Vishakhapatnam	21	Nashik	21
Nashik	18	Nagpur	22	Chandigarh	22
Bhopal	23	Madurai	23	Bangalore	23
Chandigarh (UT)	23	Gangtok	24	Nagpur	24
Kochi	23	Bangalore	25	Faridabad	25
Thiruvananthapuram	23	Bhopal	26	Agra	26
Ujjain	23	Kolkata	27	Bhopal	27
Agra	28	Coimbatore	28	Thiruvananthapuram	28
Amritsar	28	Meerut	29	Ujjain	28
Jabalpur	28	Varanasi	30	Chennai	30
Lucknow	28	Aizwal	31	Jabalpur	31
Bhubaneshwar	32	Patna	31	Meerut	32
Kanpur	32	Itanagar	31	Varanasi	33
Mathura	32	Jammu	31	Bhubaneshwar	34
Meerut	32	Srinagar	31	Kanpur	34

(*contd.*)

Annexure VI (*contd.*)

Nanded	32	Shillong	31	Shimla	34
Shimla	32	Kanpur	31	Mysore	37
Varanasi	32	Imphal	31	Dehradun	38
Dehradun	39	Guwahati	31	Guwahati	38
Delhi	39	Agartala	31	Kohima	38
Faridabad	39	Dehradun	31	Ludhiana	38
Guwahati	39	Kohima	31	Raipur	38
Kohima	39	Nainital	31	Gangtok	43
Ludhiana	39	Puducherry	31	Haridwar	44
Puri	39	Raipur	31	Nainital	44
Raipur	39	Ranchi	31	Patna	44
Haridwar	47	Thiruvananthapuram	31	Agartala	47
Nainital	47	Bhubaneshwar	31	Aizwal	47
Panaji	47	Ludhiana	31	Imphal	47
Patna	47	Shimla	31	Itanagar	47
Agartala	51	Ujjain	31	Jammu	47
Aizwal	51	Haridwar	31	Puducherry	47
Bodhgaya	51	Jabalpur	31	Ranchi	47
Dhanbad	51	Cochin	54	Shillong	47
Gangtok	51	Chennai	55	Srinagar	47
Imphal	51	Mathura	56	Kochi	56
Itanagar	51	Mysore	57	Mathura	57
Jammu	51	Dhanbad	58	Delhi	58
Jamshedpur	51	Delhi	59	Puri	58
Puducherry (UT)	51	Puri	59	Panaji	60
Ranchi	51	Bodhgaya	ND	Dhanbad	61
Shillong	51	Jamshedpur	ND	Bodhgaya	62
Srinagar	51	Kochi	ND	Jamshedpur	62
Cochin	ND	Panaji	ND	Cochin	64

*Combined rank obtained by the averaging of the rank of the city in each of the index, of reforms achieved and % ACA released.

Source: Based on http://jnnurm.nic.in/nurmudweb/defaultud.aspx, accessed on 20 December 2008.

7

Effective Delivery of Public Services

The Executive Agency Model

S.K. DAS

This chapter seeks to find an appropriate institutional mechanism for effective public service delivery. To do so, I examine the institutional mechanisms for service delivery adopted by several countries across the world. The goal is to find an appropriate mechanism that strengthens the capacity of the civil service to deliver effective public services. The chapter examines the experience of five countries selected on the basis of their success in instituting institutional reform for the improvement of service delivery, balancing autonomy and accountability in a way that has a positive impact on service delivery and strengthens the capacity of the civil service to deliver services. In it, I also examine the effectiveness of the existing institutional mechanisms in the Indian government with regard to autonomy, accountability, and service delivery outcomes.

INTERNATIONAL EXPERIENCE

Executive agencies have been set up to conduct service delivery functions on behalf of governments: countries that have established them have given them managerial flexibility, while holding them accountable for results.

Several countries have adopted the executive agency model to deliver public services (World Bank 1997: 87). The executive agencies are direct subsidiaries of ministries and function under public law or general administrative processes as applicable to the ministries of the government (World Bank 2005: 22–3). Their principal difference from the traditional ministries is that they are given greater managerial freedom and function within a management and performance contract negotiated with the departmental minister (Ibid.: 23). The minister has formal control, while the chief executive of the agency holds operational control. The agencies have specific mandates and annual performance agreements for purposes of accountability. The agreements specify services to be provided by the agency during a financial year; the system provides for bonuses to be earned for good performance and removal for poor performance (Das 1998: 93).

Learning from International Experience: Benefits and Costs

The executive agency model has balanced autonomy and accountability in ways that strengthen the capacity of the civil service to deliver effective public services. There are, however, pitfalls in the model that need to be ameliorated.

Benefits

The greatest benefit is that the civil servants working in the agencies are given autonomy, flexibility, and incentives to achieve results by relaxing the traditional centralized control over the use of financial and human resources (World Bank 1997: 87–90). The model enables the objectives and tasks of management to be specified a great deal more clearly than is possible when the activities are departmentally managed (Holmes and Wileman 2001: 44–5). Specification of purpose and task is accompanied by substantial devolution of managerial authority (Campos and Pradhan 1997: 24). In exchange for greater flexibility and autonomy, there are stringent performance requirements and enhanced accountability. Accountability is strengthened by recourse to contractual approaches entailing performance agreements, performance measurement, and reporting requirements (Ibid.: 25). In the agency model, service delivery is professionally managed:agencies are able to induct the best possible talent available in the career civil service, private sector, and civil society. The model's successful functioning has challenged the traditional concept of a unified public service (Nethercote 2003: 15).

Costs

With senior staff being hired from the open market on fixed contract at market competitive salaries, the loyalties of the staff lie with the individual agency rather than with the public service as a whole. It leads to the creation of enclaves and pay disparity between career civil servants and staff in the agencies (Nunberg 1994: 29). There is no inter-departmental mobility of the staff working in the agencies because they are recruited on the basis of specific domain competency. The functioning of the agencies with its focus on performance targets, unit costs, and individual agency independence erodes the traditional public service ethos (Ibid.). As the service delivery sector remains segmented into agencies with separate cultures and recruits coming from diverse domain backgrounds, it is necessary to instil a public service ethos to counterbalance the atomistic tendencies of the model.

On the whole, the balance of advantages seems to lie in the executive agency model as the preferred institutional mechanism for delivering public services, but its pitfalls need to be ameliorated.

THE INDIAN EXPERIENCE

The autonomous bodies set up in India for service delivery are neither truly autonomous nor accountable. This is the major reason for poor service delivery outcomes.

Both the Union government and the states in India have set up autonomous bodies such as companies, boards, and societies for public services delivery. The idea was to provide some degree of autonomy to these service delivery organizations, but in practice there is very little autonomy. There is often interference in transfers of staff as well as in the day-to-day operations of these autonomous organizations. There is hardly any accountability (Paul et al. 2006: 141). Half-hearted autonomy without accountability leads to increased corruption without commensurate improvement in performance. Very few of these organizations satisfy the minimum conditions for autonomy and accountability necessary for strengthening the capacity of the civil service to deliver effective public services.

Adoption of the Executive Agency Model in India

The pre-conditions for the adoption of the executive agency model are fulfilled in the Indian situation. As the agency-based management structure presupposes the induction of talent from a variety of sources, including the open market, there are issues regarding seniority, promotion, and pay parity vis-à-vis the career civil service. The solution is to set up a Senior Executive Service (SES).

Certain pre-conditions need to be satisfied for the adoption of the executive agency model. These include the existence of a formal, rule-based public sector, a system of credible control over inputs, and availability of skilled manpower (Schick 1998; also see World Bank 1997: 86–90). All these pre-conditions are met in the Indian situation (Das 2006: 158–62). With the adoption of an agency-based management structure and induction of talent from a variety of sources including the private sector, problems are likely to arise in relation to seniority, promotion, and pay parity vis-à-vis the career civil service. The solution to these problems is the creation of an SES consisting of all senior civil service positions at the level of joint secretary and above in the Government of India (GoI) and of equivalent positions in the state governments. The SES should be the leadership cadre of the civil service, responsible for higher-level policy advice and managerial and professional responsibilities including service delivery. Vacancies in the SES should be filled on the basis of a competitive, market-driven search, and appointments made on fixed-term contract at performance-based, market-competitive salaries.

Executive Agency Model and Civil Service Reform

The adoption of the executive agency model requires wide-ranging civil service reform and also poses risk to the coherence of the civil service by creating enclaves. It is important to map the links between the adoption of the model and the wider challenge of reforming the civil service as a whole.

The adoption of the executive agency model will require broad civil service reform as a pre-requisite. When the model is successfully implemented, it will spark wider civil service reform. The functioning of the agencies will also pose a significant risk to the traditional coherence of the civil service by promoting enclaves.

Its adoption will also require a broad separation of policy functions and service delivery. The excessive degree of central control exercised by the ministries over operational matters needs to be reduced. There should be substantial devolution of managerial authority to the agencies. An SES needs to be established.

Reform as a Result of Successful Promotion of the Executive Agency Model

Successful implementation of the executive agency model will prove that government operations should be viewed as a collection of interrelated but separately functioning businesses and managed accordingly. This will pose a challenge to the traditional concept of a unified civil service. With successful implementation of the model, the framework of enhancing accountability through stringent performance requirements will find universal acceptance across the government. It would also make a strong case for extension of accrual accounting to core departments of the government.

Risk to the Coherence of Civil Service by Promoting Enclaves

With the agencies inducting talent from the open market, loyalties of the staff will be with the individual agency rather than with the public service as a whole. This will lead to departmental atomism and erosion of public service ethos. Measures to combat enclaving should consist of (a) providing mobility to the members of the SES throughout the government, (b) a set of civil service values promoting public service ethos, and (c) training the members of the SES to give them a common view of professional standards and ethics.

Legislative Framework

The implementation of the model should be through laws that provide a clear, unified framework within which the civil service can undertake the distinctive roles and responsibilities that the executive agency model requires.

The Draft Civil Services Bill 2009, which is in its final stage of preparation, should incorporate specific provisions for the establishment of executive agencies, an autonomy and accountability framework, appointment of the chief executive, his remuneration and other conditions of service, and his responsibilities. The Bill should also include provisions for the constitution, role, and functions of the SES. In financial matters, a separate legislation should be enacted, providing for: (a) autonomy to chief executives in matters of financial management and control; (b) adoption of accrual accounting in the executive agencies; (c) an outcomes/outputs framework; (d) an annual performance agreement to be signed between the minister and chief executive; and (e) linkages between the outcomes/outputs framework and the system of outcome budgeting.

A STRATEGY FOR ACCEPTANCE OF THE REFORM AGENDA

The strategy should aim at building political and bureaucratic support for the changes that the reform will bring about.

It is necessary to build political and bureaucratic support for acceptance of the reform agenda. The politicians need to see that they stand to benefit from the adoption of the model. They should perceive that its implementation will lead to improved service delivery and, therefore, to increased electoral dividends. It needs to be emphasized that the adoption of the model will give the minister much greater control over deciding what gets included and excluded in the performance agreement, and therefore give him a greater say over what services are provided. There will be resistance from career civil servants to the creation of an SES enabling induction of talent from the open market to man senior civil service positions. It needs to be explained that in countries operating the SES scheme, the bulk of the appointments in the service are from the ranks of the career civil service. In addition, the SES will make it possible for career civil servants to earn enhanced remuneration comparable to the private sector.

The implications for the policymakers are as follows:

1. What this means is that the ministries responsible for policy advice should be separated from entities responsible for delivery of services. This will require changes to be made in the Rules of Business of the Executive Government.
2. Executive agencies should be set up for delivery of public services. The Draft Civil Services Bill 2009 should be amended to incorporate provisions on the establishment of executive agencies, appointment of chief executives, their remuneration and conditions of service, and their responsibilities.
3. Each executive agency should be required to develop and put in place a performance management system that specifies performance indicators and provides for measurement of performance actually achieved in terms of performance indicators. There should be a stipulation for monetary and non-monetary rewards for superior performance and penalties for poor performance.
4. An accountability framework should be put in place for the executive agencies. The framework should provide for an annual performance report specifying performance achieved against targets, explanations of why targets have not been met, steps taken to manage under-performance, description of significant achievements in performance, and measures taken to improve it. The annual performance report should be laid on the floor of the legislature and be made available in the public domain.

5. A framework document should be prepared for each executive agency setting out the accountability relationship between the agency and the ministry. The document should contain the following:
    i. agency's aim and objectives;
    ii. key target areas for an assessment of the agency's performance in relation to its aim and objectives;
    iii. relationship between the minister, chief executive of the agency, and officials of the ministry;
    iv. arrangement for dealing with business relating to the agency in relation to the legislature;
    v. a financial regime for the agency, specifying the process through which financial provision will be made, the extent of financial autonomy, and end-year flexibility to carry forward resources into the next financial year; and
    vi. pay, grades, promotion, and other personnel management matters to be determined by the chief executive of the agency.
6. An SES should be set up as the inter-agency leadership cadre of the civil service. The chief executives of the executive agencies should be members of the service.
7. The Central/state public service authority, as proposed in the Draft Civil Services Bill 2009, should be given the responsibility for filling up vacancies in the SES in a competitive and market-driven search process.
8. Appointment to the SES should be on the basis of a fixed-term contract. The contract should set out the terms and conditions of employment, tenure, remuneration, performance requirements, and termination. The pay for the SES position should be retained at the same level as is the present government norm for the post. A performance-related component should be stipulated which, when added to the pay, will make the total compensation package comparable to that prevalent in the market.
9. The Draft Civil Services Bill 2009 should incorporate provisions for the constitution, role, and functions of the SES.
10. The executive agencies should adopt accrual accounting to reflect accountabilities.
11. The Draft Civil Services Bill 2009 should incorporate a comprehensive charter of public service values and a code of conduct for the civil service, including the SES.

A financial management and accountability legislation should be enacted, providing for (a) financial autonomy and control to the executive agencies, (b) adoption of accrual accounting, (c) an outcomes/outputs framework, (d) an annual performance agreement to be signed between the departmental minister and the chief executive, and (e) linkages between the outcomes/outputs framework and the system of outcome budgeting.

THE ISSUE

Strengthening the capacity of the civil service to deliver more effective public services is a crucial challenge for improvement of governance in India. Several constraints limit the civil service's capacity to deliver services. Civil servants managing service delivery organizations do not remain sufficiently long on the job, nor do they have any incentive to perform (Paul et al. 2006: 141). They are not given the necessary financial and staffing autonomy, nor are they made accountable for results. A recent report (World Bank 2006b) reviewing public services delivery in India suggests that steps should be taken to (a) improve accountability, (b) give autonomy to the service providers to pursue clearly articulated goals with adequate resources, (c) delegate responsibilities for outputs and outcomes, and (d) have enforceability with teeth so that those who fail to perform are punished and those who perform well are rewarded. The challenge, then, is to have an institutional mechanism that gives civil servants autonomy to pursue clearly articulated goals while holding them accountable.

International Experience

Governments across the world are experimenting with a range of institutional mechanisms to improve service delivery. The choice of an appropriate mechanism for this has depended on service characteristics and factors such as the environment, contestability of the markets, and capability of the state to specify outputs and enforce performance (World Bank 1997: 87). Table 7.1 describes the range of mechanisms adopted for the improvement of service delivery.

A recent initiative is the adoption of the executive agency model in countries such as the UK, New Zealand, Australia, Sweden, Canada, Japan, Singapore, Malaysia, and Thailand (Ibid.: 91). An executive agency is a direct subsidiary of the ministry and functions under public law or general administrative processes applicable to the ministry.

Table 7.1 Mechanisms to Improve Service Delivery

	Service Characteristics and State Capability		
	Contestable	Easy to Specify Outputs and Enforce Performance	Difficult to Specify Outputs and Enforce Performance
Markets and the private sector	Strengthen markets through credible regulation	Contract out to for-profit or non-profit agencies	
Broader public sector	Create markets, for example, by issuing vouchers Enhance internal competition Set hard budgets and divest state enterprises	Set up performance-based agencies Corporatize state enterprises and establish enforceable performance contracts Strengthen voice mechanisms	
Core public sector			Ensure clarity of purpose and task Improve compliance with rules Strengthen voice mechanisms

Source: World Bank (1997).

Its principal difference from the traditional, vertically integrated ministry is that it is given greater managerial freedom and functions within a management and performance contract negotiated with the parent ministry (World Bank 2005: 22). The executive agency is a 'delegated' service provider as contrasted with the Public Law Administration (PLA), which is a 'devolved' service provider because it differs from a ministry as being a legal entity separate from the state and its different governance structure (Ibid.: 23). Although an executive agency is one of the many organizational forms used for service delivery, its relevance to the Indian situation lies in the unique way it balances autonomy and accountability to produce results even though it is a direct subsidiary of the ministry. We now examine the experience of five countries that have adopted the executive agency model for service delivery.

The United Kingdom

In the 1980s, the Thatcher government's Financial Management Initiative Programme undertook the scrutiny of a number of government departments to determine their efficiency (HMSO Documents 1985b). The report of one such scrutiny of management across the government (HMSO Documents 1985a) suggested three priorities for reform:

1. The work of each department must be so organized that it enhances the effective delivery of policies and services.
2. The management of each department must ensure that its staff has the relevant experience and skills required for the tasks that are essential to effective government.
3. There must be sustained pressure, on and within each department, for continuing improvement in the value of money obtained in the delivery of policies and services.

In consonance with these priorities, *The Next Steps* report recommended that the executive functions of the government, as distinct from policy advice, needed to be carried out by distinctive units called executive agencies. At the heart of this new approach was the need to reorient the systems and attitudes in the government to focus on delivery of public services and, flowing from this, on the needs of the recipients of these services (the customers) whether outside or within government (OECD 1999). The Report pointed out that real improvement in governance could be brought about only if civil servants were held accountable for results: a sense of ownership and personal identification was essential to improving performance (Ibid.).

The Next Steps report suggested that establishment of executive agencies offered the most practical way of organizing work to deliver public services. An executive agency was defined as a discrete area of work with a single named individual, a chief executive, in charge, with personal responsibility to the minister. An executive agency was structured around and focused on the task to be completed. The minister allocated resources and set annual performance targets for the results to be achieved. He delegated managerial authority to the chief executive who decided how best to run the organization and get the work done with the available resources (Ibid.). Acting on *The Next Steps* report, the government began setting up executive agencies in the late 1980s. There are now 127 executive agencies running on *The Next Step* lines, covering 78 per cent of the civil service (almost 373,000 civil servants) (Prime Minister's Office of Public Services Reform 2002).

These agencies deliver a great variety of services ranging from customs and excise collection, employment service and benefits, vehicle and driver licensing, issue of passports, child support, research and development to weather forecasting, and prison management. Notwithstanding the wide variety of public services they deliver, executive agencies have a number of common characteristics:

1. defined responsibilities and clear aims and objectives set out in a published framework document;
2. day-to-day responsibility for running the agency delegated to its chief executive with personal responsibility and managerial authority to get the job done;
3. the chief executive answering directly to the minister;
4. key performance targets covering quality of service, financial performance, and efficiency set by ministers and announced to parliament;
5. performance against these targets reported each year and published in the executive agency's annual report and in the annual *The Next Steps* report;
6. the basis of ministerial accountability remaining unchanged by agency status. Those working in the agency (including the chief executive) remain civil servants reporting to ministers who are accountable to parliament.

The chief executives are recruited on the basis of open competition. More than half of the chief executives are from outside the civil service. They are appointed on a fixed term contract and given substantial operational autonomy both in terms of management of finances and manpower, and are free to hire and fire staff. The agencies are authorized to give performance-related pay and negotiate with the unions the extent of the performance-related pay component. The mandate of the agency is described in a framework document which spells out the policy framework, the agency's missions and objectives, and the resources and other operational constraints under which the agency is required to function. The departmental minister approves the annual budget and performance targets of the agency and the chief executive is held personally responsible for the targeted performance. The annual report of the agency provides information on achievements against targets. The accounting of the agency is on an accrual basis. Ministerial responsibility is limited to policy and not the operational aspects of the agency. Parliamentary questions are answered by the chief executive and not by the minister. All agencies publish annual reports and framework documents setting out their aims, objectives, and outline their responsibilities. In addition, the cabinet office publishes an annual *Next Steps Review*, summarizing the performance of the executive agencies and providing comparative data.

The Department of Inland Revenues is a typical example. Prior to its conversion into an executive agency, it was responsible for the administration of duties and direct taxes in addition to providing policy advice to the relevant ministers, and valuation and other services. It had 40 million taxpayers and over 60,000 employees in 800 locations. It collected $160 billion in revenues and had a $30 billion annual budget (Khandwalla 2007: 144). It was turned into an executive agency in 1991 and there was remarkable improvement in its functioning. It replaced over 100 government grades by five broad bands and new job titles tailor-made to the department. It became more customer-oriented and changed from a culture of command, control, and investigation to one of service and support.

The steps it took to become customer-oriented consisted of:

1. merging tax assessment and collection in one location that earlier confused the taxpayers because they were carried out at separate locations;
2. setting up over 200 Taxpayer Enquiry Centres to help taxpayers with information and advice;
3. increasing the use of Mobile Enquiry Centres to reach remote communities and disabled persons;
4. designing a national telephone support service that enabled taxpayers to get access to the advice of experts who had computer access to the taxpayers' tax records;
5. redesigning forms and information brochures to make them more helpful to customers;
6. training over 40,000 staff members to provide better customer service;
7. restructuring the local office network to cut costs and improve service to taxpayers.

What has been the impact of the functioning of executive agencies? There has been significant improvement in service delivery outcomes. For example, in the Benefit Agency, which deals with income support claims from the government, the output per member of staff increased by over 20 per cent in the first two years of its conversion into an agency.

The Benefit Agency deals with a workload that would have required 15,000 more staff in 1990. Income support claims took, on an average, over five days to clear in 1990; in 1992–3, the average time taken to pay such claims was 3.5 days. In 1993, the Employment Service, which was created in 1990, met its target for setting up new claims to benefit over 94 per cent of the cases, compared to less than 87 per cent in 1990–1 (Das 1998: 114–15). In 1994–5, as against the target of placing 1.7 million unemployed people, the Service placed over 1.87 unemployed people into work (Khandwalla 2007: 261). The waiting time for driving tests was reduced from 13 weeks to less than six weeks (Das 1998: 114). The Passport Agency improved its turnaround time for processing applications from 24 to 7 days (Das 1998: 114). In 2002, the average figure was 10 days (see Alexander et al. 2002: 11).

The creation of executive agencies has led to a more sustained focus on performance in relation to both the quality of service for the customer and efficiency, strengthening accountability and greater transparency (HMSO Documents 1994). People working in them feel that the agency form has brought about significant benefits in terms of improved efficiency, greater transparency, clearer focus on the task and on the client base that the agency serves, and finally, greater scope for managers to manage without being hidebound by service-wide rules or hampered by routine high-level interventions on matters of detail (Ibid.).

In 2002, the government commissioned a comprehensive, independent review (Alexander et al. 2002) of the functioning of 92 executive agencies across the government. The review concluded that

> executive agencies brought about revolutionary changes in the culture, processes and accountabilities of these services delivered directly by the central government ... The agency model has changed the landscape of the government. Extremely flexible, it provides the most responsive and accountable framework for delivering executive functions from within the central government ... The agency model has been a success (Ibid.).

The Treasury and Civil Service Committee of the House of Commons reviewed the working of executive agencies and observed that their implementation has brought about an 'overall transformation in Government' (HMSO Documents 1995). The Committee concluded that 'Next Steps agencies represent a significant improvement in the organization of Government and that any future Government would want to maintain them in order to implement its objectives for delivery of services to the public' (Ibid.). The creation of executive agencies was characterized both by the head of the civil service and by experts giving evidence to parliament as the most significant change in the structure of the civil service since the Northcote–Trevelyan reforms of the nineteenth century (OECD 1999).

One of the objectives of the creation of agencies, namely cost containment, does not seem to have been achieved.[1] The evaluation of the Next Steps initiative showed that while the executive agencies set up to improve delivery of services had succeeded, agencies set up with the primary objective of cost containment had generally failed. The order of cost savings to the UK Government was only 0.3 per cent till 2008.[2] A clearer picture of the cost savings will emerge with the next review of the *Next Steps* by the cabinet office, but it remains true that the service improvement imperative in itself makes the executive agency model an attractive proposition.

New Zealand

New Zealand established executive agencies supported by two legislative enactments that provide the statutory basis for devolution of managerial authority to the chief executives. The State Sector Act 1988 makes the chief executives fully accountable for managing their agencies. The Public Finance Act 1989 devolves financial management and control from the Treasury to the chief executives who are made responsible for financial management, financial performance, accounting requirements, and asset and cash management of the agency. The features of executive agencies in New Zealand are (Das 1998: 92–6):

1. They are headed by apolitical chief executives appointed on contract for five years. The State Services Commission, an independent body, assembles interview panels with members drawn from the business sector, non-governmental community, and the SES for selection of chief executives.
2. The chief executive is designated as the chief financial officer for the agency by the Public Finance Act 1989. The Act gives him extensive formal delegation from the Ministry of Finance and the Treasury to enable him to autonomously manage his finances.
3. The chief executive is designated as the employing authority for all the staff under his control. He is responsible for trade union negotiations and has full authority to establish a complete human resource management system relating to his agency. The chief executive selects and appoints his own staff like a private sector employer. The staff positions are advertised and market salaries are offered.

4. A performance agreement is signed between the departmental minister and chief executive every year, detailing the services to be provided by the agency. The chief executive's performance is assessed in relation to the performance agreement. The system provides for bonuses to be earned for good performance and removal for poor performance. Assessment is undertaken by a third party: the State Services Commission.
5. There is a comprehensive system of financial and service performance reporting to the minister, cabinet, auditor-general, parliament, and government. The system requires different levels of aggregation of reporting to different authorities.

Has there been an improvement in service delivery consequent to the implementation of the executive agency model? Bale and Dale (1998: 107), who assessed the impact, had this to say:

> The framework has helped departments to understand that, just as in the private sector, survival is dependent on meeting the needs of the customer.
>
> Because their customer is interested in outcomes, departments, given sufficient competitive pressure, will strive to design and provide better public services to achieve those outcomes.

Bale and Dale make the point that the success of the agencies is based on a clear identification of the principal–agent relationship and clarification of the roles of key actors in setting and meeting performance incentives and expectations. According to them, the redefined 'managerial' role of chief executives empowered by freedom to manage, including the appointment, remuneration, and promotion of employees, is the crucial factor. Allen Schick, an international consultant, who reviewed the reform in New Zealand, said:

> In carrying out this study it has become evident that the reforms have lived up to most of the lofty expectations held for them ... the state sector is more efficient, productive and responsive, and there generally has been significant improvement in the quality of services provided to New Zealanders (Schick 1996: 1).

On the whole, the reform in New Zealand helped turn a 9 per cent budget deficit into a surplus during the 1980s and cut the unit costs of delivery by over 20 per cent in some agencies (World Bank 1997).

Australia

In 1996, the 'Government's Public Service Reform Agenda' identified a range of initiatives that might serve to improve public accountability for performance, increase competitiveness, and enhance leadership in the government. These initiatives included devolution of responsibility to the agency, giving agencies the flexibility to decide on their own systems for rewarding high performance, and streamlining administrative procedures. The Public Service Act 1999, which was an element in the 'Government's Public Service Reform Agenda', set out how executive agencies are to be established, defined the responsibilities of the heads of the executive agencies, prescribed how the head would be appointed and also his remuneration and other conditions of service, and provided for submission of an annual report by the agency to parliament through the agency minister.

The principal features of the executive agencies in Australia are (Nethercote 2003):

1. Heads of executive agencies are selected and appointed for up to five years by the minister responsible for the agency function. A vacancy is either advertised in the press or a field of applicants is identified through professional search agencies.
2. Annual performance agreements are signed between ministers and agency heads. Guidelines identify generic performance criteria that relate to human resource and financial management, and service delivery.
3. Assessment of the agency head's performance by the minister. Agency heads are eligible for annual performance bonuses not exceeding 15 per cent of their remuneration on the basis of these assessments.
4. Staffing powers are fully delegated to heads of the agencies. They are given all the rights, duties, and powers of an employer with authority to engage, terminate, and determine employment terms and conditions. Regarding remuneration, rewards, and performance pay, the agencies are given the flexibility to develop approaches to suit their culture and business needs within a government policy framework that establishes the boundaries of action.
5. Agency heads are provided flexibility and autonomy in financial management by the Financial Management and Accountability Act 1997. The Act, however, imposes various accountability requirements on agency heads: they must institute a fraud control plan and convene an audit committee, pursue debts owed to the Commonwealth, and ensure that adequate accounts and records are kept in line with the finance minister's orders.
6. Agencies are required to specify and cost their outputs against planned outcomes set by government and identify performance indicators and targets.

What has been the impact of the implementation of the executive agency model on service delivery? Since 1995, the Steering Committee for the Review of Commonwealth/State Service Provision publishes information on the performance of Commonwealth, state, and territory governments in delivering services. Its annual report uses a range of performance indicators to allow assessment of both the effectiveness and efficiency of government services, including education, justice, emergency management, health, community services, and housing. The reports show substantial improvement in the delivery of government services (Nethercote 2003: 138). A Productivity Commission Report, *Microeconomic Reform by Australian Governments 1997–98*, found accumulating evidence that the costs in both the state and Commonwealth public sectors had fallen (Ibid.). Commenting on these improvements Nethercote (Ibid.) says:

> While it is not possible to state unequivocally the factors behind these improvements, it is fair to suggest that the management reform agenda of the last two decades—focusing on managing for results and involving considerable evolution has had considerable positive impact on the budget and on the clients the APS serves. The reform agenda has facilitated improved business and corporate planning, better performance management, increased use of competition, and better management of people as well as finances.

Sweden

The separation of policy and operational functions into ministries and agencies has been a hallmark of the Swedish government for over 200 years. There are about 300 agencies for public services delivery, and approximately 99 per cent of government employees work in the agencies while the remaining 1 per cent works in the ministries (Blondal 2001). A director-general heads the agency and is appointed on a fixed term for seven years. A majority of the director-generals have a public sector background although there are quite a few from the private sector. The agencies in Sweden are wholly autonomous and are free from any control and regulation by the central government. As Blondal observes, the managers in the agencies enjoy great flexibility, with a focus on 'what they do, not how they do it, the focus is now on outcomes and outputs' (2001: 49).

The director-general is held accountable for results. Accountability is achieved through the issue of a Letter of Instruction (*Regleringsbrev*) by the ministries, specifying the desired results, which include a review of how the agency's work contributes to the government's desired outcomes, a specification of objectives and targets and how the agency should report back on the results achieved, and specification of any special assignment that the agency has been commissioned to undertake (Das 2006: 110). The agencies report the results in their annual reports, which include a report on performance. As the Ministry of Finance guidelines stipulate:

> the agency shall comment on its work performance in relation to the objectives, and in accordance with the reporting-back requirements specified in the Letters of Instruction ... The agency shall, in particular, comment on the performance reported in relation to the objectives of its work that the government has specified in the Letter of Instruction or some other decision. The particulars in the performance accounts shall be based on documented data and measuring methods. (Blondal 2001: 53)

How have these agencies contributed to improving public services delivery? Annual surveys of customer perception of service quality levels show an increasing level of general satisfaction with the quality of service delivered by public sector organizations (Ibid.). The Swedish government has also conducted extensive surveys of productivity trends in the public sector, and they reveal that this has shown significant increase. It is difficult to establish causal links, but hard budget constraints and increased managerial flexibilities are consistent with increased service quality levels and increased productivity (Ibid.).

Japan

Japan began implementing the executive agency model in April 2001 (Yamamoto 2006). Although separation of policymaking from operational responsibilities and public services delivery had long been on the agenda of the Liberal Democratic Party (LDP), this was difficult to implement in the face of resistance from powerful civil servants in the ministries. In fact, since its formation in 1955 until its splintering in 1993, the LDP was committed to high growth policies, and in this the LDP and the Japanese civil service shared a common concern. The LDP granted substantial autonomy to the civil service to shape and undertake comprehensive and long term pro-growth policies (Yamamura 1995: 111). However, within the civil service, those working in the ministries were not prepared to provide the public service delivery organizations with any form of autonomy. When, however, a survey reported that less than 20 per cent of the population rated the activities of the government as reflecting the needs of people, the executive model became an election issue in 1996 (Yamamoto 2006).

The LDP enacted a law creating executive agencies called Independent Administration Institutes (IAIs). By 2004, 105 IAIs had been set up and 224,000 civil servants were working in them (Yamamoto 2006). The departmental minister appoints the chief executive of the IAI. The latter is free to appoint staff on contract and pay them performance-related remuneration. The government gives an operating grant and a subsidy for capital expenditure to each agency, and the latter is permitted to spend the grant without any restriction by the ministries. The departmental minister sets goals for each agency for a period of three to five years, stipulating the budgetary outlay and targeted improvement in the efficiency and quality of services. The agency prepares a plan within the framework indicated by the minister and gets it approved. The former is given full managerial autonomy to implement the plan. In exchange for the autonomy, the chief executive is made accountable for the results. The Evaluation Committee in the administrative ministry evaluates the results achieved by the agency, and in turn, the Commission on Evaluation of Policies and Evaluation of IAIs in the Ministry of Public Management scrutinizes the findings of the Evaluation Committee (Ibid.).

What has been the impact of the functioning of the executive agencies? It is too early to say, but a questionnaire study of 57 agencies in 2003 (Ibid.) found that there was significant improvement in relation to four indicators of performance, namely, effectiveness, efficiency, quality, and accountability. The survey also found that the staff in the agencies had worked harder to improve quality and reduce costs, and were more customer-focused than in the period when they worked in a departmental mode. The survey also found positive improvements in relation to operational autonomy, autonomy in budget execution, the setting up of the organizational structure, and contracting out.

Benefits and Costs

The experience of these five countries suggests that with the adoption of the executive agency model, the capacity of the civil service has been strengthened to deliver effective public services. Substantial benefits have accrued from the implementation of the model but there have been costs too. The following is a general assessment of the benefits and costs.

Benefits

The greatest benefit is that the civil servants working in the agencies have been given autonomy, flexibility, and incentives to achieve results by relaxing the traditional centralized control over the use of financial and human resources (World Bank 1997: 87–90). This is a real benefit because centralized controls reinforced a focus on inputs rather than results and often got in the way of performance (Campos and Pradhan 1997: 24). In exchange for greater flexibility and autonomy, the executive agency model has introduced stringent performance requirements and enhanced accountability. The concept of an executive agency has required the civil servants in the agencies to accept responsibility, often personal, for achieving performance targets while managing within the available resources. Accountability has been strengthened by recourse to contractual approaches, often involving performance agreements together with performance measurement and reporting requirements (Ibid.: 25). The executive agency model is beneficial because it has clarified accountability. Through this, the chief executive of the agency is directly accountable to the departmental minister on the basis of a performance agreement that is defined in advance and used as a benchmark for measuring end-of-the-period performance (Das 1998: 99). In return for such ex ante specification of accountability, the chief executive is given the required autonomy to manage his agency.

Clarification of purpose and task is another benefit (Campos and Pradhan 1997: 24). The executive agency model enables the objectives of management to be specified with much greater clarity than is possible when the activities are departmentally managed. It also allows the performance of the agencies to be more readily assessed (Holmes and Wileman 2001: 44–5). It is significant that the clarification of purpose and task is accompanied by substantial devolution of managerial authority to the executive agencies (Campos and Pradhan 1997: 20).

The model is beneficial in the way it uses the key distinction between outputs and outcomes to improve efficiency and accountability in the delivery of public services (Das 1998: 99). Outputs are specific services that the executive agency delivers, and therefore the agency is held to account for the provision of outputs, which becomes the basis for evaluating its performance. Outcome is the success in achieving social goals, and it is the minister who decides the outputs that should be included so that the desired outcomes or social goals can be achieved. Therefore, the minister becomes accountable to the legislature and the electorate for the outcome, and is judged on the basis of whether he has chosen the right outputs to achieve desired social goals.

The model enables separation of policy functions from delivery of services. While policy functions are retained in central ministries, the executive agencies are charged with the responsibility of delivering services. Separation of policy functions from delivery of services has worked as a mechanism to ensure that contestable policy options are generated and the government is not captured by provider interests that unduly influence its policy options (Campos and Pradhan 1997: 20).

The agencies are in a position to attract the best possible talent available in the career civil service, private sector, and civil society. Consequently, the executive agency model makes it possible for service delivery functions to be far more professionally managed than a departmental activity. The successful functioning of the model testifies that government should be more gainfully viewed as a collection of interrelated but separately functioning professionally managed organizations rather than as a single organization managed by a unified civil service. In that sense, the executive agency model challenges the traditional concept of a unified civil service, first set out in the Northcote–Trevelyan Report of 1853 (Nethercote 2003: 15).

Costs

As senior positions in agencies are filled by professionals inducted from the open market on fixed contract at market-competitive salaries, the loyalties of the newly recruited staff lie with the individual agency rather than with the government as a whole. The result is the creation of several enclaves, with each enclave promoting an agency-centric, separate identity for its staff, which is very often at odds with the corporate identity of the government. In that sense, implementation of the executive agency model highlights the inherent contradiction between private sector models and the traditional public service ethos (Nunberg 1994: 29). In the UK, for example, questions have been raised about the role of the traditional corps of elite administrators occupying key positions in the gradually shrinking central ministries vis-à-vis the new executive agency staff (Ibid.).

The civil service manning the central ministries has traditionally been revered for its policymaking skills, and it continues to be populated by recruits with Oxbridge humanities degrees. On the other hand, the service delivery sector is segmented into agencies with separate cultures and staff recruited from diverse domain backgrounds. This is compounded by the fact that the functioning of executive agencies, with a focus on performance targets, unit costs, and individual agency independence, erodes the traditional public service ethos. If the social, administrative, and functional cleavages between this central core and the new staff in the executive agencies are not resolved, policy and implementation run the risk of becoming dichotomized and uncoordinated (Nunberg 1994: 29).

The functioning of the model has also raised the important question of pay disparity between civil servants manning the central ministries and staff in the executive agencies. In Sweden, for example, the higher civil service faces this form of tension (Ibid.). While the higher civil servants continue to be paid in compressed pay scales, managers in the agencies are on fixed contracts with individually negotiated pay. This has led to a situation in which the heads of agencies are often paid more than highly ranked civil servants in central core ministries with responsibility for agency oversight.

Countries implementing the model found it difficult, at least in the initial stages, to achieve inter-departmental mobility of staff working in the agencies because they were recruited on the basis of specific domain competency. It led to problems both for the executive agencies and policymaking ministries. For example, lack of mobility exacerbated the atomism and other enclave-like characteristics of the executive agencies. In the ministries, it resulted in uneven distribution of broad policymaking skills, leading typically to strong professional enclaves in high-profile ministries such as finance and, conversely, weak ones in less prestigious sectors such as education and health (Ibid.: 30–1).

In balance, the benefits of the executive agency model seem to overweigh the costs. Countries implementing the model have also embarked upon several corrective measures to alleviate the costs, and this is a subject to which I return.

A caveat is in order. While the executive agency model seems to have struck the right balance between autonomy and accountability to produce results, the balance relies critically on how much can be achieved in performance evaluation, which is a function of a range of factors including: (a) the ease with which the quantity and quality of particular service can be observed and contracted; (b) contestability of the relevant market; and (c) the government's capacity to manage performance evaluation and contracting.[3]

The Indian Experience

The governments both at the Centre and in the states have set up special purpose organizations to deliver public services. These organizations can be classified into three broad institutional categories. One is the statutory board established under an enabling legislation. The second category is a corporate form (a company) created under the provisions of the Companies Act 1956. The third category is a society registered under the Registration of Societies Act 1860. These bodies are in the nature of 'devolved' service providers. They are legal entities separate from the state and have different governance structures. The control of the organization vests with a governing body but is generally delegated to the chief executive. I propose to examine in the following the functioning of some of these organizations.

Delhi Metro Rail Corporation

The Delhi Metro Rail Corporation (DMRC) was set up as a company with equal equity participation from the GoI and the Government of the National Capital Territory of Delhi (NCTD). It has a management board of 14 directors; each of the two governments nominates five directors, and four are full-time functional directors. The secretary, Ministry of Urban Development, GoI, is the chairman of the board, the chief executive a nominee of the NCTD government. An empowered committee with the cabinet secretary, GoI, as the chairman meets periodically to sort out coordination problems. At a higher level, there is a dedicated Group of Ministers Committee to coordinate major policy issues. The funding for operations of the company comes from equity contributions of the GoI and the Government of the NCTD (15 per cent each), a loan from the Overseas Economic Cooperation Fund (OECF), Japan (56 per cent), property development revenues, and certain determined levies and taxes on the city dwellers.

The chief executive has a stable tenure and also significant staffing autonomy. The board approves the organization chart, and within this framework the chief executive is authorized to recruit staff. DMRC has engaged the services of general consultants, a consortium of five international and Indian consultants. The chief executive approves the composite contract based on the man-day requirement of each consultant prior to the initiation of each project. The salary scales of the chief executive and functional directors are fixed in terms of the Schedules A and B pay scales permissible to employees of a Central government public sector undertaking. The DMRC has a productivity-linked bonus scheme, which is in consonance with the Industrial Division Grades approved by the GoI. One significant incentive is the provision of leased accommodation paid for by the company. The employees' union, comprising the lower staff, has a voice in the determination of incentives.

The chief executive enjoys considerable financial autonomy. The Group of Ministers Committee approves each project of the DMRC along with its financing plan. In terms of this approval, the chief executive awards contracts to suppliers and contractors. No financial proposal is sent to the GoI or the Government of the NCTD. There is no process accountability to any ministry either in the GoI or the Government of the NCTD. This is because DMRC is neither a public sector undertaking of the Central government nor of the state government, and in that sense is not officially attached to nor subordinate to any ministry. The board, the empowered committee, and the Group of Ministers Committee periodically review the performance of the company. The performance of the DMRC has been outstanding. It was able to commission a 65.10 km route in Phase I within the stipulated timeline and is on target in phase II to commission another 121 km by 2010.[4]

What accounts for the DMRC's remarkable degree of autonomy? Structurally, there is no explanation. The way in which it is structured is very similar to any other government company delivering services. The only exception is that, because it is a joint enterprise of two governments, it was not possible to classify it either as a Central government public sector undertaking or as an undertaking of the NCTD government. Therefore, the DMRC could not be made to report to any administrative ministry of either government. It was because of this historical accident that it was able to secure the necessary space to work autonomously.

There is, however, a functional explanation. The combination of the personality, eminence, and achievements of the present chief executive—E. Sreedharan—has earned him the necessary managerial flexibility in the allocation of financial and managerial resources, stability of tenure, and ability to implement projects without the fear of interference from any government. Unlike the executive agency model, in which the autonomy is formally inscribed by legal instruments, the autonomy, in DMRC's case has been informally given. This is because of the chief executive's proven track record. The present chief executive has also been helped by his long tenures in the Konkan and Kolkata rail projects to have learnt to navigate the veto points in the governmental structure, wrest the required autonomy, and implement projects seamlessly.

There is a political explanation too. In the case of DMRC, the authorizing environment at the political level is stronger than that in the case of other public service delivery organizations. That the projects of the DMRC are sanctioned at the high political level of the Group of Ministers

Committee is a testimony to this. There is neither a group of ministers committee for other public service delivery organizations nor are they accorded such high priority. On the whole, the functioning of DMRC is the closest approximation to the executive agency model.

Bangalore Water Supply and Sewerage Board

The Bangalore Water Supply and Sewerage Board (BWSSB) was set up in 1964 by an Act of the Karnataka legislature at the suggestion of the World Bank that an autonomous board be created to manage the Cauvery Water Supply Scheme on commercial lines. The functions of the Board include:[5]

1. providing water supply and making arrangements for the sewerage and disposal of sewage in the existing and developing new regions of Bangalore metropolitan area;
2. investigating the adequacy of water supply for domestic purposes;
3. preparing and implementing plans and schemes for supply of water for domestic purposes to the required standards;
4. preparing and implementing plans and schemes for proper sewerage and disposal of sewage; and
5. levying and collecting water charges on a 'no loss no profit basis'.

The Government of Karnataka appoints the chairman and other six members of the board. The chairman, who is the chief executive, is usually an IAS officer on deputation from the state government and works on a full-time basis with BWSSB. There is no fixed tenure for the chairman, and there have been 34 chairmen since the Board was constituted in 1964, making the average tenure of the chairman a little over a year.

BWSSB does not depend on the government for funding. While it is able to meet its recurring expenditure from its revenues, it mobilizes finance for its capital works from various sources, including Japan Petroleum Energy Centre (JPEC) and the World Bank. It does not have full autonomy in financial matters. For example, it is not authorized to pay performance-related incentives to its staff without the approval of the government. In matters relating to acquiring land for the organization and obtaining water, it needs clearance from the government. In personnel matters, approval of the government is required to appoint staff by direct recruitment. Promotion to the higher echelons, such as the chief engineer's grade, requires approval of the government. Increase in wages for staff is through collective bargaining with the employees' union, but any wage settlement is subject to the approval of the government.

Thus, there are many constraints that limit the organization's ability to deliver services. Civil servants posted as chief executives do not continue for long on the job and are therefore not in a position to provide stable leadership to the organization. The chief executive does not have full autonomy in financial and staffing matters. There is no system of providing incentives related to performance and therefore the staff does not evince strong motivation to perform tasks. Accountability is weak, with no system of annual target-setting and no system for assessing achievement against targets.

Bangalore Electric Supply Company

Karnataka embarked on a major reform of the power sector in 1999. As a first step, the erstwhile Karnataka Electricity Board was dissolved and in its place, the Karnataka Power Transmission Corporation Limited (KPTCL) was incorporated. This was followed by the constitution of Karnataka Electricity Regulatory Authority (KERC) in November 1999. In the next phase of the reform process, the transmission and distribution business managed by KPTCL was unbundled. Four new distribution companies were formed to distribute power in Karnataka. Bangalore Electric Supply Company (BESCOM) was set up in June 2002 as one of the four companies to supply electricity to consumers in the six districts of Bangalore Urban, Bangalore Rural, Kolar, Tumkur, Chitradurga, and Davangere. BESCOM has about 6 million customers spread over an area of 41,092 sq km. It raises a revenue demand of about Rs 5,000 crore and its collection efficiency is of the order of about 97 per cent.[6]

The company is managed by a board which has a chairman, a chief executive, and six other members. The managing director of the KPTCL is the chairman of the company, as he is for all other electricity distribution companies in the state.

The company has a staff of 15,000 distributed over four categories: A, B, C, and D. The chief executive is appointed by the government but without a fixed tenure. The last three chief executives (the present one is the fourth) had an average tenure of a little over a year. Employees from the A and B categories are appointed by KPTCL because they can be transferred to any of the other electricity distribution companies in the state. The recruitment of A and B staff is done centrally and is subject to the approval of the government. Therefore, the chief executive has no real control over either the recruitment or movement of his staff from the A and B categories. BESCOM shares with other power distribution companies financial and legal staff as well as the services of a company secretary. The company generates the bulk of its finances, but in financial matters it does not have full autonomy. Issues relating to wage increases and payment of performance incentives to the staff are decided centrally and approved at higher levels, with the result that BESCOM has no control over the process of incentivizing its own staff.

Accountability is poor because key performance targets are not specified ex ante. A combination of the abbreviated tenure of the chief executives, lack of continuity, and weak incentive to perform has detracted from the efficiency of the company, its long-range planning, and performance orientation. This is further compounded by the fact that the chief executive has not been given the necessary financial and staffing autonomy.

Central Board of Direct Taxes

The Central Board of Revenue, as the apex body of the Income Tax department, came into existence with the enactment of the Central Board of Revenue Act 1924. Initially, the Board was concerned with both direct and indirect taxes, but as the size of the taxes grew, it was split in January 1964 into two: the Central Board of Direct Taxes (CBDT) and Central Board of Indirect Taxes. The bifurcation was effected under Section 3 of the Central Board of Revenue Act 1963.

The CBDT is responsible for the administration of direct taxes, but the officials of the Board in their ex officio capacity also function as a division of the finance ministry, dealing with matters relating to levy and collection of direct taxes. The Board has 27 million taxpayers and 60,000 employees in 514 locations. The total tax collected is Rs 2.3 lakh crore and the annual budget of the Board is Rs 1,530 crore.[7] The Board has a chairman and six members who are appointed by the government. The chairman is the chief executive of the Board. No fixed tenure has been prescribed for the chairman. The government sets the target for tax collection annually and reviews the progress.

The Board, though designated as the apex body for tax administration, has no financial power and no financial autonomy. In regard to budgetary allocation, the 600 and odd budgetary authorities in the Income Tax Department send proposals to the financial adviser located in the ministry of revenue for approval. In matters of expenditure appraisal and approval, the Board has no powers. The Board has no functional autonomy in personnel matters either. In terms of allocation of work, the transfer and postings of officers in the cadre of chief commissioners and commissioners of income tax are decided by the chairman of the Board, while transfer and postings of deputy commissioners and assistant commissioners are the responsibility of the member (personnel) of the Board. In practice, however, all transfer and postings of officers, from assistant commissioners up to chief commissioners, are done only at the level of the ministry.

Clearly the Board has not been given the independence to undertake its assigned responsibility as the apex body of tax administration. It has neither functional autonomy nor any financial power or authority. Interestingly, the chief commissioners and commissioners, nominally under the control and supervision of the Board, have been given financial powers independent of it. The government itself decides their transfers and postings, and they report to the government for budgetary outlays and expenditure incurred. The chief executive of the Board has no fixed tenure. Small wonder, then, that the chairman of the Board has very little accountability for what happens in tax administration.

As the examples clearly indicate, the problem with these organizations (with the exception of the DMRC) is both with autonomy and accountability. The autonomy given to them is only half-hearted and there is very little accountability. Half-hearted autonomy without accountability can translate into more opportunities for rent-seeking without an improvement in performance.

Is the problem with these organizations structural or functional? The problem is primarily structural. In fact, the autonomy concerns of these organizations are capable of being addressed within the existing structural forms by giving them greater functional autonomy. However, when it comes to accountability, the concerns cannot be addressed within the existing structural forms. In view of the corruption that plagues the working of these organizations, there is need to exercise accountability for processes in addition to outcomes. This is not possible within the existing structural forms because they are legal entities separate from the state and have governance structures technically independent of the government. What is required in the Indian situation is a structural form that can operate under general administrative processes applicable to the departments of the government, but can be given staffing and financial autonomy within an accountability and performance framework. As the analysis of the international experience shows, it is only the executive agency model that provides such a structural form.

Adoption of the Executive Agency Model in India

The question, then, is: can the model be adopted in India? Schick (1998) counsels that for countries that have not succeeded in instituting credible controls over the use of inputs, it is not a viable option. He suggests:

> Politicians and officials must concentrate on the basic process of public management. They must be able to control inputs before they are called upon to control outputs; they must be able to account for cash before they are asked to account for cost; they must abide by uniform rules before they are authorized to make their own rules; they must operate in integrated, centralized departments before being authorized to go it alone in autonomous agencies. (1998: 130)

In other words, the country should have a formal, rule-based public sector before making the transition to a system in which managers are accorded discretion to run their organizations. India has a formal, rule-based public sector that has well-established systems and procedures used by government organizations to exercise credible control over inputs, incur expenditure within budgetary limits, and assure compliance with rules. Civil servants in India have a long history of operating in integrated, centralized ministries/departments. Arguably, India satisfies the pre-conditions for making the progression to an executive agency model.[8]

Schick also stipulates that the country should have skilled human resources to meet the requirement of an agency-base management structure (Schick 1996; also see Rose 2003). The executive agency model presupposes the induction of competent professionals drawn from a variety of sources, including the open market.

Finding competent professionals to man these agencies should not be difficult in India, considering that, in addition to career civil servants with domain competency, India has about 100,000 managers in the corporate public sector with equal numbers in the civil society and private business sector.

As professionals inducted to the agencies would be called upon to work in what are essentially civil service positions, problems are likely to arise in relation to, inter se, the seniority of these professionals vis-à-vis career civil servants. Lateral entry of professionals will also affect promotions in the civil service. Payment of market-related compensation to professionals will create anomalies in the governmental set-up. In the international context, countries implementing the executive agency model encountered similar problems. To deal with them, they took steps to isolate the management of senior civil service personnel from others in the civil service by creating an SES (Nunberg 1994: 27) to resolve problems of: (a) wage erosion in comparison with the private sector and wage compression in relation to lower civil service echelons; (b) difficulty in attracting highly qualified professionals away from the private market; and (c) the absence of a public-spirited, inter-agency, service-wide corps (Nunberg 1994: 27). The features of the SES are:

1. a group of functionaries appointed to top-level positions across the government;
2. works in policymaking or leads operating agencies;
3. drawn from all sources, including the private sector;
4. limited in size, constituting under 1 per cent of the civil service;
5. hurdles to entry makes it selective;
6. receives greater training than the general civil service;
7. rewarded by higher rates of remuneration, and sometimes reputation;
8. career progression determined by performance;
9. held to a distinctive set of ethical standards and values, such as a distinctive code of conduct.

An SES should be established in the Indian government as a leadership cadre to make the civil service at senior levels more open, mobile, and competitive, and also to achieve a greater degree of management leadership in the development and placement of senior staff. Apart from enabling the government to induct talent from non-civil service sources, it will reshape the cadre of senior civil servants into a more competent corps responsible for higher-level policy advice and managerial and professional responsibilities, including public service delivery. It will also provide a solution to issues of inter se seniority, promotion, and pay parity of career civil servants vis-à-vis those who are laterally inducted. The SES should consist of all senior civil service positions at the level of joint secretary and above in the Government of India and of equivalent positions in the state governments.

The Central Civil Services Authority, as proposed in the Draft Civil Services Bill 2009, should advertise the vacancies in the SES, invite applications from eligible persons in the open market and career civil service, conduct interviews, and select the best person for the job. The Authority should then process cases for approval of the Appointments Committee of the Cabinet. Appointment to the SES should be on the basis of a contract setting out the terms and conditions of employment, tenure, remuneration, performance requirement, and termination. The pay for the SES position should be retained at the same level, as is the present government norm for the post. The idea should be to incorporate a performance-related component which, when added to the pay, will make the total compensation package comparable to that prevalent in the market.

Executive Agency Model and Civil Service Reform

The adoption of the executive agency model will entail several civil service reform initiatives. Some of these will need to be undertaken as a prerequisite for implementing the model. In addition, when the executive agencies begin functioning successfully, it will spark wider civil service reform. It is also likely that the functioning of executive agencies will pose risks to the traditional coherence of the civil service by promoting enclaves. It is, therefore, necessary to map the links between the implementation of the executive agency model in India and the wider challenge of reforming the civil service.

Civil Service Reform as a Pre-requisite

The prerequisites for implementing the executive agency model are given below:

1. Policy functions need to be separated from service delivery functions. In terms of concrete reform measures, it will mean that policy functions should be dealt with in the ministries while the executive agencies deliver services. This also ensures that contestable policy options are generated, free from provider interests (Campos and Pradhan 1997: 20).
2. The excessive degree of central control exercised by ministries over operational matters should be eliminated. This requires the emphasis on system-wide conformity to be replaced with a combination of guidelines and minimum standards. The abolition of central control will lead to a focus on results and performance.
3. There should be devolution of managerial authority to executive agencies. This calls for flexibility to the agencies in using budgetary allocations to produce results in accordance with performance targets. The agencies need to be given staffing autonomy as well.
4. An SES should be set up. Because the SES will be open and competitive, it will be possible for the government to induct competent professionals from the public and private corporate sectors, civil society, and existing pool of career civil servants. The establishment of SES will also enable payment of compensation linked to performance.

Reform as a Consequence of Successful Promotion of the Executive Agency Model

The following reforms of the civil service may result due to the implementation of the executive agency model:

1. Successful functioning of executive agencies with staff appointed on contract with differential terms of employment and levels of remuneration will spark similar practices across the government. This will be beneficial in the longer term because it will make the government sensitive to the costs of a unified civil service based on the idea of lifetime employment in contrast to the benefit it offers.
2. Successful implementation of the model will validate the usefulness of measuring performance through mechanisms that highlight results by focusing on benefits derived from the utilization of public money. In that case, the government will wish to extend the principle of results-orientation to all its core activities.
3. With successful promotion of the model, the framework of enhancing accountability through stringent performance requirements should find acceptance across the government spectrum. This will mean using performance agreements throughout the government, including in its core activities.
4. Successful use of accrual accounting in the agencies will suggest its extension to core departments of the government. This will give core departments the capacity to generate information on how to enhance decision-making, reflect accountability, and ensure control over the long-term consequences of government policies.

Risk to the Coherence of the Civil Service by Promoting Enclaves

Countries implementing the executive agency model encountered, at least in the initial stages, a degree of enclaving that posed a threat to the coherence of their civil services. The loyalties of personnel inducted from the open market on fixed contract came to lie with the individual agency rather than with the public service as a whole. While this had advantages for the agency in terms of loyal, dedicated employees, it resulted in departmental atomism and erosion of public service ethos. This happened in the UK, Australia, and New Zealand (Nunberg 1994: 27–30). These countries took three corrective steps.

1. Creation of an inter-agency, corporate identity for the senior staff of the executive agencies by facilitating their mobility throughout the

government. This meant the establishment of an SES whose members, while working in an individual agency, acquired a broader identity as part of a cohesive group at the top covered by a common, shared framework. The idea was to shape the SES into a unified inter-agency, elite corps responsible for higher-level policy advice and managerial and professional responsibilities across the government.

2. Inculcation of a set of civil service values that focused on establishing public service ethos. In New Zealand, the State Services Commission took the lead in raising awareness about public service values and ethos by issuing a Code of Conduct for civil servants. In the UK, a Civil Service Code was drawn up and incorporated into law, which came into force on 1 January 1996. The Code, apart from restating the integrity and loyalty required of civil servants, is a clear and concise statement of the responsibilities of civil servants and also forms part of civil servants' terms and conditions of employment. In Australia, the Public Service Act 1999 contains a declaration of Public Service Values and a Code of Conduct for Australia's civil service.
3. Training the members of the SES to instil a common view of public service ethos and professional standards and ethics. The UK government evolved a comprehensive framework of combined training for all the new entrants to the SES and a continuing training programme for existing members.

Similar steps need to be initiated in India to deal with the potential risk of enclaving to the coherence of the civil service.

Legislative Framework

Legislation plays a pivotal role in defining and establishing the core principles and characteristics that create the distinctive ethos of the civil service. It also provides a clear, unified framework within which the civil service is enabled to carry out its roles and responsibilities. It is heartening that the Draft Civil Services Bill 2009 is in its final stages of preparation. It seeks to provide for:

1. Appointment to the civil service based on merit, and fair and open competition (chapter II).
2. The strengthening of common civil service values (chapter III).
3. A civil service code.
4. Performance management and accountability (chapter V).
5. An authority known as the Central Civil Services Authority comprising a chairman and members to be appointed by the president on the

recommendations of a committee consisting of the prime minister, home minister, and leader of the opposition in the Lok Sabha (section 11).

6. An authority to review the civil service and recommend changes, advise the government on the formulation of the several codes for which the Bill provides, and advise the government on all aspects concerning the civil service (section 15).
7. An authority to submit an annual report indicating compliance with the provisions of the Bill by ministries/departments, the reasons for non-compliance, and the steps to be taken to ensure compliance (section 17).
8. An annual report to contain recommendations of the authority for improving the conditions of the civil service in general, new career development issues, pay structure and related issues (section 17).

How good is the proposed legislation? For a benchmark, we need to look at civil service legislation enacted in other countries. They provide for:

1. a legal basis for the legislature to express the important values and culture it wants in the civil service;
2. a mechanism to implement government decisions;
3. a framework for setting out the roles and powers of the heads of the agencies and departments, and their relationship to the ministers, publicly and with clarity;
4. an unambiguous statement to those within the civil service and to the people, of what is expected of the civil service;
5. public service standards and ethical values and how they should be applied;
6. a framework of public accountability;
7. employment principles covering such areas as merit selection and equity in employment; and
8. a basis for vesting employment powers in the heads of departments and agencies.

In comparison with this benchmark, the Draft Civil Services Bill 2009 fulfils most of the requirements, except in laying down a framework for the adoption of the executive agency model and establishing the SES. For example, Australia's Public Service Act 1999 provides for the establishment of executive agencies, appointment of the heads of the agencies, their remuneration and other conditions, and the responsibilities of the heads of the executive agency, including the form of their accountability to the agency minister. Section 20 of the Act stipulates that the head of the agency will have all the rights, duties, and powers of an employer in relation to the staff in the agency. Section 22 gives the head of the agency the power to employ staff, and Section 24 gives the power to determine the remuneration and other terms and conditions of their employment. The Draft Civil Services Bill 2009 should lay down a framework for the adoption of the executive agency model. With regard to the establishment of the SES, the Public Service Act 1999 of Australia provides for the constitution, role, and functions of the SES in Sections 34 to 38. It may be necessary for the Draft Civil Services Bill 2009 to incorporate provisions for the constitution, role, and functions of the SES.

The Draft Civil Services Bill 2009 provides for a Public Services Code of Conduct and Ethics to be prepared, also stipulating a set of values such as: (a) patriotism and upholding the national pride; (b) allegiance to the Constitution and the law of the nation; (c) objectivity, impartiality, honesty, diligence, courtesy, and transparency; and (d) maintenance of absolute integrity. This is a step in the right direction. However, we need to recognize that civil servants have special obligations because they deliver services to the community and take vital decisions that affect all aspects of the citizen's life. It is, therefore, necessary that the Bill should enshrine values pertinent to the special obligations of civil servants, covering areas such as: (a) the civil service and its relationship with the government and legislature; (b) the civil service and its relationship with the public; (c) the civil servant and his/her relationships in the place he/she works; and (d) personal behaviour of the civil servant. In Australia, for example, Section 10 of the Public Service Act contains a declaration of 15 APS values, and the code of conduct in Section 13 provides for 13 imperatives, covering all these four aspects. If the Public Services Code of Conduct and Ethics and values in the Draft Civil Services Bill 2009 are made comprehensive, covering these aspects, it will be in a position to obviate the risk of enclaving.

In financial matters, it has been the practice to enact a separate legislation. For example, in New Zealand, the Public Finance Act 1989 devolves financial management and control from the Treasury to the agencies and makes the chief executives responsible for financial management and performance. It also provides for the adoption of an outcomes/outputs framework and a system of performance agreement as the basis of accountability relationship between ministers and chief executives. In Australia, the Financial Management and Accountability Act 1997 gives the agency heads autonomy in financial management. In India, there is need for a financial legislation that provides for: (a) autonomy to chief executives in matters of financial management and control, (b) adoption of accrual accounting by the executive agencies, (c) outcomes/outputs framework, (d) an annual performance agreement, and (e) linkages between the outcomes/outputs framework and the present system of outcome budgeting.

Policy Recommendations

The establishment of executive agencies and implementation of associated civil service reform will require several policy changes. The policy changes recommended are:

1. Separating policy functions from those relating to service delivery. This will require changes to be made in the rules of business of the executive government.
2. Control exercised by ministries over service delivery and the requirement of system-wide conformity to be replaced by guidelines and minimum standards. This needs to be effected through financial legislation to be enacted for the purpose.
3. Setting up executive agencies for delivery of public services. This has to be effected by incorporating suitable provisions in the Draft Civil Services Bill 2009.
4. Defining the accountability relationship between the agency and ministry on the basis of a framework document. The document should contain the following:
    - i. the agency's aims and objectives;
    - ii. key target areas on the basis of which the performance of the agency can be assessed in relation to its aim and objectives;
    - iii. the relationship between the minister, chief executive of the agency, and officials of the ministry;
    - iv. arrangements for dealing with legislature business relating to the agency;
    - v. a financial regime for the agency describing the process through which financial provisions will be made, the extent of financial delegation, and the flexibility to carry forward resources into the next financial year;
    - vi. the responsibility for pay, grades, promotion, and other personnel management matters to be delegated to the chief executive; and
    - vii. an annual performance agreement to be signed between the departmental minister and chief executive.

5. Establishing a comprehensive performance management system for the agency. This will include an annual performance report specifying the performance achieved against targets, explanations of why targets were not met, steps taken to manage under-performance, description of significant achievements in performance, and measures taken to improve performance. The annual performance report should be laid on the floor of the legislature and made available in the public domain.
6. The SES to be set up as the inter-agency leadership cadre of the civil service. The chief executives of the executive agencies should belong to the SES.
7. The Central/State Civil Services Authority as proposed in the Draft Civil Services Bill 2009 should fill up vacancies in the SES on the basis of a competitive, market-driven talent search. The Authority is to obtain approval of the Appointments Committee of the Cabinet for the proposed appointments. The annual report of the Authority to the legislature is to invite attention to cases in which its recommendation has not been accepted.
8. Appointment to the SES to be on a fixed term contract. Contract provisions should set out the terms and conditions of employment, tenure, remuneration, performance requirements, and termination. The pay for the SES position should be retained at the same level as the present government norm for the post. There should be stipulation of a performance-related component which, when added to the pay, will make the total compensation package comparable to that prevalent in the market.
9. The Draft Civil Services Bill 2009 to incorporate provisions on the constitution, role, and functions of the SES.
10. The executive agencies to account on an accrual mode to reflect accountabilities.
11. The Draft Civil Services Bill 2009 should incorporate a comprehensive charter of public service values and a code of conduct for the civil service, including the SES.
12. To enact a financial management and accountability legislation providing for financial autonomy and control to the executive agencies, adoption of accrual accounting, an outcomes/outputs framework, annual performance agreement, and linkages between the outcomes/outputs framework and the system of outcome budgeting.

A Reform Strategy

It will be necessary to adopt a coordinated strategy for the implementation of the reform agenda. At a minimum, the strategy should aim at building political and bureaucratic support for the changes that the reform will be expected to bring about. The reform agenda may sound impressive with its international credentials but it has to be accepted by the politicians and bureaucrats. This is critical because the agenda requires radical shifts in inherited behavioural patterns and a fundamental change in the functioning of the civil service. Interference in day-to-day functioning and the arbitrary nature of some transfers and postings are problems faced by such organizations. At the state level, it has become common to appoint politicians as chairpersons of these organizations with pay, perks, and privileges on par with ministers.

However, if politicians can be persuaded to look beyond these short-term gains, they will perceive that the adoption of the executive agency model will give them much greater control over service delivery. On the basis of the annual performance agreement signed between the minister and the agency, the former will be in a position to decide what gets included and excluded in the agreement, and will therefore have a greater say over the services that are provided. In New Zealand, the executive agency model gave the ministers far greater control over services to be delivered, enabling them to make changes in priorities (Little 1993: 9; also see Scott 1994: 173).

In addition, with the adoption of the executive agency model, there will be great improvement both in the processes and outcomes of service delivery, and this will help politicians to achieve their welfare goals and also bring them electoral gains. This happened in Tamil Nadu. Politicians there supported the civil service with autonomy and additional resources to enhance programme delivery. The support was based on the perception by the politicians that effective programme delivery will bring electoral returns and signal a common ideological emphasis on welfare policies (World Bank 2006a: 54–9). What is necessary is an effort to make the politicians conscious that the adoption of the executive agency model will further their longer-term political interests.

The idea of an executive agency per se may not encounter resistance from the civil service. There are indeed a large number of talented civil servants scattered throughout the civil service who are deeply frustrated with the present dispensation and are keen to exercise greater management authority and lead changes in their organizations. The idea of an SES will, however, meet with resistance because it will be seen as a repudiation of the traditional concept of a unified career civil service. Career civil servants will not take kindly to the idea of professionals from outside being laterally inducted to man senior civil service positions in the government. It needs to be explained that the SES will be an integral part of the unified civil service, albeit its leadership cadre. If the experience of countries with an SES scheme is anything to go by, the bulk of the appointments to the SES will be from amongst members of the career civil service itself. In the American SES, careerists occupied 90 per cent of the positions in 1994 (Nunberg 1994: 28). While the size of the American SES has increased from 7,000 in 1994 to 8096 in 2007, the percentage of careerists is more or less of the same order.[9] This is because of the stipulation that at least 70 per cent SES positions government-wide must be filled by individuals with five years or more of current continuous service immediately before initial SES appointment to assure experience and continuity.[10] In Australia, recruitment from careerists has ranged between 75 per cent in 1992–3 and 86 per cent in 2000–1 (Nethercote 2003: 79). In addition, the SES will incentivize performing civil servants through enhanced remuneration on par with the private sector.

A Road Map for Implementation

A key lesson that emerges from the experience of countries with the executive agency model is that it requires adequate preparation. I now draw a road map that shows how this process should be organized by the Indian government.

Nudging the Government

The essential first step should be to nudge the government towards the adoption of the model. Arguably, it is a radical reform by Indian standards. The Indian system rarely proposes a radical reform initiative unless it first emanates from a high-powered committee or a reforms commission.[11] It is indeed fortunate that the Second Administrative Reforms Commission has recommended the adoption of the executive agency model (Second Administrative Reforms Commission 2008: 303).

Legislative Action

As I pointed out, the legislative framework necessary for implementation of the reform will consist of two specific legislations: a public services act and a financial management and accountability act. The Draft Civil Services Bill 2009 will require certain amendments. These need to be proposed and piloted through government channels and through the legislature. The financial management and accountability legislation will be a new initiative altogether, and in that sense it will require elaborate preparatory work and consultation with stakeholders before being processed and piloted through the legislature.

Allocating Roles and Responsibilities

An appropriate ministry in the government needs to be designated as the lead agency for implementation of the reform agenda with responsibility for (a) developing policy proposals; (b) piloting them through the cabinet; (c) preparing the necessary legislative proposals and piloting the bills through the legislature; and (d) setting out suitable milestones for their implementation and evolving a set of trigger-points and monitoring them.

The implementing ministries and departments need to be assigned responsibility for (a) taking steps to separate policy functions from delivery of services by instituting the necessary changes in the Rules of Business and (b) compiling a list of eligible institutions for conversion into executive agencies.

Setting Up a Task Force

The government should set up a task force under the lead agency to suggest formats for the framework agreement, autonomy and accountability framework, and reporting framework for the executive agencies. The task force should also be asked to specify the contents of the performance agreement between the minister and the executive agency.

SUMMING UP

The executive agency model provides for greater clarity of purpose and task, greater managerial autonomy in the allocation of financial and human resources, and greater accountability than the existing 'devolved' service providers such as boards, companies, and societies. The executive agency model balances autonomy and accountability in ways that strengthen the capacity of the civil service to deliver effective public services. This chapter recommends the adoption of the executive agency model on a wide scale in India to improve both the processes and outcomes of service delivery. However, instituting the model will require important shifts in the existing legal and institutional framework, including civil service reform, that necessitate building political and bureaucratic support.

NOTES

1. I am grateful to Ranjana Mukherjee of the World Bank for this suggestion.
2. This information is courtesy Ranjana Mukherjee of the World Bank. It refers to overall saving till 2008.
3. I am grateful to Chunlin Zhang, the lead private sector development specialist (China) of the World Bank, for pointing this out.
4. Author's conversation with E. Sreedharan, MD, DMRC.
5. Author's conversation with Latha Krishna Rau, Chairperson, BWSSB.
6. Author's conversation with Tushar Girinath, MD, BESCOM.
7. Information obtained from the Central Board of Direct Taxes.
8. For a discussion on Schick's pre-conditions as applicable to the Indian situation, see Das (2006: 158–65).
9. *Recruitment of SES in the US*, http://www.opm.gov/ses/recruitment/allocate.asp.
10. *Recruitment and Selection*, http://www.opm.gov/ses/recruitment/merit-staffing.asp.
11. I am grateful to N.C. Saxena for pointing this out.

BIBLIOGRAPHY

Alexander, P., S. Hinkley, A. Sharples, and W. Thompson (2002), *Better Government Services: Executive Agencies in the 21st Century*, report commissioned by the British Government.

Bale, M. and T. Dale (1998), 'Public Sector Reform in New Zealand and its Relevance to Developing Countries', *The World Bank Research Observer*, 13(1): 103–21.

Blondal, J.R. (2001), 'Budgeting in Sweden', *OECD Journal on Budgeting*, 1(1): 27–58.

Campos, E. and S. Pradhan (1997), 'Building Institutions for a More Effective Public Sector', background paper for the *World Development Report 1997*. Washington D.C.: World Bank.

Das, S.K. (1998), *Civil Service Reform and Structural Adjustment*. Delhi: Oxford University Press.

__________ (2006), *Rethinking Public Accounting: Policy and Practice of Accrual Accounting in Government*. Delhi: Oxford University Press.

Holmes, John W. and T. Wileman (2001), *Towards Better Governance: Public Service Reform in New Zealand (1984–94)*, available at http://www.oag-bvg, gc.ca/domino/other.nsf/html/nzbody/html, accessed on 20 April 2008.

HMSO Documents (1985a), *Improving Management in Government: The Next Steps*. London: HMSO.

__________ (1985b), *Making Things Happen: A Report to the Prime Minister on the Implementation of Government Efficiency Scrutinies*. London: HMSO.

HMSO Documents (1994), *Raising the Standard: Britain's Citizen's Charter and Public Service Reforms*. London: HMSO.

_________ (1995), *The Civil Service: Taking Forward Continuity and Change*. London: HMSO.

Khandwalla, P. (2007), 'Redesigning the Union Government of India', Background paper to the Reports of the Second Administrative Reforms Commission, Government of India.

Little, S. (1993), 'Improving Financial Performance: Public Sector Management Reform in New Zealand', address to National Association of State Auditors, Comptrollers and Treasurers, Washington D.C., 20 July.

Nethercote, J.R. (2003), *The Australian Experience of Public Sector Reform*. Canberra: Commonwealth of Australia.

Nunberg, B. (1994), 'Managing the Civil Service: Reform Lessons from Advanced Industrialized Countries', World Bank Discussion Papers 204, World Bank, Washington D.C.

OECD (1999), *Strategic Review and Reform: The UK Perspective*. Paris: OECD.

Paul, S., S. Balakrishnan, G.K. Thampi, S. Sekhar, and M. Vivekananda (2006), *Who Benefits from India's Public Services? A People's Audit of Five Basic Services*. New Delhi: Academic Foundation.

Prime Minister's Office of Public Services Reform (2002), *Better Government Services: Executive Agencies in the 21st Century*, available at www.civilservice.Gov.uk/agencies.

Rose, A. (2003), 'Results-Oriented Budget Practice in OECD Countries', Working Paper 209, Overseas Development Institute, London.

Schick, A. (1996), *The Spirit of Reform: Managing the New Zealand State Sector in a Time of Change*. Wellington: State Services Commission, available at http://www.ssc.govt.nz/Documents/Schick-report.pdf, accessed 17 March 2010.

_________ (1998), 'Why Most Developing Countries Should Not Try New Zealand Reforms', *The World Bank Research Observer*, 13(1): 123–31.

Scott, G. (1994), 'Strengthening Government Capacity to Manage Human Resources: The New Zealand Experience', Proceedings of a Conference on Civil Service Reform in Latin America and the Caribbean, World Bank Technical Paper No. 259, Washington D.C.: World Bank.

Second Administrative Reforms Commission (2008), *Tenth Report: Refurbishing of Personnel Administration*. New Delhi: Government of India.

World Bank (1997), *World Development Report 1997*. Washington D.C.: World Bank.

_________ (2006a), *Reforming Public Services in India: Drawing Lessons from Success*. New Delhi: World Bank and Sage Publications.

_________ (2006b) *Inclusive Growth and Service Delivery: Building on India's Success*, Development Policy Review Report No. 34580-IN 2006, Washington D.C.: World Bank.

World Bank (2005), *China: Deepening Public Service Unit Reform to Improve Service Delivery*, Poverty Reduction and Economic Management Unit, East Asia and Pacific Region, Report no. 32341-CHA, July. Washington D.C.: World Bank.

Yamamoto, K. (2006), 'Performance of Semi-Autonomous Public Bodies: Linkages between Autonomy and Performance in Japanese Agencies', *Public Administration and Development*, 26: 35–44.

Yamamura, K. (1995), 'The Role of Government in Japan's "Catch-Up" Industrialization: A Neo-institutionalist Perspective', in K. Hyungaki, M. Muramatsu, T.J. Pempel, and K. Yamamura (eds), *The Japanese Civil Service and Economic Development*, pp. 109–27. Oxford: Clarendon Press.

8

Implementation of the Right to Information

Ideas for India from Canada, Mexico, and South Africa

TOBY MENDEL

India adopted a national Right to Information (RTI) Act in 2005[1] after a long and hard-fought campaign. The 2005 Act was preceded by a 2002 Freedom of Information Act,[2] as well as the adoption of right to information laws in a number of Indian states.[3] In contrast to the 2002 law, which was weak and subject to widespread criticism, the 2005 Act has been hailed globally as an example of best practice.[4]

The campaign to adopt the 2005 Act was characterized by a unique set of interactions that absorbed into the new law better international practice and global norms, and yet organically adapted it to the local context. A good example of this is the broad definition of information in the law as including material recorded in any form, in line with international standards. The definition, however, breaks new ground by specifically listing 'samples' as a form of recorded information. This reflects the uniquely Indian experience of taking samples of materials to assess whether construction projects, for example of roads or buildings, meet the stipulated standards.

Another example is the time limit for responding to requests set out in the law. The default time limit in the Indian law, of 30 days, reflects the practice of a number of other countries. However, the Indian law once again breaks new ground by establishing a shorter time limit, of 48 hours, where the information concerns the life or liberty of a person.

This no doubt reflects, at least in part, the Indian experience of rooting the right to information in the right to life, and linking access to information with the right to basic minimum wages and other livelihood entitlements.

The central objective of right to information legislation is to bring about a structural change in the approach to governance and in relations between the government and people. It is important not to underestimate the paradigmatic significance of this change. In most countries, implementation of the right to information is the first real opportunity for citizens to engage in direct, horizontal, demand-driven accountability from government. A direct result of this is that realization of the full potential of the right to information is a long-term challenge.

The adoption of progressive right to information legislation is often a struggle, but it is only a first step. The fact that such legislation seeks to alter the balance of power in favour of citizens and away from officials often leads to bureaucratic resistance, sometimes of a very serious nature. As has been highlighted well in the Indian context, the right to information makes it more difficult for officials to hide corruption and other forms of wrongdoing, as well as incompetence and mismanagement. Less dramatic, but often equally important, is the impact on officials' ability to use spin to set the agenda, to control the timing and form of public communications, and to address problems internally, away from the glare of publicity. Similarly, officials and politicians are increasingly concerned about their ability to maintain control of national governance in an era of rapid change and globalization, and the right to information undermines their capacity to do so. Finally, bureaucratic resistance to change—which is often difficult, particularly when it is both significant and structural, as is the case with the right to information—should not be underestimated.

The experience of countries with longer-standing right to information regimes, like Canada, is that it requires constant effort to increase, and sometimes even just maintain, the flow of information over time. The need for constant vigilance to protect the right to information began manifesting itself early on in India. In August 2006, less than a year after the law came into force, the Cabinet approved a set of proposals to amend it, aimed primarily at removing 'file notings'[5] from its ambit. Due to widespread protests, the matter was put on the backburner, but it has again become a matter of debate. In June 2009, the president of India, in an address to the joint session of Parliament, indicated that the Right to Information Act would be strengthened 'by suitably amending the law to provide for disclosure by government in all non-strategic areas'. Campaigners, however, fear that this is code language for an attempt to reintroduce proposals to exclude file notings from the Act.

At the same time, the early signs from India are that, as with the Act itself, a rich experience of integrating good practices from other countries, but through a process of local integration and extension, is taking place. The history of the right to information in India has been built around a powerful narrative of grassroots activism focusing on delivering benefits to the poorest of the poor.[6] High-powered approaches from other countries—such as filing requests by email and over the telephone—have been adopted in India, but not at the expense of reaching out to the poor.

A recent study by the RTI Assessment & Analysis Group (RaaG) and the National Campaign for People's Right to Information (NCPRI) (2009), for example, indicates that 400,000 requests for information were filed by rural inhabitants during the first two and a half years of the Act, in comparison to about 1.6 million urban requests. Although the ratio may appear low, it compares positively with the experiences of other countries (see Fox et al. 2007). Furthermore, 30 per cent of rural applicants were from among the poor, holding below-poverty-line (BPL) or Antyodaya ration cards, while 15 per cent of urban applicants were below the poverty line. Again, these figures, while they could still be improved, are impressive when compared to analogous results from other countries (RaaG and NCPRI 2009: Executive Summary).

Experience with the right to information in India reflects a unique combination of successful integration of approaches from other countries and a creative ability to build on and adapt these to fit with the wider Indian experience. To assist in this process, this chapter looks at the approach to resolving key challenges in other countries, with a particular focus on Canada, Mexico, and South Africa. These countries have been chosen because they provide a range of different right-to-information experiences, all in the context of a democratic dispensation with a strong right to information law, which is thus analogous to the situation in India.

Canada is a wealthy, established democracy with a relatively long experience of right to information legislation. Success in implementing the system has been mixed; the government is relatively open but, at the same time, there have been serious allegations of political interference as well as obstruction from the civil service.

This perhaps reflects Canada's historical traditions of bureaucratic secrecy, which were still very strong when the right to information law was adopted. Besides, access to information in Canada has always been seen primarily as a governance reform rather than giving effect to a fundamental human right. Although many individuals and groups strongly advocate access to information, such advocacy has rarely been cast in the powerful language of human rights, and has arguably allowed for greater restrictions on access than would otherwise have been the case.

Mexico has a much shorter track record with the right to information, but it is already widely considered to be an important success story. It has a powerful oversight body which has played a very active role in promoting the progressive implementation of the law. The political context in Mexico has been relatively propitious, with the Fox administration (2001–6) putting in place right to information reforms following 65 years of rule by the Institutional Revolutionary Party (PRI). Secrecy was seen as a contributory factor to some serious abuses by the previous government, while the new government had no 'skeletons in the closet' to be exposed under a right to information regime.

Political will at the top levels of government, along with a strongly supportive network of local civil society organizations and a very strong oversight body, have been key success factors in the Mexico case. The importance of the right to information in Mexico was signalled by the adoption in 2007 of very strong constitutional provisions on this key right, a process in which the oversight body played a pivotal role. These constitutional amendments necessitate changes to the right to information legislation at the national and sub-national levels, a process which is currently underway.

South Africa, on the other hand, generated high initial expectations of openness, due in part to its very progressive law, but implementation has been weak by any measure. In South Africa, the right to information law was part of the paradigmatic changes of the post-Apartheid era. This, however, meant that the right to information had to compete for public attention with a range of other far-reaching reforms. It has been noted that, due to the particular historical context, the South African public has tended to place greater stress on equality rights, to the detriment of framework rights like the right to information. Political will has also been weak, with few senior official supporters. Finally, the structural mechanisms for implementation, as provided for in the law, are weak, in particular because they fail to provide for an independent oversight body, instead placing only limited review powers in the hands of the existing Human Rights Commission.

This chapter is based primarily on a desk study of information available from the three countries. It may be noted that far more information is available in relation to Canada than the other two countries. The goal here is to present a range of ideas and approaches regarding how other countries have addressed key challenges in the implementation of the right to information. It outlines the challenges and the responses that have been tried, and distils from these a number of 'action ideas' that might be considered. It is hoped that the various actors who affect implementation of the right to information in India (as elsewhere)—the various information commissions, Central and state, officials and official bodies responsible for implementation, including the Department of Personnel and Training (DoPT), non-governmental organizations (NGOs), academics, the media, the legal profession, and the private sector—will be interested in considering these experiences from other countries and potentially in integrating them locally.

The chapter demonstrates that implementation of right to information legislation poses a number of challenges. There is a need to address the culture of secrecy, which embraces not only administrative culture but also political considerations. Training for all public officials, and particularly for specialized information officers, is needed. The promotion of a professional cadre of information officers, with clear responsibilities and the power to deliver on them, is important. Mainstreaming the right to information into existing civil service systems and treating it in the same way as the delivery of other services—such as education, transportation, or financial oversight—can also help to address the culture of secrecy.

There is a need to put in place systems which facilitate the provision of information, and yet do so in a manner which limits the burden on the civil service. Requests should be nurtured so as to ensure that the system is active and continually being honed and improved. Efficient and broad proactive disclosure systems should be put into place. Information needs to be managed properly so that it may be identified and assessed quickly and effectively, particularly in the context of a request. Exceptions need to be interpreted narrowly and yet appropriately.

There is a need to reach out to the public to ensure that they are aware of their rights and make active use of the system. Finally, there is a need to ensure that the new bodies established by the legislation—the various information commissions in the Indian context—are able to maintain their independence and professionalism and to do their work efficiently. Adding to these challenges is the need to do all this as quickly as possible because the early years are crucially important in setting the tone for longer-term practice.

ADDRESSING THE CULTURE OF SECRECY

Calls to address the so-called culture of secrecy are a common refrain among right to information advocates. Indeed, the culture is so strong that in some contexts it has substantially subverted the law in such a way that it fails to bring about the desired changes in governance and relations between citizens and their government. It is now widely accepted that bureaucrats can pose a significant informal obstacle to transparency. In countries like Canada, Australia, and South Africa, the culture of secrecy represents one of the most enduring and difficult obstacles to achieving the goals of openness that underlie right to information legislation.

The term 'culture of secrecy' is evocative of Dickensian officials scuttling around endless passages ferrying bundles of papers in confidential folders. A more modern image is the idea of a professional bureaucrat, used to operating under a cloak of secrecy and well-versed in the official practices that support such a cloak, recognizing accountability only to those who formally outrank him and not to the public at large. Beyond these draconian images, however, lie a complex net of reasons for official failures to implement correctly right to information legislation. These range from sophisticated strategies to deny access to sensitive information—whether for larger political reasons or because it exposes wrongdoing—to hostility to openness, to indifference, to a lack of capacity, whether human, financial, or administrative.

Snell (2005), building on work done by Roberts, has developed a model for rating bureaucratic responses to right to information legislation, which describes five different levels of administrative compliance: malicious non-compliance (refusing to respond to requests, destroying records, deliberate refusal to record information); adversarialism (reliance on exceptions as a shopping list of reasons to deny access, delaying as long as the law permits, giving minimal reasons for refusing requests); administrative non-compliance (providing inadequate resources, poor information management, low priority given to requests); administrative compliance (timely decisions, narrow interpretation of exceptions); and administrative activism (requests given high priority, informal release of information, discretion exercised to waive exceptions where risk of harm is remote or minimal). Most of these apply simultaneously to a greater or lesser extent in all countries.

Even where the political culture has largely accepted the idea of openness, problems of bureaucratic resistance remain. In Mexico, for example, it is widely acknowledged that there has been a significant transformation, and that political elites and senior officials have embraced transparency. At the same time, promoting a true culture of openness remains a very significant challenge. A good example of this was the refusal of the Mexican authorities to provide access to the ballots of the 2006 Mexican election in which the vote was extremely close. Inspired by the famous 2000 Florida re-count, major Mexican media requested access to the ballots to undertake their own re-count.[7] The election commission refused, originally arguing that the ballots were not covered by the law and that to disclose them would threaten national security. The oversight body, the Electoral Tribune, rejected these arguments, but also rejected the request for the ballots on a highly technical legal analysis that failed to implement the right to information law, at least in spirit and intent.[8]

This section looks at a number of key ways of addressing the problem of a culture of secrecy. Specifically, it addresses the need for training and support to information officers, how to 'mainstream' the right to information, the role of parliament and the courts, and the challenge of politically sensitive information.

Training

Training of public officials is routinely identified by experts as one of the key needs for proper implementation of the right to information, or, to put it differently, lack of awareness and expertise among officials is a key obstacle to implementation. Although training is not a panacea, it is important. In addition to the more obvious benefits, it helps break down the culture of secrecy by inculcating in officials a sense of their obligations and by giving them the confidence to disclose information that would have hitherto been kept secret.

Training raises a number of challenges. The first and foremost is the magnitude of the task, and this is something of particular significance in India, given the vast numbers of people involved. There are questions about who should receive training, what it should cover, how it could be delivered efficiently, and whose responsibility this should be.

Different officials need different kinds of training. All officials should receive some general training on the right to information. This will help to foster a sense of openness as a core civil service value and enhance the cooperation all officials should extend to information officers. It will also help to promote appropriate classification practices. Training should also be directed at senior civil servants to promote their understanding and support for the system. In South Africa, for example, the Human

Rights Commission reported training provided to upper management staff at the South African Reserve Bank as one of its success stories (South African Human Rights Commission 2007a: 101).

Designated information officials (public information officers [PIOs] and assistant public information officers [APIOs] under the Indian law) require more focused and more intense training, and many experts recommend that such training be compulsory. Thematically, particularly important issues include training on information management and the interpretation of exceptions to the right of access. Interpreting exceptions poses a particular challenge to information officers, given the high stakes riding on 'getting it right' and the inherent complexity of this task. Where other officials have dedicated responsibilities for matters that are central to proper implementation of the right to information—for example, in the area of classification of information, proactive publication of information and/or record (information) management—they should also receive targeted training.

The experience of other countries highlights the need for training to be tailored to address the particular needs of different public authorities, or perhaps categories of public authorities (for example, working in the areas of health, poverty, financial issues, and the like) (Sobel et al. 2006 37–9). Different types of authorities will, for example, need to consider different factors when applying exceptions. Furthermore, it is important to ensure that training focuses on the real needs of information officers: all too often, training can become formalized and disconnected from day-to-day realities.

Although training needs are most intense during the initial implementation phases, this is in no way a one-off need. The Government of Canada noted in 2002, some 20 years after the Canadian right to information law was adopted, that the law was still poorly understood not only by the general public and requesters but also by public officials (Government of Canada 2002a: 3). Similar problems arise in most jurisdictions. A 2001 survey by the Open Democracy Advice Centre (ODAC) in South Africa found that 50 per cent of officials in the three branches of government were not even aware of the existence of the right to information law, let alone of how it operated, notwithstanding its high-profile adoption just a year earlier (Open Democracy Advice Centre 2007: 18).

In addition to a constant need for more and better training, even for seasoned officials, there is a chronic problem of people moving to new posts or retiring, necessitating a continuing flow of newly trained officials. In Mexico, for example, the change of presidential administration in

2006 resulted in changes to the local equivalent of information officers, necessitating a new round of training and awareness-raising activities (Bogado et al. 2008: 10–11).

Under the Indian law, governments at various levels have a responsibility, to the extent of their available financial and other resources, to provide training to information officers and public authorities. There are significant advantages to promoting a central focal point of expertise on right to information training. These include ensuring standardized training quality control and creating a central repository of training expertise. In South Africa, the Human Rights Commission has provided central training to public authorities (South African Human Rights Commission 2006: 83–4; 2007a: 101–2).

Given the magnitude of the challenge of training, it is important to involve as many different sectors as possible. Civil society groups, particularly academic institutions and NGOs, can make an important contribution in the area of training. In the UK, for example, civil society groups are responsible for providing much of the training imparted to civil servants.

The need to provide training to the staff of information commissions and to the judiciary has also been highlighted in some contexts. Given that judges sit at the apex of the right to information decision-making system, the rationale for this is clear. On the other hand, there are challenges in delivering specialized training of this kind to judges, and the nature of the administration of justice makes it difficult to target training efficiently as in most cases any judge on the relevant court could end up presiding over a right to information case.

Action Ideas

1. Integrate right to information modules into other training programmes offered to officials.
2. Develop online right to information courses to help promote efficient delivery to large numbers of officials.
3. Develop specific training modules on key issues facing information officers, such as how to interpret and apply exceptions.
4. Work with officials from different sectors/public authorities to ensure that training courses/modules are tailored to their specific needs.
5. Supplement formal training activities by providing support on an ongoing basis to information officers through an information hotline or similar electronic or telephone-based system.

6. Establish a central Internet portal providing access to training materials, as well as guidelines and other advice about how to implement the law.
7. Have a central authority develop standardized core training modules in different areas which can then be adapted to local needs as required.
8. Work with judicial training institutes to integrate right to information training into their more general training activities.

Status and Role of Information Officers

Information officers (PIOs and APIOs under the Indian law) play a hugely important role in any right to information system. They serve as the principal public interface, and they make important decisions about processing requests and, in most cases, the release of information.

In Mexico, as is common in many new right to information systems, information officers have been appointed from among existing staff, and public authorities have not been given any new resources for these posts. This is likely to lead to some sense of resentment towards the new system, which is asking for more from the same pool of officers. It is also unreasonable; the civil service cannot be expected to deliver more services without greater resources and, in practice, this would not be expected from them in other service areas.

An analogous problem identified in the Canadian context has been the lack of a systematic approach to the placement of information officers, along with a lack of status associated with this position relative to other career options (Information Commissioner of Canada 2007: 14). Various initiatives have been put in place to address this, including internship programmes and the establishment of dedicated developmental positions to attract staff from other divisions of the civil service.

A more structural solution is to take the necessary steps to promote various specialist positions for information officers (such as information coordinator, analyst, and the like) as established or certified career posts within the civil service with all that this implies: standardized training and civil service grade requirements, clear responsibilities and authority, the possibility of upward mobility within the post and to other posts (perhaps by classifying the position within a wider professional grouping such as planning or communications), clear performance standards, and the like.

Ideally, a central certification process for information officers, perhaps located at a university and overseen by a steering committee of experts from different sectors, could be developed. In Canada, the University of

Alberta has worked with various official bodies to develop the Information Access and Protection of Privacy (IAPP) Certificate Program, which is gradually being introduced as a formal qualification for information specialists.[9]

Various measures may be put in place to promote the status, independence, and visibility of information officers. One practical measure, depending upon the structure of the civil service, is to locate information officer units in the same (ideally fairly visible) part of all public authorities, or at least the principal government departments, whether this be communications, policy, the CEO's office, or somewhere else.

A more far-reaching idea is for information officers to report to a central authority, rather than the individual public authority in which they are located. An analogous approach has been adopted in the Canadian civil service in relation to lawyers, all of whom report to the Department of Justice, even when they are assigned to work in other departments. Information officers could even be responsible to the relevant Information Commission, which would significantly bolster their independence, although it might create certain problems vis-à-vis their departmental colleagues.

Information officers should be given significant authority to make decisions on disclosure. While it is recognized that highly sensitive or difficult cases might require reference to more senior officials, efficient and timely operation of the access system demands that most disclosure and related decisions (for example, relating to fees, notification of third parties, form of access and transfer to other authorities) be taken by information officers. Indeed, it is reasonable that delegation of authority to the least senior official (for example, to APIOs in the Indian system) should be the rule.

In many jurisdictions, information officers have a broad responsibility to ensure full implementation of the law in all of its aspects. This includes not only responsibility for processing requests but also a range of other obligations, such as putting in place the necessary systems for implementing the law, ensuring that proactive publication obligations are met, promoting and implementing appropriate information management and archiving systems, ensuring the provision of appropriate training to officials, and the like. This ensures a central locus of expertise and responsibility for these functions, which might otherwise be neglected. The Indian law only gives PIOs and APIOs direct responsibility for processing requests for information but they could informally be entrusted with wider duties.

Support to information officers can also be provided in the form of liaison networks. In Canada, various associations exist to provide support and knowledge to information professionals.[10] The South African Human Rights Commission recently launched the Information Officers Forum, aimed at bringing together information officers to share experiences and best practices, and to promote capacity building (South African Human Rights Commission 2006: 86).

Action Ideas

1. Provide additional resources to hire information officers (PIOs and APIOs).
2. Establish specialist positions with clear responsibilities and status as career options for PIOs and APIOs, which provide a prospect of upward career mobility.
3. Put in place standardized training packages and requirements for PIOs and APIOs, perhaps along with official certification.
4. Take steps to attract qualified staff to information officer positions.
5. Locate information officers in the same part of all public authorities to promote visibility.
6. Consider having information officers report to a central authority, perhaps the relevant information commissioner.
7. Give information officers the power to make decisions on disclosure of information, as well as related decisions; for example, on fees and form of access.
8. Locate responsibility for a range of information functions, in addition to processing of requests, with information officers.
9. Develop appropriate networks to provide support to information officers.

Mainstreaming RTI as a Core Public Service Value

One of the challenges in implementing any new set of rules is to integrate them into existing public service systems and practices, not only formally but also in terms of the operational culture. This has been attempted, in many countries, for thematic issues like the environment and women. The challenge is to create an environment in which fulfilling the right to information is seen as part of the job, an aspect of the core service being provided, rather than as an external constraint on doing the job.

It is important to take steps to integrate the right to information into the civil service workplace environment in the early stages of implementation, for otherwise an 'us and them' mentality can easily develop and, once in place, is difficult to eradicate. This has been a problem in Canada, for example, where the often latent hostility of officials to the law has seriously undermined openness in practice.

A number of steps can be taken to integrate the right to information into formal systems, depending upon the particular structures in place. Overarching documents, for example, the civil service guidelines or codes of conduct, should be revised as needed to reflect the new commitment to openness. Any focus on loyalty to the service needs to be adjusted to accommodate, and even prioritize, the obligation to be open, for this may well come into conflict with loyalty. In Canada, the Access to Information Review Task Force recommended that the Statement of Principles of the Public Service of Canada refer to openness and the obligations of civil servants, as custodians of public information, to provide access to that information (Government of Canada 2002b). Openness should be incorporated into performance review systems at all levels: not only for information officers but also for managers and other staff; not only for individuals but also for sub-departmental units, such as sections, branches, and the like.

Operationally, implementation of right to information responsibilities should be handled in the same way as other programmes, with resource planning and allocation, forward planning, systemic review and adjustment as required, and the like. A careful balance needs to be struck in setting up systems between centralization (which can concentrate expertise and promote uniformity but can also lead to bottlenecks and provide opportunities for political control) and delegation (which allows for quick decision-making). As a rule of thumb, systems should be centralized but individual decisions decentralized.

Altering the organizational culture is a difficult and long-term effort which goes beyond training and establishing systems. Eventually, the sense needs to be fostered among civil servants that provision of information is a core part of what they do, similar to their role, for example, in delivering health or education, or undertaking financial planning.

The impact of senior champions of the right to information within government, stressing the importance of openness as a core civil service value and value-added, can be significant. A good example of this is the Memorandum issued by the then US Attorney General Janet Reno in 1993, which had a profound impact on official openness.[11] The relative success of the right to information movement in Mexico has also been attributed, in part, to the strong commitment by former president Fox to openness. On the other hand, the paucity of senior support has been identified as a contributory factor in poor implementation in South Africa (Open Democracy Advice Centre 2007: 10).

It is also important to get civil servants to see the benefits to themselves of openness. It is significant that in the UK the civil service unions formally endorsed the campaign for right to information legislation. In the longer term, openness, together with other associated democratic approaches such as participation, should promote a more harmonious relationship between officials and the public; a sense of working together to deliver shared goals rather than a sense of 'us and them'. This will not only result in greater job satisfaction on the part of officials, but also help them to do their job better. Wider public input and oversight, which rely on the right to information, lead to better policies and strategies, to everyone's benefit.

In South Africa, a Golden Key Award ceremony for different categories of best practice performers—among public authorities, information officers, right to information activists, and the media—alongside the exposure of poor performers has served a number of goals, including mainstreaming the right to information and raising public awareness (South African Human Rights Commission 2007a).

Action Ideas

1. Prioritize actions to mainstream the right to information as a core public service before a negative attitude towards this new 'duty' takes root.
2. Revise organizational framework documents, such as civil service guidelines and codes of conduct, to reflect a commitment to openness.
3. Incorporate rules on openness into job profiles and, where appropriate, contracts.
4. Include performance in implementing right to information rules in institutional systems of rewards and penalties.
5. Treat delivery of openness in the same way as the delivery of any other service, incorporating it into central systems for allocating resources, planning, and the like.
6. Establish organization-wide performance measurement indicators with a view to identifying and addressing systemic blockages or problems.
7. Make efforts to get ministers and high-level bureaucrats to make statements supporting openness; for example, by providing opportunities for this at conferences and other events.

8. Popularize leading examples of the benefits of the right to information to civil servants.
9. Work with civil service unions to promote a better understanding among their members of the benefits to them of the right to information.
10. Use innovative techniques to promote and popularize the right to information, such as awards for best performers and naming and shaming poor ones.

The Role of Parliament and the Courts

Under the Indian law, as with many right to information laws, the national and state legislatures have a specific oversight role, inasmuch as the various information commissions, through the relevant government, report to them on an annual basis on implementation of the law. In addition, legislatures have an inherent power and responsibility to supervise the implementation of laws.

Where legislatures take their oversight role seriously, this can bolster the political commitment to implement the law progressively, send a clear signal that abuses will not be tolerated, and promote best practice approaches. Members of opposition parties can play a central role in this oversight, given their function of monitoring government performance. They can also play a key role in promoting reform. Although they cannot bring about reform on their own, once they launch an initiative, members of the governing party often support it, for refusal to do so would appear churlish and lose them popular support.

In Canada, the Standing Committee on Access to Information, Privacy and Ethics, which deals with right to information issues, has often played an active role, investigating alleged abuses, calling officials from public authorities whose implementation has been criticized to appear before them, imposing remedial measures on them, and promoting law reform efforts (Information Commissioner of Canada 2007: 12–13). The right to information has strong public appeal, and members of parliament (MPs) are often anxious to earn credit by pursuing it as a public interest issue. It is, for example, an issue which often receives significant media attention, which MPs normally relish.

The role of the courts in levering openness is also crucial. Courts stand at the pinnacle of right to information decision-making, and they have the authority—in strictly legal terms but also in terms of the social respect they command and the power of their reasoning and process—to impose solutions in cases of disagreement, particularly about the boundaries of the right to information. Determining the proper scope of exceptions to the right of access can be a delicate balancing exercise between competing social interests. Information commissioners should do their best to produce well thought-through and reasoned decisions on complaints, but sheer volume normally means that they cannot give the same depth and consideration to issues as can the courts. Furthermore, their constant interactions with public authorities on access to information matters, as well as the promotional role played by many information commissions, can sometimes lead the two sides to adopt entrenched positions; the courts can break these deadlocks by providing an authoritative 'external' resolution.

Action Ideas

1. Take steps to encourage parliament to take its oversight role seriously; for example, through lobbying and encouraging media attention.
2. Actively engage with parliamentary oversight committees, providing submissions and other information on implementation.
3. Work with opposition members to monitor implementation and promote reform efforts.
4. Press parties to make commitments on the right to information in the context of elections, when such promises are much easier to elicit.
5. Bring appeals to the courts to engage them in their oversight role; argue such cases well, presenting the court with best practices from other countries, as well as international standards.

Politically Sensitive Information

In many countries, serious openness problems have been observed in relation to politically sensitive information. As noted earlier, modern governments increasingly seek to control information, a process neatly captured in the phrase 'spin', for various reasons. In serious cases (for example, where the information contains evidence of wrongdoing), governments or officials may wish to prevent disclosure altogether. In other cases, the aim may simply be to control the release of the information. This can, variously, delay release until the information is less politically 'radioactive', give government time to develop a strategy to minimize the impact of disclosure, and/or allow governments to accept responsibility on their own terms, seemingly voluntarily, rather than in response to damaging media exposure.

Right to information legislation, in fairly obvious ways, undermines the ability of public bodies to control the flow of information, and a natural reaction, particularly in relation to politically sensitive information, is to try to counteract this. Roberts has analysed data on overall processing of requests in the Canadian context to demonstrate the differential treatment accorded to requests from, on the one hand, 'average' requesters and, on the other, the media and political parties. His research shows that, even when controlled for other factors, requests by the media and political parties take significantly longer to process and are more likely to result in a deemed refusal (that is, a failure to respond to a request, which is formally a breach of the rules regarding time limits for responding to requests) (Roberts 2002, 2005).

Special administrative routines have been put in place within the Canadian government to deal with politically sensitive requests, referred to variously as the 'amber light process' or 'red files'. Some public authorities undertake a preliminary risk assessment on incoming information requests and send those identified as potentially sensitive to the Minister's Office, which tags those it deems to be sensitive and then works with information officials to process them. These special processes affect a large number of requests. According to Roberts, 50–70 per cent of all requests to the department of foreign affairs[12] were amber-lighted in 2002, with the figure being 40 per cent for the Department of Defence (Roberts 2005: 8).

There is also evidence of differential treatment being meted out to 'troublemakers' and politically sensitive requests in South Africa. The difficulty of accessing the files from the South African Truth and Reconciliation Commission (TRC), for example, has been well-documented, even though the Commission itself strongly recommended that all its files be preserved and made publicly available, in the absence of compelling reasons for secrecy (McKinley 2003).

From a principled right to information perspective, this is clearly problematical; refusals to disclose should be based only on overriding grounds for secrecy, assessed against a risk of actual harm, and not on political considerations. At the same time, this is a difficult problem not susceptible of easy solution. Bureaucratic buy-in to the system is essential for its proper functioning. Government and the bureaucracy have enormous residual powers to control the flow of information, regardless of what the law or rules say. It may be preferable to accept that some form of special treatment will be accorded to politically sensitive information and, rather than trying to combat this, focus instead on attempting to ensure that the procedures are as formal and transparent as possible.

Action Ideas

1. Undertake monitoring and research to better understand any special procedures that have been developed for processing politically sensitive requests.
2. Expose instances of political interference in the processing of requests.
3. Put in place rules prohibiting ministers or the prime minister's office from getting involved in the processing of information requests.
4. As an alternative, put in place transparent internal procedures that ensure that the worst result of special procedures for politically sensitive requests is delay rather than outright denial of access.

ENHANCING THE PROVISION OF INFORMATION

Changing underlying attitudes towards transparency within the civil service is necessary for long-term success. It is equally important to put in place sound policies and mechanisms to foster the efficient application of the two key information-disclosure systems, namely, the requesting process and proactive disclosure. In other words, it is important to get the mechanics of providing information right. The experience from other countries demonstrates that a strong flow of information is key to building public support and a robust, progressive right to information system. Delivering this information efficiently is, for fairly obvious reasons, also key to limiting bureaucratic opposition.

Nurturing Requests

The requesting process is at the heart of the right to information system. If the volume of requests is low, then there is a serious risk that the entire system will wither into irrelevance. It is important that many individuals, not only educated elites but all citizens,[13] can and do in practice make requests for information. Early experience with implementation in India suggests some success in this area, which it will be important to maintain over time. Making direct requests for information from government is not something that comes easily or naturally to everyone. Indeed, for most people, a number of barriers to this exist, including the obvious ones of cost and effort but also fear of interacting with government and scepticism about whether it will be worthwhile. Making it easy to lodge requests should be a key right to information implementation objective.

In the initial phases of implementing right to information legislation, there may be very basic problems that impact negatively on openness. In South Africa, for example, cases of requests getting lost due to staff changes or delayed because the relevant staff member was on holiday and left his/her office locked have been noted (Pietersen and Dimba 2004: 6). These problems will vary from context to context.

Standardized requesting procedures across public authorities, along with centralized systems for making requests, help foster an efficient and user-friendly system. This is particularly likely where these are developed by authorities like the information commissions, which have a mandate to promote openness and hence a vested interest in putting effective mechanisms in place.

In Mexico, a key decision has been to focus on electronic requests, although it is still possible to make requests in other ways, for example, by mail or by presenting them directly to public authorities. This entails some costs in terms of accessibility but it has paid dividends for those requesters who do have access to the Internet.

The Mexican Information Commission, the Instituto Federal de Acceso a la Información Pública (Federal Institute for Access to Public Information or IFAI), has played a leading role in this area. It runs a sophisticated central electronic requesting system, the Sistema de Solicitudes de Información (or SISI, as it is popularly known), through a central web portal which allows individuals to lodge requests and complaints with federal public authorities. SISI allows requesters to monitor the processing of their requests, and complaints (appeals) can even be lodged with IFAI via SISI. It is widely acknowledged to be a user-friendly system which has made an important contribution to the very high number of requests in Mexico—some 220,000 in the four years between June 2003 and June 2007 (Bogado et al. 2008: 3)—and the overall success of the right to information system.

Efforts are currently underway to integrate SISI with the wider e-government initiative known as e-Mexico. In particular, there are efforts to provide access to SISI via the more than 3,000 kiosks providing public access points to the Internet, which should further facilitate the making of requests.

Standardized approaches can also be useful in the area of provision of assistance to requesters, with a view to promoting consistency and efficiency. Standard models can both provide guidance to public authorities as to what constitutes an appropriate level of assistance and relieve public authorities of the burden of developing their own systems.

In many instances, an excessively formal approach to processing requests is neither efficient nor productive. Instead, information officers should, as appropriate, engage in dialogue with requesters with a view to understanding what they are really looking for in order to be able to respond in a more focused and efficient manner. Often, the information really being sought is difficult to identify from poorly worded or excessively wide requests. Dialogue can help hone or narrow a request, saving time and effort for the public authority and increasing the likelihood of the request being satisfied in full and in time, to the benefit of the requester. At the same time, the right of requesters to refuse to provide reasons for their request should be respected where they do not wish to provide this information. More generally, requests should be treated on a client service model and not in an adversarial or strictly formal manner.

Careful monitoring should be undertaken of abuses of the law that inhibit the lodging of requests, such as refusals to accept requests or placing illegitimate bureaucratic obstacles in the way of lodging them. Targeted sanctions in high-profile cases can send a clear message to officials that such behaviour will not be tolerated.

Timely processing of requests is a significant challenge in most right to information systems. Delays are often closely linked to certain other features of the access regime, notably information management and exceptions. In Canada, the law allows public authorities to extend the time limit for a 'reasonable period of time' under certain conditions. Even though authorities often allocate themselves comparatively lengthy timelines to satisfy requests, they regularly breach even those limits (Roberts 2002: 186–7). The Canadian Information Commissioner is currently proposing triage rules which will enable requests with a high public interest value to be processed more quickly. Although there are clear potential benefits to this, it has been criticized on the ground that it is inappropriate for the information commissioner to judge which requests are important.

Delay is a chronic problem in the US. Amendments to the US law, adopted in late 2007, impose far more stringent reporting obligations regarding the time taken to process requests, in an attempt both to embarrass poor performers and to track the problem more scientifically. The amendments also prohibit certain fees from being charged to requesters when time limits are not met and require public liaison units to be established to assist applicants to resolve disputes involving delay. The US law also provides for 'multi-track' processing of requests based on the amount of work involved, as well as expedited processing of requests in cases where the applicant demonstrates a 'compelling need'.

In South Africa, delays are also chronic, and yet surveys suggest that public authorities rarely, if ever, formally resort to the extensions provided for in the law. Instead, they simply fail to respond to requests. A study by the Open Society Justice Initiative found that some 62 per cent of requests in South Africa were met with so-called 'mute refusals', that is, a failure to respond to the request within the established time limits (Open Society Justice Initiative 2006: 43).

On the other hand, public authorities in Mexico appear to be tackling the time limit issue with increasing success (Sobel 2006: 36). In Mexico, failure to respond within the time limit is a deemed acceptance of the request (in most countries this leads to a deemed refusal of the request) and the information must be provided to the requester unless IFAI agrees that it should remain confidential.

A related problem is the practice of indicating that information is 'not held', even when the authority does actually hold the information but it either cannot or does not want to find it. There is evidence that the increasing rate of 'not held' responses in Mexico may be due in part to a desire on the part of public authorities to avoid their openness obligations (Sobel et al. 2006: 21).

Fees can pose a serious barrier to requesters, and the idea of turning access to information into a commercial commodity is offensive to the underlying rationale for the right. At the same time, modest fees can serve to limit vexatious or abusive requests, which can waste civil servants' time and undermine support for the system as a whole. Regulations in India at the Central and state levels provide for standard fee structures which appear to be reasonable.

Action Ideas

1. Monitor request systems with a view to identifying basic problems and propose simple systemic solutions to avoid repetition.
2. Develop clear and efficient model procedures for processing requests for information.
3. Make available a central electronic facility for receiving requests for information at each level of government (that is, federally and in each state), perhaps along the lines of the Mexican SISI system.
4. Integrate information requesting systems with wider e-government initiatives.
5. Promulgate guidelines or guidance notes aimed at information officers and/or requesters, for example, on what constitutes a reasonable level of assistance or on how to hone a request, or mapping the government departments which hold information that is most commonly sought by requesters.

6. Develop specific training and central online resources for information officers to help them provide appropriate assistance to requesters.
7. Promote a more interactive approach to the processing of requests which involves dialogue between requesters and information officers, where appropriate, with a view to focusing on the real information interests of requesters.
8. Monitor request processing to identify and expose abusive practices.
9. Apply sanctions in a few high-profile cases where officials have wilfully failed to apply required procedural rules with a view to sending a clear message that such practices will not be tolerated.
10. Impose stringent reporting obligations on public authorities regarding the timeliness of responses to information requests.
11. Promote a role for information commissions in agreeing (or refusing) proposed extensions to time limits.
12. Promote the partial release of information as a first step in the processing of complex requests or requests where only part of the information potentially involves exceptions, and/or multi-track processing of requests depending on complexity and their public interest or personal need value.
13. Encourage public authorities to provide for internal mediators or liaison units to resolve problems of delay.
14. Impose sanctions on public authorities (or provide compensation to requesters) where they fail to meet predetermined standards of timeliness; for example, by failing to process more than 10 per cent of requests on time.
15. Adopt regulations that make it possible for public authorities to skip the step of consulting with third parties where it is clear that the information requested is not covered by an exception (with due attention to the rights of third parties).
16. Zealously apply the rule stipulating that requesters may not be charged for requests that are not met within the prescribed time limits.
17. Carefully monitor the imposition of fees for information requests and take measures to sanction public authorities which charge excessive fees.
18. Ensure that the provision of information electronically, which is increasingly the dominant model, is free.

Proactive Disclosure

Proactive disclosure, sometimes referred to as routine or suo motu[14] disclosure, has been recognized as central to an effective right to information system. It ensures that a minimum platform of information is publicly available, promotes access to information for the majority of individuals who will never make a request, and limits pressure on the request process. Indeed, progressive modern governments are increasingly making available large amounts of information that may be of public interest on a proactive basis.

The longer-term goal should be for all information that is clearly not covered by an exception and which may be of public interest to be available over the Internet. This both fosters the right to know and also promotes efficiency as it should reduce the need for individuals to resort to requests to obtain this information. These benefits have been recognized in the Indian legislation, which not only provides for extensive specific proactive disclosure obligations but also calls upon public authorities to make a 'constant endeavour' to make as much information available proactively as possible in order to minimize the need for the public to have recourse to requests to obtain information. At the same time, the evidence suggests that public bodies in India are struggling to meet these proactive publication obligations.[15]

It is one thing to recommend strong proactive publication regimes and another to put them in place. The early indications are that public authorities in India are struggling to satisfy their proactive disclosure obligations (Participatory Research in Asia 2008: 23). This is exacerbated by the fact that there does not appear to be any means of enforcing these rules. Various systems have been tried or recommended in different countries to prompt or facilitate more extensive proactive publication practices.

In Mexico, IFAI has a legislative mandate to set standards for proactive publication. Although, as in India, individuals do not have the right to lodge complaints regarding proactive publication failures, IFAI has taken a number of measures to promote better practice. It rates the websites of public authorities with a view both to helping to identify weaknesses and possible solutions, and to promoting healthy competition among authorities for good ratings. It also promotes uniform websites among different public authorities to make it easier for the public to navigate them, to promote best practice approaches, and to relieve authorities, particularly smaller ones, of the burden of website design.

In the UK, public authorities are required to develop and implement publication schemes, setting out the classes of information which they will publish and the manner in which they will publish them. The schemes must take into account the public interest in access to the information and in the 'publication of reasons for decisions made by the authority'. Importantly, the scheme must be approved by the information commissioner and he/she may put a time limit on his/her approval. The law also provides for the development of model publication schemes by the commissioner for different classes of public authority, which any public authority in the relevant class may simply apply, rather than developing its own. This system builds in a degree of flexibility, but with commissioner oversight, so that public authorities may adapt their proactive publication commitments to their specific operations. Importantly, it allows for the levering up of proactive publication obligations over time, as public authorities gain capacity in this area.

Linking the right to information to ongoing e-government initiatives can also help foster better proactive disclosure practices. In Mexico, IFAI is working to integrate the right to information with the e-Mexico initiative, which entails a commitment to make far more information available on a proactive basis. IFAI has also set up a Portal of Transparency Obligations which provides information on public authorities subject to the right to information law, along with links to their websites (public authorities also link back to the Portal) (Bogado et al. 2008: 11).

Steps can also be taken to ensure better dissemination of formally published information. The Canadian government runs a Depository Service Programme to promote access to government publications. A network of academic and public libraries across the country and internationally, including 52 full deposit libraries, receive copies of government publications. A list of these libraries is provided online. There are proposals to strengthen the programme by requiring all public authorities to participate and by extending coverage to include all publications, regardless of format.

Many countries require public authorities to include information about their proactive publication practices on an annual basis, to supplement the information they are required to provide about requests. This can help to highlight the importance of this mode of disseminating information and to facilitate the identification of weak performers and problem areas.

In Sweden, public authorities are not only required to publish a list of the categories of information they hold (as is the case in India), but also a list of all significant documents held. The implications of this in terms of assisting requesters locate the documents they are looking for are obvious.

In Mexico, every request, the response to it, and any information disclosed pursuant to the request are all automatically made publicly available, and the same applies to complaints. IFAI has implemented ZOOM, a searchable database of information requests, responses, and the results of appeals, linked to the central electronic requesting system, SISI, to facilitate this.

In the US, a weaker form of this applies in which the responses to all requests that may be of wider public interest are made publicly available. In Canada, a record of all requests, but not the information provided in response to them, is available online. In a Kafkaesque twist, the system is not run by the government but by a private individual who obtains the information monthly by making an access to information request for it. The information comes from the Coordination of Access to Information Requests System (CAIRS), an internal database of requests which is maintained by the government.[16]

Action Ideas

1. Provide assistance to help public authorities discharge their proactive publication obligations, such as providing off-the-shelf website designs.
2. Work to develop more interactive websites with a view to better targeting of proactive disclosure to meet the needs of requesters.
3. Require public authorities to report in detail on their activities to implement their proactive publication obligations, as part of their annual reporting requirements.
4. Rate public authorities by their performance in the area of proactive publication, perhaps awarding a symbolic prize to best performers.
5. Set minimum standards for proactive disclosure including through developing model publication schemes, as in the UK.
6. Link proactive disclosure regimes to ongoing e-government initiatives.
7. Promote better and more standardized distribution of formally published information, including 'deposit' libraries where individuals can be assured of finding all government publications.
8. Help rationalize access to publications that are electronically available, for example, by providing access via a central web portal that obviates the need for members of the public to search through the individual websites of different public authorities to locate them.

9. Encourage public authorities to make available not only a list of categories of information held, but also a full list of requests and responses to them.
10. Facilitate the aforementioned by requiring public authorities to track all information requests as part of their annual reporting requirements.
11. Publish on a central website all information available electronically which has been made public pursuant to a complaint (link this, where possible, to a central electronic requesting system, along the lines of SISI).

Information Management

Effective systems for information management, including the destruction and archiving of older records, are central not only to the right to information but more generally to modern, efficient governance. Poor information management systems lead to delays in the processing of requests and, in more serious cases, to the inability of public authorities to respond to requests (for example, when they cannot locate requested information). At the same time, this is a huge challenge for most governments. The availability of electronic information technologies, while vastly enhancing information storage capacities and reducing their cost, has also made information management far more complicated.

This is a challenge for wealthy developed countries, as it is for poorer, less developed nations. The 2002 Report of the Access to Information Review Task Force, for example, noted in relation to Canada: 'Everyone is in agreement, however, that there is a crisis in information management in the federal government, as well as in every jurisdiction we have studied' (Government of Canada 2002a: 141). In the Mexican context, it has been reported that while electronic records created since the right to information law came into effect in 2002 are reasonably well-organized, 'historic documents remain unorganized and completely impenetrable' (Bogado et al. 2008: 11). There is no simple solution for this problem. Resources have to be invested in developing and implementing good information management systems, which also ensure the necessary level of information security. Such resource allocation can easily be justified, given the importance of good information management for overall public service efficiency.

At a minimum, central responsibility should be allocated for setting and enforcing information management standards. Ideally, this should be overseen by a body that is independent of or operates at arm's length to the government. The right to information law of the UK provides one example of how this can be done. It requires the Lord Chancellor to issue a Code of Practice providing guidance to public authorities regarding the keeping, management, and destruction of their records, as well as transfer of records to the Public Record Office (the archives) and the destruction of those not to be transferred. The Code is not technically binding, although to some extent it might be considered to elaborate on binding obligations in the primary legislation. However, the Information Commission has a mandate to promote compliance with the Code, specifically by issuing practice recommendations on the extent to which public authorities are complying with its provisions. The system thus combines standard setting with a soft monitoring and enforcement model.

The question of transferring records to the archives and disposing (destroying) of those records that are not of historical value is important. As with information management, this should ideally be overseen by a body that is independent of the government. It is important that decisions about destruction of records are not based on a narrow appreciation of their potential further use to the civil service, but on wider social and cultural considerations.

Both information management and the archiving/destruction of records within the civil service are massive tasks and require dedicated, qualified staff. One option is for this to be incorporated into the role of information officers. If responsibility for information management and archiving is allocated to other officers, the aforementioned suggestions regarding the professionalization of information officer positions also apply to those officials.

Action Ideas

1. Allocate adequate resources, including dedicated staff, to the task of information management and archiving.
2. Adopt clear central standards on information management and archiving which are consistent with right to information rules and priorities (for example, ensuring that information of potential wider public interest is not destroyed).
3. Ensure that clear rules apply to the storage and destruction of electronic records, which can often be deleted at the press of a button.
4. Vest overall responsibility for implementation of information management and archiving rules in a central body or bodies that are

independent of the government, such as the Central Information Commission.

5. Promote cooperation between those responsible for information management and archiving, including the various archival institutions and information commissions, with a view to setting and overseeing proper implementation of standards and procedures.
6. Provide dedicated training on information management and archiving to officials responsible for these tasks.
7. Issue clear guidelines on how to implement information management systems to provide assistance to those responsible for this task.

Exceptions

Drawing an appropriate line between information that should be disclosed and information that should be kept secret is one of the most difficult challenges in implementing right to information legislation. The matter is made more complicated by public interest override rules, which require a consideration of all the circumstances at the time of the request. A further complication is the fact that most right to information laws, including the Indian law, grant a measure of discretion to public officials regarding the release of information, providing simply that there is no obligation to disclose information covered by an exception (and not that such information must not be disclosed).

Like the issue of information management, there is no magic solution to this problem. Ultimately, what is needed is well-trained and, to the extent possible, experienced officers with the capacity and confidence to release information in accordance with the law and the overall public interest.

The Canadian Information Commissioner has made available to all information officers the manual used to train his own officers on the proper scope of exceptions, even though it is recognized that this is not binding and is not always fully up-to-date (Information Commissioner of Canada 2007: 17–18). The South African Human Rights Commission monitors decisions by the Constitutional Court and Supreme Court which are relevant to the right to information and posts summaries of these online (South African Human Rights Commission 2007a: 102).

Much of the aforementioned should also be applied to the matter of classification of information. Although in India classification is technically irrelevant in light of a request for information, it can significantly influence the manner in which officials interpret exceptions. It is therefore very important that, to the extent possible, the scope of classification corresponds to the exceptions in the right to information law.

The Mexican system operates rather differently and (proper) classification is a basis for refusing access. IFAI is responsible for establishing criteria for the classification and declassification of information, and classification is strictly limited in time to 12 years, although this may exceptionally be extended by IFAI. Each public authority is required to establish an Information Committee, responsible for overseeing classification, which must be notified when the classification of a document is proposed. In practice, implementation of this varies considerably among different public authorities.

Action Ideas

1. Discourage public authorities from being excessively zealous in their consideration of potentially applicable exceptions.
2. Provide specialized training to officials, particularly PIOs and APIOs, on interpreting and applying exceptions, with a particular focus on the more difficult and most abused exceptions and on the public interest override.
3. Supplement training with written guidance, for example in the form of targeted briefing notes interpreting key exceptions, including simple 'rule of thumb' advice which information officers should find easy to follow. For example, it might be useful to clarify that protected commercial interests apply only where disclosure will be likely to lead to *monetary* loss, as opposed to loss of face.
4. Do the same for the public interest override and the exercise of discretion in applying exceptions; guidance on applying the public interest override might specify a number of potentially overriding interests, such as protection of human rights or the environment, or the exposure of wrongdoing or incompetence, as well as other considerations, such as that the sensitivity of information declines over time and that specific interests should override vague threats.
5. Establish a system for the central provision of specific advice on the application of exceptions; for example, via a dedicated phone or email hotline.
6. Publish synopses of court rulings elaborating on exceptions in a simplified format and disseminate to PIOs and APIOs, and other relevant decision-makers.

7. Promote the adoption of detailed legislation on data protection, which includes a clear and detailed definition of what constitutes personal data.[17]
8. Review existing classification labels and systems, which are likely to be fundamentally at odds with the right to information rules.
9. Establish clear rules for classification which incorporate time limits on classification, as well as regular review of classification, with information regularly declassified as the need for classification disappears.

Complaints

Complaints, both internal and to the information commission and courts, are an important part of the request process. Internal complaints give public authorities an opportunity to reconsider refusals to disclose and to have the matter dealt with at a more senior level. In many instances, particularly during the initial stages of applying a new right to information regime, lower-ranking officials do not feel they have the authority to release information that would previously have been kept secret. An internal complaint to more senior officials can help address that problem and also build confidence to release information in the first instance. On the other hand, if senior officials consistently support refusals to disclose, an internal complaint can simply act as a further barrier and delay access to information.

External complaints or appeals, in particular to information commissions, can function as a kind of circuit-breaker when relations between requesters and public authorities become adversarial. Such external complaints set the standards and tone for the application of the law. They are particularly important for purposes of authoritative elaboration of the scope of exceptions, but they also set standards in other areas, such as timely processing of requests, appropriate request-processing procedures, fees, and the like. Complaints also provide useful input into how the system as a whole is working. Where similar issues keep recurring on appeal, this may be a sign that systemic reform is needed. For all these reasons, the overall success of the system depends on there being a satisfactory rate of complaints from requesters.

Complaints potentially create tension between information commissions and public authorities, and therefore need to be dealt with carefully. It is important for information commissions to maintain good relations with public authorities, due, among other things, to the ability of the latter to obstruct openness. At the same time, the manner in which commissions deal with complaints (and in the Indian context also appeals) will have a significant bearing on their credibility among the public, particularly while they seek to establish themselves during the initial implementation period.

Two factors can seriously undermine the credibility of information commissions in the context of complaints. The first is inconsistency of decision-making, a particular risk where different commissioners have to process a large number of complaints within a short span of time, as is the case in many Indian jurisdictions.

Second, credibility can be undermined where decisions are poorly reasoned or not fully explained to the parties while, on the other hand, well-reasoned decisions will be more acceptable (or less unacceptable) to those against whom they go. Well-reasoned decisions also serve as a learning tool and help provide guidelines to public authorities to amend their decision-making, where applicable (that is, where the decision goes against them).

Complaints often give rise to investigations. In Canada, investigations of public authorities by the Information Commissioner, whether suo motu or pursuant to a complaint, have proven to be a source of considerable tension and have even created a backlash. When the Commissioner announced a policy of zero tolerance on late responses to requests in the late 1990s and sought to use his full investigative and subpoena powers to enforce this, the backlash was significant. There were reports of threats to the future careers of his staff and, as the Commissioner put it, when his searches, subpoenas, and questions were too insistent or too close to the top, 'the mandarins circle the wagons' (Information Commissioner of Canada 2000: 9). Partly as a result of this, considerable attention has been given, in Canada, to the question of investigations. Many commentators have called for the Commissioner to be given binding decision-making powers (at present his powers are simply recommendatory in nature).

Closely related to complaints is the question of remedies, including sanctions. The Indian law provides for a wide range of possible remedies to be imposed by information commissions, including structural measures—such as requiring a public authority to publish categories of information or to enhance its training programmes—and individual fines for obstructive behaviour. While formally binding, the law does not specifically indicate how these decisions are to be enforced. This has been a problem in the Mexican context where enforcement of IFAI's decisions has been left to the Ministry of Public Administration (Bogado et al. 2008: 12–13).

Regardless of the formal mechanism, imposing sanctions 'by force', as it were, should be a last resort. It takes time and there will always be avenues for resistance from determined public authorities. It is far preferable for an information commission to command such moral authority and respect that public authorities implement its decisions 'voluntarily'.

Action Ideas

1. Provide dedicated training to those responsible for deciding internal complaints.
2. Monitor and report on the performance of public authorities regarding internal complaints.
3. Adopt procedures that make it easy to file a complaint/appeal with the commissions and undertake public outreach to encourage requesters to lodge such complaints/appeals.
4. Put in place expedited procedures for complaints/appeals relating to matters such as fees, delays, and form of access, given that these should be relatively simple to resolve.
5. Analyse complaint/appeal decisions by the commissions with a view to identifying systemic failures at the level of public authorities and proposing remedial measures.
6. Put in place systems such as peer or central review to help promote consistency of complaint/appeal decisions by commissions.
7. Issue well-reasoned decisions on complaints/appeals at the commission level, so that they serve as authoritative and clear interpretations of the law.
8. Adopt clear procedures for investigations and allocate dedicated staff members to particular public authorities for purposes of investigations, in order to build relations and trust and to enhance their understanding of those authorities.
9. Clarify the issues being investigated at the outset, so that public authorities know 'the charges against them'.
10. Use persuasive measures, where possible, to promote compliance with complaint/appeal decisions by commissions, such as giving due publicity to such decisions, resorting to sanctions only occasionally and for more egregious breaches of the rules.
11. Clarify the rules regarding enforcement of commission decisions, preferably through court order rather than a more political route.

ENGAGING THE PUBLIC

The success of any right to information system depends in a number of ways on positive engagement with the public. First and foremost, fulfilment of the objectives of the law—in the Indian context the goals set out in the preamble to the law, namely, promoting democracy, controlling corruption, and ensuring public accountability—depends in fairly obvious ways on active use of the system. In other words, if the volume of requests for information is low, then these benefits will simply not be delivered. Second, political support for the law, central to its success, depends on broad-based public support, which in turn is possible only if it is actively used. Third, operation of the mechanisms for disclosing information, described in the previous section, can develop into a well-oiled system only when actively used; it is primarily through use that disclosure processes are honed and developed.

Public Awareness-Raising

Widespread public education and awareness-raising campaigns are central to engaging the public. It has been widely observed that the early years of implementing a right to information regime are particularly important as they set the trend and form lasting initial impressions of the value and impact of the system. At the same time, there is a need to maintain efforts over time. The 2002 Information Review Task Force noted that, in Canada, after 20 years, the right to access information is still not well understood. Indeed, there is some evidence to suggest that there has been a decline in awareness in comparison to the years following the adoption of the law (Government of Canada 2002a: 3).

Outreach campaigns face a barrier in the culture of secrecy that affects not only the civil service but also the public, which is accustomed to long-standing secrecy practices and a history of less than satisfactory interactions with government. The attitudes and value structures of members of the public around engagement with the public sector, including in relation to access to information, need to be changed.

Careful consideration needs to be given to the content of public outreach. In the Mexican context, it has been noted that although IFAI naturally wishes to publicize its mandate and role, a better focus of public awareness-raising initiatives is the overall right to information system and the benefits it can bring (Sobel et al. 2006: 44). At the same time, it is important for information commissions to build a strong constituency of support for their offices to ensure that they receive appropriate levels of support and that their independence is respected.

Public misperceptions, based on superficial awareness of the system, can also cause problems. In Mexico, the high profile of the right to information rules has led to a significant number of requests which do not involve access to information. On the other hand, in India there is an emerging picture of 'collateral' right to information successes, whereby information claims lead to the resolution of other administrative failures (Participatory Research in Asia 2008: 12–19).

Commentators regularly call for greater attention and resources to be devoted to direct outreach efforts. In Mexico, IFAI has engaged in a broad public relations campaign involving pamphlets, posters, radio and television spots, academic publications, and a massive and successful Internet drive, spearheaded by an extensive and user-friendly website. Although there is a wealth of anecdotal information and a strong track record of requests being lodged, overall levels of awareness have not been systematically measured and the causal impact of IFAI's public relations campaign has not been assessed.

At the same time, resource limitations mean that public campaigns need to be strategic. Two types of information are particularly important to building public support: information about politically or socially important events which attract media coverage and are widely viewed as access 'successes'; and information about the regular and widespread ongoing release of personal or other information which improves people's everyday lives. Real successes—which lead, for example, to the exposure of corruption, the reversal of policy or development proposals, or an increase in participation—should be distinguished from scandals, which may attract short-term media attention but which ultimately fail to build real support for the system.

People in Mexico believe that the law works because every week stories are published in the media about releases which actually affect people. For example, the right to information law is widely credited with the virtually complete disappearance of the 'aviadores' or government employees who would get paid but never actually report for work. Highlighting the role of the right to information in these stories can generate significant public awareness dividends.

On the other hand, where the role of the right to information is not highlighted, this benefit is lost. In Canada, the exposure of abuses relating to the so-called 'sponsorship programme',[18] initially discovered through right to information requests, eventually led to the downfall of the long-standing Liberal government. However, the public was generally unaware of the right to information link, and therefore relatively little support for the system was generated, notwithstanding the enormous significance of the result.

Efforts can be directed towards increasing the supply of access success stories, strengthening the right to information perspective, and enhancing media coverage. Networking among NGOs and journalists can be useful; NGOs frequently have stories of interest to journalists and can provide support to enhance the ability of journalists to take advantage of the law in developing their stories.

There is some debate about whether outreach should be directed towards those more likely to use the system or to the grassroots in order to promote truly widespread use of the system. Evidence from longer-standing systems, such as those of Canada and Australia, suggests that only a small percentage of the overall public will ever actually make a request for information, and that users tend to be heavily concentrated amongst the middle classes. For example, between 1983 and 2009, a total of 398,593 access to information requests were made in Canada, compared to a population, in 2009, of about 34 million (a rate of around 1 per cent). Given the number of repeat requests, this suggests a very small number of different requesters (Government of Canada 2009). At the same time, the rationale behind right to information legislation suggests that the entire population should be targeted. It would be ironic if a tool designed to make government accountable and responsive served instead to further privilege elites.

At a practical level, it can be very difficult to reach out to the truly disempowered; indeed, isolation is a defining characteristic of disempowerment which applies to the right to information just as it does to other aspects of social life. Discrimination against the disempowered in the context of the right to information has been documented in some cases. Surveys indicate that requesters are sometimes unable to submit oral requests, even though the law specifically provides for this, while the same problem has not been experienced by those submitting written requests (Open Society Justice Initiative 2006: 96–102).

On the other hand, in Mexico the oversight body has initiated a project called 'IFAI Comunidades', aimed at bringing together people within communities to identify and then request information that they need. The project has been successful in delivering information about health studies, the environment, corporate donations to public bodies, and so on, to local communities (Bogado et al. 2008: 5).

A dual strategy is appropriate, with a focus both on individuals and groups who are more likely to use the system and on the wider public.

Outreach to the youth can be especially important to longer-term support. The youth are more likely to embrace ideas of modern governance and, in particular, the equality and participation which access to information can fuel. They are also more likely to be comfortable using the Internet, and the public education system provides a potentially powerful and yet very cost-effective outreach system. Other natural targets for outreach include NGOs, academics, frequent requesters (who can bring special benefits due to their expertise and knowledge of the system), and businesses.

Public authorities, including information commissions, should develop strategic partnerships with NGOs and others to supplement and strengthen their own efforts at public outreach. In Mexico, businesses have proven to be important supporters based on the fact that they oppose corruption and bureaucratic red tape. Reliance on civil society groups may be important when attempting to reach out to the disempowered. The Mazdoor Kisan Shakti Sangathan (MKSS) experience in India, where the focus was on minimum wages, is an excellent example of this.

Action Ideas

1. Place particular emphasis on public outreach during the initial stages of implementation but continue outreach efforts over time to maintain a strong base of public awareness.
2. Target messages on the overall benefits of the system, while also ensuring that appropriate attention is devoted to the role of information commissions in order to build public support for these key bodies.
3. Focus on (real) success stories and ongoing releases which directly affect people.
4. Track 'success stories' over time to ensure that they really are successes in terms of delivering benefits.
5. Undertake direct dissemination of success stories.
6. Build contacts with the media to get them to both carry more right to information success stories and to attribute those stories to the right to information.
7. Enhance the ability of investigative reporters to use the right to information law through activities like training and internships.
8. Forge links with associations of investigative reporters as a conduit for training initiatives and to highlight the potential of the right to information to their work, including through exposure to international experiences.
9. Connect investigative reporters with NGOs, perhaps even through some formal mechanism.

10. Target outreach efforts at both more likely requesters and the general public, although the latter may require more basic messaging and innovative strategies, as with IFAI Comunidades.
11. Build strategic partnerships with NGOs and others to promote cooperation on public outreach; for example, with targeted dissemination of pamphlets and reaching out to disempowered communities.
12. Highlight the importance of access to information to the particular issues focused upon by different civil society groups.

The Role of Civil Society

Civil society—NGOs, but also the media and academics—plays a key role in promoting access to information. It often constitutes a very important requester group, particularly in the area of wider public interest requests. In many countries it is a key, often the key, source of political support for the right to information. It can be an important ally in outreach to the wider public, as well as in training public officials. It can also undertake a range of activities that help develop a strong right to information system, including legal challenges, research, including on best practices from abroad, strategic requesting to test the limits of openness, protesting bad practices, advocating progressive implementation, and the like. Private businesses can also be key political allies on the right to information. In the US and Canada, for example, this sector is among the more important requester groups and provides key political support from a powerful constituency.

Public authorities, including information commissions, can help maximize the impact of civil society initiatives in two key (and closely related) ways: by forming strategic partnerships with different groups to deliver common goals, and by working to build the capacity of civil society to achieve those goals.

Training is an area where extensive cooperation between officials and civil society, primarily NGOs and academic institutions, has taken place. As noted earlier, in Canada, the University of Alberta has worked to develop the IAPP Certificate Program. In the UK, private bodies, in many instances NGOs, undertake a substantial part of all right to information training for officials.

In Mexico, IFAI has taken cooperation with civil society to a high level. It has entered into formal cooperation agreements with a number of organizations, although these lack specificity regarding the nature of the cooperation and appear to be developed on an ad hoc basis rather than pursuant to a coordinated strategy (Sobel et al. 2006: 77–8, 83–4).

It also played a key role in nurturing a new NGO, Centro Internacional de Estudios de Transparencia y Acceso a la Información (CETA), which has a mandate to promote the right to information nationally and internationally.[19]

A number of steps can be taken to enhance the impact of civil society organizations (CSOs) in this area. It has been noted in both the South African and Mexican contexts that CSOs would benefit from greater coordination and cooperation among themselves in order to move away from their 'silo' approach of focusing on their core issues and to recognize the mutual benefits of more strategic work both with and targeting public authorities to deliver the right to information (McKinley 2003; Sobel et al. 2006: 4).

Many CSOs would also benefit from enhanced skills, to make effective use both of the right to information ('legal' skills) and the information they obtain ('advocacy' skills). In Mexico, training has been provided to NGOs in both of these areas (using the law and advocacy).

Action Ideas

1. Reach out to CSOs with an interest, active or potential, in working on right to information to explore possible areas of cooperation.
2. Conduct a national audit of key CSOs working on the right to information or related issues, with a view to mapping possible coordination/cooperation options both with and among them.
3. Conclude agreements with leading CSO groups to formalize cooperation with commissions.
4. Match smaller CSOs with larger groups and provide links to international expertise.
5. Provide training to civil society groups to build both legal and advocacy capacity.

Annual Reports and Public Guides

Many laws, including the Indian law, provide for the production of user-friendly guides for the public on how to take advantage of the right to information. These guides are important resources for the public and it is worth devoting sufficient attention and resources to ensure that they are accessible and informative.

The annual report that the information commissions are required to produce under the Indian law, as with many right to information laws, is a central tool for tracking progress in implementing the law, identifying problem areas, and generally understanding the use to which the law is being put. In Thailand, data on requests is not tracked at the level of public authorities but only in relation to complaints to the Information Commission, and this has proven to be a serious shortcoming in terms of understanding the operation of the system.

The quality of the report produced by the information commissions depends importantly on the information being provided to them by public authorities. There have been serious problems in South Africa, with public authorities failing to provide the oversight body, the Human Rights Commission, with the information it requires to compile its report. Indeed, in 2006 the Commission noted that the number of such reports being submitted to it was actually decreasing (South African Human Rights Commission 2006: 85–6), while in 2007 it reported that there had been an improvement in the submission of reports by national authorities and a decrease in reporting at the provincial level. It attributed this in part to the Golden Key Award ceremony which both rewarded good performers and exposed poor ones (South African Human Rights Commission 2007a: 107).

The 2006 Annual Report provided by the South African Human Rights Commission presents tables of raw data on requests, which is not very informative. Instead, information commissions should analyse the information provided to them and provide comments based on this in their annual reports.

Experience in Canada and Mexico suggests that it is useful to track a wide range of different variables relating to requests. For example, it is useful to track the age and occupation of requesters (by broad category), the type of information requested (for example, personal data, business information, and the like), fee information, including not only actual fees levied but also initial fee estimates where these are provided, timelines for provision of information, the form in which access was provided, requests which have been 'abandoned' by requesters, and the like.

Action Ideas

1. Produce a central 'model' guide which state governments could adapt to their particular circumstances as appropriate.
2. Monitor and analyse annual reports produced by the various information commissions, with a view to identifying and then profiling successes and problem areas.
3. Encourage commissions not only to present information but also to analyse it in their annual reports.

4. Require public authorities to provide high-quality annual reports to the commissions, which contain a range of relevant data, including detailed information on performance (such as the extent to which they are meeting their proactive publication obligations, the appointment of information officers, and the like).
5. Promulgate a model annual report which public authorities can use as guidance for their own reporting.
6. Adapt central electronic tracking systems for requests to facilitate the collection of a wide range of relevant data.
7. Assist smaller public authorities to put into place electronic tracking systems and provide them with training in their use.

PROMOTING EFFECTIVE INFORMATION COMMISSIONS

Oversight bodies—information commissions in India's case—can play a very important role in promoting the right to information. One of the key problems identified in relation to the South African system is its failure to establish a dedicated oversight body or to vest any other administrative body with the power to hear complaints (Open Democracy Advice Centre 2007: 11–27). Oversight bodies can, at best, serve as independent, dedicated focal points to promote progressive implementation of the right to information system, and function as high-profile champions of the right.

The ability of oversight bodies to play a positive role in implementation depends on a number of factors, including their mandate, both formally and in terms of the funding available to them, their independence, and their relations with other key players, such as the public (information users), civil society, and the public authorities they oversee.

Role

There are two principal roles played by different oversight bodies: resolving complaints and undertaking promotional measures. The role of the body in terms of resolving complaints is normally fairly clearly circumscribed by the legislation, and this is the case in India. Indeed, this is the primary role envisaged for the information commissions under the Indian legislation, which does not envisage the information commissions playing a wider promotional role.

There are a number of informal approaches, in addition to the formal complaints system, that can help to resolve problems quickly and relatively amicably. The benefits of promoting dialogue between requesters and information officers with a view to honing requests has been noted. Less adversarial approaches to resolving complaints, such as mediation and conciliation, have been proposed, for example in Canada and South Africa (Government of Canada 2002b; Open Democracy Advice Centre 2007: 22, 24), and the South African Human Rights Commission has provided some informal mediation services (South African Human Rights Commission 2007a: 102–3). The complaints system provided for in India could serve as a vehicle for mediation, although formal mediation would need to be backed up by regulations giving the commissions the power to approve mediated agreements.

Oversight bodies can potentially undertake a wide range of promotional activities, including monitoring, training, advocacy, public outreach and awareness-raising, providing assistance to requesters, making recommendations for reform, and even requiring public authorities to undertake structural reforms to better implement the law. In the Indian system, the government is seen as the primary promotional body, although the commissions are given fairly extensive powers to make remedial orders in the context of appeals and also have the power to make general recommendations for reform. In practice in most countries, these roles are shared between oversight bodies and government, and, indeed, civil society. The ability to mobilize sufficient resources for these tasks is likely to be the key factor in determining the scope of activities, rather than formal mandates.

There is a potential, or sometimes apparent, conflict between the complaints and the promotional role of oversight bodies, although most undertake both. For example, where an information commission has provided assistance to a requester, it might seem to be a conflict of interest for the commission also to consider a complaint from the same requester. In practice, this is not as significant a problem as it might at first appear. Oversight bodies are not courts, and do not need to follow the same strict impartiality rules. Separating the two functions can help minimize this problem and makes sense because they require different skill sets.

Action Ideas

1. Explore the possibility of undertaking mediation and/or conciliation with a view to resolving complaints.
2. Interpret the formal mandates of the Commissions broadly, with a view to enabling them to undertake a wide range of promotional measures.
3. Assign different staff to promotional functions and complaints/appeals.

4. Establish different divisions to deal with these two roles.
5. Seek to ensure adequate and independent funding to allow commissions to engage in broad promotional activities.

INDEPENDENCE AND ACCOUNTABILITY

Oversight bodies can only discharge their functions properly if they are independent, in the sense of being protected against political and other forms of interference. This is, to a large extent, a function of their formal structures, particularly regarding appointments and funding, as well as the presence of political will to respect independence and not to interfere.

A number of external factors may affect independence. It is essential that the oversight body build political credibility among key constituencies which can support it in the face of threats to its independence. In the Mexican context, the idea has been mooted of establishing a special support group, a Committee for the Protection of IFAI's Autonomy, consisting of distinguished citizens who are above politics, to safeguard IFAI's independence (Sobel et al. 2006: 3, 78–9).

An important factor is who is actually appointed to the post of commissioner. The previous Canadian Information Commissioner was a long-time Clerk of the House of Commons, whose principal role is to advise the Speaker and MPs on House procedure and to manage the Commons' departments and services. The commissioner before him was a leading political figure and one-time cabinet minister, but appointed under a government not run by his party. There are five Mexican commissioners from a range of different backgrounds, with a heavy focus on academics. The institutions in both countries are widely perceived to be independent.

Resources are clearly central to the notion of independence. A potentially serious constraint on the independence and effectiveness of the various information commissions in the Indian context is the fact that the government sets the salaries and terms of service of the employees, and that the budget is also provided by the government. Inasmuch as the rules on salaries are set out directly in the legislation, they may be difficult to change, but the budget rules could perhaps be amended so that funding comes directly from Parliament. Funding by Parliament can be justified on the basis that, for accountability purposes, the body reports to Parliament.

In Canada, a pilot project has been established with a view to ensuring independent and yet appropriate funding for 'Officers of Parliament', like the Auditor General, the Information Commissioner, the Chief Electoral Officer, and the like. Under the pilot project, an ad hoc advisory panel of MPs from all parties, chaired by the Speaker of the House of Commons, considers funding requests from these bodies and makes recommendations on funding to the Treasury Board. The idea is to address the problem of bodies that oversee and investigate government behaviour having to apply to government for funding. In turn, the Officers of Parliament have agreed to respect the spirit and intention of government policies on financial management and fiscal accountability, as well as to operate transparently (Information Commissioner of Canada 2007: 19–22).

IFAI's statute guarantees its 'operational, budgetary, and decisional autonomy'. In practice, it presents its budget to the president, although it is understood that it is the Congress that supervises the budget and that the president may not object to it. This understanding is probably cemented with the 2007 constitutional amendment, which basically raises the guarantee of autonomy to a constitutional level. In practice, IFAI receives generous funding.

The overall costs of administering right to information systems, although often a matter of heated discussion, are modest, as the experience of the longer-standing right to information regimes demonstrates. In Canada, for example, a 2002 estimate put the cost of the system at $30 million, or about $1 per citizen—very similar to *per capita* cost estimates in the US—compared to total federal government expenditure (in 2001–2) of over $450 billion (Government of Canada 2002a: 5).

The flip side of independence is accountability. In addition to the (generally quite limited) formal accountability mechanisms, including budget oversight, a number of informal systems can significantly enhance the accountability of oversight bodies. Direct forms of consultation with stakeholders are one means of promoting accountability. A comprehensive review of the entire right to information system every five to 10 years has been recommended in the Canadian context, along with the appointment of a retired judge to investigate complaints against the Information Commissioner (Government of Canada 2002b).

Action Ideas

1. Establish an NGO with the role of supporting the independence of the commissions, as well as monitoring their performance and making recommendations for reform, as appropriate.
2. Foster links with a range of potential supporters who may defend the independence of the commissions should this be threatened.

3. Examine the idea of an agreement on the involvement of parliament in funding commissions.
4. Adopt a transparency policy for the commissions so that they themselves operate openly.
5. Put in place a system for resolving complaints against the commissions.
6. Engage in consultation, including on the performance of the commissions, on a regular basis both with public authorities and users/civil society.
7. Undertake a formal institutional review on a regular basis, perhaps every two years, with a view to garnering input from different stakeholders.
8. Monitor the performance of the commissions and report on this.
9. Put in place internal systems to assess the performance of the commissions.

Relations with Public Bodies

It is important that oversight bodies maintain good relations with the public authorities they oversee, although this can sometimes be difficult. In any right to information system, regardless of the formal rules, public authorities retain considerable capacity to obstruct the flow of information and the work of the oversight body. The longer-term goal should be to inculcate amongst these authorities a sense of ownership over, and pride in, the right to information rather than attempt to force them to comply with their legal obligations. Amicable relations between the oversight body and public authorities can help in this.

The constant challenges the oversight body is forced to make to public authorities, particularly if it serves as a complaints body, as is the case in India, makes it more difficult to maintain good relations. Consistent and well-reasoned decisions on complaints can at least ensure that public authorities understand the basis for those decisions. Negative perceptions by public authorities vis-à-vis oversight bodies can contribute to poor relations. In Mexico, for example, IFAI is sometimes seen as superior, top–down, or lacking in understanding of the civil service. Regular consultation between public authorities and the oversight body, in particular with information officials, can help to address unhelpful perceptions.

The oversight body needs to be firm in upholding right to information principles, but it should generally seek to avoid imposing solutions that are seen by public authorities to be overly harsh. The problems arising from a firm policy on timelines in Canada have been noted. A more successful example from Mexico entailed efforts by IFAI to get public authorities to fulfil their proactive publication obligations. An initial survey indicated that only a minority of public authorities were fulfilling these obligations. IFAI wrote privately to the poor performers, indicating, however, that next time the report on performance would be widely publicized. The response was impressive and the rate of compliance jumped to over 90 per cent (Sobel et al. 2006: 74).

The oversight body should reach out to potential official allies. It has been noted in the Mexican context that state and local governments are often more responsive to implementing the right to information (Ibid.: 76). This can have a number of positive benefits, including fostering allies, promoting openness pilots and strong performers, and demonstrating the benefits of transparency. IFAI has established a special unit that reaches out to states and municipalities, and has dedicated part of its website to information on these levels of government, including a mechanism to channel requests for information, called Infomex, to them.

The various oversight bodies—the Central and State Information Commissions in the Indian context—should also seek to learn from and provide mutual support to one another, and to share best practices. In Mexico, IFAI provides some support and guidance to the state-level commissions. An informal international network of information commissioners hosts a conference every 18 months or so, although far more could be done to promote institutional cooperation at the international level. As noted, in Canada, the various Officers of Parliament, the independent oversight bodies, have come together on an informal basis to discuss common concerns regarding funding and to look for collective solutions.

Action Ideas

1. Use opportunities for cooperation between the commissions and public authorities, such as training, to promote trust and to forge personal relationships.
2. Put in place a formal programme of consultations with public authorities, perhaps by sector—health, finance, etc.—with meetings being held on a regular basis, perhaps annually or semi-annually, with a view to addressing areas of disagreement head on, so that they do not fester.
3. Explore ways of promoting compliance by public authorities with their openness obligations which do not cause tension.

4. Seek out potential allies among official bodies, perhaps by establishing a special unit to do this, and use those allies to pilot progressive ideas.
5. Establish a regular process of consultation among the commissions with a view to sharing best practices and promoting cooperation.

TO CONCLUDE

India's Right to Information Act 2005 is a recognized better practice example of its genre, providing a strong basis for ensuring access by citizens to information held by public bodies. However, adopting a strong law is simply the first step in this process. Implementation of a right to information law is long-term, complex, and a constant struggle against the inevitable marshalling of forces that oppose openness. It requires political will, a broad alliance between individuals and groups that support openness, imaginative solutions, and commitment.

This chapter has examined how three countries in particular, namely, Canada, Mexico, and South Africa, have dealt with a wide range of implementation challenges, painting a picture of some of the key hurdles and opportunities, outlining some of the approaches which have been tried, and providing a brainstorming list of possible action ideas. It is not intended to be prescriptive or even to suggest a system of prioritization. Rather, the goal is to present ideas in order to broaden the range of options that local actors may wish to consider.

Implementation of the right to information is a difficult process which requires serious commitment and effort from a range of different actors. Right to information proponents need to be creative and to adapt their strategies, depending upon the particular circumstances and by observing what is working and what is not. This chapter aims to assist those working on the right to information in India by providing them with ideas based on the experience of other countries, to help fuel their creativity.

NOTES

1. Right to Information Act, No. 22 of 2005. The Act received presidential assent in June 2005 and, in accordance with its own provisions, was phased-in but all provisions were in force by October 2005.

2. Bill No. 98-C of 2000. This law never came into force due to the failure of the government to notify it in the Official Gazette.

3. For a detailed review of earlier regional and national right to information developments in India, see Article 19, Centre for Policy Alternatives, Commonwealth Human Rights Initiative and Human Rights Commission of Pakistan,

Global Trends on the Right to Information: A Survey of South Asia (London: July 2001). Available at: http://www.article19.org/pdfs/publications/south-asia-foi-survey.pdf, accessed on 19 March 2010.

4. For a review of both the positive features and shortcomings of the Indian Right to Information Act 2005, see Mendel (2008: chapter on India, pp. 55–62).

5. In the Indian civil service, government officers involved in decision-making are required to record their opinions and advice on relevant files, and these are referred to as 'file notings'.

6. The MKSS (Mazdoor Kisan Shakti Sangathan) is a grassroots organization that has played a leading role in laying the groundwork for this narrative, their website containing a wealth of information about it. See, in particular, the section on writings, available at: http://www.mkssindia.org/node/26, accessed on 19 March 2010.

7. The votes in Florida in the 2000 United States presidential election between George W. Bush and Al Gore were extremely close and various re-counts were ordered. The United States Supreme Court ultimately decided that Bush had taken Florida and thus won the election. A detailed recount of votes in the whole state undertaken later by media outlets revealed that, in fact, Gore had garnered more votes.

8. They held, first, that as the electoral law strictly protects the ballots and then provides for their destruction, this effectively constitutes an exception to the right of access; second, that as the ballot boxes may be opened only by judicial order, there is no way in practice to grant access. Both arguments clearly run counter to the spirit and intention of the right to information law. At the time of the request, the ballots were simply waiting to be destroyed and no harm was identified that would have resulted from their release. See Ackerman (2007).

9. Investigators in the Information Commissioner's Office, for example, are required to have or to obtain IAPP certification. Information Commissioner of Canada (2007: 16).

10. These include the Canadian Access and Privacy Association (CAPA) and the Canadian Association of Professional Access and Privacy Administrators (CAPAPA).

11. The Memorandum essentially called on public officials to exercise their discretion to disclose information rather than to withhold it.

12. Formally the Department of Foreign Affairs and International Trade (DFAIT).

13. Ideally, everyone should benefit from the right of access, but this is limited under the Indian law to citizens.

14. This term is commonly used in India, although it seems anomalous to use an obscure Latin phrase when referring to a transparency idea.

15. See RaaG and NCPRI (2009: Executive Summary, p. 11).

16. Just as this chapter was going to the publisher, the Canadian government had decided to do away with the database in a move that has attracted widespread condemnation.

17. The development of a data protection law is reportedly already underway in India.

18. A Federal government programme to sponsor activities aimed at wooing Quebecers with a view to decreasing support for separatism in the province.

19. CETA later ran into problems and was wound up.

BIBLIOGRAPHY

Ackerman, John (2007), 'The Limits of Transparency: The Case of Mexico's Electoral Ballots', *Mexican Law Review*, 8, available at http://works.bepress.com/john_mill_ackerman_rose/2/, accessed on 14 June 2010.

ARTICLE 19 (1999), *The Public's Right to Know: Principles on Freedom of Information Legislation*, London, available at http://www.article19.org/pdfs/standards/righttoknow.pdf, accessed on 14 June 2010.

_________ (2001a), *A Model Freedom of Information Law*, London, available at http://www.article19.org/pdfs/standards/modelfoilaw.pdf, accessed on 14 June 2010.

_________ (2001b), Centre for Policy Alternatives, Commonwealth Human Rights Initiative and Human Rights Commission of Pakistan, *Global Trends on the Right to Information: A Survey of South Asia*, London, available at http://www.article19.org/pdfs/publications/south-asia-foi-survey.pdf, accessed on 14 June 2010.

Banisar, David (2003), *Freedom of Information and Access to Government Record Laws Around The World*, available at http://freedominfo.org/documents/global_survey2006.pdf, accessed on 14 June 2010.

Bogado, Benjamin, Emiline Martinez-Morales, Bethany Noll, and Kyle Bell (2008), *The Federal Institute for Access to Information in Mexico and a Culture of Transparency: Follow Up Report*. Annenberg School for Communications, University of Pennsylvania, available at http://www.gwu.edu/~nsarchiv/NSAEBB/NSAEBB247/Annenberg.pdf, accessed on 14 June 2010.

Buckley, Steve, Kreszentia Duer, Toby Mendel, and Seán Ó Siochrú (2008), *Broadcasting, Voice and Accountability: A Public Interest Approach to Policy, Law and Regulation*. Ann Arbour: University of Michigan Press.

Calland, Richard and Allison Tilley (2002), *The Right to Know, The Right to Live*. Cape Town: Open Democracy Advice Centre.

Campbell Public Affairs Institute (2003), *National Security and Open Government: Striking the Right Balance*. Syracuse: The Maxwell School of Syracuse University, Campbell Public Affairs Institute.

Commonwealth Human Rights Initiative (2003), *Open Sesame: Looking for the Right to Information in the Commonwealth*. New Delhi: CHRI, available at http://www.humanrightsinitiative.org/publications/chogm/chogm_2003/default.htm, accessed on 14 June 2010.

Doyle, Kate (2002), *Mexico's New Freedom of Information Law*. Washington D.C.: National Security Archive, available at http://www.gwu.edu/~nsarchiv/NSAEBB/NSAEBB68/, accessed on 14 June 2010.

Fox, Jonathan, Libby Haight, Helena Hofbauer, and Tania Andrade (2007), *Mexico's Right-to-Know Reforms: Civil Society Perspectives*. Washington: Woodrow Wilson International Center for Scholars.

Government of Canada (2002a), *Access to Information: Making it Work for Canadians: Report of the Access to Information Review Task Force*. Ottawa: Government of Canada, available at http://www.atirtf- geai.gc.ca/report2002-e.html, accessed on 14 June 2010.

_________ (2002b), *Synopsis of Recommendations/Proposals/Comments From Written Submissions Sent to the Access to Information Review Task Force*. Ottawa: Government of Canada, available at http://www.atirtf-geai.gc.ca/submissions/synopsis1-e.html, accessed on 14 June 2010.

_________ (2006), *Strengthening the Access to Information Act: A Discussion of Ideas Intrinsic to the Reform of the Access to Information Act*. Ottawa: Government of Canada, available at http://www.justice.gc.ca/eng/dept-min/pub/atia-lai/index.html, accessed on 14 June 2010.

_________ (2009), Info Source Bulletin Number 32B—Statistical Reporting, 2009, available at http://www.infosource.gc.ca/bulletin/2009/b/bulletin32b/bulletin32b00-eng.asp, accessed on 14 June 2010.

Human Rights Watch (2006), *Lost in Transition: Bold Ambitions, Limited Results for Human Rights Under Fox*. New York: Human Rights Watch, available at http://www.hrw.org/reports/2006/mexico0506/, accessed on 14 June 2010.

Information Commissioner of Canada (2000), *Annual Report, Information Commissioner: 1999–2000*. Ottawa, available at http://www.oic-ci.gc.ca/eng/rp-pr_ar-ra_2006-2007.aspx, accessed on 14 June 2010.

_________ (2007), *Annual Report, Information Commissioner: 2006–2007*, available at http://www.hc-sc.gc.ca/ahc-asc/pubs/_atip-aiprp/2007/index-eng.php, accessed on 14 June 2010.

Mendel, Toby (2005), *Parliament and Access to Information: Working for Transparency Government*. Washington: World Bank, available at http://siteresources.worldbank.org/WBI/Resources/Parliament_and_Access_to_Information_with_cover.pdf, accessed on 14 June 2010.

_________ (2006), 'Access to Information: The Existing State of Affairs Around the World', *Comparative Media Law Journal, 8*: 3–15 .

_________ (2008), *Freedom of Information: A Comparative Legal Survey*, 2nd edn. Paris: UNESCO, available at http://portal.unesco.org/ci/en/ev.php-URL_ID=26159&URL_DO=DO_TOPIC&URL_SECTION=201.html, accessed on 14 June 2010.

McKinley, Dale (2003), *The State of Access to Information in South Africa*. Johannesburg: Centre for the Study of Violence and Reconciliation, available at http://siteresources.worldbank.org/INTPCENG/Resources/state_of_access_to_information_in_south_africa.pdf, accessed on 14 June 2010.

Nauman, Talli (2005), *Mexican Right-to-Know Boosters Should Build Bridges to Environmental Disclosure Law*. Washington: Center for International Policy, available at http://americas.irc-online.org/am/791, accessed on 14 June 2010.

Open Democracy Advice Centre (ODAC) (2007), *Submission to the Review of State Institutions Supporting Constitutional Democracy: Right to Know Legislation.* Cape Town: Open Democracy Advice Centre (on file with author).

Open Society Justice Initiative (OSJI) (2006), *Transparency and Silence: A Survey of Access to Information Laws and Practices in 14 Countries.* Hungary: Central European University Press, available at http://www.soros.org/initiatives/justice/focus/foi/articles_publications/publications/transparency_20060928, accessed on 14 June 2010.

Participatory Research in Asia (PRIA) (2008), *Tracking Right to Information in Eight States: 2007.* New Delhi: PRIA.

Pietersen, Melvis and Mukelani Dimba (2004), *Digging out the Truth, Dogged ODAC Holds On.* Cape Town: Open Democracy Advice Centre.

RTI Assessment & Analysis Group (RaaG) and National Campaign for People's Right to Information (NCPRI) (2009), *Safeguarding the Right to Information: Report of the People's RTI Assessment 2008.* New Delhi: RaaG and NCPRI.

Roberts, Alasdair (1998), *Limited Access: Assessing the Health of Canada's Freedom of Information Laws*, Freedom of Information Research Project, April, School of Policy Studies, Queen's University, pp. 47–50, available at http://www.cna-acj.ca/en/system/files/APRIL%201998%20-%20Limited%20Access%20Assessing%20the%20Health%20of%20Canada's%20Freedom%20of%20Information%20laws.pdf, accessed on 14 June 2010.

_________ (2002), 'Administrative Discretion and the Access to Information Act: An Internal Law on Open Government?' *Canadian Public Administration*, 45(2): 175–94.

_________ (2005), 'Spin Control and Freedom of Information: Lessons for the United Kingdom from Canada', *Public Administration*, 83(1): 1–25.

Snell, Rick (2005), 'Using Comparative Studies to Improve Freedom of Information Analysis: Insights from Australia, Canada and New Zealand', Presented at 6th National and 2nd International Congress on the Right to Information, Mexico 8–11 November, National University of Mexico, Mexico City, available at http://ricksnell.com.au/Articles/Snell_Mexico_2005.pdf, accessed on 14 June 2010.

Sobel, David, Bethany Noll, Benjamin Bogado, TCC Group, and Monroe Price (2006), *The Federal Institute for Access to Information in Mexico and a Culture of Transparency.* Annenberg School for Communications, University of Pennsylvania, available at http://www.global.asc.upenn.edu/docs/mex_report_fiai06_english.pdf, accessed on 14 June 2010.

South African Human Rights Commission (2006), *10th Annual Report for the Year Ending March 2006.* Johannesburg: South Africa Human Rights Commission, available at http://www.info.gov.2a/view/DownloadFileAction?id=94843, accessed on 14 June 2010.

South African Human Rights Commission (SAHRC) (2007a), *11th Annual Report for the Year Ended March 2007.* Johannesburg: South Africa Human Rights Commission, available with Author.

South African Human Rights Commission (SAHRC) (2007b), *Ministerial Review Commission on Intelligence*. Johannesburg: South Africa Human Rights Commission, available at http://www.intelligence.gov.za/Ministerial%20Review%20Commission/Submission-%20SAHRC.doc, accessed on 14 June 2010.

Transparency International (2003), *Global Corruption Report 2003: Special Focus: Access to Information*. London: Profile Books, available at http://www.transparency.org/publications/gcr/gcr_2003, accessed on 14 June 2010.

Contributors

VIKRAM K. CHAND is Senior Public Sector Management Specialist at the World Bank, New Delhi, India.

S.K. DAS is Member (Finance), Space Commission and Atomic Energy Commission and Ex-officio Secretary to Government of India (Retired).

SUMIR LAL is Manager, Operational Communications, in the World Bank's External Affairs Vice Presidency, Washington D.C., USA.

DARSHINI MAHADEVIA is Professor, Faculty of Planning and Public Policy and Member-Secretary of the Centre for Urban Equity, CEPT University, Ahmedabad, India.

TOBY MENDEL is the Executive Director of the Centre for Law and Democracy, Halifax, Canada.

RAHUL MUKHERJI is Associate Professor in the South Asian Studies Programme at the National University of Singapore, Singapore.

ASEEMA SINHA is Associate Professor of Political Science at the University of Wisconsin-Madison, USA.